Black Cultural Capital: Activism That Spurred African American High Schools

A Volume in:
History of Education

Series Editor:
Jared R. Stallones

History of Education

Series Editor:
Jared R. Stallones
University of Northern Colorado

Series Books

Breakthrough: From Pandemic Panic to Promising Practice (2023)
Shirley Marie McCarther & Donna M. Davis

*Anti-Blackness and Public Schools in the Border South:
Policy, Politics, and Protest in St. Louis, 1865–1972* (2019)
Claude Weathersby & Matthew D. Davis

*Educating a Working Society:
Vocationalism, the Smith-Hughes Act, and Modern America* (2018)
Glenn P. Lauzon

Black Cultural Capital: Activism That Spurred African American High Schools

Vanessa Garry
E. Paulette Isaac-Savage
Sha-Lai L. Williams

INFORMATION AGE PUBLISHING, INC.
Charlotte, NC • www.infoagepub.com

Library of Congress Cataloging-In-Publication Data

The CIP data for this book can be found on the Library of Congress website (loc.gov).

Paperback: 979-8-88730-392-5
Hardcover: 979-8-88730-393-2
E-Book: 979-8-88730-394-9

Copyright © 2023 Information Age Publishing Inc.

All rights reserved. No part of this publication may be reproduced, stored in a retrieval system, or transmitted, in any form or by any means, electronic, mechanical, photocopying, microfilming, recording or otherwise, without written permission from the publisher.

Printed in the United States of America

CONTENTS

Endorsements vii

Preface ix
Jared R. Stallones

Introduction: Black Cultural Capital: Activism That Spurred
African American High Schools xi
Vanessa Garry, E. Paulette Isaac-Savage, and Sha-Lai L. Williams

1. Institute for Colored Youth (Cheyney University):
   Philadelphia, PA 1
   Molly E. O'Connor

2. Lincoln High School During De Jure Segregation: Exploring
   the Importance of Social and Cultural Capital 25
   Bradley Poos, Loyce Caruthers, and Marceline Cooley

3. The Sumner High School: An Educational Landmark
   Made by the Black Community 49
   E. Paulette Isaac-Savage and Vanessa Garry

4. A Historical Study of I.M. Terrell High School: Its Legacy and
   Implications for Improved Education of Black Students 73
   Tasha Coble Ginn

5. Frederick Douglass High School, Baltimore 93
   William P. Kladky

6. "We're Your Sons and Daughters...Guide Us as We Go": The Role of Harbison Junior College, Richlex School, and Their Communities in the Development of Cultural Capital 115
   Vann Holden

7. Douglass High School (1891–): A Place of Justice and Hope in Oklahoma City 135
   Autumn B. Brown and Lucy E. Bailey

8. A Labor of Love: The Origin, Development, and Legacy of A.H. Parker High School in Birmingham, Alabama 157
   Penny S. Seals

9. A Portrait of Como High School, Fort Worth, Texas 181
   Altheria Caldera

10. Beyond the Years: Dunbar High School 1916–1968 201
    M. Francyne Huckaby, Stephanie Cuellar, Michelle Nguyen, Leslie Ekpe, Rachel Brooks, Kellton Hollins, and Jonathan W. Crocker

11. For the Good of the Whole: Restor(y)ing the History of Georgia's First Black Public High School 223
    Amber M. Neal-Stanley

12. Turn Around, Reach Back, Lead: Legacy and Lives of the Howard W. Blake High School 247
    Vonzell Agosto, Jacqueline K. Haynes, and Ann Marie Mobley

Eplilogue 273
Vanessa Garry, E. Paulette Isaac-Savage, and Sha-Lai L. Williams

Biographies 277

ENDORSEMENTS

BLACK CULTURAL CAPITAL

Activism that Spurred African American High Schools

Throughout America, the freedom dreams of Black people and the intellectual currents that guided them were first unleashed within one-room schoolhouses, dilapidated shacks, and church basements that were converted into laboratories of discovery and dissent. In short – Black spaces matter and have always mattered in the struggle for Black liberation. The authors of *Black Cultural Capital* have delivered one of the most comprehensive collection of essays to date that highlight the monumental legacy and rich history of America's first Black high schools. Utilizing a vast array of sources, the authors have created an intimate portrait of the struggle to carve out historic spaces that educated and affirmed Black youth while simultaneously countering pernicious systems of white supremacy that sought to undermine them at every step. This volume of essays is a must have for any serious scholar or student of the Black freedom struggle in America.

— Jelani M. Favors
Henry E. Frye Distinguished Professor of History
North Carolina A&T State University
Author of Shelter in a Time of Storm:
How Black Colleges Fostered Generations of Leadership and Activism

This is a long-awaited, quintessential contribution to our still-incomplete knowledge and understanding of the unique but intertwined histories of Black education and secondary schools in the United States. The narratives are incisive, enlightening, and inspiring. A welcome advancement to the historical foundations of education.

— Tondra L. Loder-Jackson
Professor, Educational Foundations Program
School of Education, Department of Human Studies
The University of Alabama at Birmingham
Author of Schoolhouse Activists: African American Educators and the Long Birmingham Civil Rights Movement *and Co-editor of* Schooling the Movement: The Activism of Southern Black Educators from Reconstruction through the Civil Rights Era

At a time when there is a deservingly greater appreciation for historically Black colleges and universities (HBCUs), we must also remember that K-12 Black high schools played a pivotal role in anchoring communities and creating a sense of place and freedom for Black people. In their edited book, *Black Cultural Capital: Activism that Spurred African American High Schools*, Drs. Vanessa B. Garry, E. Paulette Isaac-Savage, and Sha-Lai L. Williams produced a timely and much-needed book about the significant role Black high schools have historically--and continue to play--in Black communities and the Black freedom struggle. With detailed historical case studies of Black high schools throughout the United States, the various authors illuminate how these schools served as pillars in Black communities.

— Jerome Morris
The E. Desmond Lee Endowed Professor of Urban Education
(in conjunction with St. Louis Public Schools)
Director of the Center for Communally Bonded Research (communallybonded.org)
The University of Missouri—St. Louis
Author of Troubling the Waters: Fulfilling the Promise of Quality Public Schooling for Black Children

By illuminating the ways in which Black communities and Black high schools mutually sustained and strengthened one another, this volume provides a valuable service to historians, educational researchers, students, and practitioners. Its elevation of institutions too long overlooked outside of their own communities significantly enriches understandings of the history of American education. Moreover, each chapter vividly illustrates and underscores the multiple forms of cultural capital that Black high schools have embodied throughout their history. This is essential knowledge for anyone concerned about the past, present, and future of American education and the struggle for racial justice.

— Walter C. Stern
Assistant Professor of Educational Policy Studies and History
University of Wisconsin–Madison
Author of The Hidden Politics of High School Violence, *in Kyle P. Steele (Ed.),* New Perspectives on the History of the Twentieth-Century American High School

PREFACE

Jared R. Stallones
University of Northern Colorado

The History of Education Book Series is sponsored by the Organization of Educational Historians (OEH). OEH was founded in 1965 as the Midwest History of Education Society (MHES) by Professor Kenneth Beasley of Northern Illinois University and Professor Gerald Gutek from Loyola University in Chicago. The two met at the 1964 annual meeting of the Midwest Philosophy of Education Society and realized the need for a regional history of education society in the Midwest. They invited historians of education at Midwestern colleges and universities to meet at Loyola University Chicago in spring 1965 to organize the society. Ten historians gathered in a seminar room at Loyola's Lewis Towers, shared papers, and agreed to convene the first meeting of the Midwest History of Education Society that fall. For the next three decades, the Society met annually at Loyola University on the last weekend in October.

The Midwest History of Education Society operated for many years without a mission statement, a constitution, by-laws, or dues. The Society was simply a convocation for historians of education. It had three officers who were elected for one-year terms at the annual meeting: a president to preside over the annual meeting, a vice-president to organize the program, and a secretary to keep minutes and send out the annual notice of the meeting. With no dues and no

---

Black Cultural Capital: Activism That Spurred African American High Schools, pages ix–x.
Copyright © 2023 by Information Age Publishing
www.infoagepub.com
All rights of reproduction in any form reserved.

funds, there was no need for a treasurer. The annual meeting consisted of papers, an evening banquet address, and a short business meeting. The meetings were informal with no official respondents to the papers but a great deal of lively conversation over the presentations. In 1973, under the leadership of Professor Edward Rutkowski from the University of Northern Iowa, the Society published its first *Annual Proceedings of the Midwest History of Education Society.* By the late 1980s, the Society had grown from its early beginnings and begun to attract members from other regions of the country. A more formal arrangement was needed, and the Society adopted a constitution, by-laws, and began collecting dues. While maintaining the Society's openness, the changes helped to ensure that it would grow into a true professional organization for scholars of education history. In 2002, the *Annual Proceedings* became a peer-reviewed journal, the *American Educational History Journal.* Then, in December 2008, the membership voted to replace the name Midwest History of Education Society (MHES) with the name Organization of Educational Historians (OEH). The Organization continues to meet each fall and remains an informal, collegial venue for the exchange of ideas about the history of education.

The present volume is especially timely. Although public schools aspire to provide high quality education for all students, inequities abound. Many of these inequities were starkly highlighted during the pandemic school shutdowns of the 2019-20 and 2020-21 academic years. Pandemic disruptions to children's learning had measurable effects which persist, with the greatest impacts often falling on those least equipped to deal with them. At the same time, school shutdowns also revealed inventiveness, resilience, and activism as families and allies came together to combat the threat to their children's and their communities' futures.

Black Cultural Capital: Activism that Spurred Historical Black High Schools provides echoes from the past of communities organizing for better schools. The authors explore the efforts of Black leaders, teachers, business leaders, and parents to ensure that Black children received a quality high school education. Each chapter profiles a school, its community, and the local leaders who fought bigotry, indifference, and bureaucratic inertia to create educational opportunity for their posterity. That opportunity, in turn, enriched not just the local community, but American society as a whole. This volume provides much-needed historical perspective to inform the ongoing national conversation about the past, present, and future of American education.

—Jared R. Stallones, Editor
History of Education Book Series

INTRODUCTION

BLACK CULTURAL CAPITAL

Activism That Spurred African American High Schools

Vanessa Garry, E. Paulette Isaac-Savage, and Sha-Lai L. Williams
University of Missouri—St. Louis

State governments after the Civil War opened segregated public schools for Black children; however, school district leaders did as little as possible to make the mandate for them a reality (Butchart, 2010; Butchart & Rolleri, 2004; Franklin, 1990; McPherson, 1970). Contingent upon the region in the nation, most of these public institutions were elementary schools, poorly constructed facilities, bereft of resources, and without Black teachers (Rabinowitz, 1974; Williams, 1920). Wanting a better life for their children than the one they experienced, Black leaders throughout the country convened in their respective communities to determine what they needed to do to galvanize White public school boards to provide an appropriate education for their children that was on par with the education provided to White children. It was a formidable task given the White majority governed the newly freed men (Rabinowitz, 1976). Yet, undeterred, Black ministers, attorneys, doctors, educators, and laymen tested their freedom as they petitioned school boards for facilities, resources, Black teachers, and above all, standalone

---

Black Cultural Capital: Activism That Spurred African American High Schools, pages xi–xviii.
Copyright © 2023 by Information Age Publishing
www.infoagepub.com
All rights of reproduction in any form reserved.

high schools (Franklin, 1990). Closed, repurposed, or opened historical Black high schools would likely not exist if it were not for Black activism.

Black Cultural Capital: Activism that Spurred Historical Black High Schools provides a deeper examination of Black high schools and the Black communities who culled their resources and made a difference in the lives of Black children. Specifically, it examines the efforts Black leaders, teachers, business leaders, and parents assumed to ensure that Black children received a high school education. The chapters in this book speak to the leadership in American Black high schools and the narratives shed light on the extraordinary Black educators who set the foundation for Black children across the United States (Walker, 2009). They demonstrate how Blacks with few resources stood their ground and fought to ensure that children received a proper education. And, as Sowell (1976) pointed out, it "was accomplished in the face of the strongest opposition confronting any American racial or ethnic group" (p. 34). The authors relied on Tara J. Yosso's (2005) cultural model to illustrate Black leaders' activism in their quest for high schools for their children. Yosso refers to opposition against oppression as cultural capital often seen in minority communities where Black leaders coalesce around issues of concern and strategize how to overcome them.

Yosso's (2005) notion of cultural capital is an important element in the establishment and maintenance of schools and serves as the common theoretical framework throughout the book. Her forms of capital were widespread in the Black community. In particular, four forms of capital are extensively represented. *Aspirational* capital is the "ability to maintain hopes and dreams for the future, even in the face of real and perceived barriers (p. 77). As will be demonstrated throughout this book, parents and teachers instilled in students a "can-do attitude." As such, students were lead to believe they could accomplish anything they set their sights on regardless of the social, economic, and racial barriers before them. Students received nurturing from the community in many different forms. Yosso described this form of nurturing as *familial* capital. Family extended beyond the biological members of one's family. It included administrators, teachers, and other families in the community. A variety of networks was present in Black communities. As many were replete with Black-owned businesses, churches, community centers, theaters, and other conveniences, they lent themselves to the establishment of networks and a wealth of community resources. This form of capital—*social*—enabled Black students to receive both "instrumental and emotional support" (p. 79) from various community members. Lastly, *resistant* capital is the "knowledges and skills fostered through oppositional behavior that challenges inequality" (p. 80). This includes the transference and maintenance of the "multiple dimensions of community cultural wealth" (p. 80). Reflecting on their battles for equality, parents, educators, and others instilled in children a sense of pride and prepared them to overcome systemic and other forms of racism.

Black leaders who made possible these historical high schools in segregated neighborhoods operated throughout the nation. The narratives of each of the following Black high schools, located in the north, south, Midwest, west, and along the east coast, have similar histories. The founding of the majority of these schools are rooted in school districts' reluctance to provide Black children with facilities and resources on par with those for White children. It is as if there was a White supremacist's guide on how not to educate Black children across America. On the other hand, the narratives reveal how Black communities countered to put these facilities on par with White schools. The storytelling of these facilities reveal not only community leaders who helped make them possible but also uncovers the principal and teacher leaders who delivered the academic content as well as developed the school culture that celebrated Black history. On the downside, the stories also illustrate how the closing of these facilities after the *Brown v. Board of Education* impacted the communities, students, faculty, and parents. Undoubtedly, resources in most Blacks schools paled in comparison to those of their counterparts. Free states were often no different from former slave states when it came to providing education for Black children. While tax revenues of middle- and upper-class White districts afforded their students a number of amenities, such as new books every year, this was not the case for Black schools. Nonetheless, since they paid taxes, Black parents insisted their tax dollars be used to establish quality schools for children. Yet, in many instances it would be years before schools for Black children began to receive simple benefits such as new books. Nonetheless, teachers and administrators, parents, and the community did what they could to support and prepare students for the future. In doing so, they incorporated forms of cultural capital to prepare the next generation of African American educators, scholars, athletes, and leaders.

Black schools were part of the fabric of the community. Once torn at the seams, with the closing of several schools, it greatly transformed the community. As demonstrated throughout the book and well documented in the literature, desegregation often did more harm than good, especially on Black communities (Morris & Morris, 2004) and educators. To illustrate, Milner and Howard (2004) reported "approximately 38,000 African American teachers and administrators in 17 states lost their positions between 1954 and 1965" (p. 286).

Although early Black high schools lacked resources, children found themselves nestled in a stable community. Parents, teachers, and administrators were part of an extended family for many students. It was not unusual for Black children to live on the same block as teachers, doctors, lawyers, and other professionals. Thus providing them with numerous role models.

We have often been "led to believe that the contributions of African Americans to education in this country were limited primarily to pioneers like Booker T. Washington and George Washington Carver" (Morris & Morris, 2002, p. 2). As this volume demonstrates, there were many unsung heroes and heroines who contributed greatly to the education of Black children in high schools. Not everyone was a teacher. Indeed, Black entrepreneurs, politicians, and alumni contributed to the success of the children's education. Morris (2004) points out, although there were "gross inequalities in the distribution of resources and the unresponsiveness to the needs of Black students by all-White school boards and state officials, some Black schools boasted strong reputations for providing an exemplary education" (p. 71). The schools discussed in this book are no different. Many well-known Black artists, politicians, educators, and others are alumni of the high schools represented in this book. Many schools were known for their progressive methods and a curriculum that celebrated Black culture. To illustrate, between 1940 and 1946, I. M. Terrell High School teachers participated in the Secondary School Study funded by the General Education Board, which further developed "their administrative, curricular, and instructional practices" (Kridel, 2018, p. vi). Furthermore, they, along with staff, were able to "reconsider the basic purpose of secondary education and to address classroom problems . . . that so greatly affected the education of back youth" (Kridel, p. vi).

Black teachers' and administrators' role in educating Black children was tantamount to the children's success. They were woven into the very fabric of students' lives. Black teachers prepared students for a better world. They knew what the children would face in a racist society and wanted them to succeed academically and professionally. Although their opportunities were limited, they believed future generations would encounter more open doors. It takes a community to raise a child. It also takes a community to educate a child.

Authors use historical documents, interviews from alumni, teachers, and administrators, as well as autoethnographies and autobiographies to illuminate the past and shed light on the current status of these formidable schools whose founders had foresight to understand the importance of not only education, but education within a community where students felt loved, cared for, and respected. Additionally, authors provide insight into the impact of desegregation on students and Black communities.

One of the earliest high schools created for Black children was the former Institute for Colored Youth (ICY) in Philadelphia. Molly O'Connor discusses how this school, established during the antebellum period, was birthed by many community organizations such as literary societies and Black churches. ICY prided itself on offering a curriculum that was culturally relevant and attractive to an elite staff. This included the longest-serving principal, Fanny Jackson Coppin, and other educators who were considered *firsts* such as Grace A. Mapps, reportedly, the first Black 4-year degree recipient from New York Central College (Smith, 1996) and Ebenezer Don Carlos Bassett, the "first Black diplomat in U.S. history" (Byrd, 2022, p. 35). ICY would eventually become Cheyney University, which is still thriving today.

Bradley Poos, Loyce Caruthers, and Marceline Cooley take us to the Midwest as they explore Lincoln High School, Kansas City, Missouri's, first segregated high school for Black children. Lincoln students had the reputation of being high-level achievers (Lincoln High School, 1970). As the authors note, the majority of the teachers attended HBCUs and many received a master's degree or doctorate from well-known institutions including Columbia University and Michigan State University, thus bringing with them a wealth of knowledge. They also bring to fore the Black leaders and professionals who supported the community in a number of ways.

E. Paulette Isaac-Savage and Vanessa Garry examine the first Black high school west of the Mississippi—Sumner High School. They provide a "narrative of the community's engagement in the evolution" of it from St. Louis Public Schools' "delayed opening of the school to its pinnacle days during the early and mid-20th century to the waning of its existence today." They employ funds of knowledge (Vélez-Ibáñez's & Greenberg, 1992) as part of their theoretical framework. Black leaders within Sumner and in the community along with teachers and principals ensured students received a proper education. They also created a family culture for students. This culture helped to produce some well-known graduates such as Arthur Ashe, Tina Turner, and Dick Gregory.

Using oral history interviews, Tasha Coble Ginn uncovers several themes in relation to students' experiences at I. M. Terrell High School. A common theme, which is indicative of chapters throughout the book, is how *faculty and staff cared for their students*. Coble Ginn's examples from alumni epitomize a sense of caring from their teachers. She explores the impact on the Black community when the school closed. In a word: disintegration. As was the case for many Black students, Coble Ginn describes how they lost role models, and the "opportunities to build social capital through familial ties" dissipated. She ponders if "the closure was really about improved access to education."

William Kladky tells the story of Frederick Douglass High School. He incorporates what he describes as an "external lens"—Black political power networks. He explains, "political integration did not lead to social and racial integration." Located in Baltimore, Maryland, numerous networks consisting of business people, ministers, educators, and benevolent organizations were instrumental "for educating and rallying the African American and advocacy communities." The *Baltimore Afro-American*, a weekly newspaper, was a prominent advocate for the community and often provided support to and awareness of issues impacting African Americans in Baltimore. Alumni have played an important role in the life of Frederick Douglass High School. They have used their political prowess to call for change and improvements to Douglass over the years.

In the only South Carolina chapter represented in this book, Vann Holden examines the story of two schools in Harbison Junior College and Richlex School. Fortunately for Holden, Vidal and Mooneyhan (2006) created the documentary "*In Their Own Words: A History of Harbison Institute, 1911–1958* (*In Their Own Words*), a film that includes interviews from former Harbison students. With it and other sources, Holden discusses how Harbison and Richlex created forms of cultural capital. He acknowledges the bi-directional relationship between Harbison and Biddle University (now Johnson C. Smith University). For example, Calvin

M. Young and J. G. Porter, who served as Harbison presidents, were alums of Biddle.

Not surprising, many African American communities named a school after the abolitionist Frederick Douglass. Oklahoma City, Oklahoma, was no different. Autumn B. Brown and Lucy E. Bailey describe Oklahoma City's Douglass High School as a place of justice and hope. In existence since 1891, the authors explore the important relationship between the school and the community. Even today, among other things, Douglass High School remains a site "of racial equality, economic growth" and resistance.

Before it became synonymous with the 16th Street Baptist Church bombing, Birmingham, Alabama, was home to A.H. Parker High School, the first 4-year public school for African Americans in the city. Interestingly, the school held its first commencement at 16th Street Baptist Church. Named after Arthur Harold Parker, an educator and principal of the high school, Penny Seals explores, among other things, the establishment of the school, attitudes and beliefs of school personnel, institutional policies, and the impact of desegregation on teachers from the context of social and cultural capital. As it is still in operation today, she further discusses how it is living out its rich legacy.

In one of three Texas high schools represented in the book, Altheria Caldera discusses the short history of Fort Worth, Texas's Como High School. The Como community epitomized what it meant to be tangibly poor, but intangibly rich. The children were fortunate to live in a close-knit family community. Teachers were like extended family members. Through numerous extracurricular activities such as the French Club, Science Club, and Speech Club, students showcased their creativity and skills. However, like other Black neighborhoods, Caldera points out how desegregation caused a juxtaposition between progress and loss for the students and the community.

Dunbar High School, in Texarkana, Texas, is yet another school that closed in the name of desegregation. M. Francyne Huckaby, Stephanie Cuellar, Michelle Nguyen, Leslie Ekpe, Rachel Brooks, Kellton Hollins, and Jonathan W. Crocker tell the story of the 52-year history of Dunbar. Dunbar provided a supportive and positive environment for its students and prepared them to engage on both the national and global stage. The authors incorporate interviews from Dunbar alumni. Unique to their chapter is the use of QR codes directing readers to actual interviews of alumni who attended the school over 50 years ago.

Amber M. Neal-Stanley relays how Athens, a small northeastern town in Georgia, became home to Athens High and Industrial School, the first Black public 4-year high school in the state. Neal-Stanley uncovers how the Black community's exclusion from White institutions, such as the University of Georgia, and resistance to racism and White supremacy spurred the community's efforts to provide education. She focuses on the legacy of Samuel F. Harris, who began teaching in the town in 1896 and eventually became synonymous with community involvement, strong leadership, and a pioneering classical and industrial educational model.

With the support of Vonzell Agosto, doctoral students Jacqueline K. Haynes, and Ann Marie Mobley share their personal experiences with Howard W. Blake High School. They incorporate the history of the school and the impact it had on Haynes and Mobley from a different lens. To illustrate, Haynes, a former Principal at Blake provides a unique perspective as she relates her observations of her father who attended Howard W. Blake High School and how the lessons he learned from the school set the stage for his 31-year. They also primed her for her future educational roles.

Using Morris's (2004) metaphorical Nazareth, when he asked, if anything good can come from it, we hope this book represents a resounding *yes*! While his focus was on urban schooling, the chapters in this book demonstrate the "good" that derived from Black communities in various contexts and the Black high schools that produced generations of successful graduates. Despite the foreboding challenges before them to educate Black children, the Black community, using its cultural capital, coalesced its human and other resources to provide a quality education that would prepare Black children for the oppressive society in which they lived.

We hope this book generates more discussion on the role of social networks in the development of African American high schools, high schools' connection to the community, prominent administrators, teachers, and students' contributions to the schools and society. We believe this book is a vehicle for historians, educators, sociologists, and others to give voice to the community stalwarts, administrators, teachers, graduates, and students, as well as for those schools still in operation, who were responsible for these neighborhood institutions. Chronicling these narratives contributes to the literature about the many African American institutions countering repressive policies and social issues that negatively affected the education of Black children.

—*Vanessa Garry*
—*E. Paulette Isaac-Savage*
—*Sha-Lai L. Williams*

REFERENCES

Butchart, R. E. (2010). *Schooling the freed people: Teaching, learning, and the struggle for Black freedom, 1861–1876*. University of North Carolina Press. http://www.jstor.org/stable/10.5149/9780807899342_butchart

Butchart, R. E., & Rolleri, A. F. (2004). Secondary education and emancipation: Secondary schools for freed slaves in the American South, 1862–1875. *Paedagogica Historica, 40*(1–2), 157–181.

Byrd, B. (2022). Ebenezer Bassett and Frederick Douglass: An intellectual history of Black U.S. Diplomacy. *Diplomatic History, 46*(1), 35–69. https://doi.org/10.1093/dh/dhab073

Franklin, V. P. (1990). Education for life: Adult education programs for African Americans in northern cities, 1900–1942. In H. G. Neufeldt & L. McGee (Eds.), *Education of the African American adult: An historical overview* (pp. 113–134). Greenwood Press.

Kridel, C. (Ed.). (2018). *Becoming an African American progressive educator. Narratives from 1940s Black progressive high schools*. Museum of Education. University of South Carolina. http://museumofeducation.info/narratives.pdf

Lincoln High School. (1970). *Garnett Wilson* [Reunion Booklet].

McPherson, J. M. (1970). White liberals and black power in Negro education, 1865–1915. *The American Historical Review, 75*(5), 1357–1386.

Milner, H. R., & Howard, T. C. (2004). Black teachers, Black students, Black communities and Brown: Perspectives and insights from experts. *The Journal of Negro Education, 73*(3), 285–297.

Morris, J. E. (2004). Can anything good come from Nazareth? Race, class, and African American schooling and community in the urban south and Midwest. *American Educational Research Journal, 41*(1), 69–112. https://doi.org/10.3102/00028312041001069

Morris, V. G., & Morris, C. L. (2002). *The price they paid: Desegregation in an African American community*. Teachers College Press.

Rabinowitz, H. N. (1976). From exclusion to segregation: Southern race relations, 1865–1890. *The Journal of American History, 63*(2), 325–350.

Sowell, T. (1976). Patterns of black excellence. *Public Interest, 43*, 26–58.

Smith, J. C. (1996). *Notable Black American women, Book 2*. Gale Research Inc.

Velez-Ibanez, C. G., & Greenberg, J. B. (1992). Formation and transformation of funds of knowledge among U.S.-Mexican households. *Anthropology and Education Quarterly, 23*(4), 313–335.

Vidal, E. M., & Mooneyhan, B. (Producers). (2006*). In their own words: A history of Harbison Institute: 1911–1958* [Video file]. https://www.youtube.com/watch?v=KzU80HbAuqc

Walker, V. S. (2009). Second-class integration: A historical perspective for a contemporary agenda. *Harvard Educational Review, 79*(2), 269–284.

Williams, H. S. (1920). The development of the Negro public school system in Missouri. *The Journal of Negro History, 5*(2), 137–165.

Yosso, T. J. (2005). Whose culture has capital? A critical race theory discussion of community cultural wealth. *Race Ethnicity and Education 8*(1), 69–91. https://doi.org/10.1080/1361332052000341006

CHAPTER 1

INSTITUTE FOR COLORED YOUTH (CHEYNEY UNIVERSITY)

Philadelphia, PA

Molly E. O'Connor
Rutgers University

The Institute for Colored Youth (ICY) in Philadelphia was founded upon the community cultural wealth (Yosso, 2005) of existing Black churches, social organizations, and learned societies in 19th century Philadelphia. The school not only owed its existence to community cultural wealth but also created and built cultural wealth of its own, beginning as a private secondary school with a primary section and growing into the first Black college in the country. As a secondary institution, ICY provided a first-rate education to its students via a demanding curriculum and outstanding faculty, while also providing educational resources to the Philadelphia Black community at-large. This historical analysis traces the origins of ICY, the unique curriculum, and its notable leaders, educators, and alumni, and finally considers the institute's legacy. The first section traces the state of education for Black Philadelphians and provides political context for ICY. The second section uncovers the crucial support of religious and community organizations and African Americans prioritizing education early through literary societies and self-education—doing both the work and the advocacy that laid the foundations of ICY. The final section illuminates how ICY's challenging curriculum delivered by politically engaged educators resulted in a strong network of high achieving alumni and programs and facilities that benefited the city's entire Black community.

Keywords: History of Education, HBCU, Black Educators, Philadelphia

INSTITUTE FOR COLORED YOUTH, PHILADELPHIA, PA

The Institute for Colored Youth (ICY) in Philadelphia was founded upon the community cultural wealth (Yosso, 2005) of existing Black churches, social organizations, and learned societies in 19th century Philadelphia. The school not only owed its existence to community cultural wealth but also created and built cultural wealth of its own, beginning as a private secondary school with a primary section and growing into the first Black college in the country. As a secondary institution, ICY provided a first-rate education to its students via a demanding curriculum and

INSTITUTE FOR COLORED YOUTH

Photo Courtesy of Documenting the American South, Libraries of the University of North Carolina, Chapel Hill.

outstanding faculty, while also providing educational resources to the Philadelphia Black community at-large.

This chapter uses historical analysis to argue that ICY was born out of the cultural capital garnered by the free Black community in Philadelphia and, in turn, the institute begat expanded opportunities for its graduates and the larger Black community, increasing the cultural capital of the next generations. Relying on primary and secondary sources, this account traces the origins of ICY, the unique curriculum, and its notable leaders, educators, and alumni, and finally considers the institute's legacy. By recognizing the types of capital the Black community of Philadelphia exercises in the founding and builds in the prospering of ICY, I use and deepen the lens of cultural community wealth as a cumulative kind of wealth that begats new and greater forms of capital out of its initial wealth.

What was cultural community wealth for this community of free Black Philadelphians? Beginning with the Free African Society (FAS) in 1787 (one of the first Black organized civic societies in the new nation), Black civic groups in Philadelphia numbered over 100 by 1850 with just over 50% of all free Black households participating, 61% participation in houses headed by former slaves, and an overwhelming 80–90% participation of the wealthiest 10% of African Americans (Hershberg, 1971–1972). FAS led to the creation of a multitude of similar mutual aid and moral societies; its leaders provided navigational capital and subsequent organizations built critical infrastructure to a community that lacked many of the public supports available to their White counterparts (Porter, 1936; Rafferty, 2016).

By the mid-1800s, Philadelphia Black residents had organized anti-slavery societies and boasted of at least 10 Black literary societies (of which records survive), strong Black churches (Mother Bethel AME, First African Baptist and St. Thomas African Episcopal), and the Philadelphia Library Company of Colored People. The new societies along with other libraries and reading rooms made up the cultural wealth in the Philadelphia Black community for a group of residents who lacked adequate access to public schooling, public or private secondary and tertiary education options, and the resources White communities typically relied to create schools (including local political power) (Porter, 1936; Villanova Library, n.d.-c). These organizations created wealth for Black Philadelphians by providing them with spaces to teach and learn knowledge held by elite Whites with access to education, to organize toward community and political goals, and to preserve and create their own knowledge, history, and identity as Black Americans. ICY was built upon this wealth and multiplied it by becoming a resource to the community, making political activism an intentional part of the curriculum, emphasizing a positive sense of Black identity, and equipping its students with the education and consciousness to navigate unchartered territory in business, politics, and the academy.

The first section of this chapter traces the state of education for Black Philadelphians and provides some political context for ICY. The second section uncovers the crucial support of religious and community organizations and African Americans prioritizing education early through literary societies and self-education—doing both the work and the advocacy that laid the foundations of ICY. These factors led to a demand and means for secondary education in the bustling city. The final section and bulk of the chapter relies heavily on original archival research to illuminate how ICY's challenging curriculum delivered by politically engaged educators resulted in a strong network of high achieving alumni and programs and facilities that benefited the city's entire Black community. The strong leadership of educators and administrators, a competitive, relevant curriculum, and an engaged alumni network led to student exposure to a national and international community of African Americans who were successful, politically engaged in pursuing citizenship, and globally connected with Black communities around the world.

SETTING THE SCENE FOR ICY: ANTEBELLUM PHILADELPHIA POLITICS AND EDUCATION

When the Philadelphia public school system was established in 1834 with the passage of The Free Public School Act and the city's first all-White high school in 1836, the public options for African American students included very few primary schools and a grammar school (Department of Public Instruction, 1934). By 1850, 240 public schools existed in Philadelphia County (essentially co-terminus with the modern city of Philadelphia) for White students versus three for Black students (United States Census Bureau, 1850; Silcox, 1973a). The rise of the public school system for White students and the prosperous Philadelphia economy, which few free Blacks were able to take part in, led to a call for two things by Black businessmen and community leaders: (a) schools to educate African American children in skilled trades and (b) trained African American teachers to staff schools. These goals drove the founding of ICY in 1837 by the Philadelphia Quaker community. ICY provided its graduates with an education that equipped them to break legal, educational, and social barriers. They also helped create a network and legacy of what would later be called Historically Black Colleges and Universities (HBCUs). Prior to becoming Cheyney University, ICY offered African Americans in the Philadelphia area a secondary education for nearly a century before awarding its first college degrees in 1932. The decades that preceded ICY were fraught with resistance to basic education for Black Philadelphians, an equally difficult struggle for political recognition, and a large free and growing Black population which increasingly organized for community advancement.

1820s: Philadelphia Public Schooling Established

In the decade preceding the founding of ICY, public education was a recent development and hard to come by for Black Philadelphians. In 1822, the first Philadelphia public school for Black males opened, followed by a school for girls in 1826. Just two years later, the two schools merged into the Lombard Street School, after the building was deemed too rundown for White students (Bacon, 2005). The 1827 Controllers of the Public School reported the limited success of Lombard, noting, "Of 324 pupils on the roll, only 64 had progressed to the elementary stages of the alphabet. Also, only 12 per cent studied the more difficult skill of writing. This reflected the least accomplishment in any Philadelphia public school" (Silcox, 1973a, p. 452). The school was under-resourced and, as a result, poorly performing compared to the local White schools. While schools for Black students existed in antebellum Philadelphia, many Black families lacked access to formal schooling and to quality instruction—something the ICY sought to redress.

1830s: On the Eve of ICY

By 1834, the governor had signed the Free Public School Act, providing free, universal public education for White students and free public education for few African American students (as there were few public schools for students of color). The act updated 1809 legislation, which provided free education only to students who were in poverty, effectively stigmatizing (mostly White) students as paupers (Department of Public Instruction, 1934). It was at the end of this decade that ICY was founded on a farm outside of Philadelphia briefly under the name the African Institute, chartered in 1837 with property acquired in 1839 (James, 1958). Only a year later, the Commonwealth of Pennsylvania disenfranchised free Black men (The Convention, 1838). Unfortunately, this decade would end by codifying disenfranchisement for Black males across Pennsylvania and with an attempt to curtail educational opportunity for Black students in Philadelphia. The political freedoms seemed to be narrowing as restrictions continued to be codified, but ICY began to widen educational opportunities available to Black Americans.

1840s: A Slow Start for ICY

Despite the passage of the Free Public School Act, the Philadelphia Board of Education moved to close the Lombard Street School in 1840, due to the poor management of the consistently under-resourced school and the Lancasterian system falling out of political favor (a system in which older or more advanced students teach younger students). This movement away from Lancasterian education favored White schools which already employed numerous trained, assistant teachers who easily could be assigned smaller, individual classes. The Lombard Street School had a nearly 200:1 student-teacher ratio for boys and 250:2 for girls (Silcox, 1973a). Instead of increasing resources for Lombard to hire more teachers or opening additional schools, the Philadelphia school board proposed replacing the school with a single primary school for each gender, effectively reducing the education provided to Black students to only three years.

Prominent Black, local businessman James Forten, supported by the Abolition Society, leveraged his social capital, and created resistance capital to keep the Lombard Street School open (Forten, 1831). As a successful, local business owner and skilled tradesman, Forten had garnered the respect of the White Philadelphia business community and was a successful emissary on behalf of Black Philadelphians to White leadership in the city. His success in business had given him both access to and influence among White power networks, which he wielded when he addressed the public school board with a plea to keep the Lombard Street School open; his plea was ultimately successful. Forten was motivated by his desire to promote education and economic self-sufficiency for the good of the community, even though he himself retained private tutors to educate his large family. The city opposition and resistance to providing Black students with basic education created not only an opening for a private, community-supported secondary school like the ICY but also the only way such a school would happen in the political climate.

Educational inequality between Black and White Philadelphians continued to grow with the opening of Philadelphia's first public high school for White boys in 1836 and for White girls in 1848. Meanwhile, there was no high school option or grades beyond grammar school open to African American students in Philadelphia, save for a short-lived private high school, supported by the Pennsylvania Abolition Society (Bacon, 2005). Given the dearth of primary schools and single grammar school (grades 4–8) for African American students in the newly established Philadelphia public school system, few Black students were prepared for high school level coursework. Aspirations for a better future—one in which being educated meant greater access to living wage jobs and provided further justification for enfranchisement—lay at the foundations of ICY. Quakers founded ICY; though it was administered by Black leadership and staffed by Black teachers. ICY began by offering Black boys a rigorous combination of manual labor training and academics for 11–12 hours daily in Bristol township until a temporary closure in 1845 (now part of present-day north Philadelphia, Bristol township was then farmland outside the city) (James, 1958).

1850s: ICY Moves to Center City Philadelphia

Struggling for adequate facilities and funds, ICY regrouped and re-opened in 1852 in center city Philadelphia; it was in the heart of Philadelphia's Black community that ICY began to earn its illustrious reputation (James, 1958). Given the state of education in Philadelphia for Black families, it is all the more impressive that a first-rate secondary school was founded. By the 1850 Census, one third of free Black adults in Philadelphia were categorized as unable to read and write, compared to only 5.5% of the White population. Just over 40% of African American children were not enrolled in Philadelphia schools in this period. Many Black families, though free, remained without access to education in Philadelphia. This included institutional access for children or basic literacy for adults (United States Census Bureau, 1850).

Here in the center of Philadelphia, ICY would both be at the center of the Black community and of the rising political tension in Philadelphia. Despite having been the reality in Philadelphia for decades, segregated (and inferior) schools in the Commonwealth of Pennsylvania were officially authorized in 1854 (Commonwealth of Pennsylvania, 1854). The 1830s and 1840s had brought the curbing of political and educational freedoms for Black Philadelphians as the number of free Black residents in the city increased, riots raged across the city, Nat Turner's Slave Revolt in Virginia had sparked fear in White communities across the country, and Black communities began politically organizing through the Colored Conventions and other political activities (Foreman et al., 2021; Negro Insurrection, 1831). The Fugitive Slave Act (1850) had added a new level of terror at the national level to the ongoing local race riots (occurring nearly annually or every few years during these three decades) and to the refusals of service African Americans faced daily. The Supreme Court affirmed publicly sanctioned, second-class treatment for African Americans when it handed down the *Dred Scott v. Sanford* ruling in 1857—explicitly denying that free Blacks were afforded the rights and privileges of American citizenship (U.S. Supreme Court & Taney, 1860). The success of ICY was far from assured in this climate, even as it re-opened in 1852 under new, Black leadership, head teacher Charles L. Reason (James, 1958).

The intimate connection between the political status of African Americans and their educational opportunities is foundational to understanding how and why the ICY developed and (eventually) flourished. Making ICY a success in such an oppositional environment required both navigational and aspirational capital. In response to the obstacles placed by the Philadelphia school board and general resistance to Black education, the re-opened ICY began to offer some non-traditional elements of education to the Black community that spoke to the social and political climate: a primary program to prepare students for an academically rigorous secondary education, a public reading room for its library, and lecture series or night courses to expand their reach, among other resources.

THE ROOTS OF ICY: COMMUNITY ORGANIZATIONS IN PHILADELPHIA

The early development of secondary education for Black Philadelphians evolved from the strong presence of literary societies (home to more learned groups than any other U.S. city), economic success in the Black community, and a strong network of community organizations. Though literary societies were not so robust as to be institutions of formal education in themselves, they gave shape to an influential secondary education of high academic quality that fostered a unique community and formed future leaders. ICY housed administrators and faculty who saw and enacted education as part of a wider vision of racial uplift, emancipation, and political equality, and provided spaces for an international Black identity to become salient.

Community Organizations That Influenced the Development of ICY

A critical building block of secondary and higher education in antebellum Philadelphia —of which ICY is the first such institution on both accounts—was the work of many community groups that championed education more broadly. Education in Antebellum and even post-war Philadelphia was not provided to African Americans—it required advocacy, organizing, and financial resources. The compelling reasons driving a community demand for education were two-fold: first, as some free Black workers experienced economic success, they wanted to ensure similar growth for the community to which they belonged and for future generations. Forten relied on his expert skills crafting sails and was highly influential in agitating for educational opportunities so that other young men would be able to gain a skilled trade and make profit. Beyond a concern for economic self-sustainability and the goal of social mobility, Philadelphia's growing free Black population and the city's more progressive politics (including a strong abolitionist Quaker community) made the city a hotbed of American politics, where education was viewed as a way to equality and respectability. These two goals—economic self-sufficiency and political equality—are seen throughout the work of ICY.

In the absence of adequate public education, churches, mutual aid societies, and civic groups all helped make education available or more accessible. The Pennsylvania Abolition Society started private schools, Clarkson Hall and Clarkson Hall Evening Association, to provide Philadelphia African American children and adults with basic instruction (Pennsylvania Society for Promoting the Abolition of Slavery, 1911; Newman, n.d.). Churches often founded schools or helped to sponsor students' tuition. African American churches such as Mother Bethel African Methodist Episcopal Church, First African Baptist, and the African Episcopal Church of St. Thomas not only helped to start schools, but also served as a community rallying point for other societies and hosted society meetings, like the Colored Conventions (Nash, 1991). In these ways, Black community organizations and Quaker allies leveraged existing community capital to create educational opportunities for others and in providing basic education created a demand in the city for a secondary school.

Working together to sponsor mutual aid societies, educational organizations, and civic groups, the Quaker and Black communities in Philadelphia had come together many times before Quaker benefactor Robert Humphreys left money to finance ICY in his will. These two communities were joined by a common understanding of community as a collective. A predominantly White religion, the Quakers were formative in both providing educational opportunities for African American children (through their designated Board of Education) and advocating for their rights (through groups like the Pennsylvania Abolition Society) (Bacon, 2005). Mutual aid societies sometimes overlapped with organizations advocating for reforms. Black and Quaker leaders again joined forces to realize the vision for ICY and the membership of the Philadelphia Abolition Society Board of Education (not to be confused with the city's Board of Education) also overlapped significantly with Black ICY leaders and instructors (Bacon, 2005).

Religious denominations and community organizations were crucial in helping newly freed, manumitted, and escaped slaves meet basic needs and acquire jobs, as well as paving the way for primary level education for children and adults. Societies preparing children and adults with basic literacy and numeracy and advocating for secondary education opportunities set the groundwork that enabled Black students to be prepared for secondary education and trained the earliest teachers. ICY's eventual success with high school, teacher preparation, manual training, and the classical course programs were initially made possible by these societies organizing, advocating for access, funding, and founding these educational institutions.

African American Literary Societies

The eighteenth-century learned societies in particular allowed for the rise of African American community leaders and intellectuals, as well as the diffusion of knowledge within the community. Several African American literary and debating societies began during this time, and the popularity of libraries and reading rooms grew (Porter, 1936). Members of Black literary societies gave and sponsored lectures, essays, and debates, practicing skills that were only usually acquired in White educational spaces. Society members gained access to the social capital that comes from fluency in and exposure to literature, history, philosophy, and the sciences—but they also held aspirational capital, maintaining hope that this knowledge would help their communities attain equality economically and politically. Several of the members published articles in the African American-run newspapers and journals—a public testament to their capabilities and sharpening their counterclaim to all too often-presupposed racial intellectual inferiority. Today, there is little surviving information on how the early leaders and founders of these literary societies were themselves so well-versed in subjects such as mathematics and chemistry, when laws and institutions limited their access to knowledge.

In these intellectual societies, members debated different strategies for achieving abolition and how to best educate themselves and their children with debate topics like, "Is it right for our people to approve all persons who publicly advocate emigration to Liberia?" and "Has slavery been beneficial to the African race?" (Martin, 2002, pp. 309–310). The literary societies and libraries were crucial given the state of education for Blacks in Philadelphia and trained many early Black intellectuals. These organizations and the resulting scholarship members produced were active forms of resistance to a White majority society that tried to withhold and restrict educational opportunities from its Black members. These writing, reading, and debate skills—skills used to argue and persuade—would be the backbone of ICY's curriculum.

THE WORK OF ICY: EXCELLENCE IN SECONDARY EDUCATION

An 1833 newspaper editorial cited the "establishment of libraries, reading- rooms, and debating societies" (Porter, 1936, p. 562) as a chief source of racial uplift for the Philadelphia Black community. "The subjects of discussion generally relate to their own rights and interests and frequently result in decisions from which the prejudiced mind of the white man would startle and shrink with apprehension," the article author noted (Porter, 1936, p. 562). Through debates, public orations, and penning persuasive essays in the local Black papers, society members sharpened their skills to advocate for their platform. It is this innate coupling of emancipation and education—an explicit education for full citizenship and the activism required to achieve that—of which ICY takes up the mantle. These same skills are seen in the ICY program through the curriculum and community, its extraordinary educators, helping students form a positive Black identity, serving as community resource and outpost of the diaspora, and the successes of its alumni.

Curriculum and Community

Though ICY began as a farm school in the Bristol Township in Philadelphia County (near present-day La Salle University's campus) in 1837 as the African Institute (James, 1959), it was with its 1852 move to center city Philadelphia that the school began fulfilling benefactor Richard Humphreys's desire to provide more equitable educational opportunities for students of color (G., 1833). There, ICY offered private, secondary, and primary education led by Black administrators that was unavailable to Black Philadelphians in the public system. No high school was available to Black students and the Lombard Street School did not have enough teachers or resources to serve the whole community. As the first secondary school serving African Americans in the country, ICY offered students from Philadelphia and beyond an elite education on par with White elite schools, while also offering curriculum that was culturally relevant and programs that served the wider local community.

In May 1864, alumnus and administrator Octavius Catto gave an address on the institute's history at the 12th annual commencement, published by the Alumni Association with a summary of the school's commencement exercises. He detailed the founding of what became ICY by an 1842 act of the Pennsylvania Legislature, incorporated by the Society of Friends (Catto, 1864). A Quaker philanthropist, Richard Humphreys initially funded the school with a gift of $10,000, in attempts to reduce the disparity between the two races (Catto, 1864). Humphreys and fellow Quakers, like the Philadelphia Black community, saw education as the key to the realization of civil rights and equal treatment under law based on citizenship and not on skin color. Humphreys set out to create an institution of learning that would prepare Black youth for mechanical arts and teaching, addressing both the economic and educational problems faced by the Black community (Pennsylvania Legislative Session of 1842). By 1852, the African Institute moved to downtown Philadelphia and was rechristened ICY with a high school for each gender. Later ICY added primary sections and focused primarily on teacher training, fulfilling Humphreys's full original intention for the school (Coppin, 1913). These programs and others offered by the school would grow the cultural community wealth in the Philadelphia Black community upon which the ICY was founded and create new, expanded forms of capital for its graduates.

The school's mission dictated its curriculum, and it was informed by Humphreys' aspirations for the school and Black businessmen and their societies. Humphreys bequeathed his fortune to the cause of higher education for African Americans—so its first mission was providing equal educational opportunities to and training in the trades to increase future career opportunities for students of color that were already available to their White peers. ICY's mission was also formed by a combination of advocates for education; drawing on the minds from the Black business community, mutual aid societies, and literary societies that advocated for education in Philadelphia more broadly and that helped shepherd the demand for this school. The curriculum was targeted at providing teacher education to expand education opportunities for Black students and to provide instruction in skilled labor, so workers could access higher paying jobs in mechanics and agriculture (Catto, 1864). Academic excellence became a hallmark of the school, so much so that ICY drew students from as far as Virginia and the Carolinas in addition to a strong regional and local student base and that it grew into one of the first Black colleges in the nation. The curriculum reflected both the needs and the aspirations of the Black community in Philadelphia—from the need for more teachers to the call for skilled labor and to the political debates and lectures at the heart of the learned societies.

Graduates were free to pursue the career of their choice, though administrators made a special effort to ensure students interested in teaching had the opportunity to attend. The school began with a classical academic-focused curriculum and developed mechanical and agricultural training under the long tenure of Principal Fanny Jackson Coppin, the third principal of the school. Swept up in the zeitgeist of Booker T. Washington in the early 20th century, ICY evolved to focus more intently on its teacher training program and agricultural work.

A rigorous curriculum provided students the foundation to break new societal barriers. The culmination of ICY's academics was brought to the fore in the days prior to commencement; students were given a "public examination…in Greek, Latin, Mathematics, and higher English studies" (Catto, 1864, p. 3). The published graduation pamphlets recounted the exam contents for each subject, highlighting the classical, rigorous curriculum provided by ICY. In the subject of Greek alone, students were expected to master the "Greek Testament, extracts from Homer, Lucian, and Anacreon" (Catto, 1864, p. 3). Successful scanning Greek poetry and fluency in grammar were also skills expected of students. Students and alumni both took part in reading original oratories.

The school was committed to more than teaching the tomes of Western civilization; ICY equipped students with an education that would liberate them and counter White justifications for enslavement and second-class status of Black Americans:

> It is wise to pause and remember, that the principles of right, equity, and justice; the very ideas of an improved civilization, more benign and general in its diffusion; the very moral conception of individual and mutual rights of property, contract and government, upon which the people of the North justify their attitude in the present conflict, have never been more successfully and generally promulgated than through the teachings of the School. (Catto, 1864, p. 10)

If the South had had equivalent education, Catto argued, "for the masses, irrespective of class or color...we to-night [sic] would not be at the crisis of a civil war" (Catto, 1864, p. 10). Education for Black or White students was inseparable from politics. Catto argued that education was vital to the preservation of the State.

During Principal Fanny Coppin's impressive tenure, arriving as a teacher in 1865 and serving as head principal from 1869 to 1902, she strove to provide students with a classical education and an accessible, practical education with which students could make a living. With the purchase of Cheyney farm in 1902, the school would shift its curricular focus from strenuous academics to teacher certification and manual labor. By 1905, the first-year classes were offered at the new Cheyney campus—Booker T. Washington's concept of manual training for teachers dominated the curriculum and Washington himself would deliver the opening address (Brooks & Stark, 2011). Despite the classical course falling out of favor, the school continued to churn out graduates who were trailblazers, to host renowned Black leaders as speakers and educators, and to build a library with funds from Andrew Carnegie in 1909. As part of serving the community beyond the average 100-student daily attendance in 1862 (growing to nearly 200 by the end of Ebenezer Bassett's tenure as the institute's second principal), ICY multiplied the community wealth it created by providing education and resources to the community via evening courses, a public reading room, and summer institutes—and would later become home to some African American social service organizations (Biddle & Dubin, 2010; *The Christian Recorder*, 1862). By its 12th annual commencement in 1864, ICY had four divisions—two high schools and two elementary schools, divided by gender.

Extraordinary Educators

The exceptional African American faculty was crucial in forming a generation of educated pioneers for both the economy and the academy. Of the school's six teachers, three of them were ICY alumni—evidence that the school was fulfilling its mission. In addition to graduates, ICY employed teachers from the elite network of highly educated African Americans, including some of the first Black graduates of Harvard and Yale as teachers—Richard Greener and Edward Bouchet (Bass &

Branch, 2014; Coppin, 1913;). Sarah Mapps Douglass was the first principal of the girls' division and Charles L. Reason the head of the school. Reason was an activist as well as an educator; he served as an education reporter for the Colored Conventions Movement (Williams, 2001). Perhaps its best-known administrators were Ebenezer Bassett and the longest serving principal, Fanny Jackson Coppin.

From the time of its re-location to Philadelphia, the school's principals and educators were a reflection of the community it served. The Quaker managing board specifically advertised for administrators and teachers of color (*The National Era*, 1852). Thought to be the first Black woman to earn a four-year college degree from New York Central College, Grace A. Mapps was the first teacher hired and the first principal for females, named in 1852 (Smith, 1925; Smith, 1996). An accomplished academic, Charles L. Reason led the school for three years before leaving to head another school out of state (James, 1958). The second principal, African American Ebenezer Bassett, took the helm in 1857; he was the first Black graduate of Connecticut Normal School and teacher in New Haven (Wynes, 1984). Growing ICY's network abroad, in 1869, Bassett was appointed as minister to Haiti and the Dominican Republic, the first ever Black diplomat to represent the United States.

The institute's first principal, Charles L. Reason, was a son of Haitian immigrants. He envisioned and enacted an institution where:

> families would submit application and pay ten dollars for tuition, books, and stationery; the poorest pupils could attend free. Boys and girls alike would study algebra, trigonometry, poetry, the classics, and the sciences. In keeping with Richard Humphreys' will, students would learn to teach. (Biddle & Dubin, 2010, p. 157)

Bassett would later add "trigonometry, higher algebra, Latin and Greek to the curriculum," (Biddle & Dubin, 2010, p. 182) a curriculum that rivaled White elite schools. Reason used his personal "contacts in the black intelligentsia to arrange guest lectures; these too were open to all" (Biddle & Dubin, 2010, p. 157) and opened an impressive public reading room with about 450 visitors annually, making 4,088 book loans and hosting 1,554 visits to the reading room (Biddle & Dubin, 2010; Librarians' Second Annual Report, 1855). He grew the student body from six students at the start of his tenure in 1852 to 118 students by 1855 (Williams, 2001).

Born enslaved in the District of Columbia, Fanny Jackson Coppin came to ICY as a teacher after graduating from Rhode Island State Normal School and then from the gentleman's course at Oberlin (the gentleman's course was the collegiate degree—Coppin noted that the Oberlin gentleman's course was the same curriculum taught at Harvard College) (Coppin, 1913). After serving as principal of the female division under Bassett, Coppin was quickly elevated to principal of the entire school in 1869 (only four years after her arrival), a position she held for 33 years; she was the first Black woman to become a principal (Campbell, 1995). Coppin oversaw the development of ICY maintaining both fidelity to the classical curriculum and a dedication to an education that was accessible and taught practical skills. In her autobiography, *Reminiscences of School Life, and Hints on Teaching*, Coppin writes:

> In the year 1837, the Friends of Philadelphia had established a school for the education of colored youth in higher learning. To make a test whether or not the Negro was capable of acquiring any considerable degree of education. For it was one of the strongest arguments in the defense of slavery, that the Negro was an inferior creation; formed by the Almighty for just the work he was doing. It is said that John C. Calhoun made the remark, that if there could be found a Negro that could conjugate a Greek verb, he would give up all his preconceived ideas of the inferiority of the Negro. Well, let's try him, and see, said the fair-minded Quaker people. And for years this institution, known as the Institute for Colored Youth, was visited by interested persons from different parts of the United States and Europe. Here I was given the delightful task of teaching my own people, and how delighted I was to see them mastering Caesar, Virgil, Cicero, Horace and Xenophon's Anabasis. We also taught New Testament Greek. It was customary to have public examinations once a year, and when the teachers were thru examining their classes, any interested person in the audience was requested to take it up, and ask questions. At one of such examinations, when I asked a titled Englishman to take the class and examine it, he said: "They are more capable of examining me, their proficiency is simply wonderful." (Coppin, 1913, pp. 19–20)

Before Coppin developed the mechanical and industrial training department, helping to fulfill Humphreys additional intentions for the school, training in a skilled trade was only available to Black boys through the prison system or the House of Refuge, an alternative to prison (Coppin, 1913). To establish and fund the new departments, she spoke "before all the literary societies and churches where they would hear me; in Philadelphia and the suburban towns; in New York, Washington and everywhere" (Coppin, 1913, p. 24). The school that depended on the larger Black community to get its start, also depended on them for growth. In turn ICY would provide graduates educated in the following trades: "For boys: bricklaying, plastering, carpentry, shoemaking, printing and tailoring. For the girls: dressmaking, millinery, typewriting, stenography and classes in cooking, including both boys and girls. Stenography and typewriting were also taught to the boys, as well as the girls" (Coppin, 1913, p. 25).

Some of ICY alumni would return to serve as teachers as well. Building a network of educators and administrators who were well educated and well connected, not only provided students access to knowledge, but provided access to higher education or skilled jobs that otherwise would have been much harder for students to obtain. As graduates of Harvard, Yale, Oberlin, and more, ICY teachers leveraged their experiences from respected universities and colleges to teach Black youth, equipping them with academic and cultural capital that would enable them to do the same for the next generation. They also provided students with connections to White colleges and universities and were also able to help students navigate barriers in these still predominantly White institutions (Yosso, 2005). The teachers and administrators brought their reputations to the school and the institute garnered a reputation of its own. Such connections and increased levels of education provided increased social and cultural capital for students, which led to greater civic engagement.

Forming Black Identity and Staking a Place in the Diaspora

An important part of the curriculum was the solidification of a Black identity and a connection to the African Diaspora. Faculty members' experience spanned the diasporic experience—ranging from former enslavement to being born to immigrant parents or immigrating themselves and from advocating for equality in the United States to moving outside of the United States in hopes of a more equal future. In addition to being taught by extraordinary educators, ICY students heard guest and commencement speakers who were activists in the African American freedom struggle and in the international African diaspora. In fostering the common kinship among members of the African diaspora and encouraging students to pursue education or other fields that lifted up the Black community as a whole, faculty members built familial capital. Guest speakers were not an add-on or accidental to the curriculum—but part and parcel, providing "a sense of community history, memory, and cultural institution" (Yosso, 2005, p. 79). ICY was a school that provided both the dissemination of Black knowledge and formed creators of that knowledge. ICY speakers included Frederick Douglass, Booker T. Washington, Carter G. Woodson, Mary Church Terrell, and Mary McLeod Bethune (*The Christian Recorder*, 1863; Institute for Colored Youth Historical Marker, n.d.). W.E.B. Du Bois addressed students on three separate occasions (Institute for Colored Youth Historical Marker, n.d.). ICY was intentionally cultivating future activists that would not only advocate for political change but spread this mission as administrators and teachers in HBCUs and public schools (for other examples of this explicit "second curriculum" for activism throughout K–12 Black education, see Anderson, 1988; Favors, 2019).

In addition to hosting political and social activists, ICY administrators and faculty often wore multiple hats, teaching concepts in the classroom and working toward change beyond the walls of the school, embodying scholar Tara J. Yosso's concept of resistance capital. Sarah Douglass Mapps often wrote for William Lloyd Garrison's abolitionist newspaper, *The Liberator* and was a founding member of the Gilbert Lyceum, a literary and science society (Lindhorst, 1998; Porter, 1936). The faculty's well-connected political and social networks in the African American community paved a path for ICY graduates to pursue higher education, get work in the skilled trades, and advocate for equal rights—ultimately fulfilling Forten's goals. In pursuing higher education and in their activism, ICY graduates exemplified what social science research has shown: that there is a positive correlation between higher levels of education and civic involvement (Helliwell & Putnam, 2007). The social and political capital possessed by the ICY community led to many and begat many more successful firsts for graduates, as well as fostered a salient and positive Black identity from which students drew pride. This shared identity created a class of professionals, teachers, and laborers who were united in their pursuit of equality.

The impressive lecturers that made their way through ICY over the years supported identity formation and international diaspora connections. In 1913, Arthur Schomburg addressed the summer teaching institute at then Cheyney Institute with "a plea for the establishment for a chair of Negro history in our schools and colleges" (Schomburg, 1913, p. 1) –a campaign to make Black history part of the formal, explicit curriculum. "Where is our historian to give us, our side view and our chair of Negro History to teach our people our own history?" Schomburg asked his audience (Schomburg, 1913, p.18).

An ICY education equipped its students with resistance capital, preparing them to be the first African Americans in their professional fields, to create an infrastructure for Black education, and to advocate for political, social, and economic equality in the face of tremendous opposition. Coppin, in her autobiography, paints a bleak picture of the discrimination she faced upon her arrival in Philadelphia in contrast to her experiences at Oberlin. Catto's death is a testament to the violence perpetrated against men of color trying to exercise their right to vote, even in a northern city like Philadelphia with its sizeable free Black community and significant abolition efforts. An ICY education, according to Coppin, was intended to challenge arguments of Black inferiority, routinely used to perpetuate and protect the institution of enslavement.

Alumni

ICY alumni are some of the strongest examples of Yosso's navigational capital, as they broke barriers to receive education and professional training for a world in which they did not yet live—a world that valued the talents and skills of Black citizens on par with their White counterparts. In his 1864 graduation address, Catto said:

> Probably, there is no better way of judging the worth of the Institute than by glancing at the positions its graduates hold in the sphere of usefulness to their fellow-men, and the amount of intelligently directed labor they may be performing, to contradict the aspersions which have been cast upon the people with whom they are identified. (Catto, 1864, p. 14)

The first class of one student graduated in 1856 with a high school diploma, and only 14 total students had graduated from the institution by the 1860 commencement (Villanova Library, n.d.-b). Among these early graduating classes were future teachers and principals of the institute and of Philadelphia public schools, the second African American female doctor (the first to graduate from the Women's Medical College of Pennsylvania), and many future community leaders (National Institutes of Health, n.d.; Silcox, 1973b) ICY graduates were also breaking barriers as they furthered their education as the first Black graduate at the University Pennsylvania, the first Black student and graduate of the University of Pennsylvania's architecture school, the second Black woman to earn a M.D., and some of the few Black artists to receive training from the Philadelphia Academy of Fine Arts, to name just a few (Villanova Library, n.d.-b).

Forerunners in industry, the academy, and public service, graduates' success spans architecture, medicine, government, education, ministry, and law, among other fields. Julian Abele became a renowned architect, contributing to the city's art museum and designing the Widener Memorial Library at Harvard (Penn University Archives & Records Center, n.d.). Rebecca Cole was the second Black woman to earn a medical degree and practice medicine in South Carolina, Philadelphia, and eventually Washington, D.C. (National Institutes of Health, n.d.). John Wesley Cromwell was an activist and the first Black lawyer to argue a case in front of the Interstate Commerce Commission (Ruffle, n.d.). Another activist alumnus, Robert Douglass, Jr. was both an accomplished artist and an active leader in the National Colored Conventions (Dickinson et al., 2013/2016). John Smythe served as the U.S. ambassador to Liberia, as part of a career in the federal government (Villanova Library, n.d.-b).

In academia, Josephine Silone Yates was a chemist and possibly the first Black woman who achieved the rank of full professor (Culp, 1902; Kremer & Mackey, 1996). James B. Dudley—also an attendee of freedmen's schools and public schools in the South before attending ICY—became president of North Carolina A&T in 1896 (NC A&T University Archives, n.d.) Finally, Jacob C. White, Jr. became a major civil rights leader—a long-time friend of classmate turned colleague Catto—serving as an ICY teacher and part of the Black intelligentsia (Biddle & Dubin, 2010). White also played a key role in establishing a Black baseball club, the Philadelphia Pythians. These few ICY alumni success stories accompany many others, especially of pioneering teachers and administrators who went on to lead and teach in other institutions, fulfilling a founding mission of the institute. As part of building cultural community wealth, ICY graduates also went down south to teach in the Pennsylvania Abolition Society freedom schools (Bacon, 2005, p. 24). The school not only formed youth into educated leaders through the day school, but also held community lectures and amassed a library with a publicly accessible reading room (The Institute for Colored Youth/Rakestraw, 1853).

Teachers College to University

In 1902, Principal Fanny Jackson Coppin retired. ICY bought Cheyney farmland outside of Philadelphia and began offering courses there in 1905 to a class of 14 students, marking a major shift in the history of the school (The Cheyney Training School for Teachers, 1914–1915; Conyers, 1990). Hugh Browne, its new principal, would embrace Booker T. Washington's manual labor education philosophy, at the behest of the school's managing board (Catto, 1902). By 1914, ICY was renamed Cheyney Training School for Teachers by Browne's successor, Leslie Pickney Hill (The Cheyney Training School for Teachers, 1914–1915). Hill would grow the 14-student enrollment to over 500 and oversee its growth from a Quaker-supported private secondary school to a full-fledged college. The school began awarding state teacher certifications in 1920, was bought by the state of Pennsylvania in 1922, and awarded its first college degrees in 1932 (Slater, 1994). Cheyney was elevated from a state college to a state university in 1983, the only HBCU in the Pennsylvania State System (Cheyney University, n.d.-d). Today, Cheyney is a liberal arts university with just under 630 undergraduates, offering masters level degrees in education (Cheyney University, 2020).

Cheyney University proudly promotes its role as the first HBCU. What looks the same in the 21st century? It has remained at the same location just outside of Philadelphia for over a century and retained a strong teacher education program and a liberal arts core identity. Their major offerings are targeted toward liberal arts and social science programs in the "helping professions," education, business, and scientific research (Cheyney University, n.d.-a). In line with their history as the first HBCU, they continue to prioritize "responding to the needs of the community" as the heart of their educational mission. Cheyney University continues to create cultural community wealth for their students and the larger Black community which they serve by focusing on community-oriented majors, prioritizing social mobility for their students, and providing an accessible college education (the school ranks number one in the state for social mobility and nationally as best public HBCU for scholarships) (Cheyney University, n.d.-b).

ICY'S LASTING LEGACY: A MISSION THAT ENDURES

Despite Philadelphia's northern location, sizable free Black population, and reputation for abolition activity, the city also contained the same racially-motivated violence found elsewhere. Having fought and won the fight for Black male suffrage with Pennsylvania's ratification of the 15th Amendment, beloved alumnus and teacher Octavius Catto was shot, some think, on his way to vote or at least on his way to protect other Black men exercising their right in the first election they were eligible (Biddle & Dubin, 2010). By that October 10, 1871 election day, Catto would have only been 32 years old. Philadelphia and the surrounding area in the first half of the 19th century were both hyper local and national in how African Americans experienced everyday life. The violence, abuse, legal restrictions, social discrimination, professional exclusion, and lack of regard for Black lives were all also part of the Northern antebellum experience. As the free Black population grew, Northern Whites felt their social and economic dominance increasingly threatened. The early development of secondary and higher education for Black students in Philadelphia is replete with common struggles faced by African Americans seeking to be educated and recognized as full persons and full citizens.

Both the formal and informal education initiatives in Philadelphia built on the community cultural wealth of its participants prepared a class of educated, elite Black leaders to fight for equal rights and expand opportunities available to African Americans. Though these educational opportunities relied on the aspirational capital of ICY faculty and students who made the institution a success—and the all-important literary societies, and community leaders who preceded them.

Basic education had to be available for a community to need secondary and higher education. Secondary education opportunities held within it hopes of accumulating the social capital to influence social and political change—with the ultimate goal of achieving full citizenship. ICY not only helped provide early entrée into all-White institutions (graduate schools, leadership position, etc.) but, more importantly, would grow into Cheyney University, beginning the work of building Black higher education institutions and professional schools which would continue to educate students for freedom and equality—politically, economically, and socially.

REFERENCES

31st U.S. Congress. (1850). *Fugitive slave act of 1850.* http://legisworks.org/sal/9/stats/STATUTE-9-Pg462.pdf

American Society of Free Persons of Colour. (1830). *Constitution of the American Society of Free Persons of Colour, for improving their condition in the United States; for purchasing lands; and for the establishment of a settlement in upper Canada, also, The Proceedings of the Convention with their Address to Free Persons of Colour in the United States.* University of Delaware Library. http://coloredconventions.org/items/show/70

Anderson, J. D. (1988). *The education of Blacks in the South, 1860–1935.* University of North Carolina.

Bacon, M. H. (2005). The Pennsylvania Abolition Society's Mission for Black education. *Pennsylvania Legacies, 5*(2), 21–26. http://www.jstor.org/stable/27764999

Bass, C., & Branch, M.A. (2014). Yale College's first black grad: it's not who you think. *Yale Alumni Magazine.* https://yalealumnimagazine.com/blog_posts/1719

Biddle, D. R., & Dubin, M. (2010). *Tasting freedom: Octavius Catto and the battle for equality in Civil War America.* Temple University Press.

"Book Notice." (1862, June 21). *The Christian Recorder,* (Philadelphia, Pennsylvania). http://www.accessible.com.proxy.libraries.rutgers.edu/

Brooks, F. E., & Starks, G. L. (2011). *Historically Black colleges and universities: An encyclopedia.* ABC-CLIO, LLC.

Campbell, J. (1995). *Songs of Zion: The African Methodist Episcopal Church in the United States and South Africa.* Oxford University Press.

Catto, O. V. (1864, May 10). *Our alma mater: An address delivered at concert hall on the occasion of the twelfth annual commencement of the Institute for Colored Youth, May 10th, 1864.* The Alumni Association. Historical Society of Pennsylvania Collections. http://digitallibrary.hsp.org/index.php/Detail/Object/Show/idno/5242

Catto, O. V. (1902, July 3). Our alma mater. "Commencement at Institute for Colored Youth." *The Christian Recorder.* http://www.accessible.com.proxy.libraries.rutgers.edu

Central Connecticut State University. (n.d.). *Ebenezer D. Bassett, Class of 1853.* Central Connecticut State University. http://www.ccsu.edu/bassett/

The Cheyney Training School for Teachers. (1914–1915). *Annual report of the Cheyney Training School for Teachers (Institute for Colored Youth)*. The Cheyney Training School for Teachers. Cheyney, PA. https://hdl.handle.net/2027/uiuo.ark:/13960/t1ng5wd2s

Cheyney University. (2020). *Cheyney University of Pennsylvania fact sheet.* https://cheyney.edu/admissions/

Cheyney University. (n.d.-a). *Academics The department of social and behavioral sciences.* https://cheyney.edu/academics/academic-departments-programs/the-department-of-social-sciences/

Cheyney University. (n.d.-b). *Home page.* https://cheyney.edu/

Cheyney University. (n.d.-c). *Cheyney timeline.* http://www.cheyney.edu/library/Cheyney-Timeline.cfm

Cheyney University. (n.d.-d). *Who we are.* https://cheyney.edu/who-we-are/the-first-hbcu/#:~:text=As%20a%20charter%20member%20of,HBCU%20in%20the%20state%20system

Commonwealth of Pennsylvania. (1854). *Excerpts from Pennsylvania Act No. 610 for the regulation and continuance of a system of education by common schools.* http://explorepahistory.com/odocument.php?docId=1-4-247

The Convention. *National Gazette and Literary Register*. (1838, January 23, p. 3. Readex: America's Historical Newspapers. https://infoweb-newsbank-com.proxy.libraries.rutgers.edu/apps/readex/doc?p=EANX&docref=image/v2%3A109C8F89B2698480%40EANX-11C2E9580C248D10%402392398-11C2A99F433A33D0%402-12A04C7DF95E2A0C%40The%2BConvention

Convention for the Improvement of Free People of Color. (1830, 1831, 1832, 1833, 1835, 1855). *Minutes and proceedings for 1830, 1831, 1832, 1833, 1835, and 1855 Conventions. Conventions by year*. Philadelphia, PA. University of Delaware Library. http://coloredconventions.org/convention-by-year

Conyers, C. H. (1990). *A living legend: The history of Cheyney University, 1837–1951*. Cheyney University Press.

Coppin, F. L. (1913, 1999). *Reminiscences of school life, and hints on teaching* [electronic edition]. University of North Carolina at Chapel Hill Academic Affairs Library. https://docsouth.unc.edu/neh/jacksonc/jackson.html

Culp, D. W. (Ed). (2006). *Twentieth century Negro literature or, a cyclopedia of thought on the vital topics relating to the American Negro. 1902.* https://www.gutenberg.org/files/18772/18772-h/18772-h.htm

Department of Public Instruction. (1934). *100 years of free public schools in Pennsylvania.* https://archive.org/details/100yearsoffreepu00penn

Dickinson, M., Alspaugh, J., & de Vera, S. (Eds). (2013, 2016). *Robert Douglass, Jr. The fight for Black mobility: Traveling to mid-century conventions.* An exhibit in the collection of the Colored Conventions Project: Bringing 19th-century Black Organizing to Digital Life. https://coloredconventions.org/black-mobility/delegates/robert-douglass-jr/

"The Examination of the Pupils of the Philadelphia Institute for Colored Youth," (1861, May 11). *The Christian Recorder.* http://www.accessible.com.proxy.libraries.rutgers.edu/

Favors, J. M. (2019). *Shelter in a time of storm: How Black colleges fostered generations of leadership and activism.* University of North Carolina Press.

Foreman, P. G., Casey, J., & Patterson, S. L. (Eds.). (2021). *The colored conventions movement: Black organizing in the nineteenth century.* University of North Carolina Press.

Forten, J. (1831, March 19). Letter to William Lloyd Garrison. *The Liberator.* http://www.accessible.com.proxy.libraries.rutgers.edu/

G. (1833). The free Blacks, and the will of Richard Humphreys. *The Friend: A Religious and Literary Journal, 6*(15), 113. https://archive.org/details/sim_friend-a-religious-and-literary-journal_1833-01-19_6_15/page/114/mode/2up

Geffen, E. M. (1969). Violence in Philadelphia in the 1840s AND 1850s. *Pennsylvania History: A Journal of Mid-Atlantic Studies, 36*(4), 381–410. Penn State University Press. http://www.jstor.org/stable/27771810

Helliwell, J. F., & Putnam, R. D. (2007). Education and social capital. *Eastern Economic Journal, 33,* 1–19. http://dx.doi.org/10.1057/eej.2007

Hershberg, T. (1971–1972). Free Blacks in antebellum Philadelphia: A study of ex-slaves, freeborn, and socioeconomic decline. *Journal of Social History, 5*(2), 4–29. http://www.jstor.org/stable/3786411

"The High School Examination." (1863, May 16). *The Christian Recorder.* http://www.accessible.com.proxy.libraries.rutgers.edu/.

"The Institute for Colored Youth," (1862, May 10). *The Christian Recorder.* http://www.accessible.com.proxy.libraries.rutgers.edu/

Institute for Colored Youth Historical Marker. (n.d.). [Photo]. ExplorePAhistory.com. http://explorepahistory.com/hmarker.php?markerId=1-A-37D.

The Institute for Colored Youth. (1864). *Objects and Regulations of the Institute for Colored Youth, with a list of the Officers and Students and the Annual Report of the Board of Managers, 1864.* Richard Humphreys Foundation Records, 1837–1982, Friends Historical Library of Swarthmore College.

Institute for Colored Youth. (1867). [Program] Order of exercises of the Fifteenth Annual Commencement of the Institute of Colored Youth, Philadelphia, Fifth and Sixth days, Twelfth mo. (Thursday and Friday, December), 19th and 20th. Pennsylvania Historical Society Collections.

James, M. M. (1958). "The Institute for Colored Youth." *Negro History Bulletin, 21*(4), 83. https://www.proquest.com/docview/1296729740/fulltextPDF/980F243ED5ED4B93PQ/7?accountid=13626

James, M. M. (1959). A note on Richard Humphreys. *Negro History Bulletin, 23*(1), 4. https://www.proquest.com/docview/1296783606/fulltextPDF/4A7C5495BDD34052PQ/1?accountid=13626

Kremer, G. R. & Mackey, C. M. (1996). Yours for the Race: The life and work of Josephine Silone Yates. *Missouri Historical Review, 90*(2), 199–215. https://digital.shsmo.org/digital/collection/mhr/id/47884

Levinson, B. A. U. (2016). Symbolic domination and the reproduction of inequality: Pierre Bourdieu and practice theory. In B. A. Levinson, J. P. K. Gross, C. Hanks, J. H. Dadds, K. Kumasi, & J. Link (Eds.), *Beyond critique: Exploring critical social theories and education* (pp. 113–138). Routledge.

Lindhorst, M. (1998). Politics in a box: Sarah Mapps Douglass and the Female Literary Association, 1831–1833. *Pennsylvania History: A Journal of Mid-Atlantic Studies, 65*(3), 263–278. https://journals.psu.edu/phj/article/view/25504

Librarians' Second Annual Report. (1855, April 27). *Frederick Douglass' papers*. American Memory, Manuscript Division, LOC. http://memory.loc.gov/ammem/doughtml/

Martin, T. (2002). The Banneker Literary Institute of Philadelphia: African American intellectual activism before the war of the slaveholders' rebellion. *The Journal of African American History, 87*(3), 303–322. http://www.jstor.org/stable/1562480

Nash, G. B. (1991). *Forging freedom: Formation of Philadelphia's Black community, 1720–1840*. Harvard University Press.

The National Era. (1852). *Chronicling America: Historic American newspapers*. Library of Congress. https://chroniclingamerica.loc.gov/lccn/sn84026752/1852-06-17/ed-1/seq-4/

National Hall-National Hall Frederick Douglas [sic]. (1863, April 11). *The Christian Recorder*. http://www.accessible.com.proxy.libraries.rutgers.edu/

National Institutes of Health (NIH). (n.d.). *Rebecca J. Cole. Changing the face of medicine*. National Institutes of Health. https://cfmedicine.nlm.nih.gov/physicians/biography_66.html

Negro Insurrection. (1831, September 6). *National Gazette and Literary Register*, 1. Readex: America's Historical Newspapers. https://infoweb-newsbank-com.proxy.libraries.rutgers.edu/apps/readex/doc?p=EANX&docref=image/v2%3A109C8F89B2698480%40EANX-11C4F03998E60218%402390067-11C0A7980001CCF0%400

Newman, R. S. (n.d.). *The PAS and American Abolitionism: A century of activism from the American Revolution Until the Civil War*. The Historical Society of Pennsylvania. https://hsp.org/history-online/digital-history-projects/pennsylvania-abolition-society-papers/the-pas-and-american-abolitionism-a-century-of-activism-from-the-american-revolutionary-era-to-the-c

PA Historical and Museum Commission. The Institute for Colored Youth Historical Marker. (n.d.). https://explorepahistory.com/hmarker.php?markerId=1-A-37D

Penn University Archives & Records Center. (n.d.). *Julian Francis Abele 1881–1950*. https://archives.upenn.edu/exhibits/penn-people/biography/julian-francis-abele

Pennsylvania Legislative Session of 1842. (1842). *An Act to Establish an Institution by the Name of 'The Institute for Colored Youth.'* Laws of the General Assembly of the Commonwealth of Pennsylvania.

Pennsylvania Legislative Session of 1842. (1842). *An Act to Establish an Institution by the Name of 'The Institute for Colored Youth.'* Laws of the General Assembly of the Commonwealth of Pennsylvania. https://books.google.com/books?id=e88_AQAAMAAJ&lpg=PA299&ots=Ytek_E0d1Q&dq=Pennsylvania%20Legislative%20Session%20of%201842.%20(1842).%20%E2%80%9CAn%20Act%20to%20Establish%20an%20Institution%20by%20the%20Name%20of%20%E2%80%98The%20Institute%20for%20Colored%20Youth.%E2%80%99%E2%80%9D&pg=PR1#v=onepage&q&f=false

Pennsylvania Society for Promoting the Abolition of Slavery. (1911). *The oldest abolition society, Being a short story of the labors of the Pennsylvania Society for Promoting the Abolition of Slavery: The relief of free Negroes unlawfully held in bondage, And for improving the condition of the African race*. The Society. https://hdl.handle.net/2027/loc.ark:/13960/t1gh9kz8f?urlappend=%3Bseq=12

Porter, D. B. (1936). The organized educational activities of Negro literary societies, 1828–1846. *The Journal of Negro Education, 1*(4), 555–576. http://www.jstor.org/stable/2292029

Presidents & Chancellors. (2021 January 30). University Archives. North Carolina A&T. http://www.library.ncat.edu/resources/archives/leaders.html

Rafferty, J. R. (Ed.). (2016). Free African society. *Encyclopedia Britannica.* https://www.britannica.com/topic/Free-African-Society.

Rakestraw, J. (1853). *Library in the reading room.* [photo] The Institute for Colored Youth. Printed by. Historical Society of Pennsylvania Collections.

Ruffle, K. (n.d.). John W. Cromwell (John Wesley), 1846–1927. *Documenting the American South.* University of North Carolina. https://docsouth.unc.edu/church/cromwell/bio.html

Saunders, P., & Augustine Education Society of Pennsylvania. (1818). *An Address Delivered at Bethel Church, Philadelphia on the 30th of September 1818 before the Pennsylvania Augustine Society for the Education of People of Color.* Printed by Joseph Rakestraw.

Schomburg, A. A. (1913). *Racial integrity: A plea for the establishment of a chair of Negro history in our schools and colleges, etc.* Negro Society for Historical Research, Occasional Paper 3. Read before the Teachers Summer Class at Cheney [sic] Institute, July 1913. A. V. Bernier. https://babel.hathitrust.org/cgi/pt?id=emu.010000894583&view=1up&seq=1&skin=2021

Silcox, H. C. (1973a). Philadelphia Negro educator: Jacob C. White, Jr., 1837–1902. *Pennsylvania Magazine of History and Biography, 97*(1), 75–98.

Silcox, H. C. (1973b). Delay and neglect: Negro public education in antebellum Philadelphia, 1800–1860. *The Pennsylvania Magazine of History and Biography, 97*(4), 444–464. https://journals.psu.edu/pmhb/article/view/42993

Slater, R. B. (1994). The Blacks who first entered the world of White higher education. *The Journal of Blacks in Higher Education, 4,* 47–56. http://www.jstor.org/stable/2963372

Smith, A. B. (1925). The Bustill family. *The Journal of Negro History, 10*(4), 638–644. Association for the Study of African American Life and History. http://www.jstor.org/stable/2714143

Smith, J. C. (1996). *Notable Black American women, Book 2.* Gale Research Inc.

United States Census Bureau. (1830). *1830 Returns of the Fifth Census Abstract of the United States.* Aggregate Population by State and County. https://www.census.gov/library/publications/1832/dec/1830b.html

United States Census Bureau. (1850). *1850 seventh census-Pennsylvania. Population by County—Classification of Age and Color—Aggregates.* https://www2.census.gov/library/publications/decennial/1850/1850a/1850a-24.pdf.

United States Supreme Court, Taney, R. B. (1860). *The Dred Scott decision: Opinion of Chief Justice Taney.* Van Evrie, Horton & Co. https://www.loc.gov/item/17001543/

Villanova Library. (n.d.-a). *A great thing for our people: The Institute for Colored Youth in the Civil War Era.* Digital Exhibit. Villanova University Library. https://exhibits.library.villanova.edu/institute-colored-youth/

Villanova Library. (n.d.-b). *Graduates.* Villanova Library Institute for Colored Youth Digital Exhibit. https://exhibits.library.villanova.edu/institute-colored-youth/graduates/

Villanova Library. (n.d.-c). *Mapping the Institute community.* Villanova Library Institute for Colored Youth Digital Exhibit. https://exhibits.library.villanova.edu/institute-colored-youth/test-map/

Williams, S. W. (2001). *Charles L. Reason. Mathematicians of the African diaspora.* Mathematics Department. The State University of New York-Buffalo. http://www.math.buffalo.edu/mad/special/reason_charles_l.html

Wolfinger, J. (2013). African American migration. *The encyclopedia of Greater Philadelphia.* http://philadelphiaencyclopedia.org/archive/african-american-migration.

Wynes, C. E. (1984). Ebenezer Don Carlos Bassett, America's first Black diplomat. *Pennsylvania History, 51,* 232–240. https://journals.psu.edu/phj/article/view/24462

Yosso, T. J. (2005). Whose culture has capital? A critical race theory discussion of community cultural wealth? *Race Ethnicity and Education, 8*(1), 69–91. https://doi.org/10.1080/1361332052000341006

CHAPTER 2

LINCOLN HIGH SCHOOL DURING DE JURE SEGREGATION

Exploring the Importance of Social and Cultural Capital

Bradley Poos, Loyce Caruthers
University of Missouri-Kansas City

Marceline Cooley
Kansas City Missouri School District

Kansas City's Lincoln High School was the first segregated high school for Black students. Lincoln High School emerged out of a de jure segregated public education system in the aftermath of the Civil War. Kansas City, Missouri's segregated public schools operated from 1867 to 1955. Lincoln High School has a proud history rooted in excellence and student success. In this chapter, we explore the story of Lincoln High School, once the pillar of the Black community. In particular, we examine the social and cultural capital that led to Lincoln's success during its roughly 75 years as a segregated high school. Using Yosso's six types of cultural capital—aspirational, linguistic, familial, social, navigational, and resistant—we explore communities of color as a wealth of social and cultural capital. We conclude with implications regarding contemporary segregated schooling post *Brown*.

Keywords: Lincoln High School, Cultural Capital, Social Capital, Critical Race Theory, Segregated Schooling, Anti-Blackness

LINCOLN HIGH SCHOOL DURING DE JURE SEGREGATION: EXPLORING THE IMPORTANCE OF SOCIAL AND CULTURAL CAPITAL

We regret to leave dear old Lincoln High School, but we must. We have served our term; it will always be a pleasant memory. We know we shall find ourselves longing again to stroll the corridors of this dear old building. (Dorcas Sinclair, Class of 1940)

Lincoln High School, long the prestigious educational and cultural center of the Black community, still stands up on the hill at 2111 Woodland Avenue just as it has since the building opened 84 years ago in 1936. In 1865, long before the opening of this building, Lincoln High school began as the "first elementary school to educate the black children of the newly freed slaves....This school was called Lincoln Elementary School in commemoration of the great emancipator, Abraham Lincoln" (Cooley, 2017, para. 3). No longer the pillar of de jure segregation, Lincoln College Preparatory Academy (LCPA), as it is now known, continues its reputation of excellence. LCPA is one of Kansas City Public School District's signature schools and was named the best high school in Missouri (2016) by the

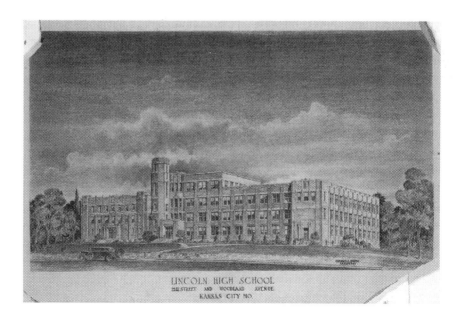

U.S. News and World Report. As a signature school, neighborhood students do not automatically attend Lincoln as they did in its early years but pulls students from across the entire district and requires certain admission criteria, including academic, behavior, and attendance requirements. We capitalize Black and White, racialized terms that recognize the "political permeance of these words as real, existing racial identities" (Thúy Nguyễn & Pendleton, 2020, para, 7).

Today, LCPA serves students of all racial, ethnic, and cultural backgrounds—38% of Lincoln's current students identify as Black/African American (Missouri Department of Secondary and Elementary Education, 2019). This is in comparison to roughly 65% of Lincoln's students who identified as Black/African American in 2006 (Randle, 2019). The trend at Lincoln of greater integration is somewhat of an anomaly both locally and nationally, as hyper-segregated schools—schools where fewer than 10% of students are White—have tripled between 1988 and 2016 (Frankenberg et al., 2019). Interestingly, greater integration at Lincoln has left some to ask whether this is a positive or negative development, which can be seen in Randle's (2019) article, "Lincoln Prep May No Longer be Majority Black: Is That a Sign of Loss or Progress?" This is certainly a complicated question and one that harkens back to the debates of W.E.B. Dubois and Booker T. Washington. It is an important question, as well, and requires a deep consideration of Lincoln's history as "the castle on the hill."

In this chapter, we ask: What role did social and cultural capital have in the success of Kansas City's Lincoln High School during years of de jure segregation? As such, we consider Lincoln's meaningful history as Kansas City's first and most prestigious segregated Black high school. Specifically, in this chapter, we describe the historical context of Lincoln High School and its neighborhoods. Our analysis is centered on the importance of social and cultural capital in the success of Lincoln, using the work of Tara J. Yosso (2005) who applied the lens of Critical Race Theory (CRT) to explore communities of color as a wealth of social and cultural capital. Thus, we address findings considering Yosso's six types of cultural capital—aspirational, linguistic, familial, social, navigational, and resistant. We conclude with implications regarding contemporary segregated schooling post *Brown* and the pervasive anti-Blackness several scholars contend surrounds its failure (Bell, 2004; Dumas, 2016; Gill et al., 2017).

HISTORICAL CONTEXT OF LINCOLN HIGH SCHOOL AND ITS NEIGHBORHOODS

Sherry Schirmer's (2016) book, *A City divided: The Racial Landscape of Kansas City, 1900–1960*, details the racialization of space in Kansas City. Within Kansas City resides a deep and stark division between Black and White; a division that was firmly established by mid-twentieth century. Racial division and tension were nothing new to Kansas City, however, as the city found itself on the precipice of conflict during the antebellum period. Torn between the Jayhawkers of Kansas and Bushwhackers of Missouri, residents of Kansas City were terrorized by raging warfare between free-staters and slave-staters.

It was not until after the Civil War and the invention of the steam locomotive that Kansas City began to experience meaningful growth. By 1880, Kansas City, Missouri, was the 24th largest city in the United States and 10% of its population was Black (Coulter, 2006). The population boom in the late nineteenth century resulted in the need to consider how to educate the growing number of children in Kansas City. Given its Southern roots, it is no surprise that the first public schools in Kansas City would educate Black and White children separately.

Missouri State Constitution, Article XI (1875) explicitly stated, "Separate free public schools shall be established for the education of children of African descent" (Section 3). And by 1889, it was unlawful in the public schools of Missouri for "any colored child to attend a [W]hite school or any [W]hite child to attend a colored school" (Missouri State Revised Statutes, 1889). The law was indeed enforced, especially in rural areas of Missouri where access to separate schools for Black children was often unavailable. Certainly, the lack of access to education, among other limited opportunities for Black families in rural areas of Missouri, led to impressive growth of the Black population in Missouri's urban areas, including Kansas City.

The Black population in Kansas City grew from just shy of 200 individuals in 1860 to nearly 14,000 by 1890; and between 1880 and 1890 the Black population grew by almost 70% (Gotham, 2002). As Blacks left rural Missouri and settled in Kansas City, many of them ended up in certain identifiable neighborhoods: Hell's Half Acre, Church Hill, Belvidere Hollow, or Vine Street Corridor, all of which were home to noticeable concentrations of the Black population (Gotham, 2002).

Church Hill was east of downtown and bounded by 8th and 12th streets, Holmes and Troost. Church Hill was home to two prestigious Black churches, Allen Chapel A.M.E. and Second Baptist Church (Schirmer, 2016); it was also where the Lincoln School was established at 11th Campbell in 1869 (Shortridge, 2012). Indeed, Church Hill was a step up from Hell's Half Acre where a considerable number of domestics resided that worked in the adjacent mansions; all Black "enclaves" and housing and residential patterns in general, at least in late 19th century Kansas City, were absent residential segregation. Blacks were not separate from Whites in housing (at least not until the early 1900s), though the same cannot be said of schooling. A firm dual system began in Kansas City with the creation of its first public schools in 1867.

By the early 1900s, segregation had become entrenched in the social fabric of Missouri, despite the fact that Missouri, unlike Jim Crow states of the Deep South, did not create ordinances of separation other than those that applied to the public school (Greene et al., 1973). Missouri, in fact, was one of only three former slaveholding states—Delaware and West Virginia being the others—that did not adopt Jim Crow. Yet, in Missouri, complete segregation was the custom, and it was widely enforced ("Local Jim Crowism," 1919). The turn of the century brought with it a certain vigor among Whites to portray Blacks as not only inferior but evil, which can be seen in a number of popular books published in the first decade of the 20th century (See Carroll, 1900; Dixon, 1902, 1905; Shufeldt, 1907). Most certainly, beginning in the early 1900s, a concerted effort among Whites in Kansas City was undertaken to reduce Blacks to a secondary status. A tightening of segregation and erosion of social gains were occurring ("Meager Accommodations for Negro Theater Goers," 1903).

After 1900, Kansas City's Black workers were losing hold on occupations once open to them. Most labor unions in skilled trades refused Blacks, whereas, before 1900 contractors might have been willing to hire Blacks at lower wages than Whites. The growth of collective bargaining between contractors and labor unions after 1900 resulted in the exclusion of skilled Black laborers ("Passing of Negro Servants," 1906). By 1907, Black people were experiencing firsthand the cruelties of segregation: Blacks could not rent public halls for meetings and public events; Blacks could not secure places to bury their dead; Black physicians were denied the right to practice in clinics at Kansas City hospitals; and residential segregation was becoming rigid.

However, with the advent of machine politics through the *Pendergast Machine*, "as soon as the machine gained control of the city government in 1926, two Negro physicians were given

posts in the city's-colored hospital and in the Health Department" (Dorsett, 1966, p. 111). (The Pendergast Machine, according to Dorsett (1966), was the creation of two brothers, who controlled politics for almost 40 years in Kansas City by providing jobs and food for the poor as well as social outlets.) Ensuring blocks of votes for the Democratic Party and parlaying political favors for middle-and upper-class citizens, machine politics benefited the election of the 33rd President Harry S. Truman (Dorsett, 1966).

Meanwhile, emerging in segregated neighborhoods were congested Black slums, characterized by poorly constructed, unsanitary houses divided into two or three apartments, often without sewers, and a high percentage of sickness and disease ("Divided We Fall," 1925). With segregation reflected in its schools, Kansas City by the early 1900s was fast becoming a divided city, aided in part by a growing school district educating Black and White children in separate schools.

Public education, by the turn of the century, had grown tremendously in popularity among Kansas City's Black and White populations. By the early 20th century system, Black schools, especially in the South (Walker, 1996, 2000; Walker & Archung, 2003) became pillars of strength and success within their respective local communities; Black teachers and administrators found means to educate children within oppressive conditions. This was, at least in part, a result of social and cultural capital, which we argue is significant to the understanding of how segregated schools—like that of Lincoln High School in Kansas City—became exemplars of great success.

THEORETICAL FRAMEWORK: SOCIAL AND CULTURAL CAPITAL

Symbiotic relations within the economy, institutions, and states, as agents of social and cultural reproduction, contributed to the phenomenon of "reproduction theory" that Bourdieu (as cited in MacLeod, 1987) defined "as the general cultural background, knowledge, disposition, and skills that are passed on from one generation to the next" (p. 12). Collins (2003) called attention to ways knowledge and the process of knowledge validation are often matters of racialized and gendered notions pertaining to maintaining the status quo and power relations in the larger society. Schools reproduce class status in areas of "class division, gender binaries, and racial/ethnic stratification" (Fergus, 2016, p. 121); reflected in belief systems of teachers and administrators and often hidden in the cultural ways of schools. While reproduction theory was largely used to explain the nature of schooling during the early 1960s and 1970s, and abandoned by the 1980s, it was replaced with theories related to agency, identity, and voice (Collins, 2009). Yet, the persistence of economic factors and inequalities through reproduction theory remains a part of the contemporary life of schools. Helliwell and Putnam (2007) viewed schools as mechanisms of sorting, not enhancing skills, knowledge, and civic engagement; hence, it is clear that despite the increase in educational attainment of the general population, social status remains a complex dilemma of the 21st century.

An understanding of reproduction theory, revealed in social and cultural capital, provides a complex framework underlying the seminal work of Bourdieu and Passeron (1977). These theorists sought to explain working-class culture through the transmission of culture via habitus. Bourdieu and Passeron defined habitus as an unconscious, internalized force, mediated amidst the social classes in which individuals were born and raised. Through "a three-dimensional space" (Bourdieu, 1984, p. 114) of economic, social, and cultural capital, individuals encounter objectivism and structuralism, resulting from the rules of structure that emanate from the symbolic power of a middle-and upper-class White culture.

Economic capital provides financial support for raw materials and labor in a capitalist society; negotiated by physical capital through skills and expertise of workers and managers. Meritocracy and the relationship between schools and the workforce reflect patterns to meet the demands of labor. Such patterns in schools are consistent with structures of tracking, access to advanced course work, discipline policies, low-level instruction, and other means to ensure the reproduction of expected labor for low-income and marginalized students. Ladson-Billings (2014) captured the essence of social reproduction through characteristics of instruction and regimentation in schools that prepare poor students for expected roles of low skills and low-pay service jobs, while their middle-class and upper-class peers are involved with innovative projects that support future roles of entrepreneurs and career professionals. Ladson-Billings's perspective mirrors Bourdieu and Passeron's (1977) summation that education persuades social subjects to remain in their natural birth places and to know their places.

Social capital is not a single entity but comprises a variety of forms with common social structures and facilitates actions as resources among individuals to create human capital (Coleman, 1988). Three forms of social capital are: (a) obligatory expectations and trustworthiness for reciprocal exchanges among actors in the social environment; (b) information to support actions through social structures with social relations maintained for other purposes; and (c) norms, accompanied by sanctions, limit negative effects or encourage positive ones (Coleman, 1988). Significant to social capital are norms that one "should forgo self-interest and act in the interest of the collectivity....[that] leads persons to work for the public good...[and to] overcome the public goods problem that exists in collectivities" (Coleman, 1988, S104–105). In turn, economic and social capital intertwine with cultural capital immersed with educational credentials.

Cultural capital provides financial advantages to certain classes in the form of educational credentials and positions middle and upper classes to use resources for economic success. Bourdieu (1977) purported educational credentials are the conduits "through which social reproduction, defined as the reproduction of the structure of the relations of force between the classes is accomplished" (p. 11). Helliwell and Putnam (2007) discovered mixed messages, when examining the use of cultural capital in different communities, considering positive externalities for social trust and negative ones for different types of social engagement. These messages stimulated the authors' further investigations of cultural capital. In general, their findings were clear that education has cumulative effects on political and community engagement; the more educated those around us, the greater the likelihood of trust increases to support actions within communities. Their analysis brings us to shifting meanings of cultural capital.

Intriguingly, Yosso (2005) refuted the traditional interpretation of "Bourdieuean cultural capital theory" (p. 70) and by using the lens of CRT, shifted the discussion of cultural capital. She reconceptualized marginalized communities as having an abundance of social and cultural capital. Multiple types of capital were identified:

1. *Aspirational capital* entails being able to maintain hopes and dreams for the future, even in the face of real and perceived oppressive conditions.
2. *Linguistic capital* consists of intellectual and social skills, attained through communication and experiences that entail multiple languages and styles.
3. *Familial capital* are forms of capital nurtured among familial (kin) to support a sense of the community's history, memory and culture.
4. *Social capital* involves networks of people and community resources; via interactions in social networks, individuals receive peer and other

social support for active and emotional sustenance to navigate the power dynamics of hegemonic and capitalistic institutions.
5. *Navigational capital* entails skills of maneuvering through social institutions; historically, infers the ability to maneuver through institutions not created with marginalized communities in mind.
6. *Resistant capital* signifies knowledges and skills fostered through oppositional behavior that challenges inequality. (pp. 77–81)

Blacks emerged from slavery with a fundamentally different consciousness of literacy and viewed reading and writing as ways to challenge oppression (Anderson, 2010). Although enslaved and forbidden by law to read and write, many employed aspirational, social, navigational, and resistant forms of capital. Today, all six types of capital contribute to markers of wealth that should be embraced and valued within communities. This wealth of social and cultural capital was apparent in the development of Lincoln High School, reflected in patterns of resistance that have been the focus of various scholars (Anderson, 2010; Franklin & Higginbotham, 2010; Richards, 2003).

METHODOLOGY

Narrative history, as Eileen Tamura (2011) posited, can be thought of as "the telling of a story to explain and analyze events and human agency in order to increase understanding" (p. 150). History is often told from a Eurocentric perspective, neglecting to give voice to the experiences of marginalized communities. Our intent was to use narrative history to untangle the role of social and cultural capital in the success of Kansas City's Lincoln High School during years of de jure segregation. In other words, a contextual link of the past was explored to understand how Black people could successfully navigate and resist a post-slavery environment to build a high school for their children; surrounded by a disinterested White community in Kansas City.

Oral history was used to collect memories and personal commentaries of historical significance, incorporating stories and narratives of pre-*Brown* graduates and alumni as well as community activists to share the story of Lincoln High School. As methods, we explored digitized historical artifacts, memorabilia, yearbooks, archived reunion booklets and school data, photographs from personal collections, and oral interviews to piece together this notable historical narrative. Documents were collected in consultation with the Black Archives of Mid-America Kansas City, the State historical Society of Missouri, and the Missouri Valley Special Collections.

HIGHLIGHTS FOR THE SCHOOL ON THE HILL

Yosso's (2005) concepts of social and cultural capital within segregated communities and elsewhere helped to address the question: What role did social and cultural capital have in the success of Kansas City's Lincoln High School during years of de jure segregation? The Black architects of Lincoln High School struggled to give their children access to literacy as the larger society looked upon them with utter contempt and anti-Black sentiments (Booth, 2008; Dumas, 2014, 2016; Shufeldt, 1907). Their stories refute the portrayal of Bourdieu's (1984) economic, cultural, and social capital with individuals constrained by the rules of structure that emanate from hegemonic subjugations of institutional racism and powerful dynamics of a dominant White society.

Drawing on historical data, we tell the story of the creation of Lincoln High school. The early creators of the only Black high school in Kansas City believed, through a collective community, they could navigate a system that attempted to maintain the peculiarities of slavery and what Hartman (1997) described as the afterlife of slavery, which can be seen in ways the Black community of Kansas City struggled to uplift the race and to eradicate anti-Blackness. We detail how social and cultural capital were used as community resources to lift up a single institution and its students—parlayed by teachers and administrators, community organizations, churches, activists, and prominent graduates.

The Creation of Lincoln High School

Kansas City's first Black public school, the Lincoln School, was originally opened as a privately funded Sabbath elementary school around 1865, before becoming part of the Kansas City School District in 1867, the district's inaugural year (Jones, 1938). The Black Sabbath schools typically operated during evenings and weekends and served as educational systems of, by, and for African Americans (Aaron, 1999). Certainly, Sabbath schools enjoyed much popularity in the antebellum and immediate postbellum period; the Lincoln School is but one example of this. Sabbath schools revealed a certain "aspirational capital" and "navigational capital" (Yosso, 2005). The struggle for formal education among the Black community was fraught with oppression and many obstacles; in the face of these oppressive conditions, they aspired to achieve and collectively navigate education for their children through campaigning for education. The aspiration for formal schooling among the Black community remained steadfast but required a commitment to working within a White supremacist context and framework.

The Sabbath School, the only school for African Americans in Kansas City, was first established in the Second Congregational Church at 10th and McGee Streets, the same church that housed the Lincoln School (Jones, 1938). The school board rented the basement of the building from the trustees of the Second Congregational Church. Thus, with 250 enumerated school-aged Black children, one teacher, Mrs. M. J. Copeland was appointed but resigned on September 24 before the school year had even begun (Howell, n.d.) and replaced by her husband (Kremer, 1978). Her resignation was likely due to women not being able to teach if they were married (Roe, n.d.). Ultimately, James Dallas Browser, who was reportedly the head of a private mission primary school in 1865, became the school's and city's first Black teacher of the newly acquired district school (Office of Housing and Community Development, 1978).

Attendance among Kansas City's Black youth was initially spotty at the Sabbath school, and the Black community was forced to employ its collective "navigational capital" through maneuvering institutional barriers (Yosso, 2005). Students were required to find their own way to and from school, regardless of their places of residence (Dennis, 2016b). Navigational capital was employed by families who took in students who lived long distances from the school and cared fro them so they could attend school. Browser (1876–1877) in the "Annual Report of the Superintendent of Schools" conveyed that in 1873 there were over 400 Black children of school age in Kansas City, and the average attendance was a dismal 165. Fifty-seven percent of eligible White children were enrolled in the Kansas City Public Schools in 1877, while only 47% of Black school-aged children were enrolled. Browser suggested that the distances that Black students had to travel, especially in rainy or cold weather, accounted for the considerable absenteeism. Browser was most certainly correct. By 1885, Black enrollment had increased to nearly 64%, a result of newly constructed Black schools in Kansas City (Smith, 1972).

Throughout the late 19th century, the Kansas City Public Schools built numerous new schools to support their growing dual system, and among them were all-Black elementary schools: Cherry Street School (1883), Douglass School (1886), Page School (1890), Attucks School (1893), Bruce School (1898), and Penn School (1899). These primary schools became "feeder" schools into Lincoln High School, which by 1882 had a district-approved four-year high school curriculum that offered such trades as, "mechanical drawing, cabinet making, carpentry, and masonry, [however] the core curriculum at Lincoln High emphasized English, science, history, and mathematics" (Dennis, 2016b, para 8) for the development of leaders.

Becoming official in January 1882, the high school course of study for Black students at Lincoln was originally introduced into the Lincoln School as a department within the elementary building. David Victor Augustus Nero, principal of the Lincoln School, had campaigned hard for an African American high school in Kansas City and gave the following rationale for its beginning:

> The greatest good derived from the public schools of our country, is their influence upon the character of the pupil. The cultivation of will-power begun in the common school, and of such vital importance to the moral condition of each individual, is carried on more effectively in the high school,....for the exercise of such power are hereby extended to him. (Nero, 1880–1881, pp. 82–83)

Nero, however, would not be afforded the opportunity to see his vision in practice. Amidst controversy, Nero was transferred to Sumner High School in Kansas and was succeeded at Lincoln by Samuel Robinson Bailey. Nero's transfer was likely out of retaliation from the White board (Dennis, 2016b) for such flattery of the Black pupil. Under Bailey's leadership, Lincoln survived its experimental phase and was formally created as a stand-alone high school in 1890, existing in a building connected to the elementary before moving to 19th Tracy in 1908 and eventually 21st Woodland in 1936 (O'Connor, 1999).

Gabriel N. Grisham, the first principal of the high school facility from 1890 to 1905, created a vision for Lincoln High school patterned after a Du Boisian approach (Dennis, 2016b; Lewis, 2019). W. E. B. DuBois's "Talented Tenth" centered on leadership and advancement for Blacks through a focus on higher education instead of the trades. Grisham's goal of lifting the race can be seen in his published work in the *Colored American*, an African American New York newspaper (Dennis, 2016b; Lewis, 2019; Sweeney, 2016). Lincoln, under the leadership of Grisham, quickly became a source of community pride, "educating future black business, cultural, and religious leaders" (Sweeney, 2016, p. 15), to name a few: Lucille Bluford, Hazel Browne, Fred Curls, Ollie Gates, Julia Hill, Leon Jordan, Basil North, Bruce R. Watkins, Dr. Robert Wheeler, Yvonne Wilson, and Reverends Samuel W. Bacote and Earl Abel.

With Lincoln School High School firmly established as a stand-alone high school building, Lincoln Elementary school was renamed Yates Elementary School to avoid the confusion of two schools named "Lincoln." It became clear during this time, as well, that there was a need among Kansas City's growing Black community, for vocational training to accompany the academic curriculum. So, in 1908, the same year that Lincoln High School was opened at 19th Tracy, R.T. Coles High School opened as a vocational high school for Black students. By 1915, R.T. Coles provided a second option for Black students and included an academic and vocational curriculum that served as the first junior high school for Black students.

Education for Black students, however, was far from a district priority. Earl Martin (1913) noted at the end of 1911 Kansas City's Black schools were valued at just over $450,000 and White schools, close to $6,000,000. Such discrepancies can be seen in the upkeep and maintenance of the district buildings as well. Of the nearly $2,000,000 expended for maintenance of district school buildings, just over $100,000 were spent on the Black schools. By 1918, there were eight Black elementary schools and one high school in Kansas City. Lincoln, by 1920, was overcrowded and lacked equipment. Among some of the most egregious complaints included classes being held in stairwells, many teachers without desks; no gymnasium or library; and leaky gas lines to the stove of the Domestic Science Department classroom, which required windows open at all times (Coulter, 2006). Despite public recognition of the deplorable conditions at Lincoln, a new high school was not opened until 1936.

Leading up to the completion of the new Lincoln High School, the Black community showed great resolve and a certain "resistant capital" (Yosso, 2005). By 1936, the campaign for a larger and better Lincoln High School facility was gaining strength. Hugh Oliver Cook, principal of Lincoln from 1921 to 1944, was instrumental in garnering the community to pressure the board for a new facility; however, a bond issue for the new facility failed in 1927 (Dennis, 2016b). Daniel Holmes, pastor of Paseo Baptist Church from 1921 to 1967, and a critic of police brutality and Pendergast machine politics of the 1930s ("Boss" Tom Pendergast of the influential Pendergast family was known for his corrupt and heavy-handed influence within the Democratic party both in Kansas City and throughout the state of Missouri), fought long and hard with the Kansas City School Board to build Lincoln High School.

Lucille Bluford, a student at Lincoln, in a 1926 editorial for the *Lincolnite* wrote about the neglect, blaming the White school board:

> The opposite race has six high schools, in which to educate its children. . . . They [the school board] have been going to do this for the last two or three years. Surely it cannot be thought the Negro citizens do not deserve a new school. Has not Lincoln as large a percentage of pupils attending college as any high school of the city? Are not two of Lincoln's graduates on the University of Kansas Honor Roll? Still with these facts we are neglected. (Sweeney, 2016, p. 16)

Lucille's father, Robert Henry Bluford, accepted the position as science teacher in 1918 and taught at Lincoln High school and the junior college for 25 years (Trout, n.d.); at the time of Lucille's editorial, her act could have caused retribution from White board members. Later, Lucille sought entrance to University of Missouri's School of Journalism but was denied; she was the second Black student to graduate from the University of Kansas's School of Journalism (Emily Taylor Center for Women and Gender Equity, 2017). Lucille Bluford's editorial in the *Lincolnite* launched her career as a journalist and "more than 65 years as a reporter and then longtime editor and publisher of *The Call*, hers was the dominant voice of Kansas City's African-American community, most powerfully during the Civil Rights era, arguably America's bravest and ugliest chapter" (Bradley, 2016, para 1).

Ultimately, H.O. Cook, a mathematics and psychology teacher and eventually a principal for over 40 years, shaped the trajectory of Lincoln High School, including its curriculum (Dennis, 2016a). Cook, with the help of community activists, pressured school board officials and established negotiations for the new Lincoln High School, which would also include a public branch library for its community members. Construction on the new high school began in 1935, completed in time for students in the fall of 1936, and could house up to 1,100 students. The "Castle on the "Hill, in reference to its stately position overlooking the cityscape atop Woodland Avenue (2111 Woodland Avenue), took on a decidedly more academic turn with the opening of the new building, which included a junior college staffed largely by the regular faculty of the high school.

Opening in the same year as the new high school, 1936, the junior college program was fully accredited and came to be known as simply, Lincoln Junior College (Aaron, 1999). Lincoln Junior College provided Black high school graduates with an opportunity to gain a high quality first two-years of college upon their completion of a high school course of study. Beginning with an enrollment of 75 students in its inaugural year, Lincoln Junior College had more than doubled its enrollment by the time of its abolishment in 1954 and merger with the formerly all-White Junior College of Kansas City (Aaron, 1999). The 1953–1954 school year marked the final year of Lincoln Junior College; and junior college students were among the first of the school district's students to be desegregated following the *Brown* decision, May of 1954.

Social and Cultural Capital in the Success of Lincoln High School

Lincoln High School served as a defining feature of the African American community from the late nineteenth century through the mid-twentieth century. This was due in large part to elements of clear and powerful "social capital" and "familial capital" (Yosso, 2005) within the Lincoln community; reflected in its history, memories, and culture. Solidarity, networking, and community (Coleman, 1988) were central to Lincoln's success.

This is not to suggest that Kansas City's Black students received an equal education; they did not. The cultural and social capital among segregated Black schools, such as Lincoln, were used to resist dominant hegemonic structures (Coleman, 1988). African Americans' collective assets consisted of economic, social, and cultural capital. Franklin (2002) noted the sacrifices individual Blacks made for the good of the race that can be seen in "the formation and development of many Black banks, orphanages…, and especially education institutions [which] came about as a result of social and fraternal groups, women's clubs and organizations, religious denominations and the social capital in the local black community" (p. 177). We provide a discussion of how these phenomena were integral to the development of Lincoln High School and reflected among and within teachers and administrators, community organizations, churches, and activists, including prominent graduates.

Teachers and Administrators

As Kansas City's preeminent Black high school, Lincoln was staffed with a superbly qualified faculty and administration. Roy Wilkens, reporter and managing editor for the *Kansas City Call* from 1923 to 1931 and later the Executive Secretary of the National NAACP, had this to say about Lincoln and Black schools in Kansas City:

> The black schools [in Kansas City] were much better than they had any right to be, partly because they were full of talented teachers who would have been teaching in college had they been white, and partly because Negro parents and children simply refused to be licked by segregation. (Dennis, 2016b, para. 1)

A *Kansas City Star* article (1915) made note of the school's impressive progress: "Lincoln High School is becoming the center of the interests of the negro communities under the influence... of J. R. E. Lee, ... He was sixteen years a professor in Tuskegee Institute under the late Booker T. Washington" (State Historical Society of Missouri Research Center, 1915). This was not only true of Lincoln High School, as the quality of education and educators were high across all Kansas City's Black schools.

Students at Lincoln received quality instruction under the tutelage of stellar teachers, including female teachers; during early years they could teach until they got married. The school board announced in March of 1944 that married teachers could be hired (Roe, n.d.). We mention some of these notable teachers—a list too long to capture within the constraints of this chapter—but included, to name a few within four decades: 1920s and 1930s—Florence Baker, Hazel Browne, Dorothy Lillard, N. Clark Smith, Williams, J. Oliver Morrison, Aaron Douglas, William Levi Dawson, Florence Rae Kennedy, and Brownlee Baird Rainey; and 1940s and 1950s—Perry Kirkpatrick, Isaiah Banks, J.K. Russell, Neal Herriford, James Jefress, Leonard Pryor, Dr. Jeremiah Cameron, Inez Kaiser, Dr. Robert Wheeler, and Garnett Wilson. An interview with Perry Kirkpatrick, teacher/basketball coach at Lincoln High School from 1948 to 1961, described characteristics of the school faculty and support staff:

> It was a most memorable and pleasant experience. From the beginning it was evident that I was becoming associated with a group of professional educators who were interested in and concerned about the full development of the young people whom we served....All efforts were directed toward raising educational standards by establishing and maintaining a teaching/learning climate conducive to maximum achievement for each student. (Lincoln High School, 1970c)

Garnett Wilson, a teacher and school counselor for 39 years in the district, taught at Lincoln from 1958 to 1963. She noted:

> The school was known throughout the state for the high level of achievement of its students. Every student was encouraged to set high individual goals and to strive to the best of his/her ability to achieve those goals. Teaching at Lincoln was a most rewarding experience. There was a cooperative spirit among parents, teachers, and students. (Lincoln High School, 1970a)

The majority of Lincoln High School's faculty during the years of segregation had a master's degree or higher and most of the faculty were graduates of Historically Black Colleges and Universities (HBCUs); also, some were graduates of major White universities and colleges. It should be noted that segregation laws forced Blacks to enroll in colleges and universities outside of the state if Missouri's HBCUs did not offer their intended field of study. The following teachers serve as exemplars of the quality and preparation of Lincoln's instructors:

1. Inez Kaiser earned her master's degree from Columbia University in 1941 and taught Home Economics at Lincoln High School.
2. Dorothy Lillard earned her master's degree from Columbia University, as well, and taught at Lincoln High School and R.T. Coles.
3. Neal Herriford, an English teacher at R.T. Coles school and Lincoln High School, graduated from the University of Kansas and received a master's degree from Harvard University.
4. Dr. Jeremiah Cameron, alumnus of Lincoln, received a master's degree from the University of Chicago, returned to the school to teach English, and later earned a Ph.D. in English from Michigan State University.
5. Dr. Robert Wheeler taught at Lincoln and received his doctorate at the University of Kansas and later became the first Black superintendent of the Kansas City, Missouri School District, 1978–1982.
6. Girard Bryant earned a master's degree from the University of Kansas in 1938, and a Doctor of Education in 1963 from Washington University in St. Louis.

The barriers of segregation kept these highly qualified and excellent Black teachers within schools like that of Lincoln High School and led to their prominence and success, so much in fact that Lincoln did not only compete with many White schools, but outperformed them, despite being under-resourced.

Inez Kaiser, former teacher at Lincoln and the first Black woman to own a public relations firm (Nelson, 2020), described how students learned, despite limited resources and poor facilities:

> Our classrooms were crowded since all the Black kids had to go to Lincoln regardless of where they lived. When Central High School was turned over to Blacks, it helped relieve the overcrowded condition. Four of us taught 35–45 students home economics in a classroom with six or seven sewing machines. The food room was as poorly furnished. We shared rooms and rotated throughout the day. Somehow the children learned in spite of the inconveniences. We taught them well. ...The name of the high school may change, but the spirit of excellence of old Lincoln will live on. (Lincoln High School, 1970b)

Dennis (2016b) described Lincoln's efforts to include students' histories and experiences in the curriculum as reflected in a quote from alumnus Dr. Jeremiah Cameron, who years later, said as students "we knew about Negro music, Negro literature, and Negro achievements." Lincoln's cultural and social capital included various community organizations and churches as well.

Community Organizations and Churches

Despite institutional barriers, Kansas City's Black community regarded Lincoln High School as a prestigious educational and cultural center. Community members—churches, local businesses, news and radio media, social clubs, doctors, lawyers, and recreational/social centers—had vested interest in the success of "their" school and insisted on better educational opportunities and conditions. As such, families moved closer to Black schools; they campaigned for better resources and school buildings and came together as a community, holding forums and debating local issues.

Examples of institutions that uplifted the community include the Paseo YMCA/YWCA, the Black Chamber of Commerce, Niles Homes for Children, The Kansas City Call, Carver Center, radio and social clubs, as well as schools, churches, and hospitals. Churches, in particular, were often advocates for change. They were structures in which African Americans defined themselves and what was important to them. Magnificent churches—like Paseo Baptist Church, ministered by Dr. D. A. Holmes (1921 to 1967) and St. Stephens Baptist Church (n.d.), ministered by Rev. John J. Williams (1944 to 1984)—were advocates for change and community members often congregated in storefronts or homes to plan collective action. Under Reverend Williams' leadership, for example, St. Stephens Baptist church stood at the forefront of the Civil Rights Movement, and he was active in advocacy and philanthropy. Williams was instrumental in raising $5,000,000 for Martin Luther King, Jr. Memorial Hospital, which opened in 1972 and served as a safe space for Black doctors (St. Stephen's Baptist Church, n.d.).

Further, a relatively small but influential group of Black professionals—through a combination of wealth, background, education, talent, and ambition—assumed positions of prominence. Many of them later formed the local political organization of Freedom, Inc. in 1961; two of the founders were graduates of Lincoln, Leon Jordan (1926) and Fred Curls (1937); others were Bruce R. Watkins, Howard Maupin, and Charles Moore. Freedom, Inc. was instrumental in desegregating public facilities, integration of housing, election of public officials, mayors, legislators, and school board members. Moreover, the Black community was self-sufficient in that it had its own businesses, churches, schools, entertainment, grocery stores, and medical facilities. It was only when Black people stepped outside their neighborhoods that the sense of deprivation set in for them. This is not to suggest that the Black community did not protest the inequities, they did and did so effectively, but segregation required the Black community to form their own separate society; its people and institutions were rich in aspirational, linguistic, familial, social, aspirational, navigational, and resistant capital (Yosso, 2005). Indeed, aspirational, navigational and resistant capital resulted in formal education for Black children. Social and navigational capital supported the growth of Black businesses and other organizations within a segregated city. Lincoln High School, its faculty, staff, and students, as well as the greater Lincoln community, were exemplars of community cultural wealth, depicted through linguistic and familial capital.

Prominent Graduates and Community Activists

Marcelene Cooley attended Lincoln High School from 1952–1956 and served as president of the Lincoln Alumni Association between 2008–2012 (Cooley,

2017). Today, she consistently maintains the history of its graduates and points to the result of a quality education and leadership from teachers and alumni that contributed to prominent graduates and activists at the local and national levels. Cooley (2017) stated: "In a world that viewed us as "second class citizens," we have become pioneers and trailblazers who have changed the social, economic, and political fabric of Kansas City by our unwillingness to compromise for less" (para. 22).

Prominent graduates include Lincoln and R.T. Coles Alumni in the subsequent areas—all of whom attended Lincoln during the years of de jure segregation and are mentioned in multiple areas. They were benefactors of social and cultural capital.

Administrators Pk–12 and Higher Education. Dr. Robert Wheeler, first Black superintendent of Kansas City, Missouri School District (KCMSD); Dr. Jeremiah Cameron, known as the dean of Kansas City's Black intellectuals, taught at the University of Missouri-Kansas City and Metropolitan Community Colleges; Robert Wedgeworth, former Dean of Columbia University and Professor and Executive Director of American Library Association, author/lecturer, and presidential appointment to the National Commission on New Uses of Copyright; Melvin Tolson, professor at Wiley College (Marshall, Texas), an American poet, educator, columnist, and politician (his biopic was depicted in 2007 "The Great Debaters," produced by Oprah Winfrey); and Dorothy Lillard, teacher and administrator for 50 years including KCMSD and three countries and invited by the Queen of England to lunch at the Lancaster House.

Entrepreneurs. Ollie Gates, owner of Gates & Sons Barbeque; Basil North, first Black manager of a Kroger food chain in Kansas City; Fred Curls, owner of real estate company, paved the way for Blacks in real estate through teaching courses.

Community Activists and Political Leadership. Samuel Jesse Cornelius, civil rights activist for the Nixon, Ford, and Reagan administrations; Ida M. Bowman Becks, American elocutionist, suffragist, and community organizer from 1911 to late 1940s; Leon Jordan, one of five founders of Freedom, Inc, three terms as Missouri House of Representative; Fred Curls, one of five founders of Freedom, Inc and promoted the expansion of the City Council to 12 members; Clifford Warren, first Black Lieutenant Colonel of KCMO Police Department; Veodist Luster, first Black Chief of Fire Prevention; Yvonne Wilson, educator/administrator and Missouri State Senator; Leon Jordan, first African American Police Lieutenant and organizer of the police force in Liberia, West Africa; and Kenton Keith, former diplomat, Ambassador to Qatar, and Senior Vice President of Meridian International Center of Foreign Service.

Legal Field and Political Service. Harold Holliday, Sr., first Black student at UMKC, attorney, magistrate judge, and Missouri House of Representatives; Basil North, first Black attorney for KCMSD; and Florynce Rae Kennedy, lawyer, feminist, civil rights advocate, lecturer, and 1997 recipient of a Lifetime Courageous Activist Award.

Journalism and Entertainment. Lucille Bluford, former publisher and journalist of the Kansas City Call; Julia Lee, jazz, rhythm and blues vocalist; Gerren Keith, producer/Director of TV Sitcom, "Good Times" (1974) and "Different Strokes" (1978); professional jazz musicians Sonny Kenner, Charlie Parker, Oscar Wesley, Eddie Saunders, and Larry Cummings, aka Luqman Hanza; and Eddie Baker, Donald Parsons, and Logan Walker, members of "5 Acres" local band.

The rich history and legacy of Lincoln High School, no longer the pillar of de jure segregation, serve as a model for contemporary schooling of African American students and other marginalized students. Yosso's (2005) notions of community wealth can be a guiding light in the 21st century for connecting schools and communities. Samudzi and Anderson (2018) insisted, "We do not need an army, leaders, or advanced weaponry to organize ourselves in our respective localities. We need self-determined people willing to work together in their communities" (p. 95). These prominent graduates displayed such characteristics.

IMPLICATIONS FOR CONTEMPORARY SEGREGATED SCHOOLS

James Anderson (2010) suggested the Black community's commitment to their schools and the education of Black youth are results of the push during the post-bellum period of ex-slaves who had been denied such opportunities prior to the Civil War. Black schools, like Black churches, served as the backbone of the community. Despite the successes of schools like Lincoln High School in Kansas City, the education of Black children in America continues as a byproduct of an unequal system. Furthermore, Dumas (2014) suggested Bourdieu's explanation of schooling and inequality among poor and working-class students is described as a "site of *la petite misère* . . .suffer a kind of *malaise* results from a growing consciousness that what they are promised as educational opportunity is unlikely to lead to greater social or educational mobility" (p. 3).

For Black children and families in America, this suffering intensified by schooling as sites of suffering, remind us that Blackness is a sign of otherness and "[W]hiteness remains invisible to itself, shrouded in a 'broad, collective American silence" (Booth, 2008, p. 689). Today, for many Black children, marked by constructions of anti-Blackness that often erode the social and cultural wealth of their communities—it is difficult to escape negative images and perceptions that are emotionally devastating to their psychological well-beings. Moreover, we have been less willing to include conversations regarding the suffering of Black youth in educational research and policy analysis (Dumas, 2014).

With the struggle to integrate schools which spanned two decades from 1971 to 1995 and the subsequent *Jenkins v. Missouri* (1984), eventually a failure, Lincoln High school became an academy in 1978 and was renamed Lincoln College Preparatory Academy in 1986 (Poos, 2014). As White parents have become more attracted to the International Baccalaureate (IB) Program and its reputation of excellence, Black students have decreased in attendance year after year (Randle, 2019). We suggest that looking to the past to identify lessons from Kansas City's Lincoln High School, especially regarding the strength of social and cultural capital during de jure segregation, might offer insight into ways to eradicate anti-blackness in today's schools and build multiple "castles on the hill" within the Kansas City Community. Yosso's (2005) forms of social and cultural capital are couched in Khalifa's (2018) notions of culturally relevant school leadership (CRSL) for meeting the educational needs of Black children and youth in the following ways:

1. Promote aspirational culture through crafting a vision in partnership with "community-based voices, staff members, and students" (p. 156) to support culturally responsive, equitable, and inclusive education.
2. Use linguistic and familial capital to incorporate knowledge and experiences of community members and parents to influence teaching practices and "humanize student identities" (p. 159). The integration of hip-hop with subject areas is one example of the use of community-based knowledge.
3. Involve networks of people and community resources via social capital to navigate hegemonic and capitalistic institutions by fostering among students' academic identity through individual helping, tutoring, and academic support programs. Every student should plan for college.
4. Navigate social institutions not created for them by identifying teachers who are culturally relevant and use community-based knowledge to mentor other teachers. Break the silence around issues of race and marginalized communities through open dialogue and sharing.
5. Challenge inequality through resistant capital and reject low expectations and deficit language regarding students and their families. Leaders help teachers become warm demanders that establish caring relationships and demonstrate belief in the success of students (p. 158).

Lincoln High School and its historical memories of dedicated principals, teachers, and community members remain a beacon of light in the Kansas City community and a model for transforming schools to serve the needs of Black children and other marginalized groups.

REFERENCES

Aaron, M. R. (1999). *The higher education of African Americans in Kansas City, Missouri: A history of Lincoln Junior College, 1936–1954* [Unpublished doctoral dissertation]. University of Missouri-Kansas City.

Anderson, J. D. (2010). *The education of Blacks in the South, 1860–1935.* University of North Carolina Press.

Bell, D. (2004). *Silent covenants: Brown v. Board of Education and the unfulfilled hopes for racial reform.* Oxford University Press.

Booth, W. J. (2008). The color of memory reading race with Ralph Ellison. *Political Theory, 36*(5), 683–707. https://doi.org/10.1177/0090591708321034

Bourdieu, P. (1984). *A social critique of the judgment of taste.* Harvard University Press.

Bourdieu, P., & Passeron, J. (1977). *Reproduction in education, society and culture.* Sage.

Bradley, D. (2016, October 18). Lucile Bluford fought for decades to help African American community in Kansas City. *The Kansas City Star.* https://pendergastkc.org/article/castle-hill-lincoln-high-racial-uplift-and-community-development-during-segregation

Brown v. Board of Education, 347 U.S. 483 (1954).

Browser, J. D. (1876–1877). *Kansas City, Missouri School District's annual report [Annual report of the Superintendent of Schools].* Missouri Superintendents (Vertical File). Missouri Valley Special Collections, Kansas City, MO.

Carroll, C. (1900). *The Negro is a beast.* American Book and Bible House.

Coleman, J. S. (1988). Social capital in the creation of human capital. *American Journal of Sociology, 94,* S95–S120.

Collins, J. (2009). Social reproduction in classrooms and schools. *Annual Review of Anthropology, 38,* 33–48. doi: 10.1146/annurev.anthro.37.081407.085242

Collins, P. H. (2003). Toward an Afrocentric feminist epistemology. In N. K. Denzin & E. J. Lincoln (Eds.), *Turning points in qualitative research: Tying knots in a handkerchief* (pp. 47–72). AltaMira Press.

Cooley, M. (2017). *Marcelene Cooley: Lincoln High School, 1952–1956.* In J. Friend, L. Caruthers, & C. Schlein. Kansas City speaks: Stories of school Desegregation. http://kcdeseg.com/?page_id=142

Coulter, C. E. (2006). *Take up the Black man's burden: Kansas City's African American communities, 1865–1939.* University of Missouri Press.

Dennis, M. (2016a). *Hugh Oliver (H.O.) Cook. [The Pendergast Years, Kansas City in the Jazz Age and Great Depression].* Missouri Valley Special Collections at the Kansas City Public Library. https://pendergastkc.org/article/castle-hill-lincoln-high-racial-uplift-and-community-development-during-segregation segregation

Dennis, M. (2016b). *The "castle on the hill:" Lincoln high, racial uplift, and community development during segregation.* [The Pendergast Years, Kansas City in the Jazz Age and Great Depression]. Missouri Valley Special Collections at the Kansas City Public Library. https://pendergastkc.org/article/castle-hill-lincoln-high-racial-uplift-and-community-development-during-segregation

Divided we fall. (1925, March 2). *Arthur A. Benson II papers* (Box 303). State Historical Society of Missouri Research Center.

Dixon, T. (1902). *The leopard's spots: A romance of the white man's burden—1865–1900.* A. Wessels.

Dorsett, L. W. (1966). Kansas City politics: A study of boss Pendergast's machine. *Arizona and the West, 8*(2), 107–118.

Dumas, M. J. (2014). 'Losing an arm': Schooling as a site of Black suffering. *Race Ethnicity and Education, 17*(1), 1–29.

Dumas, M. J. (2016). Against the dark: Antiblackness in education policy and discourse. *Theory Into Practice, 55*(1), 11–19. doi:10.1080/00405841.2016.1116852

Emily Taylor Center for Women and Gender Equity. (2017). Lucille Bluford: KU women's hall of fame & recognition award. University of Kansas. https://emilytaylorcenter.ku.edu/lucile-bluford

Fergus, E. (2016). Social reproduction ideologies: Teacher beliefs about race and culture. In D. Connor, B. Ferri, & S. A. Annamma (Eds.), *DisCrit: Critical conversations across race, class, & disability* (pp. 117–127). Teachers College Press.

Frankenberg, E., Ee, J., Asycue, J., & Orfield, G. (2019). *Harming our common future: America's segregated schools 65 years after Brown.* Center for Education and Civil Rights.

Franklin J. H., & Higginbotham E. B. (2010). *From slavery to freedom: A history of African Americans.* McGraw-Hill.

Franklin, V. P. (2002). Introduction: Cultural capital and African American education. *The Journal of African American History, 87*(2), 175–181.

Gill, C., Cain Nesbitt, L. L., & Parker, L. (2017). Silent covenants in the neoliberal era: Critical race counternarratives on African American advocacy leadership in schools. In M. D. Young & S. Diem (Eds.), *Critical approaches to education policy analysis: Moving beyond tradition* (pp. 155–174). Springer.

Gotham, K. (2002). *Race, real estate, and uneven development: The Kansas City experience.* SUNY Press.

Greene, L. J., Holland, A. F., & Kremer, G. R. (1973). *The role of the Negro in Missouri history, 1790–1970.* Von Hoffman Press.

Hartman, S. V. (1997). *Scenes of subjection: Terror, slavery, and self-making in nineteenth-century America.* Oxford University Press on Demand.

Helliwell, J. F., & Putnam, R. D. (2007). Education and social capital. *Eastern Economic Journal, 33*(1), 1–19.

Howell, W. R. (n.d.). *The colored schools of Kansas City, Missouri*: Your Kansas City. Arthur A. Benson II Papers (Box 302). State Historical Society of Missouri Research Center, Kansas City MO.

Jenkins v. Missouri, 593 F. Supp. 1485 (W.D. Mo. 1984).

Jones, C. (1938). "Lincoln first schools for blacks in Kansas City." [Newspaper article in the *Kansas City Star*]. Missouri Valley Special Collections (Vertical File: Lincoln). Kansas City Public Library, Kansas City, MO.

Khalifa, M. (2018). *Culturally responsive school leadership.* Harvard Education Press.

Kremer, G. R. (1978). *A biography of James Milton Turner.* American University.

Ladson-Billings, G. (2014). The pedagogy of poverty: The big lies about poor children. In P. C. Gorski & K. Zenkov (Eds.), *The big lies of school reform: Finding better solutions for the future of public education* (pp. 7–16). Routledge.

Lewis, F. (2019, July 3). *American Negro academy: Promoting the talented tenth.* ThoughtCo. https://www.thoughtco.com/american-negro-academy-45205

Lincoln High School. (1970a). Garnett Wilson. *Reunion Booklet.*

Lincoln High School. (1970b). Inez Kaiser. *Reunion Booklet..*

Lincoln High School. (1970c). Perry Kirkpatrick. *Reunion Booklet.*

Local Jim Crowism. (1919, April 3). [Article in the *Rising Son*, a Black newspaper]. Arthur A. Benson II Papers (Box 302). State Historical Society of Missouri Research Center.

MacLeod, J. (1987). *Ain't no makin' it: Leveled aspirations in a low-income neighborhood.* Westview Press.

Martin, E. (1913). *Our Negro population: A sociological study of the Negroes of Kansas City.* Franklin Hudson.

Meager accommodations for Negro Theater Goers. (1903, October 30). [Article in the *Rising Son*, A Black newspaper]. Arthur A. Benson II Papers (Box 303). State Historical Society of Missouri Research Center.

Missouri Department of Elementary and Secondary Education. (2019). *School data*. https://dese.mo.gov/school-data

Missouri State Constitution. (1875). *Art. XI, sec. 3, 54* [Copy of Missouri State Statute]. Arthur A. Benson II Papers (Box 303). State Historical Society of Missouri Research Center.

Missouri State Revised Statutes. (1889). [Copy of Revised Missouri State Statute]. Arthur A. Benson II Papers (Box 303). State Historical Society of Missouri Research Center, Kansas City, MO.

Nelson, C. (2020, December 29). *A portrait in Black leadership featuring Inez Kaiser.* Whatsupkansascity. https://whatsupkansascity.net/a-portrait-in-black-leadership-featuring-inez-kaiser/

Nero, V. (1880–1881). *Tenth annual report of the Kansas City public schools* (Kansas City, Missouri, Superintendents, Vertical File). Missouri Valley Special Collections.

O'Connor, P. (1999, March 11). Finding a solution to Lincoln's future. *Kansas City Star.*

Office of Housing and Community Development. (1978). *The spirit of freedom: A profile of the history of Blacks in Kansas City, Missouri*. Arthur A. Benson II Papers (Box 301). State Historical Society of Missouri Research Center.

Passing of Negro servants. (1906, May 3).[Article in the *Rising Son*, a Black newspaper]. Arthur A. Benson II Papers (Box 303). State Historical Society of Missouri Research Center, Kansas City, MO.

Poos, B. W. (2014*). Desegregation at Kansas City's Central High School: Illuminating the African American student experience through oral history* [Unpublished doctoral dissertation]. University of Missouri-Kansas City.

Randle, A. (2019, May 12). Lincoln prep soon may no longer be majority black. Is that a sign of loss or progress? *Kansas City Star.*

Richards, J. H. (2003). Samuel Davies and the transatlantic campaign for slave literacy in Virginia. *The Virginia Magazine of History and Biography, 111*(4), 333–378.

Roe, J. (n.d.). End of the marriage penalty: This week in Kansas City history. Missouri Valley Special Collections, Kansas City Public Library. https://kchistory.org/week-kansas-city-history/end-marriage-penalty

Samudzi, Z., & Anderson, W. C. (2018). *As Black as resistance: Finding the conditions for liberation.* AK Press.

Schirmer, S. (2016). *A city divided: The racial landscape of Kansas City, 1900–1960*. University of Missouri Press.

Shortridge, J. (2012). *Kansas City and how it grew, 1822–2011*. University Press of Kansas.

Shufeldt, R. W. (1907). *The Negro a menace to American civilization*. RG Badger.

Smith, C. A. (1930). *Lincoln High School* [Mounted Drawing]. Missouri Valley Special Collections, Kansas City, MO.

Smith, T. L. (1972). Native Blacks and foreign Whites: Varying responses to educational opportunities in America, 1860–1950. *Perspectives in American History, 6*, 304–310.

St. Stephens Baptist Church. (n.d.). African American heritage trail of Kansas City. https://aahtkc.org/ststephens

State Historical Society of Missouri Research Center. (1915). [Kansas City Star newspaper article about Lincoln High School]. Arthur A. Benson II Papers (Box 303). Kansas City, MO.

Sweeney, M. (2016). A short history of the celebrated Lincoln high and its 150 years of success. *Jackson County Historical Society Journal, 54*(1), 13–19.

Tamura, E. H. (2011). Narrative history and theory. *History of Education Quarterly, 51*(2), 151–157. doi:10.1111/j.1748-5959.2011.00327.x

Thúy Nguyễn, A., & Pendleton, M. (2020, March 23). *Recognizing race in language: Why we capitalize "Black" and "White."* Center for the Study of Social Policy. https://cssp.org/2020/03/recognizing-race-in-language-why-we-capitalize-black-and-white/

Trout, C. (n.d). *Lucille Bluford.* https://historicmissourians.shsmo.org/lucile-bluford

U.S. News and World Report. (2016, April 19). *Best high school rankings.* https://www.rti.org/news/us-news-world-report-announces-2016-best-high-schools-rankings

Walker, V. S. (1996). *Their highest potential: An African American school community in the segregated South.* University of North Carolina Press

Walker, V. S. (2000). Valued segregated schools for African American children in the South, 1935–1969: A review of common themes and characteristics. *Review of Educational Research, 70*(3), 253–285. https://doi.org/10.3102/00346543070003253

Walker, V. S., & Archung, K. N. (2003). The segregated schooling of Blacks in the southern United States and South Africa. *Comparative Education Review, 47*(1), 21–40. https://doi.org/10.1086/373961

Yosso, T. J. (2005). Whose culture has capital? A critical race theory discussion of community cultural wealth, *Race Ethnicity and Education 8*(1), 69–91. doi:10.1080/1361332052000341006

CHAPTER 3

THE SUMNER HIGH SCHOOL

An Educational Landmark Made by the Black Community

E. Paulette Isaac-Savage and Vanessa Garry

University of Missouri-St. Louis

Sumner High School (Sumner) located in St. Louis, Missouri, was the first Black public high school west of the Mississippi River. When St. Louis Public Schools (SLPS) delayed opening the high school for a decade, the Missouri General Assembly's 1875 amendment forced all Missouri school districts to open segregated public high schools. In 1875, SLPS opened a shuttered elementary school building to house Sumner. The former elementary school for White children closed due to the unsavory neighborhood surrounding it. The placement of the high school in a school SLPS did not want White children to attend galvanized the Black community to petition the district for a more desirable location. It took three decades for the district to relent and build a new Black high school in a more desirable location. The example of Black leaders' social and resistant capital working to provide a proper education for their children modeled for future Black leaders how to challenge White power structures in support of education Black children. The narrative reveals how Black leaders within Sumner and the community collaborated to ensure Black children's education and future prosperity. Tracing Sumner's history revealed

Black Cultural Capital: Activism That Spurred African American High Schools, pages 49–71.
Copyright © 2023 by Information Age Publishing
www.infoagepub.com
All rights of reproduction in any form reserved.

the collaboration between the community, faculty, and principals created a family-like culture. Faculty cared for students like they were their own as they prepared them for work, college, and life after graduation. They produced some of the finest graduates who went on to become educators, servicemen, scientists, engineers, doctors, and entertainers.

Keywords: Cultural Capital, Historical Black High Schools, African American Education, Advocacy

INTRODUCTION

In 1865, the Missouri General Assembly (MGA) reversed its 1847 law that prohibited Blacks from attending public schools. It amended the 1865 law that permitted all Black children to attend public schools. However, in 1875, the MGA amended the 1865 law to compel state school districts that failed to open Black secondary schools to do so (Evans, 1938). In 1875, St. Louis Public Schools (SLPS) complied by opening Charles Sumner High School (Sumner), the namesake of the Massachusetts abolitionist, Senator Charles Sumner. SLPS housed the high school in an abandoned elementary school building that was previously a school for White children but shuttered it due to its unsavory setting. Surrounded by a saloon, jail, and funeral parlor, Sumner became the first public high school west of the Mississippi River for Black children (Buckner, 2013).

The Sumner High School

As Black children strode to Sumner, secondary school-age girls walked past saloon patrons, along with elementary-age children, since the district combined the upper and lower grades when they opened the high school (Tandy, 1875). Deemed inappropriate for White children, the district's decision to send Black children to this facility is an early example of its willful neglect in educating Black children (Tandy, 1875). Outraged, the Black community leaders petitioned the district to relocate the school to the bucolic Elleardsville (later changed to The Ville) where surroundings were more conducive for educating children. After decades of lobbying the school board, the community's eventual success was likely the catalyst that spurred generational community support for Sumner ever since (Buckner, 2013; Tandy, 1875).

This chapter is a narrative of the community's engagement in the evolution of Sumner from SLPS' delayed opening of the school to its pinnacle days during the early and mid-20th century to the waning of its existence as of 2022. Throughout its history, the Black community played a pivotal role in its development and survival. For example, after the Civil War, as the American Missionaries Association established schools run by White liberals, Blacks attempted to arrest control so they could have greater participation (McPherson, 1970; Rabinowitz, 1974). This was true in St. Louis after the war as Black St. Louisans in the early years at Sumner desired greater participation since education represented freedom to Blacks— freedom to learn, grow, and advance (Butchart, 2010). However, Black children's acquisition of a proper education at Sumner was and remains contingent upon the community's activism. This was Sumner's reality from its inception through the Jim Crow era and for its existence years after desegregation.

Framework

The theories utilized to undergird this Sumner narrative are the funds of knowledge (Rios-Aguilar et al., 2011) and cultural capital (Yosso, 2005). Both help unpack the Black community's leadership's response to SLPS' neglect in establishing novel Black schools. They reveal how Black people relied on their own expertise to counter the school board's oppressive actions throughout the Jim Crow era and desegregation that prevented their children from receiving a proper public education. The frameworks illuminate Black leaders' creation of networks of people resources called upon to undo unfair local laws and use of the court system to battle repressive federal and state laws.

The term "funds of knowledge" is Vélez-Ibáñez's and Greenberg's (1992) reinterpretation of Eric Wolf's (1966) concept of replacement funds. Their research of Latinx communities along the southwest border states revealed these communities were self-reliant due to their redeployment of resources and trading expertise among themselves to care for the needs of their families. Funds of knowledge gained considerable attention in the late 1990s as researchers revealed Latinx parents were untapped reservoirs of knowledge. These parent resources were underutilized in schools and when welcomed as partners, their knowledge, referred to as capital, benefitted the education of children (Moll et al., 1992; Vélez-Ibáñez & Greenberg, 1992). Decades later, Esteban-Guitart and Moll (2014) continued to refer to funds of knowledge as an "approach based on the simple principle that people are competent and have life experiences; consequently, they have accumulated knowledge of 'forms of capital'" (p. 35). We define Sumner's Black stakeholders' "funds of knowledge as strategic and cultural resources" they used to claim and protect their inalienable rights (Vélez-Ibáñez & Greenberg, 1992, p. 313).

As research on the funds of knowledge proliferated, Llopart's and Esteban-Guitart's (2018) literature review of funds of knowledge research uncovered three themes. The first was justice and social change; the second, dialogue with other theoretical approaches; and the third was the development and particularities of the funds of knowledge notion (Llopart & Esteban-Guitart, 2018). The second of the three, dialogue with other theoretical approaches, revealed the interrelatedness of funds of knowledge and Yosso's (2005) community cultural wealth model. Yosso (2005) challenged Bourdieu's theory that "cultural capital is not just inherited or possessed by the middle class, but rather it refers to an accumulation of specific forms of knowledge, skills and abilities that are valued by privileged groups in society" (p. 76). Similar to funds of knowledge, Yosso (2005) asserts cultural capital comprise knowledge, skills, and abilities used by communities of color to resist oppression. Of the six forms of capital included in Yosso's model, social capital and resistant capital are the two that best reveal the actions of the St. Louis' Black community's leadership in their quest for parity. According to Yosso (2005), social capital is a network of people who help others navigate society's institutions. She defines resistant capital as the knowledges and skills nurtured through resistance to subordination. Both of these forms of capital are witnessed throughout Sumner's history.

Internal (Principals and Teachers) and External (Black Community) Activists Fight for Sumner's Existence

Two cadres of Black leaders, non-SLPS and SLPS employees, used their technical and tactical skills to fight for African American children's education in St. Louis for most of its existence. In the school's early years, non-SLPS employees or external leaders/activists such as Black attorneys, newspapermen, ministers, and politicians petitioned SLPS' board to afford Black children their rights to a public education and pushed for integration. For example, when the school first opened, Black activists advocated for its relocation from 1875 to 1908 and the hiring of Black teachers in 1877. They also petitioned the district to align the Sumner's principal's school management duties with his White peers in 1929 to facilitate integration (Dreer, 1955). Throughout Sumner's heyday in the years leading up to *Brown v. The Topeka Board of Education* (*Brown*) landmark case, community leaders' efforts enriched the school's neighborhood with a hospital, community center, and teachers' college making it into a thriving middle-class enclave. Conversely, during Sumner's decline, external leaders were comprised mostly of alumni. In the early twenty-first century, they helped save Sumner from closures in 2013 and played a minimal role in keeping the school open as other entities took the lead in 2021.

During the Jim Crow era, internal leaders/activists were Black SLPS employees who surreptitiously reported inequities to the external Black community (Dreer, 1955). They, in turn, used the information to disrupt the status quo and petition the district for educational parity for Black children. Internal Black community activists included long-term serving principals who advocated for support from the district and community to ensure Sumner was on par with the White schools. In particular, although Sumner had existed for 146 years as of 2021, four principals out of a total of twenty-four served a combined 111 of the 146 years (Sumner's Alumni Association, n.d.). Their long tenure enabled them to develop relationships inside and outside the district and leverage the relationships to support continued improvements of Sumner. Along with principals, teachers as activists during the early to mid-twentieth century used life skills curriculum to teach students ways to help overcome life obstacles after graduation.

Influences from Policies and Court Decisions

In addition to the influences of both leadership factions, Sumner's development was contingent upon the push/pull impact of social and policy issues like Jim Crow that bolstered segregation versus court judgment such as the 1954 Supreme Court's decision for *Brown* that sluggishly unraveled it. Still, federal, state, and local policies influenced the development of The Ville neighborhood, which in turn, impacted Sumner. For example, St. Louis' 1916 Ordinance prevented Blacks from purchasing houses in White neighborhoods but The Ville, then situated along the outskirts of the city, was unencumbered by real estate covenants. Thus, in the early 1900s, Blacks rented houses or purchased land and built homes in The Ville; eventually, developing it into a Black neighborhood with homeowners. On the other hand, St. Louis' 1930s zoning practices disrupted Black neighborhoods like The Ville and its decade-long 1950s urban renewal projects affected their demise (Gordon, 2008). For instance, in the 1930s, the city imposed commercial zoning on The Ville's multi-family zoned neighborhood (Toft & Bailey, 1975). Compounding the zoning problem was the city's mid-century urban renewal projects. In the 1950s through the 1960s, city workers leveled the Mill Creek Valley enclave in the central corridor of St. Louis to build highways connecting the city to its surrounding suburbs (Gordon, 2008). The dismantled community left many Black citizens scrambling for housing in already densely populated Black neighborhoods such as The Ville (Gordon, 2008).

Whereas local policies caused displaced Black citizens to overpopulate already dense Black neighborhoods, court decisions paved the way for the Black middle class to exit them. In 1948, the U. S. Supreme Court decided in the *Shelley v. Kraemer* case real estate covenants were unenforceable by the courts (Brooks &

Rose, 2013). The Shelley house, located in the Greater Ville neighborhood surrounding The Ville, somewhat cracked the door open for Blacks to pursue housing outside of Black neighborhoods but states remained in authority over the matter. On the contrary, the 1968 federal law Fair Housing Act, prohibited discriminatory practices in real estate and states had no sovereignty over the statute and could not undo it (Gordon, 2008). It opened the door for Blacks to pursue housing in enclaves previously closed to them and The Ville's middle class exercised their right. The arrival of displaced low-income multi-families renting the single-family homes vacated by the middle class contributed to the erosion of The Ville and along with it, Sumner (Todd, 1992).

1875–1910: Politicians, Ministers, and Businessmen Win a Place for Sumner

Reconstruction in St. Louis invigorated the Black community as they attempted to claw back rights denied by White supremacists before, during, and after the Civil War. Their fight for their children's education was necessary since community leaders viewed their children's education as a requirement for advancement in society. Thus, when the state lifted its ban on public education for Black children, various community factions routinely convened to address the SLPS' board's disparate policies such as overwhelmingly inferior facilities and the lack of Black teachers (Buckner, 2013). One high priority during the school's inception was convincing the school board to move the high school to an area that was more conducive for teaching and learning. Leading the charge in 1877 was the fearless firebrand Republican Charlton Tandy. He wrote a scathing letter to the local newspaper editor exposing the board's decision to locate Sumner to a shuttered elementary school building for White children. A decade later in 1887, a 10-member committee reaffirmed the community's angst with the school's location (Buckner, 2013). They wrote a letter to the board entitled, "To the Honorable Board of President and Directors of the St. Louis Public Schools" asking them for their consideration in relocating the school. In 1907, to reignite the petition to relocate Sumner, another committee of prominent Black leaders wrote an expanded version of the 1887 letter. Their letter included illustrations to support their argument. They entitled it, "A Complaint with Illustrations to The Board of Education of St. Louis" (Buckner, 2013).

A skilled orator, Tandy's letter was characteristic of the captain—forthright. He was a second generation abolitionist, and unlike the first generation who believed the oppressor would relent, the second believed they could not wait and needed to be aggressive and expedient in their pursuit of freedom (Quarles, 1969). Therefore, Tandy wrote his letter to the editor of the *St. Louis Globe-Democrat* to expose the board's hypocrisy of making taxpaying Black citizens' children attend a school located in an unsavory neighborhood they did not want their children to attend. The following is a portion of Tandy's published letter:

It is no place for the moral advancement of our children, with a bar and beer saloon directly fronting the school-house door. Consistently, I cannot see why the place should be set apart for a schoolhouse for our children, when we proportionately pay our taxes towards the support of our public schools. Another reason, it is not centrally enough located to accommodate the bulk of the colored children, they [living] in the Seventh, Eighth and Ninth Wards. I ask any and all fair-minded and impartial citizens: Is this right? Is this just? It is not, but is ridiculous in the extreme, and an imposition upon us. It cannot truthfully be said that our people are disposed to the grumblers, when we consider all things, especially the action of the School Board, who refused to employ competent teachers of our own race, but accepted incompetent white teachers, who only care for the dollars and cents, and not for the advancement and progress of our children in morals and education.

— *Respectfully, etc., Charlton H. Tandy*
(Tandy, 1875, p. 3)

Tandy's letter sounded the alarm of the lack of parity of Black and White school facilities and other community leaders continued the fight for a new home for Sumner. The next two complaint letters written by Black community leaders in 1887 and 1907 included similar reasoning. In fact, their letters appear to use Tandy's article as a blueprint; however, they augmented them with rich details to illustrate the loathsomeness of Sumner's location and the community's justification for making the request to relocate the school.

In 1887, the board was steadfast in not conceding to the Black community's demands nor did the community acquiesce to the board's decision. Instead they selected 10 of its members to present its petition for a new location for Sumner to the board. Chairman Jas. W. Grant and the other nine members peppered the beginning of the complaint letter with tamed words like "your Honorable Body" and "it's our duty." Then its members informed the board its duty to its community was to inform them of Sumner's appalling location and petition them to relocate the school. They stated the environment was worse than when the elementary school for White children was located there and the district closed it then for the same reason the Black community wanted the board to relocate Sumner. Additionally, it requested a high school not mixed with elementary and secondary-school-age children but one for high-school-age children only and a building with all the amenities similar to the White Central High School. The Black leaders followed up their request with another one—pay Sumner's teachers the same as Central's teachers. In other words, pay Sumner's teachers with "salaries graduated according to the rank" (Buckner, 2013, p.2). At the end of the letter, the committee members respectfully requested an invitation to attend the SLPS committee meeting when they convened to discuss the petition. It is unknown if the board invited the committee to a follow-up meeting but its members did not budge on its decision not to relocate Sumner.

In 1906, the community convened yet another committee called the Colored Citizens Council to revive the campaign to relocate Sumner and chose Reverend George E. Stevens to serve on it. Stevens, raised by parents educated at the Institution for Colored Youth (ICY) a school known for its Black alumni activists, attended mixed schools growing up in the North, and graduated from Lincoln University in Pennsylvania (Dreer, 1956). In 1903 he moved from New York to the border state to lead Central Baptist Church (Adams, 2014; Dreer, 1956). A stalwart agitator for integration, Stevens was the archetype of the son of parents taught by ICY's teachers who rigorously taught students about their culture (Favors, 2019). Stevens, as a core member of the committee, pressed the board to relocate Sumner. It was the beginning of his long fight for public education parity for Black children in St. Louis.

The SLPS' official record of the board meeting on April 10, 1906, revealed the council petitioned the board to stop making improvements on Sumner and move the school farther west (Saint Louis Missouri Board of Education, 1905-07). They shared a map with the board that illustrated the location of the school in relation to where its students lived. It supported the community's rationale for relocating Sumner to The Ville neighborhood since most Black families lived at the outer limits of the proposed site and more families were moving into the neighborhood. It, along with photographs, were noteworthy evidence that distinguished the 1907 complaint letter from the others. The lack of parity of Sumner's facilities and curriculum compared to the White schools was obvious from the council's meticulous work in collating the complaint letter. Harriet A. Hubbard Clem, a 1900 Sumner graduate and later one of its math and history teachers, corroborated the council's findings as she recalled the school's location when she was a student.

> Graduating from Banneker, I entered Sumner High School, then located in some desolate place in the lowest of St. Louis slums. I cannot recall much of the year or so I attended school in that God-forsaken hole. As I remember it, I was scared to death most of the time. Over what? I do not know save that everybody cautioned me to be careful and "look out for anything." (Buckner, 2013, p. 17)

Oscar M. Waring, principal of Sumner from 1879 to 1908, had the following to say about the Eleventh and Spruce site.

> Though the community and patrons had confidence in the school, the present location has long been the subject of just complaint. He stated that he had apologized to citizens and strangers for the utterly unsuitableness of the building and surroundings (at Eleventh and Spruce) to the extent that he had, RUN OUT OF REASONS WHY. (Buckner, 2013, p. 6)

Black community activists were clear-eyed about not accepting the school district's unsafe placement of Sumner in the former White elementary school at Eleventh and Spruce Streets and its 1895 location on Fifteenth and Walnut Street. Nor did they acquiesce to the district's customary practice of not providing Sumner with the proper secondary school amenities. Their almost three-decade long campaigns revealed their perseverance to successfully convince the board to move Sumner to the community's desired location, 4248 West Cottage Avenue, and equip it as a premier high school of its day. It also proved that Blacks would not accept anything less than they were owed as taxpaying American citizens. The tenacity of these leaders to demand their rights and their willingness to continue the fight until they received some semblance of parity, modeled respectability and steadfastness for the Black community that became an integral part of the Sumner pride. Their fortitude to stand up against the White power structure for their children's freedom makes the place where Sumner continues to exist in 2022 hallowed grounds.

1877–1968: PRINCIPALS CREATE SUMNER PRIDE— SCHOLARSHIP, DISCIPLE, AND CULTURE

In 1877, Superintendent William Torrey Harris hired SLPS' first Black teachers after Tandy and other Black community leaders petitioned the district to do so. While Torrey spoke about the new Black hires as an experiment, the Black community received them as community members invested in the education of their children (Gersman, 1972). One of the first Black hires was Oscar M. Waring, who, in 1879, became Sumner's first Black principal. Waring replaced Webster, Missouri resident Alva C. Clayton who left the position to become principal of the then recently opened Lincoln Institute, now called Lincoln University in Jefferson City, Missouri (Marshall, 1966). His task was taking the fledgling Black high school and executing on the community's expectation—putting it on par with the White high school. Meeting the community's expectations was likely very challenging for Waring and the faculty since the White and Black high schools were disparate facilities. Therefore, Black principals' and teachers' advocacy included focusing on things they could impact like rigorously instructing students and convincing them to work hard.

From all accounts Waring appeared to be an easy-going principal. Born in Virginia and educated at Oberlin College, Waring's background made him a good fit for the job. A former lawyer, he garnered teaching experience by serving as a math instructor at the then newly founded Alcorn College (now Alcorn State University) and honed his high school principal leadership skills while guiding teachers and students at a Louisville, Kentucky high school. Respected by Sumner's teachers and the superintendent, Waring served 29 of his 31 years with SLPS at Sumner ("St. Louis Colored Schools Celebrate Their Twenty-Ninth Year Under Negro Teachers" 1906). Julia Davis, Sumner graduate, SLPS teacher, and local historian was a student during the last few years of Waring's tenure and the first year of Principal Frank L. Williams' tenure. Davis and Birdie Arbuckle Price, two '09ers as the 1909 graduates were known, reminisced about their alma mater in their booklet entitled "Down Memory Lane." Their biographical sketches of faculty and recollections of Sumner reveal school life under Waring's leadership and the beginning of Williams' principalship. Accordingly, Waring was a reticent linguistic intellectual who focused more on scholarship and less on discipline. He spoke several languages fluently and often poked his head in Sumner classrooms to speak to students in foreign languages or ask them to share a pun with him. Seeking students' approval, he discouraged teachers from evoking his name when threatening or disciplining them (Buckner, 2013). The two '09ers summed up Waring's educational philosophy with his quote, "None can do his best work in all its richness without a sound fundamental education and greatest of all a sterling character" (Buckner, 2013, p. 6).

Like Waring, most of Sumner's first teachers such as Gertrude Wright, C. G. Morgan, William H. Gibson, Simon Lott, John B. Vashon, Douglass H. King, and J. Arthur Freeman were also scholars (Donaldson, 1948). Though many were long gone when the '09ers arrived, a second generation of scholars replaced them. A few of the out-of-state Sumner teachers during the early 1900s included English teacher George C. Poage; chemistry, trigonometry, and geometry teacher Elmer Campbell; and English, mathematics, mechanical drawing teacher, Harry Laird Phillips. All attended distinguished universities that prepared them to teach at the secondary and college levels. For example, the first Black Olympian, Poage, born in Missouri, spent most of his early life in Wisconsin and graduated from the University of Wisconsin. Campbell was an alumnus of Howard University while Phillips was an alumnus of the University of Pennsylvania. Although most of Sumner's early Black teachers grew up outside of St. Louis in the Midwest and North, there were some St. Louisans who returned to the city to teach. Sumner and Howard University graduate Harriet A. Hubbard Clem taught history, geometry, and algebra and Frank Roberson, former student of Oberlin and University of Karlsruhe, taught art. Frank was the son of wealthy barber William Roberson, who served on the Educational Council with other leaders who petitioned SLPS for Black teachers. Additionally, the first Black graduate of Washington University's (in St. Louis) manual training program, August "Gus" Thornton implemented the program first at L'Ouverture then at his alma mater, Sumner (Buckner, 2013).

Faculty's firsthand experience of pursuing an education as Black Americans motivated them to strongly encourage students to do their best. It was slow progress but their persistence appeared to work. Davis stated that although each year students in her class dropped out of school, fewer exited each passing year (Buckner, 2013). Enrollment stability was an achievement for the faculty during Sumner's early years. Nothing illustrates this better than the increase in graduates during Waring's tenure from the first two graduates, Emma L. Vashon and John F. Pope in 1885 to a yearly average of 13 graduates during the last few years before his retirement (Buckner, 2013).

In 1908, Waring retired due to illness. The same year, SLPS appointed superintendent, who then selected the Kentuckian, Frank L. Williams, to replace Waring. Like Waring, education was his second career. In an interview with Williams for his dissertation on the Black leadership in St. Louis, Herman Dreer, Sumner teacher and administrator, learned Williams enrolled in Berea College because he realized he needed more schooling (Dreer, 1955). Williams' degree from Berea culminated in a career change from business to the field of education. He secured a teaching job afterwards, then a principalship, and later a principal position at William Grant High School in Covington, Tennessee, so he could enroll in graduate school at the nearby University of Cincinnati in Ohio.

Accepting Blewett's offer, Williams was the dichotomy of Waring. The experienced principal had all the characteristics Blewett wanted in the next Sumner leader—someone who could implement the most up-to-date curriculum and run the school aptly. At the beginning of Williams' tenure, the school and community leader did not let the local politics distract him from moving forward with the goals for the school. Case in point, his appointment coincidentally commenced after the district conceded to the Black community and agreed to build a new Sumner in The Ville neighborhood. Williams missed the Black community's decades-long campaigns petitioning the SLPS board to relocate Sumner, but he was present to witness the White community's crusade against the district's construction of the high school in their neighborhood. Their mission failed and Sumner opened in The Ville in 1910. Although the White community lost its Sumner battle, their ongoing campaign eventually won the segregated housing war as they convinced enough citizens to vote for the 1916 Ordinance. It called for the separation of White and Black neighborhoods and marginalized Blacks to mainly four St. Louis areas (Gordon, 2008). The consequences of long-term segregated housing in St. Louis was a harbinger of the school's future; nevertheless, during the first half of the twentieth century, the Black community sprouted up around Sumner.

In 1910, the new brick Sumner building, a symmetrical Georgian-style structure had identical wings on each side of the entry and its wide steps leading up to the main doors created a dramatic entrance. Above the building's pediment perched on the roof to allow for air circulation is its signature cupola, a distinct feature of the building. Once inside, wide masonry steps open up to the first landing where expansive east and west hallways lead to large classrooms. Similar to the first floor, large windows allow natural light to flood into the second floor classrooms which create bright and airy spaces characteristic of SLPS' architect, William B. Ittner's school buildings (Gyure, 2001). The third floor houses the school's library and from its majestic windows one can easily see its rectangular football field flanked by shuttered buildings that were once flourishing Black institutions. A street separates the Sumner building from its track and football field and tennis courts where track, football, and tennis athletes like Dick Gregory, Juan Farrow, and Arthur Ashe respectively, practiced.

Similar to the generation of Black leaders who convinced the school board to build the high school in The Ville, some of those same leaders, along with the next generation of Black leaders, effectively organized and garnered support to build institutions in The Ville to serve their race. In 1917, St. Louis millionaire Annie Turnbo Malone built Poro College a block west of Sumner that included a school, manufacturing facility for Black hair products, auditorium, and a rooftop garden open to the public. In 1922, Annie Malone's Children's Home relocated to the street adjacent to the east side of Sumner's football field. Three years later,

SLPS built the Turner School for children with special needs north of the football field facing Sumner. In 1937, well over a decade after the initial talks with the then St. Louis mayor, the fruits of the labor of Black Attorney Homer G. Phillips, other Black leaders (including Williams), St. Louis mayors, and voters, the new Homer G. Phillips Hospital opened in The Ville. The doctors of the historic hospital trained many residents from Howard University in Washington, D. C. and Meharry Medical College in Tennessee. A year later in 1938, east of Sumner's field, the Tandy Community Center (namesake of Charlton Tandy) opened. In 1940, just northwest of Sumner's football field, Stowe Teachers College moved into its own new building for the first time after initially being co-located with Sumner (Sumner Normal School), then an elementary school. The enclave became self-contained as merchants opened stores along Easton Avenue (now Martin Luther King) south of The Ville. In 1992, according to auto-parts store owner, James Wright, "You couldn't find a place to park." (Todd, 1992, p. 1C). The neighborhood often referred to as middle class comprised homeowners or renters who were entrepreneurs (e.g., laundresses, drivers, and cooks), teachers, doctors, and nurses (Lang, 2009). No matter their economic background, The Ville community along with other Black St. Louis neighborhoods desired an appropriate education for their children to elevate their lives. The Sumner principals collaborated with the community to ensure children received what the community expected.

In 1929, although Williams made significant contributions to Sumner and The Ville, his Sumner principalship ended abruptly when the board transferred him to the Black manual training school. Two noteworthy accomplishments during his tenure were Sumner's North Central Association of Secondary Schools and Colleges accreditation and its membership to the National Honor Society in 1911 and 1924, respectively. Additionally, under his leadership the faculty expanded the curricula, athletic program, and clubs, as well as cultural programs. Regardless, the board moved Williams due to turmoil in the Black community caused when word spread that they were considering making him superintendent of the colored schools (Dreer, 1955). It is not surprising the administration considered Williams for such a position. Sometime after his arrival in St. Louis, he became the Black man White leaders in the community would consult regarding matters of race (Dreer, 1955). The community respected the ambitious Williams whose community work included leadership roles in the segregated Pine Street YMCA, New Age Federal Savings and Loan Association (founder), and Citizens Committee for the Homer G. Phillips Hospital; however, the power he garnered from his relationship with White leaders concerned the Black community.

Additionally, Williams managed Sumner, the Black teachers' college, and the Cottage laboratory school unlike his White counterparts who managed one school. According to some in the community, his assignment eliminated two Black principal positions and suppressed the development of the college (Dreer, 1956). Reverend Stevens, a race man and others like him, did not believe Williams spoke for all African American St. Louisans (Dreer, 1955). They were interested more in school integration than the advancement of one Black man. Although Williams' supporters wrote a letter to the newspaper editor condemning his transfer, in the end, the community prevailed which led to the change in Williams' assignment. The foiled promotion resulted from the collective efforts of Blacks coming together to remove obstacles preventing integration. It is another example of how they bonded around a common interest and fought oppressive regimes even when one of their own was perhaps innocuously part of a ruse to impede their advancement.

Fortunately, the work started by Williams continued with George D. Brantley who was his assistant 2 years before the board promoted him to principal to backfill the vacancy left by Williams. Beginning in 1929 and ending in 1968, Brantley, Sumner's longest serving principal, started his principalship during the Great Depression and concluded it at the end of the Civil Rights Movement. Over halfway through Brantley's tenure, the 1954 *Brown* decision compelled SLPS to integrate schools. Yet, similar to the district's response to opening Black schools in 1865 or hiring Black teachers in 1877, they did the bare minimum. What minor changes the SLPS made benefitted White communities since school boundaries barely changed. In particular, in 1954, the district merged the teachers' colleges and, as a result, they closed Stowe and transferred Black students to the White teachers' college—Harris (now Harris-Stowe State University). The decision caused the displacement of Stowe's Black female president and its faculty and forced Stowe students, who were role models for college-bound Sumner students, to leave their supportive neighborhood to attend a college void of their culture. Sumner's 1963 alumnus, retired United States Army Major Kenneth Lee said, "I wanted to be one of them (Stowe student). When the high school or Stowe students at that time were not disruptive and went about their business in a distinct way" (K. Lee, personal communication, December 7, 2021). The following year, the district integrated the high schools; however, the demographics remained the same since the school district used neighborhoods to define school boundaries. Through all the external and internal challenges, Brantley prevailed as principal of Sumner for almost 40 years.

Whereas Waring's strength was building relationships and Williams was instilling discipline, Brantley's forte was developing Sumner culture. Dr. Lynn Beckwith, 1957 alumnus who served the St. Louis region as a teacher, principal, superintendent, and professor, called Sumner culture—Sumner pride (L. Beckwith, personal communication, December 2, 2021). Brantley exemplified pride by collaborating with the community, being visible in and outside of the high school, and connecting with students. Standing outside Sumner each morning, he greeted passing students and the ones he missed, he wished them a good day as he made his rounds to the classrooms (M. Green, personal communication, February 4, 2022). To distinguish SLPS' Sumner from other American schools named after the abolitionist Senator Charles Sumner, Brantley referred to the high school as "The Sumner" (L. Beckwith, personal communication, December 2, 2021). Illustrations of Sumner pride include ways students, faculty, and the community bond as family and live Sumner's motto—truth, industry, and loyalty.

Alumni, administrators, and faculty living in and around The Ville during Brantley's tenure thought of it as being among family who looked out for each other. Beckwith, then a resident of the Greater Ville neighborhood surrounding The Ville, said the area had a richness to it since the insulated neighborhood encompassed its own movie theatres, bowling alley, shops, and restaurants. Class of 1957 Sumner alumnae and graduate of the University of Missouri, Anita Brooks stated her family lived in The Ville. She asserted, "(We) all lived together no matter your professions . . . we treated everybody the same" (A. Brooks, personal communication, December 17, 2021). It was common to see Sumner teachers and administrators, who lived in The Ville, walking to school or walking home. Lee stated, "Ms. Woods (Sumner counselor) lived across the street from us . . . we were all part of the neighborhood . . . she could walk across the street and tell mama" (K. Lee, personal communication, December 7, 2021). John D. Buckner, principal after Brantley, lived one block south of Sumner and walked to work as well as to Annie Malone's Children's Home where he served on its board (Garry, 2017).

With their lives intertwined, students, parents and faculty could easily chat about students' progress off campus (e.g., on someone's front porch or in church). Additionally, if students' actions in the neighborhood warranted reporting, neighbors did so. Edward Langford, 1967 Sumner alumnus and graduate of Central Missouri State University, stated, "he felt comfortable at Sumner because it was like a family and everyone supported each other" (E. Langford, personal communication, January 24, 2022). As of 2021, he remains in touch with about 13 of his former Sumner football teammates and they get together annually before the Christmas holiday. These examples of teachers' and administrators' advocacy for students on and off campus revealed their commitment to the community and their goal—providing Black children with an appropriate education.

Evidence of the faculty's success during Brantley's tenure were the countless students who embraced Sumner's motto and were able to either secure employment or attend college after graduation. Arthur Sharpe, Jr., who graduated from Sumner in 1947, stated he and his small group of friends never thought for a second they would not attend college. When he graduated from Sumner, he told his friends he was going to Northwestern, which was Stowe Teachers College located on the northwestern corner of Cottage and Pendleton (A. Sharpe, personal communication, December 17, 2021). The former SLPS principal who was the head of numerous middle schools mentioned he had very good teachers at Sumner and aspired to be a doctor in high school. Nevertheless, while attending Stowe, his teachers influenced his decision to become an educator. Another 1947 Sumner alumnus, Agustus "Gus" Bell, Jr. completed Stowe's 2-year program and soon afterwards, the army drafted him. Upon his return to Missouri, he used his G. I. benefits to attend Lincoln University in Jefferson City, Missouri, where he completed his Bachelor of Science Degree in Business Education and a master's degree. Bell served on Lincoln's staff for 6 years. Returning to St. Louis and assigned to teach at his alma mater, Bell professed, "I wanted to transfer to my students what I learned and experienced" (A. Bell, personal communication, December 14, 2021). He later became the chairman of Sumner's Business & Distributive Education Department.

Sumner students were able to obtain their desired goals because of industry or arduous work instilled in them by both their parents and their teachers (loco parentis). Its faculty cultivated students' study habits knowing from experience the work demands required to obtain an education. According to alumni, Sumner's teachers used thought-provoking questions, encouraging words, or admonishment in an attempt to motivate them to learn. Thirty-four year SLPS veteran teacher and instructional coordinator, Ora Langford (Edward's sister) spoke about the ways her teachers motivated them. For example, after proof-reading students' papers, English teacher Cheryl S. Vaughn encouraged students by telling them to "add a little local color to this" which meant to add more modifiers and descriptors (O. Langford, personal communication, January 24, 2022). One of Ora's favorite instructors, chemistry teacher Preston D. Ingram, preferred the following admonishment for students who were not working, ." . .fail now and avoid the June rush" (O. Langford, personal communication, January 4, 2022). It was his way of reminding students they needed to stay on task in order to graduate. According to Edward Langford, the public speaking teacher, N. J. Gerdine used her ruler to rap students' knuckles if they said 'huh' instead of a word. He said today he avoids saying 'huh' because Gerdine reminded them it was not a word (O. Langford, personal communication, January 24, 2022). Regardless of what they taught, Vaughn, Ingram, Gerdine, and other Sumner teachers used whatever strategies they had at their disposal to motivate students to learn the content.

Yet, students needed more than motivation. If they planned to attend college or pursue professional job opportunities, they also needed instructors adept at teaching them high school content. Attending mostly northern or Black institutions, since Jim Crow and border states did not admit Black students to White colleges and universities, Sumner's teachers graduated from top-notch institutions and were more than qualified. They graduated from prestigious White colleges and universities such as the University of Chicago, University of Illinois, Harvard, Columbia, and the University of Kansas. Others received degrees from elite Black universities and colleges like Howard University and Talladega College.

Sumner faculty, similar to their peers during the 1930s and 1940s, were progressives and used practical applications to teach students complex topics. Faculty taught students the academics by "adapting to circumstances and demands" which prepared students well for life after Sumner (Kridel, 2015, p. 5). Some of the academic courses included geometry, algebra, trigonometry, economics, social studies, chemistry, public speaking, English, Latin, and history. Furthermore, students received training in the practical arts, fine arts, and health and physical education.

All Sumner interviewees doted on the music program and its teachers, University of Kansas and Northwestern graduate, Wirt D. Walton and Northwestern graduate and Sumner alumni, Kenneth B. Billups. Alumni stated the support from the two teachers enabled them to grow as singers and musicians. As music students, they were able to travel with either the instrumental or vocal groups outside of St. Louis to compete against other bands or participate as choir or glee club members at Sumner or out-of-state programs. Class of 1974 Sumner graduate Michelle Green used her cousin's address so she could attend Sumner to study under Billups. She never dreamed he would become one of her staunchest advocates. For instance, while preparing for a music program on one of the choir's biannual trips along the east coast, he furtively had her audition for the dean of Howard University's music program. Though her peers knew what Billups was up to, she only found out when he told her about it once all the students were on the bus. She decided not to apply, nor did she accept the Lincoln University full scholarship he secured for her because she decided to remain in St. Louis and care for her aging parents. Two of her fondest memories as pianist's accompanist was playing with the St. Louis Symphony and for U. S. President, Gerald Ford. Two of the many distinguished alumni who were Sumner choir standouts were artists Grace Bumbry and Robert McFerrin.

Students' enrollment in Sumner's academic courses was contingent upon their abilities defined by their junior high school assessments and grades. For example, students who ranked the highest were able to take accelerated courses. Referred to as tracking, it was typical in the public education system in the first half of the twentieth century for school administrators to group students by their abilities. They enrolled students with similar abilities in the same classes and they remained together throughout the day. Anita Brooks, the often highest scoring student in her math classes, liked taking classes with students with similar abilities, "I appreciated accelerated classes . . . It gave us a better education because it did not throw everyone in the same class" (A. Brooks, personal communication, December 17, 2021). She also appreciated Sumner's teachers' interest in placing girls in math and science classes which was avant-garde at the time. Having an affinity for math and experiencing upper level mathematics courses at Sumner bolstered her undergraduate accounting studies as well as an early accounting career at a firm in the District of Columbia. Conversely, another alumnus' perspective on ability grouping was not in deference to accelerated classes but that students enrolled in the upper tier courses received the best teachers, which alluded that those on the other end of the spectrum did not.

In addition to teaching academic courses throughout the day, in the morning before the first class, students attended homeroom where teachers were advisors to them and taught students skills to prepare them for life during and after Sumner. Whereas the academic courses prepared them intellectually, the life problems curriculum helped them examine problems of the day or ones they would encounter after graduation. Faculty were as adept at teaching the second curriculum (e.g., Black culture) because of lived experiences. O. Langford said this about Sumner's advisement program, "In Sumner you had your advisors. Once I got to that point I felt a little more comfortable because it felt like somebody cared . . ." (O. Langford, personal communication, January 24, 2022). O. Langford's experience adeptly describes the intent of an advisement program that affords youngsters adult support and guidance throughout their high school career.

Students were also active contributors in Sumner's development as they helped create the school rules with the approval of the principal and participated in numerous athletic programs and clubs listed in the booklet. In particular, the 1945 Sumner handbook, 51 pages bound in a four inch by five inch booklet informed students about curricula and regulations. For example, the students' auditorium etiquette included stopping all conversations when a guest stood behind the podium. Lee shared his auditorium experience, "we would be talking, but as immediately as Mr. Brantley entered the auditorium it became quiet" (Major Lee, personal communication, December 7, 2021). Beckwith corroborated Lee's assessment commenting, "we would be buzzing and so forth in the auditorium and he (Brantley) would walk to the stage . . . he would not have to say a word . . . silence" (L. Beckwith, personal communication, December 2, 2021). The behavior described by the alumni is very impressive since Sumner enrolled upwards of 2,000 students at that time. Sumner's rules helped maintain a positive learning environment and the modeling of the rules by adults demonstrated for students the desired everyday etiquette citizens adhered to in their daily lives. Students were to live up to Sumner's motto then and throughout their lives because once a Sumnerite, always a Sumnerite!

During the middle of Brantley's tenure, The Ville and surrounding neighborhoods prospered as Blacks collectively coalesced around strategies to acquire excellent public education, health care, and housing for their community. However, in 1968, at the end of his tenure, court decisions and federal laws enabled residents to seek housing in enclaves that once shunned them. As the middle class slowly moved away from The Ville, it began its slow decline. As an illustration, the 1954 Supreme Court's *Brown* decision signaled what was to come as it prompted the slow demise of segregation, the impetus for the development of The Ville neighborhood. A decade later, the Civil Rights Act obliterated Jim Crow law by providing voting rights, ensuring equal opportunity employment, and desegregating public facilities. In 1968, the same year Brantley retired, the Fair Housing Act would soon eradicate segregated housing. Though many statutes and court decisions influenced schooling during Brantley's tenure, his legacy is one of the most endearing ones remembered by alumni.

1969–PRESENT: PRINCIPALS COME AND GO, ENROLLMENT DECLINES, AND ALUMNI ADVOCATE—SUMNER'S DESCENT

When Brantley retired, Superintendent William Kottmeyer reorganized SLPS' leadership and promoted Julia Davis' son, John Buckner, as the Sumner principal. Prior to his appointment Buckner taught math at Sumner, then moved to the district office to supervise secondary education. He served as principal for only 2 years. With few exceptions, 2 years became the average tenure for principals after Brantley. For example, from 1968 to 2021, a span of 53 years, 20 individuals served as Sumner principals.

During Buckner's tenure, with a continued increase in student enrollment at the high school, he augmented the administration team and assigned each a specific responsibility. He continued programs implemented by Brantley with the exception of the addition of the Black Student Union. Throughout the 1970s, students demanded unions, a product of the Black Power Movement, when attending predominantly White schools bereft of Black culture. It was different for Sumner students since the Carter G. Woodson Negro History Club was in existence and Sumner's faculty historically taught Black culture to students. According to 1976 Sumner graduate Sharon Fisher, "(Sumner teachers) did not just teach (Black history) during Black history month . . . they taught that year round" (S. Fisher, personal communication, February 5, 2022). In 1971, SLPS Acting Superintendent Ernest Jones reassigned Buckner to his former district position.

The 1970s was also a period of continued White flight from the city to the suburbs while businesses followed; thereby, hollowing out the city's tax base. The aftermath of St. Louis' loss of inhabitants and businesses were empty buildings. This was evident in the small neighborhood of The Ville. Public and private institutions in the neighborhood closed one by one—Stowe closed in 1954, Poro College razed in 1965, and Homer G. Phillips Hospital closed in 1979. These institutions that were the bulwarks of the middle-class neighborhood shuttered because White administrators in power determined which college (Harris or Stowe) or hospital (City Hospital Number 1 or Homer G. Phillips) remained open—the White or Black facilities. It was likely a foregone conclusion that the White facilities would remain open and their neighborhoods preserved. Another blow that was hard for Sumner to overcome was the loss in student enrollment due to the outcome of the 1972 *Liddell v. Board of Education for the City of St. Louis* legal case. The court's decision in 1983 allowed SLPS students to attend county schools which further reduced SLPS' enrollment as Black parents enrolled their children in county schools. One SLPS district administrator said she and her peers thought the students would return but they never did (Garry & Uchitelle, 2019).

The nation, St. Louis, and The Ville went through significant changes as America slowly desegregated its society and all that was associated with it. For example, SLPS integrated Sumner's faculty and staff during the 1970s but Sumner remained an all-Black high school because SLPS continued to use neighborhoods as school boundaries. Although the race-mixed faculty gave the appearance of integration, they did not prepare students for an integrated society the way their former Black colleagues helped students adjust to a Jim Crow culture. Therefore, as more White colleges and universities enrolled Black (Sumner) students, they had to contend with lack of visibility on campuses and microaggressions. One common microaggression by their peers and faculty was the questioning of their acceptance to predominantly White institutions (PWI) without affirmative action.

Case in point, Dr. Sheri Betts, 1976 Sumner graduate, executive coach, and author graduated from Washington University in St. Louis and earned a subsequent degree from UCLA. While attending PWI, she recalls feeling invisible and the need to prove herself even though she graduated at the top of her high school class (S. Betts, personal communication, December 14, 2021). Betts credited her success in college to the teachings by Sumner faculty, Ella B. SiLance (English), William Ahrens (bookkeeping), and Michael Kappel (math). Her counselor, Ruth LaValle, guided her to a college preparation program and assisted her with getting into Inroads, an internship program for college-bound students, which afforded her a 4-year internship in cost accounting with Blue Shield, a health insurance plan provider (S. Betts, personal communication, December 14, 2021). She reciprocated her good fortunes by giving back to the community when she became Executive Director of the Inroads program in Los Angeles.

LaValle, former third grade teacher and Sumner counselor to 1976 alumnus and Tennessee State graduate Roosevelt Hernton, also made a difference in Hernton's life. According to certified public accountant Hernton, "(LaValle) talked to me about higher education and going to college . . . (she) was a big part of me going to the next level" (R. Hernton, personal communication, May 13, 2022). She had a greater impact on him when he was a third grader and she asked him to stand and recite the multiplication facts for six and as he described it, he messed up. Not liking that feeling, he made a pledge to himself that he would always be prepared. Living that pledge in college he treated his studies like an eight-hour day job by going to the library immediately following his last class for the day (R. Hernton, personal communication, May 13, 2022).

Samuel Miller served his last year as principal the year Betts and Hernton graduated. Alumni who interacted with him as students commented on how supportive he was to them. After serving as principal of Sumner, Miller became the director of security in the SLPS. His departure, along with Buckner's, foreshadowed the future challenges SLPS' administration would have in recruiting and retaining top principal talent like Brantley. In addition to the revolving door of principals, The Ville continued to decline. Yet, Sumner parents along with teachers continued to encourage children to do their best. For example, 1976 Sumner alumnus and Tennessee State graduate, Anthony "Tony" Lee, whose mother was also a Sumner graduate, said his mom did not expect him to get any Cs on his grade card. According to his mother, if you were getting Cs you were merely "dusting off seats" in school (T. Lee, personal communication, December 17, 2021). Lee, like other alumni interviewed, felt supported by faculty such as track coach Harold L.

Thompson and football coach Lawrence E. Walls. Alumni of Sumner, Thompson ran track and both Walls and Thompson played football. They returned to their alma mater to teach physical education and both teachers supported Lee by permitting him to use their office to study. Lee said, "they saw me as a promising student" (T. Lee, personal communication, December 17, 2021).

In the 1980s and 90s, as Sumner's parents and teachers continued to push their children to excel, the explosive use of crack-cocaine across America threatened neighborhoods like the one surrounding Sumner. The wide-spread drug usage across America prompted both Presidents Ronald Reagan and George H. W. Bush to wage wars against drugs. Still, Blacks were not the beneficiaries of their battles. Instead, Black communities bore the brunt of them as incarceration of Blacks for drug related crimes ballooned disproportionately to the Black population (Tonry, 1994). Sumner students, whose lives were upended due to dependency on drugs, received support from Sumner faculty. Teachers and counselors could do little to abate the war outside of Sumner but they did assist children dealing with drug problems. According to 1976 Sumner alumnae Fisher, Ms. White, a Sumner counselor, invited her to mentor and support girls at risk. "Ms. White was telling me that I could be a good mentor to some of the girls. When she had one-on-one meetings I would be there with her . . . you know . . . to tell them this is not the way" (S. Fisher, personal communication, February 5, 2022).

From 1976 to 1996, back-to-back Principals Virgile R. King and Joseph DuBose Jr., were the only two principals after Brantley to serve more than a few years. When they left Sumner, most of the principal short termers served no more than 2 or 3 years. Meanwhile, The Ville's fleeting promise of revival during DuBose's tenure never materialized (Todd, 1992). Therefore, Sumner's existence could no longer rely on the community's support but instead it had to depend on the district, faculty, students, and parents to bolster it. Still, the closed businesses along Martin Luther King Avenue (formerly Easton), boarded up cottage houses, and empty lots where houses once stood illustrated The Ville's fall in stature. Conversely, although Sumner's teachers were still trying to influence students' lives, the building showed its age, the yearbooks got thinner, there were a lot less extracurricular programs, and the student population continued to shrink. Yet, according to 2011 alumnae and University of Missouri-St. Louis graduate, Raven McNeil, Sumner faculty was like her family. Her father and mother transferred McNeil and her twin brother from an Ohio high school to Sumner; thus, the school's history was completely foreign to her. Both she and her brother were very successful in high school. He was the captain of the football team in his senior year and she traveled out of state with the Future Business Leadership of America program. It was there she honed her public speaking and networking skills. According to McNeil, "teachers saw a lot of things in us that we did not see in ourselves . . . All of this investment poured into me. I saw it as an opportunity and I decided to seize the moment" (R. McNeil, personal communication, December 14, 2021).

In 2021, SLPS entered into its second partnership to revitalize Sumner. The first was in 2013 with the alumni which ended prematurely. Nevertheless, SLPS Superintendent Kelvin Adams stated though everyone had good intentions, it did not work out for several reasons with one being principal turnover. Adams, commencing his post in 2008 and scheduled to retire in 2022, was present both times Sumner was at risk of closure. Each time he collaborated with community partners to help revitalize the school. According to Adams,

> ..the legacy of Sumner no longer exists today because the Sumner alumni attended was driven by a strong principal (Brantley), strong faculty and staff, and community support. Now it (Sumner) is a school without a community. While the alumni speaks glowingly and how great Sumner was, that was not transferred to kids. (K. Adams, personal communication, May 2, 2022)

Last, he spoke about the misfortunes of The Ville, which include low housing stock and elevated crime surrounding an isolated Sumner. Therefore, he thinks the new partnership is a wonderful opportunity for all involved. The following statement is the vision of the 2021 arts program.

> We envision an innovative partnership between SLPS, local cultural/heritage institutions and community organizations in The Ville that offers Sumner students rigorous and engaging training in the Arts & Activism informed by a foundational understanding of St. Louis Black History centered around The Ville and Sumner High School. (4theVille, St. Louis Shakespeare Festival, Sumner Renaissance, Sumner PRFC & Market Analytics, LLC, 2021)

Local arts collaborators include St. Louis organizations such as St. Louis Shakespeare and the Black Rep, Contemporary Art Museum, Craft Alliance, Dance Integration, La Voûte, Ballet 314, and the Opera Theatre of Saint Louis. In the first year and second years, partners taught elective courses and, subsequently, added activism and history to the curriculum. The arts instructors collaborate with the existing Sumner faculty and staff by infusing an arts theme in the curriculum and teaching art electives at the end of the school day. SLPS is fully supportive of the program and Adams surmises it has a good chance of being successful. When asked if Sumner was worth saving, Adams said, "Yes, or I would not have made the recommendation. It is the future model for what can be done" (K. Adams, personal communication, May 2, 2022).

REFERENCES

Adams, M. A. (2014). *Advocating for educational equity: African American citizens' councils in St. Louis, Missouri, from 1864 to 1927* [Doctoral dissertation, University of Missouri-St. Louis]. University of Missouri, St. Louis IRL@UMSL. https://irl.umsl.edu/dissertation/261/

Brooks, R., & Rose, C. (2013). *Saving the neighborhood: Racially restrictive covenants, law, and social norms.* Harvard University Press.

Butchart, R. E. (2010). Black hope, white power: Emancipation, reconstruction and the legacy of unequal schooling in the US South, 1861–1880. *Paedagogica Historica, 46*(1–2), 33–50. DOI: 10.1080/00309230903528447

Buckner, J. (2013, October 16). *Sumner high school programs.* State Historical Society of Missouri (S1114, Box 3, Folder 96).

Buckner, J. (2013, October 16). *A complaint with illustrations to the Board of Education of St. Louis.* State Historical Society of Missouri (S1114, Box 4, Folder 151).

Buckner, J. (2013, October 16). *To The Honorable Board of President and Director of the St. Louis Public Schools.* State Historical Society of Missouri (S1114, Box 4).

Buckner, J. (2013, October 16). *Down Memory Lane* (p. 17). State Historical Society of Missouri (S1114, Box 4, Folder 132).

Buckner, J. (2013, October 16). *Down Memory Lane* (p. 6). State Historical Society of Missouri (S1114, Box 4, Folder 132).

Donaldson, U. S. (1948). *The Negro and education in Missouri* [Unpublished master's degree thesis]. Indiana State Teachers College.

Dreer, H. (1955). *Negro leadership in Saint Louis: A study in race relations* [Unpublished doctoral dissertation, University of Chicago].

Dreer, H. (1956). George E. Stevens, pioneer champion of integration. *Negro History Bulletin, 19*(5), 99–101.

Esteban-Guitart, M., & Moll, L. C. (2014). Lived experience, funds of identity and education. *Culture & Psychology, 20*(1), 70–81. https://doi.org/10.1177/1354067X13515940

Evans, J. W. (1938). A brief sketch of the development of Negro education in St. Louis, Missouri. *The Journal of Negro Education, 7*(4), 548–552.

Favors, J. M. (2019). *Shelter in a time of storm: How Black colleges fostered generations of leadership and activism.* The University of North Carolina Chapel Hill.

4theVille. (2021). *St. Louis Shakespeare Festival, Sumner Renaissance, Sumner PRFC & Market Analytics, LLC.* Sumner High School recovery proposal.

Garry, V. (2017). St. Louis citizen John D. Buckner: Community activist from Jim Crow to post civil rights. *Vitae Scholasticae, 34*(1), 32–47.

Garry, V., & Uchitelle, S. (2019). The upside to one urban district's school closings: African Americans achieve in income balanced schools. *Education and Urban Society, 52*(2), 194–214. https://doi.org/10.1177/0013124518819758

Gersman, E. M. (1972). The development of public education for Blacks in nineteenth century St. Louis. *The Journal of Negro Education, 41*(1), 35–47.

Gordon, C. (2008). *Mapping decline: St. Louis and the fate of the American city.* The University of Pennsylvania Press.

Gyure, D. A. (2001). *The transformation of the schoolhouse: American secondary school architecture and educational reform.* [Unpublished doctoral dissertation]. University of Virginia.

Kridel, C. (2015). *Progressive education in Black high schools: The secondary school study, 1940–1946.* http://www.museumofeducation.info/publications.html

Lang, C. (2009). *Grassroots at the gateway: Class politics & Black freedom struggle in St. Louis, 1936–75.* University of Michigan Press.

Llopart, M., & Esteban-Guitart, M. (2018). Fund of knowledge in 21st century societies: Inclusive educational practices for under-represented students. A literature review. *Journal of Curriculum Studies, 50*(2), 145–161. https://doi.org/10.1080/00220272.2016.1247913

Marshall, A. P. (1966). *Soldier's dream: A centennial history of Lincoln University 1866–1966*. Lincoln University.

McPherson, J. M. (1970). White liberals and black power in Negro education, 1865–1915. *The American Historical Review, 75*(5), 1357–1386.

Moll, L. C., Amanti, C., Neff, D., & Gonzalez, N. (1992). Funds of knowledge for teaching: Using a qualitative approach to connect homes and classrooms. *Theory Into Practice, 31*, 132–141. DOI: 10.1080/00405849209543534

Quarles, B. (1969). *Black abolitionists*. Oxford University Press.

Rabinowitz, H. N. (1974). Half a loaf: The shift from White to Black teachers in the Negro schools of the urban South, 1865–1890. *The Journal of Southern History, 40*(4), 565–594. https://doi.org/10.1016/0014-4983(84)90011-1

Rios-Aguilar, C., Kiyama, J. M., Gravitt, M., & Moll, L. (2011). Funds of knowledge for the poor and forms of capital for the rich? A capital approach to examining funds of knowledge. *Theory and Research in Education, 9*(2), 163–184. DOI:10.1177/1477878511409776

St. Louis colored schools celebrate their twenty-ninth year under negro teachers. (1906, June 17). *St. Louis Globe-Democrat*, p. 33. Newspapers.com

Saint Louis Missouri Board of Education. (1905–07). *Official Report*.

Sumner's Alumni Association. (n.d.). Charles Sumner High administrators 1875–2018. https://explore.searchmobius.org:443/record=b1131517

Tandy, C. (1875, September 18). The school board and the colored people. *St. Louis Globe-Democrat* (p. 3). https://www.newspapers.com/search/#query=Charlton+Tandy&t=18366&ymd=1875-09-18

Todd, C. (1992, August 30). A vision for The Ville. *St. Louis Post-Dispatch*, 1C. Newspapers.com

Toft, C. H., & Bailey, C. (1975). *The Ville: The ethnic heritage of an urban neighborhood*. Missouri Historical Society.

Tonry, M. (1994). Race and the war on drugs. *University of Chicago Legal Forum, 1994*(1), 25–81. http://chicagounbound.uchicago.edu/uclf/vol1994/iss1/4

Velez-Ibanez, C. G., & Greenberg, J. B., (1992). Formation and transformation of funds of knowledge among U.S.-Mexican households. *Anthropology and Education Quarterly, 23*(4), 313–35.

Wolf, E. R. (1966). *Peasants*. Prentice Hall.

Yosso, T. J. (2005). Whose culture has capital? A critical race theory discussion of community cultural wealth. *Race Ethnicity and Education. 8*(1), 69–91. DOI: 10.1080/1361332052000341006

CHAPTER 4

A HISTORICAL STUDY OF I.M. TERRELL HIGH SCHOOL

Its Legacy and Implications for Improved Education of Black Students

Tasha Coble Ginn
University of North Texas-Dallas

The history often taught, showcases the first Black segregated high schools as inferior to the schools attended by their White counterparts. While there were inequities in the distribution of resources, the students who attended these schools acquired a high level of cultural capital that supported their academic and personal success. This study directly focuses on examining the educational experience of Black students at I.M. Terrell High School in Fort Worth, Texas, before the school system's desegregation plan that required its closure. Interest convergence and counter-story telling tenets of Critical Race Theory (CRT) are the theoretical frameworks utilized in the qualitative research study. Additionally, the cultural capital framework through the CRT lens was considered in research analysis. Oral history interviews were analyzed to uncover six themes in response to the research questions. The themes, in summary, desire to achieve more than the prior generation, faculty and staff cared for their students, students were held to high expectations, the faculty were upheld as role models, familial bonds, the school's closing negatively impacted the Black community.

Keywords: Black High Schools, I.M. Terrell High School, Brown v Board School Closures, High Expectations for Black Students

Shujaa (1996), in exploring the role of desegregation in relation to the current academic achievement of Black Americans, states, "with respect to public education, the model established in *Brown* has failed to deliver the desired result of educational equality for African Americans" (p. 39). Unfortunately, Black students have not received the quality education promised with the passing and implementation of school desegregation laws. Educators and Black families are left to wonder if desegregation resulted in long-term negative impact on the teaching and learning of Black students (Ford, 2004). In fact, some Black schools during segregation provided a high level of quality education that resulted in the academic success of their students (Morris & Morris, 2002). One such school known for providing a top-quality education is I.M. Terrell High School in Fort Worth, Texas. Given the need to determine how to better serve Black students since desegregation has not served as the solution hoped for by many, the study of a school like I.M. Terrell

I.M. Terrell High School. This file is licensed under the Creative Commons Attribution-Share Alike 3.0 Unported license.

High School may provide insight into how educators can better educate Black students. Such studies can also bring overdue attention to the benefits the schools provided their students and the Black community overall.

I.M. Terrell High School was the first high school in which Black students could receive an education in Fort Worth during segregation. Until the 1950s, it was the only high school for Black students. Not only did students from Fort Worth attend I.M. Terrell High School, but students faced with no other schooling option in several Tarrant County cities—Arlington, Bedford, Mansfield, and Weatherford—also attended Terrell. At the height of its student enrollment, the school provided an education to as many as 1,747 students. Despite the large number of students and limited resources, it is known for providing a learning environment that promoted achievement (Miller, 1973). I.M. Terrell High School was established in 1877 when Fort Worth established their first public schools in conjunction with their first White public school and was known as the Ninth Street Colored School until 1910 when it was named the Fort Worth Colored School after undergoing a relocation due to growth in the student population. One of the school's principals, Isaiah Milligan Terrell, is the namesake whose legacy prompted the renaming of the school in 1921 (Hanson, 2017).

Like many other Black schools during segregation, students at I.M. Terrell knew they received subpar materials and often used hand-me-downs from the White schools; however, the education and culture in the building still left students believing that obtaining an education was the only option and that they could achieve greatness. Walker (1996) expresses the legacy of segregated schools in the following words:

> ...to remember segregated schools largely by recalling only their poor resources presents a historically incomplete picture. Although black schools were indeed commonly lacking in facilities and funding, some evidence suggests that the environment of the segregated school had affective traits, institutional policies, and community support that helped black children learn in spite of the neglect their schools received from White school boards. (p. 3)

In fact, in 1940 I.M. Terrell participated in the Secondary School Study, which was established to support teachers with pedagogical practices. The Rockefeller Foundation's General Education Board funded the Secondary School Study. The leaders of the study hoped to include only the most "promising schools." Selection to participate in the study included an evaluation of a school's methodology regarding the staff's use of curricular materials and the level of school leadership. During the time of the study, I.M. Terrell focused on the development of an "integrated core program based on personal and social problems" along with increased "student growth and teacher professional development" (Kridel, 2015, p. 17). In addition to the study, Terrell graduates showed success in college despite the cost of a higher education that was often a deterrent for many Black students at the time. A study conducted by Fort Worth Independent School District (ISD) in 1969 indicated that I.M. Terrell students had fewer failures in college than their counterparts who graduated from White Fort Worth high schools such as Paschal, Carter-Riverside, and Diamond-Hill Jarvis (Wilson, 2012). Again, further showing why the study of I.M. Terrell could provide guidance to modern day educators.

Titus Hall, a graduate of I.M. Terrell, told Madigan during an interview with the reporter that he wants the school to be thought of as the mother school of Fort Worth. He believes it "should be the high school, an emblem of what can be, not of yesteryear" (Madigan, 2002). He is not alone in his regard for his alma mater as it is affectionately remembered as a "beacon on a hill" by many. Hall's words represent the spirit of this research. Is there a lesson for current day educators about how Black students were educated that led to so many successes that can possibly change the narrative of the current outcomes of Black students? Can I.M. Terrell be an "emblem" of what can be for the education and achievement of Black students? Unfortunately, before it could serve as such a representation, it was closed without regard to the positive, unparalleled legacy associated with the school.

Despite the desirable outcomes I.M. Terrell had based on both the academic and career success of so many of its graduates, Fort Worth ISD closed the doors to the school in 1973. The school board indicated that the closure was a result of their efforts to uphold the desegregation laws of the time that had not previously been upheld by the school district and its constituents. Desegregation resulted in the closure of several Black schools because of the many White parents refusing to send their students to a Black school. Such closures have left scholars wondering if such acts associated with desegregation actually undermined its promises (Ford, 2004).

I.M. Terrell High School in Fort Worth, Texas has a reputation of providing a quality education that resulted in many of its former students succeeding as civic, education, and business leaders. The school culture of I.M. Terrell that was shaped by highly educated Black educators may inform how current day educators can better educate Black students.

The findings included in this chapter are a result of conducting oral history interviews with 27 former I.M. Terrell students before its closure in 1973. Twenty-six interviews lasted 30–90 minutes and were held via Zoom or telephone and one interview was conducted through an email exchange. Interviews were recorded and then transcribed and coded.

RESEARCH QUESTION

The following research questions guided the study and the presentation of the findings:

1. How do people describe the experience of being a student at I.M. Terrell High School?
2. How was the education of Black students impacted by the closing of I.M. Terrell High School?

THEORETICAL FRAMEWORK

Critical Race Theory (CRT) is the theoretical framework that underpins this work. CRT explores the unstated intentions of individuals when making decisions, policies, and laws that have racial implications or are connected to racial differences between the policymaker and those who will experience the impact of the policy (Chapman et al., 2013; Zamudio et al., 2010). The specific areas of the framework that guided the research and analysis are construction of narratives, interest convergence, and the use of revisionist histories. The framework was applied to ultimately use the historical context to make meaning of the contemporary context (Ladson-Billings, 1995). CRT allows individuals to understand how it is possible that those who experienced the same time in history interpret the period and events differently (Adams & Adams, 2014).

Interest convergence is the idea that White people will only support racial justice policy when it is clear to them that they can benefit by moving forward with said policy (Bell, 2004). In other words, White people will uphold policies that support justice for Black people only when they believe the benefit intersects with an opportunity for their own advancement.

Construction of narratives and revisionist histories reflects the process and opportunity to reintroduce history through an interpretation from those whose voices are traditionally not a part of the original historical record. The narratives allow for the telling of the counter story by those who were oppressed and not members of the culture that shaped and told the dominant narrative (Brown, 2010). Despite its name, CRT is meant to look at race related policies with the attempt to help bring redemption, not merely criticism (Ladson-Billings, 2013). The counter-narrative process allows for the preservation of history from the perspective of the oppressed (Mungo, 2013). Through the preservation comes the use of the reconstruction of an earlier time to aid in the understanding of the present (Donato & Lazerson, 2000). Revisionist history allows for the exploration of how the result of actions in history may have been influenced by the dynamics amongst those with and without power and wealth (Donato & Lazerson, 2000).

In addition, the cultural capital framework through the CRT lens was considered in the analysis of the research. Specifically, consideration of aspirational capital, familial capital, and social capital provided a foundation for the research process (Anzaldúa, 1990). Social capital propels the academic success of students (Coleman, 1988). Social capital in an education setting comes as a result of trusting relationships with those who have the power (formal and informal) to provide motivation, resources, and/or accountability for a certain academic standard that may otherwise not be achievable (Coleman, 1998). In Black schools prior to *Brown*, it was often thought that by reaching a high academic standard one could also reach a high level of civic influence and expand their ability to positively impact the race as a whole (Malone, 2008). As a result, members of the Black community made personal and financial sacrifices to help Black children gain access to an education. The efforts of the educators as a form of culture capital is coined by Savage as Extraordinary Service (2002).

Research Methods

A qualitative historical ethnographic was utilized to address the research questions. The rich description that comes from qualitative research is well aligned with the purpose of this study. An ethnographic study allows the researcher to learn the key elements of a specific group (Merriam, 2009). I.M. Terrell's culture was studied through oral history since it is no longer in existence.

The oral history process is similar to that of interviewing in traditional qualitative research, but because of its essence for the overall research process, it tends to include more in-depth questions. Oral history is a process that allows for memories and personal explanations to capture historical significance through the process of interviews that are recorded (Ritchie, 1995). The capturing of the oral histories often unveils information that is not already available to the researcher or the historian through other methodologies. Oral history provides an opportunity to retell important historical events from the vantage point of those who were disregarded in other accounts of history (Adams & Adams, 2014). Given the process of historical research and the foundation of CRT, the two can be easily interwoven through the research process.

QUALITATIVE INQUIRY

Qualitative research allows a researcher to focus on context and rich descriptions to answer research questions. The level of exploration that comes as a result of qualitative research allowed me to understand the experiences of former I.M. Terrell High School students. Specifically, the research methodology allowed me to gain insight into how the former students make sense of the time period when they were high school students (Merriam, 2009). The process allowed me to uncover the meaning that former students bring to their experience at I.M. Terrell, especially given the context of desegregation.

The process is inductive in nature because the qualitative research process allowed me to gather information that results in an increased understanding of my subject along with their lived history that shapes their perspective (Denzin & Lincoln, 2005). In addition, connections to the literature were made.

Participants

The oral history in this project focused on the experience of individuals who were part of the schooling experience at I.M. Terrell High School. To best capture the educational experience of all who attended, the participants are diversified across gender, year of graduation, and residential neighborhood at the time of attendance. There are thirteen male participants and fourteen female participants. Their graduation years span across 30 years and all participants resided in one of the Black segregated neighborhoods within the city of Fort Worth when they attended I.M. Terrell.

Participants were recruited using social media, communication with the alumni association, and through my personal network. In addition, the use of snowball sampling increased the number of participants. For example, several of the narrators gave the interviewer names of peers at the end of each interview when they were asked for suggestions of any other individuals who should be considered for participation in the study.

Respondents were informed about the nature and purpose of the research, so they could determine their interest in participating. Every participant was required to sign a consent form granting their permission to participate in any facet of the study. The oral consent was secured before the start of each interview.

FINDINGS

After the completion of the interviews I listened as many times as needed to create accurate transcripts. After interviewing and transcribing, the data was sorted by both subject areas and themes. During the multiple readings of each transcript, I made note of any parts of interest that could possibly answer the research questions or had a connection to the interest convergence tenet of CRT and the culture capital theory.

The initial notes taken allowed me to begin the open coding and categorizing process. Coding in qualitative research is a term or short phrase that represents a cumulative and significant meaning to a portion of the data derived from interview transcripts or artifacts during the research process (Saldana, 2016). The foundational step in coding is identifying and marking data that shows any applicability to discovering answers to the research questions. The marking then informed grouping and coding of common threads across multiple interviews and archival research (Merriam, 2009). The common threads were then utilized to create categories based on data that appears multiple times (Saldana, 2016).

The Mindset of Achieving More than the Prior Generation Created a Strong Value of Receiving an Education

Black teachers who would have a choice for a more prestigious career if not for the color of their skin set aside any feelings of self-pity or anger and geared all of their energy to making sure their students understood what was possible if they earned a great education. As a result, the students at I.M. Terrell learned to appreciate the value of education and that had a direct impact on the effort they gave each day in the classroom. The transfer and ultimate sharing of education as a value contributed to the students' cultural capital. This was epitomized by Nelda Harris, Class of 1969.

> What we learned was that we were survivors, that we could excel, that we could "compete" Most of the teachers felt, they were teaching us to master the content

so their students could achieve the goals they had for themselves that they could not actualize because they were Black. They had something to offer, and they were encouraging us to accept what they had, and by their desire to nurture and encourage most of the students accepted what was offered.

According to Harold Diggs, Class of 1969, based on what the teachers shared with them, the students knew that "education was the key" to them being better than their teachers and parents. The sentiment resulted in students having a sense of obligation that all the students "had to be better" than those that had gone before them because so many sacrifices had been made so much effort was being poured into his generation. Devoyd Jennings, Class of 1966, in recounting what he believed was the mindset of many teachers based on his experience, shared, "I didn't win this round, but I'm going to teach these kids and they'll win for me."

Working to achieve a great education was not just about each individual student, but represented respect to the Black people who had gone before them and made receiving such a high caliber of education possible. Brenda Moore, Class of 1966, affirmed such representation, "We were held accountable because so many people had been through so many things to get us to the point where we were." According to Linda Brewster, Class of 1969,

> The education offered within the walls of I.M. Terrell High School was about furthering the lives of each student and all those who could be impacted by their achievements. It was a springboard to get you started for a productive life; a better life.

The obligation was also felt because of all that had occurred in the efforts towards civil rights for Black people. To illustrate, Myra Burnett, Class of 1973, said, "We had an obligation to achieve all that we could because it was a special moment...following the civil rights acts. A special moment to really join as full citizens of the United States." Ms. Burnett furthered her opinion by sharing that the teachers at I.M. Terrell would openly tell the students that they would have the opportunity to do things and go places that Black people had not before and that preparation was necessary for when that door of opportunity finally opened.

The students were very aware of all the teachers had sacrificed (some by choice and others because of the color of their skin) and came to a feeling of not wanting to disappoint their teachers as shared by Myrna Burnett, Class of 1973. "Certainly we didn't want to let them down, so we tried hard to keep our level of achievement up for them." Burnett's desire to keep up her achievement level resulted in her becoming a faculty member at Spelman College.

Ultimately, I.M. Terrell's faculty had hope not only for their students' academic future but also for the racial equity they hoped would come soon and they wanted to prepare their students for all they hoped would come. According to Bob Ray Sanders, Class of 1965, "They were trying to prepare us for days of change that was coming. A change they would not necessarily see, but they thought they could see it for us." The efforts were exemplified daily in how the faculty treated and instructed their students. The hope for change helped the students establish aspirational capital despite the racial challenges that remained present during the time the school's doors were open. Looking ahead and believing that better days were possible fueled the students at I.M. Terrell, and contributed to their commitment doing well academically. Sander's fueling resulted in becoming a well-known journalist.

Teachers and School Administration cared for Their Students

The faculty utilized their personal knowledge of each student as a conduit to reach students' hearts and minds. Three participants used explicit language to emphasize that they were known by name at I.M. Terrell, only to be later regarded only by a social security number after graduation. According to Harold Diggs, Class of 1969, the "teachers took an active interest" in their students because they were concerned about their success. Not only did teachers know them by name, but they also knew their temperament, as recounted by George Williams, Class of 1964, who went on to share how he had no doubt his teachers genuinely cared about him.

The care teachers had manifested itself in forms of not giving up and in the use of affirmative language. Carolyn McBride struggled to learn but said her I.M. Terrell math teacher stayed after school to tutor her. Her teacher modeled the instructional process in multiple ways and assured her that, despite being difficult for Carolyn, she was certain the content would eventually be mastered. Brenda Moore, Class of 1966, still keeps close to her heart the words of an I.M. Terrell teacher who shared that if there was something she wanted to do, it was always important to try because failure is okay. Moore left that conversation believing she could do anything she put her mind to. The type of care that was affirming and inspiring, resulted in Moore, along with other students, loving school. Moore's love of school and the inspiring words of her teacher are still alive through the work she does as a reading tutor and mentor to children in the Fort Worth community as a part of her life in retirement. Brenda Jones Piper, Class of 1973, shared similar sentiments, "They told us you're going to do good. You can do whatever you want, whatever you put your mind to, you're going to do it. They were encouragers and we believed them. I believed them." Opal Lee, Class of 1943, reinforced the same sentiment. "Teachers knew when you were struggling to get some material and if [the teacher] had to give you some extra attention." Florida Ward, Class of 1965, further affirmed this point, stating, "If we didn't understand, they were always willing to get us to an understanding before we left the classroom. They didn't want us to go thinking 'I wonder how to do this.'" There was a relentless level of responsibility taken by the teachers to ensure all their students learned.

Faculty members' care led to students finding them approachable and committed to creating an enjoyable learning environment. This "level of care" was further illustrated by the ease of accessibility to faculty, according to Fred Alexander, Class of 1960.

> The level of everyday encouragement that we got...If I had a problem in a class, I didn't necessarily have to schedule a meeting two weeks out with a teacher to talk about whatever that problem was. I mean, I could probably go right after the class or at the end of the day and spend ten to fifteen minutes with that teacher to get it if I had questions or problems about a class. I could get that answered right away. I didn't have to go through a lot of red tape to get that done. They made time for us.

Ann Collins, Class of 1969, characterized her teachers as "intelligent, but they were also fun loving. They made the learning environment, the classrooms, enjoyable."

The affirming and welcoming approach also resulted in students engaging with subject matters that they once considered unappealing. Fred Alexander, Class of 1960, had this type of dichotomous relationship with Ms. Jones in the area of history, "I remember Ms. Jones, who was one of my favorite teachers of all, taught history. Now, this is kind of a weird situation because I hated history, but I loved Ms. Jones... One of the best teachers there. She just had a friendly manner to get her point about history over." Fred Alexander said he now loves history, showing how the delivery and care of the teachers shifted the perspective of their students.

The care was further extended when a student had a financial need. Nelda Harris, Class of 1969, shared there were situations when teachers would purchase clothing items for a student in need or pay for a school outing so the child would not miss a learning opportunity. Opal Lee, Class of 1943, recalled teachers paying for meals and learning materials for students, and Ann Collins, Class of 1969, mentioned teachers providing snacks to students if teachers noticed students were hungry because they did not eat breakfast. Clearly, there was a belief that teachers would make every effort to remove barriers that could conceivably prevent a student from achieving academic success.

Caring went beyond the content, it was shown in addressing the personal needs of the students. It was expressed in making sure students had a path for their life beyond high school. While many words and stories during the research captured the high level of care, it is profound that eight different participants used the word "caring" to describe the faculty or the environment at I.M. Terrell High School. In addition, an additional seven participants used the word "encouraging." The faculties' commitment and care are aligned with many other educators from the first Black high schools who felt personally accountable for their students' learning (Franklin, 2002).

The faculty utilized their personal knowledge of each student as a conduit to reach the hearts and minds of their students. As a result of this level of education and care, the teachers were held in the highest regard by all in the Black community according to Myra Burnett, Class of 1973. The students had familial capital because of the strong relationships that resulted in a level of trust that mirrored what one might have with extended family.

Paired with relationships and interaction with students were the trusting and supportive relationships held with parents. Some parents whose children attended I.M. Terrell High School had not had the opportunity to earn a high school diploma. They believed the education at I.M. Terrell was the best, even if it was the only option for their children to reach a life that allowed them to flourish economically and socially. Furthermore, the parents trusted the teachers because they lived in the same community. They regularly interacted with the teachers in their neighborhoods, churches, and Black-owned businesses. Parents considered teachers an extension of their families who shared the responsibilities of rearing their children. Therefore, they held the same expectations and values at home for the schooling process. One participant shared, "My parents expected us to do it, to give respect to our teachers as well as to make sure we excelled." Another participant shared that she had a choice to attend I.M. Terrell or a newly integrated high school closer to her home. Her parents made it clear that they knew that there was no way the integrated high school's teachers would invest the same time and effort as I.M. Terrell's teachers. Specifically, she remembers them saying, "We are not sure how you are going to be treated, if it's going to be some racial overtones." Her mom went on to tell her, "I'm not sure that you'll be treated fairly." Emerson Kincade, Class of 1959 spoke positively about the connection that was a part of his experience as a student at I.M. Terrell. He said the people that taught at I.M. Terrell either lived in your immediate neighborhood or were part of a community connection such as the local church. "They knew you; they knew your parents."

Energized by feeling good and eager to become good citizens, the students were poised to meet the high expectations and culture of excellence involved in attending I.M. Terrell High School.

High Expectations of the Faculty Members Ensured Each Student's Readiness for Life Beyond High School

The students at I.M. Terrell had the opportunity to learn from teachers who were overqualified by today's standards for a high school teacher. Many of the teachers were educated to the masters or doctoral level, but due to the limitations of segregation were not able to pursue careers that aligned with their intellect and knowledge of their content area.

Equipped with a superb understanding of their content, teachers refused to allow students to fail. Teachers tutored after class and after school to make sure all students had access to learn the material. According to Opal Lee, Class of 1943,

> So the teachers were gifted to say the least. And they had our interest at heart. The teachers were extremely good and that's putting it mildly. The teachers knew the material that you were struggling to get. If they had to give somebody some extra

attention, if they didn't do it themselves, they knew students that could help. So it was just like a family. Everybody looked after everybody else.

The expectation for learning was also repeatedly shared through affirmative statements. Due to the teachers being experts in their content, they were able to secure or direct students to materials to supplement the subpar learning materials provided from the local school system. Several participants even mentioned that it did not seem to matter that they had less or inadequate instructional materials. In fact, Nelda Harris, Class of 1969, commented "they were all exceptional teachers, so they made up for anything that lacked in terms of equipment, books or even the facility itself."

Students were taught to go beyond just the content that was present in Fort Worth ISD's curriculum, and to become brilliant thinkers and writers. Bob Ray Sanders, Class of 1965, fondly recounts his teachers' "constant challenge" to think about subject matter and ideas, and situations. In fact, these thinking and writing skills helped so many Terrellites succeed in college and beyond. Fred Alexander, Class of 1960, credits the frequent communication and level of expectation of his teacher, Ms. Phillips, to his success in college that resulted in his long standing career as an architect. Personal accountability manifested into a form of social capital by instilling a standard of excellence in the students that resulted in great academic, professional, and civic achievement.

Knowledge of content was not viewed as enough for students to succeed, but there was a belief that students also had knowledge of their history as Black people and presented themselves with grace, dignity, and confidence. I.M. Terrell teachers told the students that they could do anything they put their mind to doing, and the students believed them. Ann Collins, Class of 1969, recalls that Black history came alive through the personal testimonies and connections her teachers shared across content areas. The empowerment Collins felt from learning Black history took her through law school and her current role as a judge.

Roderick Grimes, Class of 1969, shared that his parents "reinforced the notion that if I was going to make anything of myself, I need a good education and college was not something that was a thought or an ideal. It was something that I could work hard enough to make happen."

Grimes' aspirational capital resulted in him attending Northwestern University through the support of his I.M. Terrell school counselor by way of helping him navigate the selection process and securing an academic scholarship.

Unquestionably, the faculty's intellect and care equipped the students with an extraordinary level of social capital. Furthermore the revisionist history as retold in this study contradicts what is commonly studied about pre-*Brown* segregated schools as exemplified by Gladys Moore, Class of 1969, remarked:

> Well, basically when I think of I.M. Terrell, first of all, I think about the teachers that we had because I think we would not have received the kind of education that we did receive if it had not been for the dedication of those teachers. The demand at

I.M. Terrell was that you would achieve excellence. They wouldn't accept anything else. And that was something that really kind of pushed us and it wasn't like we felt the pressure. It was a good thing. It was something that made us feel like we could all become leaders and there was nothing that we couldn't do or couldn't achieve, if we tried.

Gladys, like most participants in the study, without probing shared how well they were equipped to face society. There is no dwelling and in fact minimal mention of the subpar materials that often lace the stories of Black segregated schools.

One participant, along with several other participants, shared that he recalls one of the English teachers required excellence and even expected students to redo their work until they reached at least a B-level performance, not only using her skills and education at I.M. Terrell but also contributing to the curriculum across the full public school system. Daryl Glenn, Class of 1969, speaks to this sense of excellence.

> We had exceptional teachers. They were very talented. Many of them would've been in other fields if not for the color of their skin. They gave us what they had. The teachers permitted us to think, and we had to expound on our thinking. It wasn't just straight down the line, You do this, you do that. You had to be a thinker.

Along those same lines, Devoyd Jennings, Class of 1966, stated,

> You had an abundance of very smart people, teaching us. They taught us how to survive in the future that they thought we would have, and it made us really, really, really, competitive. The teachers because of segregation were limited on the fields in which they could work. They wanted to equip the students to be prepared for the future opportunities they were hoping the students would have.

Teachers were thought of as providing an excellent delivery of instruction combined with high expectations. According to George Williams, Class of 1964, the teachers

> led by example. Because everybody was well respected, all the teachers were well respected. We just wanted to be like them when we grew up. We just wanted to be able to do something and do something that was really going to make a difference.

Nelda Harris, Class of 1969, does not "recall any teacher who did not have great expectations for the students. I just don't recall it." James Cash, Class of 1965, echoed the same sentiment. "There were no low expectations for anyone. We needed to excel or understand that we were not working hard enough." The expectation for academic excellence empowered the students with vital cultural capital (Franklin, 2002). The students understood that their teachers' expectations were part of the shared valued system that would help not only them individually, but the Black race collectively. I.M. Terrell students further had the connection made between high achievement while in high school with access to the ability to build wealth. The high expectations became the needed foundation to build aspirational capital.

The great care and academic programming left students feeling prepared for the career or higher education choice that would follow. The confidence in their level of preparation gave them the type of hope associated with aspirational capital. The students had aspirations for their future and strongly believed the aspirations would materialize. Daryl Glenn, Class of 1969, demonstrated this when he said, "When I got to college, I realized I could do it. The tools that I received there (I.M. Terrell), as an average student, propelled me through the University of Houston."

Given that my interviews included many K–12 educators, a high ranking city official, a publication professional, two CEOs, multiple nurses, along with those who made great progress in careers that did not require a four-year degree, I think it is without question that I.M. Terrell High School's culture and instruction offered the necessary foundation for its students to flourish after graduating from the beacon on the hill. More important than career success were the sentiments and continual commitment and advocacy to the Black community. Opal Lee, Class of 1943, recently recognized for her leadership in advocating for Juneteenth being declared a federal holiday. Devoyd Jennings, Class of 1966 is renowned in Fort Worth for his leadership surrounding the building of economic empowerment within the Black community. Bob Ray Sanders, Class of 1965, continues to use his experience as an award-winning journalist of the city's leading newspaper and his work in radio and television to engage the city's youth and provide civic leadership across many areas. The positive legacy of I.M. Terrell's former students continues to impact the city of Fort World and the entire country.

The faculty's burning desire and hope for the next generation of Black people fueled their relentless high expectations for their students. Roy C. Brooks, Class of 1967, captures so much in one simple remark, "They expected that I would do my best in all things. They expected that I would learn." Ann Collins, Class of 1969, says excellence was a tradition based on all the students who had attended the school before her. Excellence was expected in all things, including their assignments, presentation of their clothing, timeliness, and making whatever sacrifices were needed to learn. In fact, to supplement the learning materials, to teach study skills, and to teach the use of reference materials, students were expected on many occasions to use the public library. At the time, the only public library the students could use was in downtown Fort Worth, which often meant coordinating transportation. There was simply no excuse for not meeting the expectations, as recalled by Ann Collins, Class of 1969.

I.M. Terrell's Faculty Served as Role Models and Examples of Excellence

I.M. Terrell teachers' educational experience and professionalism became an icon of excellence to their students. The students were eager to learn how the teachers could achieve their stature so they too could have great outcomes in their lives.

While many faculty members were remembered fondly by name amongst the participants, Hazel Harvey Peace's name unquestionably was shared most frequently. Hazel Harvey Peace is synonymous with I.M. Terrell High School because of the favorable memories held by her former students. It is nearly impossible to have a conversation with someone about the school without her quickly becoming the subject of a heartfelt story. Myrna Burnett, Class of 1973, described Ms. Peace as being an "icon of educated, sophisticated Black womanhood." Ms. Burnett wanted to be just like her which only pushed her further in her educational pursuits. Hazel Harvey Peace was also favorably remembered by Opal Lee, Class of 1943. Ms. Lee shared, "she knew what excellence was and she wanted us to strive for it. And she gave us the tools to strive."

The faculty's leadership extended beyond the walls of I.M. Terrell High School into the overall Black community. When referring to the teacher, Pamela Cash, Class of 1966, remembered, "They were just good examples for upstanding citizens in the academic community and in the whole city, the whole Black community." The community connection likely helped spur the camaraderie across the student body and faculty that existed at I.M. Terrell.

A Strong Familial Bond Existed Between Those Associated With I. M. Terrell High School

The family bond complimented and was a catalyst for the educational process at I.M. Terrell. Ann Collins, Class of 1969, described it as "more like a family environment so it was more expected of you as well in that environment."

A large number of participants indicated they simply were unable to describe what it meant to be a student at I.M. Terrell. Words like family and camaraderie were interjected through almost every interview. A few examples follow.

For Linda Brewster, Class of 1969, "It was really more of a family feel to it, a family unit." Gladys Moore, Class of 1969, expounded even further.

> It was the building, it was the people, the camaraderie, the compassion in that building every day when you would go in. I can't even explain it to you, because you have to have lived it, but it was an honor. Something you just felt when you went there. I don't consider them as classmates, I consider them as family. And that was another thing I.M. Terrell instilled in us that we were a family. And when you walked in that building, you didn't feel like you were coming to school, you thought you were coming home. It wasn't school, it was home.

Speaking of home, Myra Burnett, Class of 1973, indicated, "So I think in many ways it was a home, it was something to be proud of." Ann Collins, Class of 1969, shared that the teachers, counselors, and school administration treated the students as if they were family. The sentiment was shared by George Williams, Class of 1964, who stated, "The environment was real close, like a real family-like environment." When speaking of his electronics instructor, Harold Diggs, Class of 1969, said Warren T. Bennett was his father away from home and what he taught him ultimately about life saved his life. He goes on to describe how Mr. Bennett taught him skills to help him earn money and most importantly, trusted and believed in him. Carolyn McBride, who attended I.M. Terrell High School for one year before going to an integrated high school, remembers Terrell as a place where they were taught to love one another.

The camaraderie and familial ties resulted in the students having familial capital (Yosso, 2006). Students developed a broader understanding of a bond that can go beyond biological kinship lines. The bond helped establish a deep connection and community between the faculty and the students and amongst the student body. The familial capital that results from ties of this magnitude help shape not only the students as individuals but positively impact the collective Black community (Franklin, 2002).

Most Feel the Closing of I. M. Terrell had a Negative Impact on the Black Community

The study indicates many negative consequences that came after the closing of I.M. Terrell High School which left most Black families with no other option than to send their children to newly integrated predominately-White high schools. In the White schools, students experienced a much different level of care than those who attended I.M. Terrell, which negatively impacted the quality of education. The burden of integration was put on the backs of Black children as they had to enter an unknown community, school, and culture given that there appears to not have been any effort to require White families to send their children to Black high schools.

The community disintegrated. Gerrod Anderson, Class of 1948, viewed I.M. Terrell High School as the "hub of the Black community." He as others do find a direct correlation between I.M. Terrell's closing and the loss of the Black community that soon followed. Myrna Burnett, Class of 1973, felt then and now

> that we were losing something of our culture and that were giving that up too easily for the cause of integration. And when I look at where we are with resegregated schools, it seems like perhaps it was for not. We hoped for something that did not manifest.

Pamela Cash, Class of 1966, in thinking about role models she had in teachers at I.M. Terrell High School, said integration took the role models away from Black students. Using the feedback from these alumni narrators, you can conduct a deeper analysis of their perspectives. For example, examine what they gave up for the current "resegregation"—the absence of role models then and now.

The value of education in the Black community was greatly jeopardized by the lack of access to teachers who had the level of care and commitment as the teachers at I.M. Terrell High School. Furthermore, students no longer had a space for an educated Black person to openly share a healthy balance of the possibilities that could come by being educated with the challenges they may face. Students who could no longer attend I.M. Terrell were often left to attend integrated schools and were now taught predominately by White teachers.

The opportunities to build social capital through familial ties and the empowerment that Black teachers at I.M. Terrell disappeared without a clear path to gain such capital within their academic experience. Black students were left without teachers who planted a strong desire for what could be, which diminished the aspirational capital that had been the legacy of I.M. Terrell. The intersectionality of social capital and high achievement that existed was lost because of the integration plan in Fort Worth ISD that resulted in the closure of the beacon on the hill.

Discussion and Implications

It is often taught and presumed that *Brown v. Board* was needed because Black students did not have access to excellent learning opportunities within the walls of Black high schools. The slow school desegregation process that occurred after *Brown* assumed that as a result of integration Black children would receive a better education at the predominantly White schools they would now attend. The study of I.M. Terrell High School and close consideration and analysis of CRT completely debunks the message given for nearly 60 years.

The revisionist counterstories that the 27 participants shared painted a clear, consistent picture that extraordinary learning took place for decades at I.M. Terrell High School. The education prepared its students for success in college and careers and taught the value of their personal history and how that history should be used as both a motivator and bonding agent between them and their classmates.

Simultaneous consideration of the participants' response and the tenets of interest convergence suggest concern and wonderings regarding the real reason a community pillar such as I.M. Terrell was closed. Further research should be conducted to determine if there were any benefits to the greater White community that lead to the closing. Such research could then inform future decisions and processes for school closures that may disrupt Black communities. The research may also give voice to all parties, therefore, promoting equity in the decision-making.

The students at I.M. Terrell had access to school and community leaders who supported their career aspirations which revealed their experiences modeled the expected outcomes when social capital is present. The strongest seems to be the familial capital actively created by their faculty. The faculty's efforts lead to a high level of aspirational capital that spurred so many graduates to unimaginable success. How do educators and the Black community recreate this for current day Black students?

Given that the social capital had such a strong influence on the outcomes of the students in a segregated high school, it is worth considering and making active efforts to create such capital for Black students in current day schools. To start, educational policy makers should consider establishing a required study of the positive contributions of Black people both within schools and as part of educator certification coursework. To avoid only a surface level study, rigorous standards and guidelines should be included. Secondly, more effort has to be given to recruiting Black educators. Similar to how many systems give signing bonuses or stipends to bilingual educators, Black educators should receive supplemental pay as well. The last area that should be explored are required opportunities for educators to examine their expectations for Black children. Do they see the potential in each of their Black students or do they unconsciously lower their expectations because they do not think their Black students have the same intellect or academic ability as their non-Black peers?

Conclusion

I.M. Terrell High School was closed in 1973 after providing an education to Black students for nearly 100 years. The true reason for its closing is still in debate across its alumni and Fort Worth's Black community. It therefore leaves one wondering if the closure was really about improved access to education.

The legacy of I.M. Terrell High School is shaped by the Black educators who unselfishly chose to prepare their students for a world of integration and the equitable opportunities they hoped would follow. The students were immersed in a level of social and cultural capital that fostered their ability to courageously go onto navigate a newly integrated predominantly-White society with courage and confidence.

The I.M. Terrell High School study revealed that the unequal facilities, financial support, and instructional resources did not prevent students from learning. The knowledge, expectations, and care of the faculty far out measured what was lacking. The teachers' backgrounds, professionalism, and commitment became a source of racial pride for the students. Student life outcomes debunk the false narrative that Black segregated high schools could not provide an excellent education. The false narrative became the steppingstone for the push for integrating schools. Sadly, the profound thirst for the dream associated with attending an integrated school caused Black people to surrender their race's educational and economic progress.

Time will not allow us to go back and make the implementation of school integration one of true equality and not just of convenience or the White people who did not want their children to attend schools like I.M. Terrell. However, it is not too late to let our Black children know they are intelligent beings who can achieve at the same level (if not higher) than their White peers.

It is time to end naming Black people who have success academically and professionally as exceptions to the race. It is time that all know that extraordinary, intelligent Black people were the model for the race before actions laced with acts of superiority by White people tried to camouflage it. No matter their race, all of our children deserve to benefit from the recommendations brought forward in this chapter. It is time that we adequately prepare educators to teach Black students while holding an expectation that each student can soar to success. It is time to reconsider the lack of representation of Black people and their voice in most curriculum choices and how history is taught.

The study of I.M. Terrell shows what is possible for Black children when they receive what they deserve within a school setting. I.M. Terrell is a model of what can and should be for education.

REFERENCES

Adams, J. H., & Adams, N. G. (2014). "Some of us got heard more than others": Studying Brown through oral history and critical race theory. *Counterpoints*, *449*, 189–202. doi: 10.2307/1340546

Anzaldúa, G. (1990). *Making face, making soul =: Haciendo caras: Creative and critical perspectives by feminists of color.* Aunt Lute Foundation Books.

Bell, D. (2004). *Silent covenants: Brown v. Board of education and the unfulfilled hopes for racial reform.* Oxford University Press.

Castleman, J. (2013). *I.M Terrell High School* [Photograph]. Wikimedia. Creative Commons Attribution-Share Alike 3.0 Unported. https://commons.wikimedia.org/wiki/File:I.M._Terrell_High_School_building,_eastern_exposure,_Ft._Worth,_TX_01.JPG

Chapman, T. K., Dixson, A., Gillborn, D., & Ladson-Billings, G. (2013). Critical race theory. In Irby, B. J., Brown, G., Lara-Alecio, R., & Jackson, S. (Eds.), *The handbook of educational theories* (pp. 1019–1026). Information Age Publishing, Inc.

Coleman, J. S. (1988). Social capital in the creation of human capital. *The American Journal of Sociology, 94*, S95–S120. https://www.jstor.org/stable/2780243

Denzin, N. K., & Lincoln, Y. S. (Eds.). (2005). *The Sage handbook of qualitative research.* Sage Publications, Inc.

Donato, R., & Lazerson, M. (2000). New directions in American educational history: Problems and prospects. *Educational Researcher, 29*(8), 4–15. https://www.jstor.org/stable/1176628

Ford, R. T. (2004). Brown's ghost. *Harvard Law Review, 117*(5), 1305–1333.

Franklin, V. P. (2002). Introduction: cultural capital and African American education. *The Journal of African American History, 87*, 175–181.

Hanson, G. W. (2017, July 12). Terrell, Isaiah Milligan [I.M.]. *Handbook of Texas online.* http://www.tshaonline.org/handbook/online/articles/fte56.

Kridel, C. (2015). *Progressive education in Black high schools: The secondary schools study, 1940–1946.* http://www.sc.edu/study/colleges_schools/education/research/museum/publications/index.php

Ladson-Billings, G. (1995). Toward a critical race theory of education. *Teacher College Record, 97*(1), 47–68. http://dx.doi.org/10.1177/016146819509700104

Ladson-Billings, G. (2013). Critical race theory—What it is not! In M. Lynn & A. D. Dixon (Eds.), *Handbook of critical race theory in education* (pp. 34–47). Routledge.

Madigan, T. (2002, October 7). *Separate but superior.* Fort Worth Star Telegram. http://www.pbs.org/weta/twoschools/thechallenge/telegram/telegram_2.html

Malone, B. (2008). Before Brown: Cultural and social capital in a rural Black school community, W. E. B. DuBois High School, Wake Forest, North Carolina. *Historical Review, 85*(4), 416–447. http://www.jstor.org/stable/23523968

Merriam, S. B. (2009). *Qualitative research: A guide to design and implementation.* John Wiley & Sons, Inc.

Miller, K. (1973, June 2). Terrell era ends. *Fort Worth Star Telegram* (p. 4).

Morris, V. G., & Morris, C. L. (2002). *The price they paid: Desegregation in an African American Community.* Teachers College Press.

Mungo, S. (2013). Our own communities, our own schools: educational counter-narratives of African American civil right generation students. *Journal of Negro Education, 82*(2), 11–122. http://ww.jstor.org/discover/10.7709/jnegroeducation.82.20111

Ritchie, D. A. (1995). *Doing oral history.* Twayne Publishers.

Saldana, J. (2016). *The coding manual for qualitative researchers* (3rd ed.). SAGE Publications.

Savage, C. (2002). Cultural capital and African American agency: The economic struggle for effective education for African Americans in Franklin, Tennessee, 1890–1967. *The Journal of African American History, 87*, 206–235. doi:10.2307/1562464

Shujaa, M. J. (1996). *Beyond segregation: The politics of quality in African American schooling.* Corwin Press, Inc.

Walker, V. S. (1996). *Their highest potential.* The University of North Carolina Press.

Wilson, S. A. (2012). *Vanished legacies and the lost culture of I.M. Terrell High School in segregated Fort Worth, Texas.* [Master's thesis]. University of Texas, Arlington. ProQuest. https://rc.library.uta.edu/uta-ir/handle/10106/11502

Yosso, T. J. (2005). Whose culture has capital? A critical race theory discussion on community cultural wealth. *Race Ethnicity and Education, 8*(1), 69–91. doi:1080/136133205200341006

Zamudio, M., Russell, C., Rios, F., & Bridgeman, J. L. (2010). *Critical race theory matters: Education and ideology* (1st ed.). Routledge. https://doi.org/10.4324/9780203842713

CHAPTER 5

FREDERICK DOUGLASS HIGH SCHOOL, BALTIMORE

William P. Kladky
American Institutes of Research

This chapter examines Baltimore's Frederick Douglass High School (Douglass) through an external lens—Black political power networks. There is an examination of the causal reasons why political integration did not lead to social and racial integration, why de facto racial segregation returned, the role of urban changes and historical factors, why Douglass has deteriorated, and implications for the future. The theoretical perspective of this chapter is Yosso's (2005) theory of cultural capital, along with explanations by Franklin (2002). Essentially, because of the perpetual social injustices and the failure of societal racial integration, the African American community was forced to develop Douglass when the public school system failed to do so. Financial and other support by the African American community was essential for even basic daily functioning, much less significant strides. African American achievement of political office in Baltimore elections has not been sufficient to overcome continued—if not increased—opposition on the state and federal level to develop a more equitable public school system in Baltimore. The roles of community groups, individual actors, the prevailing Black culture, and the political economic interaction of these forces have been critically important.

Keywords: Frederick Douglass High School, Cultural Capital, African American Social Networks, Community

FREDERICK DOUGLASS HIGH SCHOOL

This chapter examines Frederick Douglass High School Baltimore's Frederick Douglass High School (Douglass) through an external lens—Black political power networks. The rationale for an external view is because of the perpetual social injustices and the failure of societal racial integration which forced the African American community to develop a high school when the public school system failed to do so. In the process, there is an examination of the causal reasons why political integration did not lead to social and racial integration and why de facto racial segregation returned. The role of urban changes and historical factors, why Douglass has deteriorated, and future implications also will be treated.

The theoretical perspective of this chapter is scholar Tara J. Yosso's (2005) theory of cultural capital, along with explanations by V.P. Franklin (2002). "Centering the research lens on the experiences of people of color in critical historical context reveals accumulated assets and resources in the histories and lives in the communities of color" (Yosso, 2005, p. 77). This is why Douglass's story is being viewed from the lens of alumni and the Black community as an asset and resource for the development of the school. The financial and other support by

Frederick Douglass High School. Note: Eminonuk, CC BY-SA 4.0

the African American community to the public schools is essential for basic daily functioning much less significant improvement. African American achievement of political office in urban elections has not been enough to counter continued—if not increased—opposition on the state and federal level to more equitable public school systems in urban areas. The huge social capital gap with White communities has meant that African American communities must supply the little they can to serve their own interests. The roles of community groups, individual actors, the prevailing Black culture, and the political economic interaction of these forces are critically important.

History

After the Civil War, the Baltimore African American community's agitation end with the June 25, 1867 passage of Baltimore City Council resolution #79 that made the City responsible for African American public schooling. Both before and after the Civil War, facilities for African Americans were separate and strikingly inferior to those for White children. The official funding formula was school taxes paid by Whites would go to White schools, while taxes paid by African Americans would go to African American schools, thus guaranteeing that they would remain substandard (Olson, 1980). African American schools were taught and run by White teachers and principals.

The educational progress in Baltimore was enhanced by the 1870s–1880s arrival of a new generation of African American political leaders, such as lawyer Everett J. Waring and Union Baptist Church's Reverend Harvey Johnson, who migrated to Baltimore from rural Virginia and Maryland. Some were trained in the ministry. They marshaled the Black community and formed the Mutual United Brotherhood of Liberty, Baltimore's first civil rights organization. Their congregations' activism and legal suit against the state (Black Laws) finally led to the 1888 muting of the Black Laws and the hiring of African American teaching professionals, but at lower wages (Seyler & Norcio, 2012). This was the beginning of the importance of the mobilization of the African American social community in achieving any educational progress.

By 1880, African Americans lived throughout Baltimore City, making up over 10% of the population in three fourths of the 20 wards and not over one-third of any ward. But after the continuing influx of lesser skilled African Americans migrated to Baltimore and other northern cities from the South and from rural areas of Maryland, segregation solidified. With Baltimore's population passing 500,000, the City Council passed three ordinances before 1917 outlawing African Americans from moving into White neighborhoods. Though overturned in the courts by 1919, the actions illustrated the level of housing discrimination that had become entrenched (Olson, 1980). Douglass's history would be increasingly negatively affected by the resultant racial segregation and diminished African American political power in both the city and state.

The Beginning

Douglass began in 1883 when the Grammar School for Colored Children opened, which became the Colored High School in 1885 with a staff of a principal and several assistants. The school was a separate unit within the high and grammar schools. In 1897, a separate building was constructed for the high school students. When it relocated in 1901, the school included both normal and polytechnic departments. The training school was separated from the high school in 1909. These changes were the result of lobbying by the African American community and educational groups such as the Alumni Association of the Colored High School, the Civic Aid Association, and the Defense League.

The continuing 1920s African American urban population surge, increased wealth, and political mobilization led to the construction of a new school during 1923–1925 that finally had the usual high school components of a gymnasium, cafeteria, and library. The new school's name was changed to honor Frederick Douglass, and Douglass and Dunbar of Washington, D. C. became the first African American high schools east of the Mississippi. Douglass was the only city secondary school for African American students until 1931. Used in the day and evening for education, Douglass was also a center for the African American community's cultural, social, and related activities during the evening and the summer; however, Baltimore's 234 Protestant churches were African Americans' cultural and institutional core. The *Baltimore Afro American* (*Afro*), the African American weekly newspaper established in 1892 was particularly important in rallying African American opinion into action (Skotnes, 2013). It brought issues to the public's attention, publicized important meetings, and strongly advocated for racial equality. The 93% growth of the African American population during 1900–1933 pushed its school population up 170%. In 1925, with the added political and community support of the Baltimore branch of the National Association for the Advancement of Colored People (NAACP), the Maryland State Colored Teachers Association, and the NAACP's national office, African American public school teachers achieved almost total salary equality with White teachers. Kentucky-born Francis M. Wood (1878–1943), who also led several state and national educational and civil rights organizations, became the city's first African American "Director of Negro Schools" in 1925 and served until his death. With each having 38 schools for African Americans and its own educational division, Baltimore and Washington, D. C. then were the nation's most comprehensive public school systems for African Americans. They achieved this feat because of the combined efforts of numerous African American political and social organizations working together. The roughly 400 African American social clubs and 216 Baltimore churches as of 1934 (Skotnes, 2013) pushed any potentially friendly politicians and sympathetic community leaders to aid in their endeavors.

Overall illiteracy in the Baltimore African American community fell from 25.7% in 1900 to 7% in 1930. Political power largely produced these gains, as African American candidates won City Council seats in 13 of the 18 elections between 1890 and 1930. During this time, the city was almost unique in having a continual presence of African Americans in elected public office (Skotnes, 2013). These gains resulted after the dominant power players defused the impact of the increasing African American voting power with the 1920s municipal redistricting and the state legally enforcing racial segregation and inequality. However, progress was limited compared to White public education. Baltimore remained segregated, separate but unequal, with the African American community having its own social clubs, fraternal organizations, professional baseball team, Druid Hill YMCA, Parent-Teacher Associations, businesses, etc. In the early 1930s, $67.61 per year was spent on each White city school student, but only $48.01 on each African American student. Because of funding disparities, every African American teacher had to use their own professional inventiveness and personal resources to provide necessary teaching materials. For example, even all the students' art paper and pencils had to be purchased from the teacher's own funds. The African American social clubs and churches helped as best they could with donations of money and school materials, as well as volunteers for mentoring and enrichment. Combined with everyone being held to high standards, many Douglass students excelled (Robinson, 2005).

The near doubling of African American voters between 1940–1952, stirred by key leaders and community groups, produced more political victories. One very important group was the Colored Democratic Women, which mobilized support for sympathetic White candidates like Mayor Theodore McKeldin who supported better housing, improved neighborhoods, and wider employment opportunities for African Americans (Gately, 1993a; Olson, 1980). Baltimore elected its first African American State Delegate in 1954. School standards continued to be high, with virtually every student receiving the school's personal attention. Douglass was called "the public private school" by many (White, 2004).

However, most Baltimore African American schools still had dilapidated buildings deemed unfit for use for White students: no libraries, cafeterias, or playgrounds; not enough textbooks; and so overcrowded some operated on split sessions. Douglass, designed for 900, had 1,900 students. A 1947 state survey found most African American schools were physically deficient and had overcrowded classrooms (Crockett, 1988).

More racial integration occurred, thanks to biracial political pressure by a coalition of advocacy and community organizations (including the NAACP and the Baltimore Urban League) which demanded African American admission to the White schools, such as the advanced Baltimore Polytechnic Institute (Poly). Nursing and other schools at the University of Maryland started admitting African American students in 1951 followed by Poly admitting 13 African American students the next year.

With the Supreme Court's landmark *Brown v. Board of Education* decision in 1954, Baltimore schools fortunately desegregated with little rancor. Baltimore was one of the first cities south of the Mason-Dixon line to comply. In 1954, a racially integrated faculty taught at Poly's Summer Center evening adult education school with some Douglass students attending. Douglass moved into a new facility on Gwynns Falls Parkway near Mondawmin Mall also in 1954. But the desegregation overall was minimal and Douglass's best teachers and brightest students left for better, mostly more integrated, schools (Olson, 1980).

Like most urban centers in America during the later 1950s and early 1960s, more and more Whites moved to suburbia, partly related to the negative stimulus of large-scale construction of public housing (as part of urban renewal), and segregation intensified. Poor African American households moved into the Douglass area from other parts of Baltimore. Tensions arose between their children and those of White and African American middle-class families who traditionally had attended the school. Baltimore began its long (and continuing) population decline, especially after the April 5–12, 1968 riots that killed six and burned entire swaths of the city (Baltimore's Civil Rights Heritage, 1977). The riot was only contained after the local and state police, National Guard, and Federal troops arrived to quell the riot. While the April 4th assassination of the Rev. Dr. Martin Luther King, Jr. was the immediate cause, African American anger had been building because their East and West Baltimore neighborhoods had poor housing, high infant mortality, much higher unemployment, and more crime. Further, the government response to these conditions had been minimal. The riots scared significant numbers of Whites to flee to the suburbs, to be followed by the African American middle class.

In response, community associations worked with area churches to improve housing, sanitation, education, employment, and to fight crime. This was enhanced by key White supporters and groups. As African Americans became more of the electorate, their political representation surged. More African Americans were elected to the City Council, and African American State Delegates increased from 9 to 16 during 1969–1979. But despite constituting over half the city's population by 1980, African Americans still held less than 30% of the City Council seats.

In 1971, Ronald N. Patterson (1929–1982), considered an "outsider" from Washington, D. C., became Baltimore's first African American school superintendent after 14 White incumbents. He had a rocky tenure, mostly due to White resentment and pressure because of this achievement of African American control of public education. This was exacerbated because the school system was the first major institution to come under African American control (Olson, 1980); Baltimore did not have an African American mayor until Clarence H. "Du" Burns in 1987 (Lofton, 2015). Plan for busing to achieve more integration was fought by White residents and their elected officials eventually leading to his 1975 dismissal. Community political pressure led to some desegregation but minimal efforts to achieve real equal education. Many Baltimore schools remained totally segregated until 1974, when federal agents forced city authorities to seek racially balanced schools through compulsory student and staff assignments.

Under Mayor William Donald Schaefer (1971–1986), Baltimore's downtown was redeveloped and the new Douglass opened in 1984 after a $10.8 million renovation. Douglass was largely rebuilt as a result of a general state education facilities upgrade as well as considerable political pressure by African American social clubs, churches, and the Historic Frederick Douglass High School Alumni Association. The school had two gymnasiums, 32 classrooms, a 1,000 seat auditorium, a library, and a swimming pool. *Time* called Baltimore the Renaissance City, but the reality in many African American neighborhoods was very different. Conditions worsened when city spending was slashed and school budgets fell 25% during the 1970s. Unemployment jumped from 4% to 11%, poverty increased from 4% to 11%, and median family income dropped over 20% (Olson, 1980). Attributed to crack cocaine, Baltimore's much higher crime rates than surrounding counties led to accelerating 1980s–1990s population losses. Large scale abandonment of housing and boarding-up of houses and graffiti became prevalent as both the White and African American middle class moved to the suburbs.

By the mid-1980s, remaining middle class African American parents sent their children to private or parochial schools, or moved to suburbia when their young reached school age. Baltimore, Douglass, and the culture within the African American community changed. As more joined the drug culture, even more children were abandoned and homeless. Many Douglass students lived in single parent and very low-income families within violent neighborhoods where drug dealers were the most visually successful, and abject poverty, hopelessness, and failing parents were the norm. Some principals and teachers no longer lived near Douglass, and some ninth graders never showed up the first day.

In 1987, Baltimore first elected an African American mayor, Kurt Schmoke, who pushed literacy in schools but was criticized by African American leaders as being distant, focused on business, and uncaring about the community. Schmoke did begin programs in education, housing, public health, and economic development that made limited improvements. He started a private foundation and a cabinet-level city agency to fund and enlarge adult literacy programs, supported educational innovation, and successfully waged a campaign to establish a city partnership with the state that provided more state funding for the public schools.

The School's Alumni Association worked very hard to raise the standards at Douglass, but lacked resources. They lobbied officials and criticized the school district for the lack of textbooks, the dilapidated and unheated building with holes in the classrooms' floors, and their non-response to repair requests. The Association painted the building, gave support, joined and worked with the attendance team, and funded scholarships because the school district lacked enough resources to help the needy students. However, Poly and some of the other White and middle-class schools had their walls painted, got many computers, and had repairs fixed quickly. This was due to both the state and the city being dominated by the White power establishment that had ruled the state for years. Not only were the White schools more supported by their richer alumni and friends, their needs were prioritized by connected politicians and local foundations. With the school system lacking adequate funding to begin with, what was there was monopolized by the forces supporting White schools. One Douglass principal said they had enough money to buy a few needed supplies for teachers, but had to borrow textbooks from other schools (Neufeld, 2006). Principals of African American schools supplemented the inadequate public funding with funds, materials, and services donated by an array of alumni, community, individual, and nonprofit contributors. They networked with friendly private schools to arrange education for students better suited for alternative environments.

In 1989, the city finally sold Old Douglass to a developer and it became an apartment building. The building's owner is currently Brick Lane, an apartment management and investment company. Four years later, Douglass celebrated its 110th anniversary amidst continuing improvement efforts by the alumni and its administrators. There were visits from successful African Americans, tutors, establishment of a job preparation, and a job apprentice program at the nearby Mondawmin Mall. Like the old Douglas, however, the Mall was beginning its long decline, from being a prosperous upscale retail center to a crime-ridden one loaded with hair salons, sneaker and jewelry shops, fast food stores, two rehab centers, a parole office, and a WIC office. Douglass along with its college partners hosted college and career fairs and rewarded excelling students with Mall coupons. For example, one local institutional partner, the University of Maryland Medical System's mentorship program paired 57 students with 54 employees (Gately, 1993b; Sherer, 1993). The program stemmed from the African American community putting political pressure aided by some White education advocates.

But youth violence had increased to unprecedented levels compared to the 1980s, with almost daily student violence in classrooms and occasional assaults and fighting. Douglass even closed for two days in 1993 so that teachers and staff could receive disruptive student training. Violence was increasingly normal on school grounds and in the schools. Incidents involving guns rose, including assaults, robberies, and firearms possession. Douglass's incidents rose from 47 to 67 during 1992–1994 (Gately, 1993b), while all city schools' weapons assaults, armed and unarmed assaults, and arrests spiked. After many criticized the ineffective school security, the City Council investigated the violence and Baltimore's school superintendent instituted conflict resolution classes to confront violence. Baltimore's police started community policing and increased drug raids during the late 1980s–1990s, which helped raise resident morale. Despite this, local organizations were still threatened by drug dealers, the raids minimally diminished the drug networks, there were protracted court delays, and the city's detention center overcrowding became acute. A respite of sorts was provided by a surprising drop in the city's crime rate in 1994 for the first time in 10 years, though this was part of the national trend.

After a state analysis found that the funding disparity between poor and wealthy school districts had grown wider, advocates and the community demanded change (Shwe, 2020). Major Maryland ACLU lawsuits in 1978 and its *Bradford v. Maryland State Board of Education* lawsuit in 1994 challenged the state's funding system, prompting a gubernatorial commission that studied funding policy and recommending alterations. Reform efforts strengthened in 1996 after a Baltimore City Circuit Court judge ruled the state was not providing city students an adequate education (Shwe, 2020). As a result, the school district and the state worked under a consent decree that provided more funding and rearranged the schools' governance. Douglass teachers now had more school supplies, the halls were repainted, and many small repairs were done. After 1996 and 2000 litigation, in 2002 the state adopted a modern, standards-based finance system ("Bridge to Excellence") to send more funding to high-need districts. This increased state funding to city public schools over $2 billion. Accompanying the funding was a state-conducted standards review. In 1994, Douglass was marked by the state to be closed because of poor performance, though this decision was reversed after community outcry. The state kept it open and approved a comprehensive improvement plan after intensive lobbying from the school system, its friendly city and state politicians, and numerous African American civic and social groups, especially the Douglass Alumni Association. With the funding and review, Douglass restructured into separate academic and career-preparation groups and replaced 130 staff (ACLU of Maryland, 2021; Gately, 1994a; Gately, 1994b; Shwe, 2020; Vicino, 2008).

By the late 1990s, though, most Douglass students were African American, many were low income, and student attendance and achievement were very low. Located in one of West Baltimore's most crime-ridden neighborhoods, Douglass had bars on the windows, high metal gates around the entrance, graffiti walls, and dim hallways. Blaming the school district for many of the problems, numerous state lawmakers accused it of fiscal mismanagement. This produced the 1997 abolition of the mayor-appointed city school board within a state partnership. After state-instituted school standard tests (e.g., Maryland State Performance Assessment Program [MSPAP]), the school district decided to close some low-performing schools like Douglass, but the "Save Our School Douglass Coalition" formed to successfully oppose the takeover (Gately, 1994). The Coalition included Douglass alumni, members of the Douglass Alumni Association, local church leaders, and a few White advocates.

Various city church networks provided help. Enrichment programs were tried to improve the schools—such as the late 1990s–2006 Muse 360 program that educated Douglass students about arts and culture from an African American perspective (Obee, 2016). Another bright public-private partnership was the 1990–1996 Barclay School, Johns Hopkins University, Homewood Friends Meeting Barclay, and Calvert project enabled by the Abell Foundation (Lally, 1996). The local Foundation, funded by the Baltimore family that had owned *The Baltimore Sun*, provided significant funding for a variety of educational, health, and recreational improvements. In 1993, a U.S. Department of Defense grant enabled establishing

Douglass's assistive technology academy (Parrish, 2019). This program, a partnership with local medical institutions, introduces students to possible careers in physical therapy and prostheses manufacturing.

Douglass then was restructured on an academy model around a career theme emphasizing closer teacher-student relationships. The school also added Academy 2000 for ninth graders; started a business, finance, and management academy; and began the Cab Calloway academy for the arts, music, and humanities. Grant funds provided a mural, hallway plants, and benches; painted the welcoming sign; repainted the school; and hired a resource center to design curriculum and industrial training programs; institute academic and occupational competencies; and purchase computers, computerized milling machines, and other equipment. The various improvements were designed to bring Douglass up to date in technology, programming, and student preparation.

These efforts pushed Douglass's 1993–2008 attendance rate from 63% to 82%, though in 2004 Douglass was just two White students shy of being as segregated as 1925 (Olson, 1980). After completion of the innovations, things deteriorated in Baltimore again, as realistically portrayed in *The Wire*, HBO's lauded crime drama (2002–2008). Having in 2003 a $54–64 million deficit, the school district extensively cut teachers and staff. Many Douglass 11th and 12th graders then were not attending school because they needed to work, while many absent 9th graders were in the drug trade sub world (Raymond, 2008). For 2004–2005, Douglass had 10 teacher vacancies in critical areas. Teachers faced a shortage of textbooks, with students sharing outdated textbooks, sometimes four to a book, and materials. There were 50 students in a classroom, multiple disciplinary problems, and many students often did not stay a year. In 2006, more disruption came as Douglass enrolled 16-and 17-year-old youths just released from incarceration who were placed in classes with ninth-graders as young as 12 (Video Vérité, 2008). This stemmed from court-mandated mainstreaming, as students with special needs joined general students in classes.

In 2007, because Douglass had not met the adequate yearly progress standards set by the No Child Left Behind Act, the state intervened again and replaced the administration and the principal. This restructuring also caused many teachers and support staff to leave. Illustrating the tumult, Video Vérité's 2008 *Hard Times at Douglass High* film chronicled the school's struggles to meet academic standards. The schools and the teachers union continued to be political footballs, as politicians and the media faulted them for seemingly every problem in the city. The school district increasingly was blamed for the chaos, such as in the 2007 *Baltimore Sun* investigative article detailing extensive errors in the school budget. In a poll that year, 2% of city residents gave the school system an A, 10% percent gave it a B, 32% C; 22% D, 20% Fail, and 15% unsure, with a mean grade-point average of about D-plus. At that time, some 66% of the Douglass teachers were not certified, despite most having worked in the system at least 20 years (Neufeld, 2007, 2009; Video Vérité, 2008).

Improvement began again. More males graduated after Douglass began a College Bound Program. Beginning in 2010, Baltimore City Public Schools began an ambitious plan to redesign and rebuild aging school facilities. The subsequent 2012 "Jacobs Report"—an independent analysis commissioned by the city which assessed the physical condition of all schools—found many school buildings could not adequately support quality instruction. Criticism intensified after a *Baltimore Sun* study that year again found the school budget was not being carefully monitored. Cutbacks had produced a thin staff working overtime at higher wages, such as the school superintendent's driver earning double his salary in overtime and exceeding Governor Martin O'Malley's (Green, 2012).

In 2012, the district's new plan and a $4.2 million federal School Improvement Grant, coupled with support from the alumni association and community groups, helped Douglass cut its dropout rate 50%, dramatically increased test scores, and boosted English language arts proficiency from 41% to 53% and math proficiency from 32% to 44%, the first time meeting its goals in 18 years (U.S. Department of Education, 2013). The principal had opened a night school for tutoring or credit recovery, encouraged student leadership, and arranged a dual enrollment program with nearby Baltimore City Community College. After years of community advocacy and pushing by School Superintendent CEO Andrés Alonso, in 2013 the state established the 21st Century School Construction and Revitalization Program as a partnership between the city, the Maryland Stadium Authority, Baltimore City Public Schools, and the Interagency Committee on Public School Construction (Hopson, 2013).

But improvement efforts stalled with the 2015 Baltimore riots after police-victim Freddie Gray's New Shiloh Baptist Church funeral. Protests arose across the city, including by Douglass students and others outside the school building. The peaceful protest suddenly became a riot after police overreacted to a milling of students and others around the Mondawmin Mall area near Douglass. Some blamed Douglass students for starting it all, but this was never verified. Only 75–100 Douglass students were involved, with over 700 not participating in the protest. The negative media attention drew well-meaning advocates and outsiders to come to the aid of the students. However, little changed after the media, city leaders, and celebrities subsequently appeared at the school and promised football field lights, frequent check-ins, etc. The original protest itself was somewhat odd for Douglass students to do, which did not have a history of activism except during the Civil Rights Movement.

Beginning in 2016, the Maryland Commission on Innovation and Excellence in Education (Maryland Association of Boards of Education, 2021) again revised the state's education funding formula and recommended education reforms. In 2018, the year Baltimore was declared the most dangerous American city (Taylor, 2001), Douglass's current and former students were among crime's victims. Baltimore's schools made national headlines that same year because students in multiple schools were wearing hats, gloves, and winter coats in freezing classrooms.

This partly happened because nearly half of Baltimore's schools were built in the 1960s or earlier, with just 3% built after 1985.

Partnerships helped provide learning tools and opportunities that the school could not afford. In 2019, a non-profit and the Old Douglass owner partnered to convert part of the building into a dormitory-style residence for people coming out of prison. That same year, Associated Builders and Contractors of Baltimore hosted its first workforce development presentation for 30 Douglass students about available career and education opportunities in the construction industry (Rodricks, 2019).

Obstacles to improvement were huge. With 58 murders per 100,000 residents in 2019, Baltimore was easily the deadliest large American city. After a shooting at Douglass that year, the City's School Board supported arming school officers. Many Douglass students saw the school as their safe haven, and felt teachers were not given adequate support and their positive attitude and contributions were used against them. The city enacted a Trauma Responsive Care Act that provided assistance to identify disruptive or students who had been mentally traumatized by the violence (Kennedy, 2020).

Douglass's improvement also has been limited by the occasional attacks on administrators and teachers by family members of disciplined students. A 2019 city security assessment required under the state's 2018 Safe to Learn Act found many problems at Douglass: the classrooms' interior doors could not be emergency locked, surveillance cameras were limited, video security footage was incorrectly collected, emergency and exterior lighting was poor, and metal detectors were not used consistently. Douglass students said the Mondawmin neighborhood conditions affected their learning, they experienced trauma regularly, and the school's hallways smelled like spoiled milk in a building crawling with bugs (Campbell & Anderson, 2019; Richman, 2019).

In 2019, the state legislature first debated *The Blueprint for Maryland's Future*, an ambitious educational improvement plan to address funding and performance inequities. It incorporated the Kirwan Commission's final recommendations. The Commission had been created by the Maryland General Assembly in 2016 to set a standard for education in the state and lead efforts to achieve it. Foundations continued to try to help, such as the Cal Ripken Sr. Foundation, the Major League Baseball—Major League Baseball Players Association (MLB-MLBPA) Youth Development Foundation, and Fields & Futures in Oklahoma City that provided funding so that Douglass's baseball and softball teams no longer had to play on concrete surfaces as well as basic equipment for the teams (Parrish, 2019).

As of 2021, the city's public schools' total enrollment was 79,187, with 76.6% African American and 13.5% Hispanic or Latino. Though enrollment declined 5,789 during 2015–2019, the fourth largest in the state. Some 50.4% of students were low income and 14.6% had a disability. In its 26 high schools, proficiency rates were 9% for math and 16% for English language arts (Papst, 2021). A 2017 Maryland state testing data (found that 88% of parents felt their student was safe at his/her school. The district continues to close schools and relocate students, dispose of surplus buildings, and revamp programs. At $15,793, the City schools rank fifth nationally in per-pupil spending, though five other Maryland districts are in the leading 17. Regarding administration, Baltimore's mayor appoints the Board of School Commissioners (school board) that oversees the schools and hires the chief executive and chief academic officers (Baltimore City Public Schools, 2021; Papst, 2020).

According to the latest Baltimore City Public Schools data (2020), Douglass currently has 850 students in grades 9–12, with enrollment by a choice lottery, and an 18:1 student-teacher ratio. In 2019, the school had an 88% 4-year graduation rate, above the city average and a significant improvement from previous years. In overall testing, Douglass ranks in Maryland's bottom half, with 20–24% math and 6–9% reading proficiency rates. With 99% African American, 1% Hispanic, and 0.3% White students, Douglass's diversity score is 0.02, far below the state average of 0.72. Diversity has stayed relatively flat for several years. In 2021, the school district's role in the problems continues to be criticized and politically exploited. Poor oversight was blamed when in 2021 media reported that a student at the public Augusta Fells Savage Institute of Visual Arts passed 3 classes in four years but ranked near the top half of his graduating class with a 0.13 GPA.

Revelations from Douglass's Checkered History

The following section highlights the most important influential trends and factors in the ups and downs of Douglass's history. Particular emphasis is placed on findings applicable to the community context.

The Role of African American Social Networks

Many positives in Douglass's past and present have occurred and are occurring because of its loyal alumni and the various religious and social networks entwining African American Baltimore. These networks—ministers, social clubs, benevolent organizations, business people, attorneys, other professionals, educators, and interested lay—were responsible for educating and rallying the African American and advocacy communities to change efforts and political battles supporting the development and improvement of African American schools. Because many alumni reside in the city and suburbs, they stay in touch with news about Douglass and often provide whatever assistance is needed. While their help cannot hope to truly address the problems that require substantial financial resources, it does make a difference for many individual students.

Throughout most of its history, Douglass has been the source of much pride for the African American community. During the first decades after the school's founding, one-third of Douglass graduates went to college or normal school. After *Brown*, the school exemplified how segregation was a double-edged sword: excluding African Americans from White institutions, while unifying them in their own institutions in which they flourished.

Encouraged and sometimes led by the Frederick Douglass High School Alumni Association, the Douglass alumni's political connections and power has been significant in compelling the city and state to be aware of and step-up their level of improvements to Douglass. Probably the primary movers have been the many African American churches, for example, Bethel A. M. E., New Shiloh Baptist Church, and New Psalmist Baptist Church, and the myriad of African American social clubs, (e.g., the Arch Social Club founded in 1912). Their efforts have been supplemented and sometimes stirred—by media like the Baltimore *Afro American* and some radio stations; as well as friendly White-dominated advocacy and social services groups, including those funded by Associated Black Charities. Each improvement and positive development during Douglass's history has been the result of extensive lobbying and pressure being applied by the alumni and its allies on political and school leaders. When Douglass declined in the 1980s, the Douglass alumni stepped up its support to at least cushion the negatives on the school. Unfortunately, in a pattern that is generally characteristic in other schools and social institutions, the involvement of Douglass's army of alumni and volunteers has varied considerably. This is understandable given the multiple pressures on the typical volunteer, especially volunteers with limited financial resources. There is only so much that volunteers can do.

The active advocacy by the weekly *Baltimore Afro-American* has been critical in raising the African American community's awareness and support for positive political change. The *Afro* is the longest-running African American family-owned newspaper in the country. In the 1920s and 1930s, editor Carl J. Murphy fought Jim Crow and pushed for African American hiring by Baltimore's police and fire departments, African American legislative representation, and a state supported university to educate African Americans. The *Afro* collaborated with the NAACP on several civil rights cases, including the 1950s collaboration in the latter's suit against the University of Maryland Law School's segregationist admission policies that bolstered the 1954 *Brown v. Board of Education* decision which outlawed segregated public schools. It continues to be a change agent today, such as with its current, long-running "Clean Block" campaign to spruce up streets and reduce crime.

The Role of the Community

The various African American communities in Baltimore have played crucial roles in the history of Douglass and Baltimore. Below is a brief historical summation, followed by a political analysis, a discussion of the importance of White nonprofit organizations and foundations, and a look at influential factors in the key changes.

Early African American educational improvements in the 1920s and 1930s were the direct result of Baltimore's urban concentration and the relative wealth and political mobilization of Baltimore African Americans. The resultant strength pushed state and city politicians toward constructing a new "colored" school in

1925. Crucially, this was done fully within institutionalized segregation, which remained in the schools legally until 1954 and beyond in actuality.

Where gains were made during the 1940s and 1950s, the community again had a deciding role. Community pressure was important in upholding standards at Douglass and other schools, despite the inferior facilities and sorely inadequate funding. These deplorable conditions had resulted from Baltimore's extreme and pervasive level of racial segregation, racial prejudice, White local politicians catering to their constituencies, and the indifference of the state to the African American community's needs. Teachers were faced with a stark choice: improvise and contribute personally to buy at least some needed materials, or largely abandon the students to a very inferior education. Similarly, the community's continued push for integrated schools eventually led to some racial integration before the 1954 *Brown* decision.

The importance of nonprofit and political organizations promoting African American interests cannot be underestimated in Douglass's history. It was political lobbying by the Baltimore branch of the NAACP, the Maryland State Colored Teachers Association, and the NAACP's national headquarters in Baltimore that directly led to early improvements in African American teacher salaries and conditions at Douglass. African American political power did not result in Douglass and other majority Black schools achieving parity with the White schools, but resulted in Baltimore being good for African American public education through the 1950s. Improvements during these decades were due to the continuing political pressure exercised by the advocacy organizations, the Douglass alumni, the general African American community, and some key White advocates.

White advocates in local nonprofits and foundations have greatly helped Douglass and other parts of the public schools. For example, from 1986 to the late 1990s a very effective curriculum program by Success for All Foundation in Baltimore (an outgrowth of Johns Hopkins University) brought significant benefits. Now in 46 states, the controversial "Success for All" program began again in Baltimore in the late 2000s, though not all educators are supportive of the program. The Abell Foundation has been instrumental in Baltimore's various improvement efforts, and continues to fund innovative and ongoing efforts in education.

Extra help also has come to Douglass because of African American Baltimore's pride in Douglass as an institution and for its history. This began early and has continued. Douglass was the flagship African American local school and has had additional support that many other African American schools have not received. Ongoing financial, political, and advocacy support by Douglass's extensive social network has supplemented the mostly meager school system support. While especially beneficial during the 1920s through the 1950s, this individual direct assistance is comparatively limited by most current African Americans in Baltimore being mostly of middle and lower-income.

As Baltimore changed from being a majority White city to mostly African American, political power shifted on the local level. The momentous change was because of extensive White and middle-class African American flight, structural racism, and the move by businesses and social amenities to the suburbs. The big population drop meant fewer state representatives in number and in percentage of state elected officials and fewer dollars to support the school district. Baltimore's population and economic decline made City Hall much less powerful than it had been when the area was prosperous. The city simply has less financial resources to address problems and less political influence in state politics. After 2000, the city's political status in state politics has been worse than it was during most of the 1920s–1970s period. Maryland today is supportive of Baltimore's improvement primarily in its urbanized areas, with elsewhere almost totally unsympathetic because of economic and racial factors. Baltimore's various problems, such as education, have deteriorated faster and deeper as a result.

Douglass's Contribution to the Community

From its beginnings, Douglass-trained African American graduates often have become the leaders of the community. Many worked as educators and administrators, especially in the City's public schools. For example, Edith C. Gibson, a 1953 Douglass graduate, earned a bachelor's degree in 1957 from what is now Morgan State University, and was sent out of state at taxpayer expense to attend Columbia University in New York because African Americans were not allowed to attend the University of Maryland. She became the first African American woman to supervise secondary art education in Baltimore public schools. Other educators who graduated include Ellen L. Johns (Douglass, 1941), who was a school principal, church leader, and political activist. Alumnus Charles G. Gaskins (Douglass, 1950) Sr., was a city public schools principal at several schools in the 1980s, as well as a physical education teacher, Sunday school superintendent, church leader, and coach. Verda Freeman Welcome (Douglass, 1930) was the first African-American woman to serve as a state senator. Other community leaders who either graduated or attended Douglass include U.S. Supreme Court Justice (1967–1991) Thurgood Marshall (Douglass, 1925); Lillie Mae Carroll Jackson (Douglass, 1909), longtime leader of the community; and Carl J. Murphy (Douglass, 1907), editor of the *Afro-American*. Graduates have excelled in medicine, business, government service, and numerous other areas. For example, Rev. Ernest M. Sewell (Douglass, 1957) was an AT&T executive and pastor (Rasmussen, 2020, 2021).

Douglass's graduates also have enriched the national and international community. The list of illustrious alumni includes former U.S. Representative Parren J. Mitchell (D-Maryland, 1971–1987) of the seventh congressional district who graduated in 1940; Roger G. Brown (Douglass, 1959), Baltimore Circuit Court judge; and NFL pro-football star Raymond Chester who played for the Baltimore Colts and Oakland Raiders (1970–1981). Douglass's alumni who pursued noted careers in the entertainment field include jazz singer and bandleader Cab Calloway (Douglass, 1925), jazz singer Ethel Ennis (Douglass, 1950), and international dancer Avon Long (attended Douglass 1925–1927), who played "Sportin' Life" in the original cast of *Porgy and Bess*. The contribution of Douglass employees to the community has been considerable and is continuing. Further, the majority of the Douglass teaching staff always have contributed their own resources and volunteered their time to work with students before and after school. Many mentor children. During the 1980s, for instance, each teacher would mentor five children, though most ended up with 25. They helped both those who wanted to be helped and those who did not.

Reasons for Hope

Despite the lack of overall progress in the Baltimore school system over the past 40 years, a number of productive approaches have been identified, tested, and verified. However, the impact of these improvement efforts have been significantly reduced by continuing (and increasing) structural racism.

The ongoing multiple partnerships between the schools and business, educational, governmental, and nonprofit organizations is a very encouraging sign, as is the continuing involvement of Douglass alumni. This represents what Yosso (2005) calls aspirational capital, how the Black community's desire for educational excellence led them to fight for change. Several foundations like the Abell Foundation have partnered with city schools—including Douglass—on successful pilot programs. For example, the Middle Grades Partnership, supported by the Morton and Jane Blaustein Foundation, arranged nine public/private school partnerships serving 350 students by the end of 2015. The school district continues to explore partnerships with local organizations like the Digital Equity Coalition and various local businesses.

Involvement of Baltimore area universities and colleges in improvement efforts already has produced positive change. The University of Maryland Medical System, Johns Hopkins University, and Towson University have partnered successfully with several schools including Douglass. The social work program at Coppin State University, walking distance from Douglass, has hosted a Helping Everyone Affirm Life Day, a community resource fair with free haircuts and hair care services. Another foundation-supported success is the Thread youth charity improvement program with 1,000 volunteers mentoring 288 students in 2021. Thread included Douglass in its student improvement initiative in 2017.

Pushed by the African American community and leaders, advocacy, and multiracial organizations, the State of Maryland continues to try to help. Of course, state support for the Baltimore city schools varies considerably depending upon the prevailing political winds. The ascendancy of African American political leaders to power positions in Annapolis—such as the 2022-elected Governor Wes Moore and the current Maryland House of Delegates Speaker Adrienne Jones—will hopefully lead to improved efforts to assist Baltimore and its schools. For instance, the state's 21st Century School Construction and Revitalization Program and other programs promise real improvements. Michael Steele, Maryland's first African American elected to statewide office and served as Lieutenant Governor from 2003–2007, observed that the schools in the poorer neighborhoods never have the books, supplies, and computers they need, but other schools do. This eventually led to slightly increased state funding but with little attention to deeper problems.

There are now a number of laws that, if fully enforced and implemented, would greatly aid the schools. For example, state law mandates each school system conduct a safety evaluation for each building and identify any patterns of concern. Unfortunately, politics upends many improvement efforts. For example, the governor-vetoed Kirwan Commission's *Blueprint* would have doubled City Schools funding per student to $30,117 in 2030.

Some Douglass students are continuing to excel despite whatever obstacles. In 2002, the boys' top-ranked "Mighty Ducks" basketball team won the Class 3A state final, its first. Students are starting businesses as part of a "Millionaire's Club," and have placed in national debate and robotics competitions (Davis, 2019; Gaskill, 2020). The students' collective results on state academic assessment examinations have, however, not budged much from a persistent low level. Some individual students, though, do go on to higher education and successful careers. Douglass's sports teams often have been prominent.

As has been demonstrated, Douglass's historical improvements, like that of African American education generally in Baltimore, have resulted from the political pressure virtually continuously applied by the African American community, advocates, nonprofits, key White supporters, Douglass teachers and students, and concerned individuals. Despite the problems caused by various social, economic, and political factors in a changing urban environment, Douglass has survived and even thrived occasionally thanks to its supporters. With the increase in African American political power, strides have been made on the city and state level toward addressing the long-standing problems and disadvantages of a modern urban school. It is true that Douglass's academic achievements remain mired in mediocrity and plagued by petty crime on site. However, there currently are a myriad of exciting, innovative efforts to improve the preparation of the students for future careers. The involvement of local foundations like the Abell Foundation and national ones like Open Society has been critical. The alumni association and the African American community continue to help where and when they can. Baltimore has had African American leadership in City Hall and North Avenue (the School System's headquarters) for several decades now, and it is hoped that this added political power will continue to make progress in the long-present problems of public education. The causes of that plight have been demonstrated to be the structural racism that has led to severe racial segregation and continuing racial discrimination. The fact that Baltimore is now labeled as an African American city rather than as an American city has worsened its political power on the state level. The continual critical support of the community, including alumni, groups, organizations, nonprofits, and individuals, is essential for future improvements in Douglass and Baltimore in general.

REFERENCES

ACLU of Maryland. (2021). *Kirwan: Maryland's Commission on Innovation and Excellence in Education.* https://www.aclu-md.org/en/kirwan-marylands-commission-innovation-and-excellence-education

Baltimore's Civil Rights Heritage. (1977a). *1885–1929: Segregation and the Fourteenth Amendment.* https://baltimoreheritage.github.io/civil-rights-heritage/1885-1929/

Baltimore's Civil Rights Heritage. (1977b). *1966–1976: After the unrest.* https://baltimoreheritage.github.io/civil-rights-heritage/1966-1976/

Baltimore City Public Schools. (2021). *FAQs.* https://www.baltimorecityschools.org/faq

Campbell, C., & Anderson, J. (2019, February 11). Frederick Douglass shooting suspect was confronting staffer about disciplining relative, Baltimore police say. *The Baltimore Sun.* https://www.baltimoresun.com/news/crime/bs-md-ci-douglass-shooting-report-20190211-story.html

Crockett, S. (1988, November 27). Breaking the color barrier at poly: 9 braved taunts to attend school. *The Baltimore Sun*, 1A.

Davis, P. (2019, April 11). At school safety hearing, Baltimore officials discuss violence, role of social media, ways to address trauma. *The Baltimore Sun.* https://www.baltimoresun.com/education/bs-md-ci-handle-care-20190410-story.html

Eminonuk. (2016). *Frederick Douglass High School* [Photograph]. Wikimedia. Creative Commons. BY-SA 4.0 https://creativecommons.org/licenses/by-sa/4.0

Franklin, V. P. (2002). Introduction: Cultural capital and African American education. *The Journal of African American History*, 87(2), 175–181. https://www.journals.uchicago.edu/doi/10.1086/JAAHv87n2p175

Gaskill, H. (2020, November 23). Some counties push to remove police from schools—But who has the authority to make the call? *Maryland Matters.* https://www.marylandmatters.org/2020/11/23/some-counties-push-to-remove-police-from-schools-but who-has-the-authority-to-make-the-call/#:~:text=During%20the%202018%2D2019%20school%20year%2C%2062%20students%20were%20arrested,executed%20by%20school%20resource%20officers

Gately, G. (1993a, October 29). Douglass troubles cloud anniversary. *The Baltimore Sun*, 1A. https://www.baltimoresun.com/news/bs-xpm-1993-10-29-1993302015-story.html

Gately, G. (1993b, October 20). Douglass to close for two days: Teachers to learn how to handle unruly students. *The Baltimore Sun*, 1A. https://www.baltimoresun.com/news/bs-xpm-1993-10-20-1993293067-story.html

Gately, G. (1994a, April 22). *Douglass intervention denounced. ProQuest Historical Newspapers.* The Baltimore Sun, 2B. https://www.lib.umd.edu/dbfinder/id/UMD08200

Gately, G. (1994b, April 20). State won't take control of Douglass High: Major changes look likely for Patterson High. *The Baltimore Sun*, 1A. https://www.lib.umd.edu/dbfinder/id/UMD08200

Green, E. L. (2012, March 1). City schools pay $14 million overtime in four years. *The Baltimore Sun.* https://www.baltimoresun.com/maryland/baltimore-city/bs-md-ci-schools-overtime-20120301-story.html

Hopson, J. M. (2013, December 13). Is Frederick Douglass High School due for another name change? *The Baltimore Times.* http://baltimoretimes-online.com/news/2013/dec/13/frederick-douglass-high-school-due-another-name-ch/

Kennedy, S. (2020, February 7). "The Wire" is finished, but Baltimore still bleeds. *Wall Street Journal*. https://www.wsj.com/articles/the-wire-is-finished-but-baltimore-still-bleeds-11581119104#:~:text=With%2058%20murders%20per%20100%2C000,half%20of%20Baltimore's%202016%20rate

Lally, K. (1996, March 2). Md. tests torpedo successful program Barclay School ends Calvert partnership after scores falter. *The Baltimore Sun*. https://www.baltimoresun.com/news/bs-xpm-1996-03-02-1996062025-story.html.

Lofton, R. (2015, July 1). *A brief history of Baltimore City public schools*. Third Colloquium, Johns Hopkins School of Education.

Maryland Association of Boards of Education. (2021). *Priority issue: The Kirwan Commission & the blueprint for Maryland's future*. https://www.mabe.org/adequacy-funding/

Neufeld, S. (2006, June 13). Douglass students want attention paid to school. *The Baltimore Sun*. https://www.baltimoresun.com/news/bs-xpm-2006-06-13-0606130113-story.html

Neufeld, S. (2007, April 9). School budget full of errors. *The Baltimore Sun*. https://www.baltimoresun.com/news/bs-xpm-2007-04-09-0704090131-story.html

Neufeld, S. (2009, Mar 4). Michael Steele takes a cheap shot at Frederick Douglass High. *The Baltimore Sun*. https://www.baltimoresun.com/bs-mtblog-2009-03-baltimore_schools_michael_stee-story.html

Obee, M. (2016, July 9). Baltimore students to study African diaspora in Cuba. *The Baltimore Afro-American*, D1. https://issuu.com/afronewspaper/docs/washington-baltimore_afro-american__15e9e25e334e43

Olson, S. H. (1980). *Baltimore: The building of an American City*. Johns Hopkins University Press.

Papst, C. (2021, March 4). Governor Hogan calls for investigation of city school failing hundreds. *Fox45 News*. https://foxbaltimore.com/news/project-baltimore/governor-larry-hogan-calls-for-investigation.

Parrish, K. Jr. (2019, September 18). *Baltimore's Frederick Douglass High gets a new field of dreams*. Black History Always. https://theundefeated.com/features/baltimores-frederick-douglass-high-gets-a-new-field-of-dreams/

Rasmussen, F. N. (2020, July 4). Ellen L. Johns, a Baltimore public schools principal and active member of Union Memorial United Methodist Church, dies. *The Baltimore Sun*. https://www.baltimoresun.com/obituaries/bs-md-ob-ellen-johns-20200704-bc-szmc2x5ratviaghjsfum5lsq-story.html

Rasmussen, F. N. (2021, February 22). Edith C. Gibson, the first Black woman to supervise secondary art education in Baltimore public schools, dies. *The Baltimore Sun*. https://www.baltimoresun.com/obituaries/bs-md-ob-edith-gibson-20210222-2qwka6omb-jgzjb2t4jfue2zkpm-story.html

Raymond, A. (2008). *Isabelle Grant Interview*. VideoVérité. http://videoverite.tv/pages/filmdouglasinterview.html

Richman, T. (2019, August 20). Broken locks, poor lighting: Baltimore schools found to have "significant security and safety issues." *The Baltimore Sun*. https://www.baltimoresun.com/education/bs-md-baltimore-schools-security-20190820-ya7omntjz5h2hnembneaijs55u-story.html

Robinson, J. (2005). *Education as my agenda: Gertrude Williams, race, and the Baltimore public schools*. Palgrave Macmillan.

Rodricks, D. (2019, May 31). In Sandtown, a new and needed mission for Old Douglass. *The Baltimore Sun*. https://www.baltimoresun.com/opinion/columnists/dan-rodricks/bs-md-rodricks-column-0602-story.html

Seyler, A., & Claire N. (2012). *Roberta Sheridan (ca. 1864–d. 1918)*. Archives of Maryland. (Biographical Series). https://msa.maryland.gov/megafile/msa/speccol/sc3500/sc3520/012300/012385/html/12385bio.html

Sherer, J. L. (1993). Elizabeth Shire's helping hands. *Hospitals & Health Networks, 67*, 18. https://collections.nlm.nih.gov/ocr/nlm:nlmuid-7807587X36-leaf

Shwe, Elizabeth. (2020, December 16). Civil Rights groups push for funding to address Inequities at Baltimore public schools. *Maryland Matters*. https://www.marylandmatters.org/2020/12/16/civil-rights-groups-push-for-funding-to-address-inequities-at-baltimore-public-schools/#:~:text=Since%20then%2C%20Baltimore%20City%20public,%E2%80%9CThornton%E2%80%9D%20education%20funding%20formula.&text=By%202017%2C%20Baltimore%20City%20schools,Department%20of%20Legislative%20Services%20report

Skotnes, A. (2013). *A new deal for all? Race and class struggles in depression-era Baltimore*. Duke University Press.

Taylor, R. B. (2001). *Breaking away from broken windows: Baltimore neighborhoods and the nationwide fight against crime, grime, fear, and decline*. Westview Press.

U. S. Department of Education. (2013, December). *Better times at Douglas High*. https://sites.ed.gov/progress/2013/12/better-times-at-douglass-high/

Vicino, T. J. (2008). *Transforming race and class in suburbia: Decline in metropolitan Baltimore*. Palgrave MacMillan.

Video Vérité. (2008). *Hard times at Douglass High: Isabelle Grant interview*. Video Vérité. https://videoverite.tv/pages/filmdouglasabout.html

White, T. (2004, May 16). Douglass still struggling. *Baltimore Sun*. https://www.baltimoresun.com/opinion/op-ed/bal-pe.md.douglass16may16-story.html

Wikipedia. (n.d.). *Frederick Douglass High School* [Picture]. https://en.wikipedia.org/wiki/Frederick_Douglass_High_School_(Baltimore,_Maryland)

Yosso, T. J. (2005) Whose culture has capital? A critical race theory discussion of community cultural wealth. *Race Ethnicity and Education, 8*(1), 69–91. doi:10.1080/1361332052000341006

CHAPTER 6

"WE'RE YOUR SONS AND DAUGHTERS... GUIDE US AS WE GO"

The Role of Harbison Junior College, Richlex School, and Their Communities in the Development of Cultural Capital

Vann Holden
University of South Carolina

This chapter focuses on the history of South Carolina's Harbison Junior College and Richlex School, the schools' relationships with the communities they served, as well as the forms of cultural capital produced by the two schools, their students, and their communities. Both schools connected their students to essential resources and networks, created familial bonds among their students and faculty, developed cultural wealth with their students and community, and served as important centers of community activity. These topics are explored through an analysis of the narratives of Harbison and Richlex's former students and teachers. While the stories of these students, educators, and schools are specific to the Chapin, Dutch Fork, and Irmo communities of South Carolina, they also reflect larger themes and trends in

Black education during the segregated era and add depth to our understanding of the history of Black education in the South.

Keywords: Segregation, Community Cultural Wealth, Social Capital, Familial Capital, Resistant Capital, Historical Analysis, Narrative Inquiry, Oral History, Critical Race Theory

INTRODUCTION

The history of southern Black communities creating schools for their children predates the end of the Civil War and has continued in spite of efforts to outlaw, control, and undermine the education of Black children (Anderson, 1988). After gaining their freedom, Black families fought to ensure universal public education for all children and found early success, establishing schools for hundreds of thousands of Black children in the South in the years after emancipation (Anderson, 1988; Bullock, 1967; Du Bois, 1935). Segregated Black schools have been celebrated for their "1) exemplary teachers, 2) curriculum and extracurricular activities, 3) parental support, and 4) leadership of the school principal" (Walker, 2000, p. 264). In addition to their roles as instructional leaders, the primary recruiters of Black teachers, and role models for students, Black principals emerged as prominent voices in Black communities (Floyd, 1973; James, 1970). Efforts

Rosenwald/Richlex/Dutch Fork Elementary

to expand public education for Black children, however, were not supported by southern Whites (Anderson, 1988).

South Carolina was the site of numerous examples of this overall pattern of Black communities striving to realize their vision of public education in the face of widespread efforts to derail their progress. Schools for Black students were founded throughout the state's Pee Dee region in the years after the Civil War, and the Black communities of nearby Camden established twenty-two schools serving more than four thousand students by 1867 (Anderson, 1988). At Burke Industrial School in Charleston, Black educators created an academically-focused curriculum and programs in the arts, rejecting the White district leaders' plans for the school's instructional program to reinforce the city's existing, racialized economic hierarchy (Baker, 2006). In Clarendon County, the Black community fought at the local, state, and national levels to ensure that their students were provided with equal resources. The Black community's petition for one school bus and the board's subsequent denial of this request resulted in *Briggs v. Elliot*, one of the cases that was consolidated into the *Brown v. Board of Education* desegregation case (Allen, 2019; Hine, 2004).

The lead attorney for the plaintiffs in the *Briggs* case was Harold R. Boulware of Irmo, South Carolina, the counsel for the state branch of the National Association for the Advancement of Colored People (Boulware, 1980; Moore & Anderson, 2018). Boulware's role in the fight for equal educational opportunities is well-documented, but his family also played a major role in advancing educational opportunities for Black students and communities. Mabel Boulware, Harold's mother, taught at Harbison Junior College for several decades, and Robert Boulware, Harold's father, was Harbison's long-time dean (Biddle University, 1904–1919, 1921; Johnson C. Smith, 1922–1926, 1928–1930). Margaret Boulware, Harold's wife, led Line School and taught at Richlex School in Irmo for more than a decade (Hawkins, 1973; Montgomery, 2002).

Between 1911 and 1966, Harbison and Richlex were the only high schools available to Black students in the Chapin, Dutch Fork, and Irmo communities of South Carolina. The educators at Harbison and Richlex, including the Boulware family, played a vital part in both the education of generations of Black students and the long-term development of the surrounding areas. This chapter examines the history of the two schools and their roles in developing and spreading cultural capital in their communities. This research attempts to answer the following questions:

1. What is the pre-desegregation history of high schools serving Black students in the Chapin, Dutch Fork, and Irmo communities?
2. How did Black schools in these communities create and share cultural capital with their students?

METHODS

This research draws on the practices of historical analysis, narrative inquiry, and oral history. This includes the collection and analysis of archived material, narratives, oral histories, and other resources. Different types of resources were utilized in the research on Harbison and Richlex. The analysis of Harbison relies on photograph collections, books, theses, dissertations, university publications, and the works of other scholars. Archived material on Harbison was accessed from the Presbyterian Historical Society Pearl Digital Collections, the North Carolina Digital Heritage Center, and the University of South Carolina. During the research on Richlex School, archived material from School District 5 of Lexington and Richland Counties (School District Five [District 5]) was examined. This included school board meeting minutes, letters, newspaper clippings, and internal planning documents.

Many readily available sources, however, omit marginalized voices and are thus incomplete (Morris & Parker, 2019). Narrative research and oral histories serve as important methods in this research as they focus on stories and experiences that are often absent from the archival sources and documents (Alridge, 2020). Researchers and participants engaging in narrative research examine their stories and make meaning of their experiences (Glesne, 2016). As story-telling and meaning-making are natural parts of human life, narrative research is particularly useful to those seeking to understand "the ways humans experience the world" (Connelly & Clandinin, 1990, p. 2). This study utilizes the analysis of narratives form of narrative research; this is characterized by the collection of stories, the identification of themes in the stories, and an emphasis on excerpts from participants' narratives in the writing (Polkinghorne, 1995). Oral history is a type of narrative and interview inquiry focused on historical events, skills, ways of life, or cultural patterns (Glesne, 2016). The method employed in this chapter is collective oral history, defined by Janesick (2010) as a collection of "individual stories around a particular theme or stories in which all people share a particular experience" (p. 2).

Former Harbison students were interviewed and highlighted in the film *In Their Own Words: A History of Harbison Institute, 1911–1958* (*In Their Own Words*), and all of the Harbison stories included in this research are from that documentary (Vidal & Mooneyhan, 2006). Larry Haltiwanger, Norma Jean Corley Mackey, Shirley Portee Martin, Michael Reeves, and James Washington attended Richlex and were interviewed by the author during the research process. These interviews utilized the methods of narrative research and oral history. Three participants were graduates of Richlex (Haltiwanger, Reeves, Washington), and two participants attended Richlex as well as desegregated schools in District 5 (Mackey, Martin). The three Richlex graduates are all Black men, while the two participants who attended both the segregated and desegregated schools are Black women.

The findings of this research are divided into separate sections on the histories of the schools and the forms of cultural capital created by the schools and their communities. Though archival material and secondary sources are used in the discussion of the two schools' histories, the Harbison section relies more on the use of secondary sources while the Richlex section heavily utilizes archival material. The findings section then focuses on the forms of cultural capital described by former students in their interviews, oral histories, and *In Their Own Words*. The stories are grouped by theme, and the themes are organized around forms of cultural capital identified by Tara J. Yosso (2005). At least three forms of cultural capital were present in the students' stories: social capital, familial capital, and resistant capital. Each of these forms of capital is defined and discussed in separate parts of the findings. While these forms of capital are the focus of the analysis and have been separated here to better illustrate specific themes in the data, Yosso (2005) notes that these forms of capital "are not mutually exclusive or static, but rather are dynamic processes that build on one another" (p. 77). Though the stories are categorized here according to a specific form of cultural capital, the former students' narratives often represent or reinforce additional forms of cultural capital.

Like most histories, one limitation of this research is the absence of artifacts. Some documents related to Black education and educators have been intentionally destroyed (Walker, 2000). In other cases, written documentation may not exist because of the long-lasting impacts of laws designed to prevent Blacks from learning to read and write (Morris & Parker, 2019). The primary sources that have survived are often those of the dominant group or that support the dominant group's narrative of history. These issues were present in this research as well. The land and buildings that were once home to Harbison are now a satellite campus for Midlands Technical College, and current administrators for the college shared that the school no longer stored Harbison-related files. Richlex documents and trophies have also been lost over time as the campus was repurposed during desegregation.

THEORETICAL FRAMEWORK

Critical Race Theory (CRT) is a framework that was first used in legal contexts to examine the impact of race and racism and has since expanded into education and other fields (Crenshaw, 2011; Ladson-Billings & Tate, 1995; Lynn, 2019). CRT is useful in historical and narrative analysis due to its emphasis on documenting and understanding previously marginalized voices and experiences (Morris & Parker, 2019). Solorzano and Yosso (2002) identified key elements of methods grounded in CRT, and this research emphasizes three of those elements: the challenge to the dominant ideology, the centrality of experiential knowledge, and the commitment to social justice.

In Western society, histories play a pivotal role in the communication of the dominant ideology (Appleby, 1998). Histories, however, are not universal truths. Historical questions, analysis, and findings reflect the values, worldviews, and eras of the historian (Carr, 1961; Morris & Parker, 2019). CRT-informed research presents counter-stories to the dominant narratives about race, racism, and education, helping audiences better understand the relationship between the past and the present (Berry & Cook, 2019; Carr, 1961; Morris & Parker, 2019).

Narrative research and historical analysis in CRT focus on marginalized voices and stories, emphasizing the lived experiences of participants and those at the center of the story. The inclusion of these narratives lifts up the people and history that were previously ignored by the academy, further challenging the dominant narrative (Malagon et al., 2009). Historical research situated within CRT also adds significant layers to our understanding of the current inequities in our world, and this is essential to social justice (Alridge, 2015). There is a need for research that examines the cumulative impacts of historical racism on the current educational opportunities available to Black students (Donnor, 2019). This type of analysis situates current challenges and racialized disparities within their historical roots, creates new questions, and allows new discussions (Alridge, 2015; Donnor, 2019).

THE HISTORY OF HARBISON

The school that would become Harbison Junior College began as Ferguson Academy in Abbeville, South Carolina between 1882 and 1886 (Helsley, 1988; McMillan, 1952; Richings, 1903; Vidal & Mooneyhan, 2006). Rev. and Mrs. Emory W. Williams, a Black couple from Washington, D.C., founded the school, but it was acquired by the Board of Missions for the Freedmen of the Presbyterian Church U.S.A. (Board of Missions) in 1891 after accruing some debt (McMillan, 1952; Richings, 1903). Rev. Thomas Amos became principal and led the school for 14 years, increasing enrollment from 62 to 350 between 1892 and 1904 (Biddle University, 1904; Richings, 1903). The school also secured additional funding from Samuel P. Harbison and was renamed in his honor during Rev. Amos's tenure (Helsley, 1988; McMillan, 1952).

Members of Abbeville's White community opposed Rev. Amos's leadership and Harbison's existence, and increasing pressure resulted in Rev. Amos's resignation in 1906 (Helsley, 1988). Rev. Calvin M. Young was named the school's new leader, and he closed Harbison for four months to ease tensions. Shortly before its 1907 reopening, the school's Ferguson Hall was destroyed in a fire (Board of Missions, 1907). Rev. Young and the Board of Missions publicly stated that the fire was not intentionally set (Board of Missions, 1907; Helsley, 1988). Like Rev. Amos's departure and the temporary closure of the school, these statements may have been attempts to de-escalate the conflict (Johnson, 2009).

Opposition to the school's presence in Abbeville continued to rise despite Rev. Young's efforts. Hostility towards Harbison culminated on March 17, 1910. As students slept in their rooms, the campus's main building was lit on fire. Carl Duckett, Samuel Jenkins, and Edward DuBose were killed in the blaze while other students were injured as they jumped from the burning building (Helsley, 1988; McMillan, 1952). The murder of the three Harbison students erased any hope that the school's leaders had for remaining in Abbeville. Shifting from their strategy of appeasing those who opposed the school, Harbison's leaders publicly attributed the fire to "the work of an incendiary" and declared their intention to find a new home for the school (Board of Missions, 1910).

Irmo, South Carolina, was selected as the site for the new Harbison, and the plan was for the school to be part of a community of Black-owned farmers, businesses, and homes (Helsley, 1988). The school eventually acquired 4,100 acres of land, 500 to be used for farming at the college and 3,600 to be divided into 25-acre parcels and settled by Black Presbyterians (Helsley, 1988). The school's enrollment initially declined due to the impact of the 1910 fire and the Harbison family's requirement that the school become an all-male institution, a status it retained until 1933 (Board of Missions, 1912; Helsley, 1988). The annual catalogs of Biddle University (1911–1919, 1921) and Johnson C. Smith University (1922–1926, 1928–1930) indicate that Harbison's enrollment ranged from 72 to 158 between 1911 and 1930. During this time, Harbison also operated a parochial school (Vidal & Mooneyhan, 2006).

THE ORIGINS OF RICHLEX

Harbison's move to Irmo occurred at the same time that the area's Black communities were expanding educational opportunities for their children. St. Peter Baptist Church, located less than 10 miles northwest of the new Harbison, donated land for a school serving Black children in 1918 (R. L. Floyd Foundation, Inc., 1996). The Rosenwald Fund provided 30.8% of the funds to build the school, and the school adopted the name of Rosenwald School in recognition of this funding source (Fisk University, 2001; R. L. Floyd Foundation, Inc., 1996). Pine Grove Rosenwald School opened in 1923, just to the southeast of the Harbison campus (Fisk University, 2001; Richland County Recreation Commission, n.d.). Other known schools for Black students in the area included Line School and Boyd Hill School, both founded in the 1930s (Montgomery, 2002). Harbison's parochial school, however, remained the only available high school for Black students (Vidal & Mooneyhan, 2006).

Momentum for school desegregation grew during the 1940s (Baker, 2006). South Carolina Attorney General T.C. Callison took office in 1951 and advised school districts that a failure to provide Black students with high schools could result in courts ordering White high schools to enroll Black students (Callison, n.d.; Tolliver Cleveland Callison Papers, n.d.). It was recommended that, in order to maintain segregated systems, smaller districts consolidate in order to increase resources and establish Black high schools (Callison, n.d.). More than a half-century after *Plessy*, the state's desire to maintain the segregated schools forced it to make minimal progress towards the equal portion of the "separate but equal" doctrine.

Amid this statewide effort to delay desegregation, Chapin District #9 and Irmo District #8 of Lexington County combined with Dutch Fork District #6 of Richland County to form Lexington District #5 (District 5) in 1951 (Harmon & Harmon, 1951). While White students were assigned to schools located in the part of the district where they lived (Chapin, Dutch Fork, or Irmo), all Black students were sent to a centralized school located at the site of the Rosenwald School that had served Black students since 1918. The campus was improved through funds from the Educational Finance Commission, another statewide program intended to delay desegregation (Baker, 2006; District 5, March 9, 1953; Dobrasko, 2005). The school was renamed Richlex School by district leaders, and Mr. Robert Lee Floyd was named principal (District 5, September 28, 1953; R. L. Floyd Foundation, Inc., 1996).

In 1954, Richlex graduated nine students in its first class (R. L. Floyd Foundation, Inc., 1996). From 1952–53 through 1963–64, Richlex was the largest school in the district. During that time period, its enrollment climbed, peaking at 625 in 1965–66 (South Carolina State Department of Education, 1953–1966). Despite its size, the school was consistently provided with fewer resources than the White schools in the district. Black students faced larger student-teacher ratios than White students (South Carolina State Department of Education, 1953–1966). Mr. Floyd and other staff were paid less than their peers, and the district provided Richlex with less support for its academic, athletic, and art programs (District 5, 1953–1968).

Though considerable attention could be paid to the unequal resources provided to Richlex, the next phase of this chapter's analysis draws on the framework used by Vanessa Siddle Walker in *Their Highest Potential*. In her research on Caswell County, North Carolina, Walker examined what the Black communities and educators created in spite of or, in some cases, because of the neglect of White policymakers and school boards (Walker, 1996). This framing keeps the focus on the practices, values, and characteristics of the segregated Black schools as well as their importance to the students and communities they served (Walker, 2000). Working within this model, we will examine the narratives of those who experienced Harbison and Richlex to understand the two schools' roles in the creation of social, familial, and resistant capital.

SOCIAL CAPITAL AT HARBISON AND RICHLEX

The analysis of evidence on Harbison and Richlex indicates the development of social capital in both schools. Social capital refers to networks connecting people, communities, and resources (Yosso, 2005). These networks and connections assist members as they progress through their education, career, and life. This was seen in the form of professional networks, support to alumni as they navigated post-secondary opportunities, and assistance to students and community members in need.

Harbison was one of at least 60 schools in the Carolinas that were under the direction of the Board of Missions by 1910, and this connected Harbison to a large network of educators (Board of Missions, 1910). One of Harbison's most important ties was to Biddle University (now Johnson C. Smith University). Founded in 1867 in Charlotte, North Carolina, as a school for Black men, Biddle aimed to prepare its graduates for religious and educational leadership (George, 1955; Hartshorn, 1910). By 1903-04, at least three Biddle alumni, including Robert W. Boulware, were members of Harbison's faculty (Biddle University, 1904). Boulware became the school's dean in 1922 (Johnson C. Smith, 1923). Rev. Calvin M. Young, Harbison's president from 1906 to 1929, earned multiple degrees from Biddle and served on Biddle's Board of Trustees (Biddle University, 1909; Johnson C. Smith, 1929; Johnson C. Smith, 1930). Succeeding Rev. Young was a

Biddle alumnus named J. G. Porter, a member of Harbison's faculty since 1912 (Biddle University, 1913; Biddle University, 1930). Between 1904 and 1921, at least 11 other Biddle graduates taught at Harbison (Biddle University, 1904–1919, 1921). The Biddle-Harbison pipeline worked in two directions. After graduating from Harbison, both Harold Boulware and his brother Ralph Harbison Boulware went on to Johnson C. Smith (formerly Biddle) (Johnson C. Smith, 1934).

The pipeline is evidence of social capital in the form of a professional network connecting Biddle graduates with career opportunities. Harbison's students appear to have created a similar professional network after leaving the school, with alumni such as Telicious Kenly Boyd, Thomas Kenly, Zadie Morris, Vernetta Riley, and Rubie Nixon Schumpert becoming teachers at Richlex School after completing their education (R. L. Floyd Foundation, Inc., 1996; Vidal & Mooneyhan, 2006). Margaret Boulware, the wife of Harbison alumnus Harold Boulware, was a member of the Richlex faculty by 1955 and would remain there until her retirement in 1968 (Hawkins, 1973; R. L. Floyd Foundation, Inc., 1996).

The Richlex teachers also facilitated their students' entry into and navigation of the workforce. Michael Reeves, a 1967 graduate, discussed his relationship with Mr. Kenly, his former teacher and coach, after high school:

> When I first went in the military, the last person I saw from Richlex was Mr. Kenly. The first person I saw when I got back was Mr. Kenly. The person that caused me to get the job that I did, that caused me to leave Columbia and come to Atlanta, was based on a referral from Mr. Kenly.

After a chance encounter with a district manager for a pharmaceutical company, Mr. Reeves was called about submitting an application. He was required to submit a reference, and Mr. Reeves said, "I only put down one person. I said, 'The only person that knows me better than anybody else in this whole world is a guy named Mr. Kenly.'" He recalled the importance of that reference:

> And I said, 'Well, what was the game changer that made you guys hire me?' He said, 'Mr. Kenly was the reason we hired you. See, we talked to that guy, ... he was the most amazing man we'd ever met. We'd never met anybody like that. Then he talked about you and he said that you had a brother that played pro ball at that time, that was the first Black to play at Clemson, but that I was probably the better ball player out of the group.' Then they immediately went on into character references, and so he just became my guy. I went from a job making, at that time, about $6,000, which was okay at the time, to a job where I was making $30,000 with a company car and everything, and then bonuses on top of that. Ended up being that first, second year, around $45,000, which was great money. And so, I was ever indebted to him for that.

Mr. Kenly connected other Richlex students to post-secondary opportunities. Larry Haltiwanger, a 1967 graduate, went on to play college football after graduating from Richlex, and Mr. Kenly played a crucial role in this:

> He was our football coach. He carried me to my first college football game. He and my brother, we went to South Carolina State. I remember too, he carried about me and a couple of guys to our first college football game.

Richlex School taught its students early on that the faculty and school community would support them as they pursued these endeavors. The Richlex alma mater, written by Mrs. Juanita Melrose Floyd, an English teacher and the wife of Mr. Floyd, declares, "When troubles face us, in this world of toil and woe, your arms embrace us, guide us as we go" (Floyd, n.d.).

The faculties' professional networks and encouragement of students as they navigated colleges and careers are indicators of the social capital present at both Harbison and Richlex. The development of social capital is also reflected in Harbison's efforts to connect students and the community to key resources. Mrs. Boyd, a Harbison graduate who became a teacher at Richlex, mentioned Harbison's North Room, a place for students and the community to access essential resources. Mrs. Schumpert, another Harbison graduate who went on to teach at Richlex, further described this program:

> Another thing they had while I was there, I might mention this was a room they called the North Room. You know a lot of boys came to Harbison without means. They were short on things, and the National Board of Missions...did a lot of supporting of the students while they were there, and it kind of flowed over into the community. People in the community were allowed one day to come over and pick out items that they could use for their children or for their household...They had clothes from infants to grown-ups, female and male.

Harbison was also actively involved in encouraging and supporting Black education in the wider community, ensuring Black children had educational opportunities not otherwise available to them. Mrs. Boyd discussed Harbison's work in this area:

> They also had a club known as the Big Sister's Club. It was a club that was organized to raise funds to pay the teachers two months in the Pine Grove area. Students there were only going to school four months. So this club was organized to raise money to pay the teachers two extra months.

Harbison and Richlex were vital parts of the networks connecting students, alumni, educators, the community, and resources. These networks helped educators and former students navigate their careers. They also benefited the wider community by serving as an essential resource for students and community members in need and promoting the expansion of educational offerings in the community.

FAMILIAL CAPITAL AT HARBISON AND RICHLEX

Familial capital consists of the culture, histories, and understandings which are developed and communicated within or among families (Yosso, 2005). The concept of family in familial capital is inclusive of extended families and those that share communal bonds, and familial capital can be developed in school settings

(Yosso, 2005). Participants in interviews about Richlex frequently discussed the family climate within the school and provided examples of how the bonds between the school and community strengthened both. The stories of Harbison featured in the documentary *In Their Own Words* demonstrated similar themes of a faculty, student body, and community that treated one another as family.

Richlex's 1965 valedictorian James Washington described the school as "a big family," and added that the teachers "cared for you as a whole person." Mr. Haltiwanger added additional detail on the familial relationships in the school, stating the teachers "were like our parents away from home." The Richlex alma mater expands on the language used by Mr. Haltiwanger, referring to the students as the school's "sons and daughters" in three separate lines (Floyd, n.d.).

Some of these relationships were cultivated by the extensive connections between the faculty and community outside of the school. Mr. Reeves provided examples of the teachers' presence in local churches and the community:

> So the way the classes were at Richlex and the way the teachers were, it was a family affair more than it was a structural affair. These were family, and you saw these guys... I saw Mr. Kenly at Pine Grove AME church. He was the bass guy. He sung bass on that choir, and so, you saw him at his church, you saw him at our church when they came to visit or something like that. You saw Ms. Riley the same way when she was at St. Peter right nearby Dutch Fork. You saw her, saw Ms. Corley at Pleasant Spring. You saw Ms. Bowman at Pine Grove. You know, things like that. I could go to all the teachers and tell you where they went to church, and they knew things about you that... if you messed up at school during the day, sometimes they would hold classes and put you in their car and go home with you. And so what that meant was that, they'd pull up and said, 'Well, I know your father's working on a job over on such and such and Creek Road, Nancy Creek Road, so I'm going to take you over there because you're just a little bit to manage for your britches.'

Norma Jean Corley Mackey, who attended Richlex and graduated from the desegregated Irmo High in 1971, also shared her perception of the school and her teachers' relationships with the parents:

> To me, it was more of like a big huge family. Because everyone knew everyone. And even though it was a huge, a large family, it was almost as if you knew each, every... not just knew them by name, but you *knew* them. You knew their families. They knew your families. Most of the teachers knew the kids and knew the kids' families, knew where they lived. And didn't seem to have a problem if they needed to, to go ride to the kid's house if there was a problem or something going on within the school. They just had that kind of relationship with the parents.

Like Mrs. Mackey, Dr. Shirley Portee Martin attended Richlex before graduating from the desegregated Irmo High in 1972. Dr. Martin elaborated on another element of the community's relationship with the teachers at Richlex:

> Well, some of the interesting things that stand out was that feel of community. My granddaddy was also a farmer. At certain times of the year, whatever he'd farm, he'd

send bags of that to my teachers. I knew that when I got on the bus, I'd have five brown paper bags of collard greens that I've got to deliver to Ms. Outten, Ms. Ritter, and Ms. Corley. I mean, it was just such a sense of family. Everybody, there was just that kind of closeness.

Mr. Haltiwanger echoed these sentiments, "They knew our parents personally, most of them did, because they lived in the area." Mr. Reeves recalled being invited to the Boulware house on Saturday mornings and shared a story of the time Mr. Bowers, the janitor at Richlex, caught him and a group of his friends with beer while out in the community:

(He) came up to me and said, 'Now, y'all give me all that beer you got, put it in my car, and I'm going to take it to Roll's house and tell him this is what y'all buying with your money like this. This not something you supposed to be doing. And especially if you go to school at Richlex, I'm not going to let it happen.'

The partnerships and meaningful relationships between the Richlex faculty and parents were critical to the development of the students and the community. While this section focuses on the broader definition of kinship and family, it should also be mentioned that some members of the Richlex faculty were directly related to the students. Larry Haltiwanger's brother was Cecil Haltiwanger, a science teacher, and Mrs. Mackey's aunt was Martha Corley, a first grade teacher. Members of Dr. Martin's family also taught at Richlex. Mrs. Mackey explained how these relationships and other factors contributed to the climate of the school when discussing Mrs. Corley:

She was able to be there in the one building with these students from first grade, many of them on through high school. There was that relationship, not just with that one student, but with probably that student and all of their siblings. There was that connection there. You knew certain things not to do, certain behaviors not to display because you knew that relationship, you knew that these teachers knew that, well I knew that they knew my aunt. And my aunt was my daddy's sister.

Mr. Haltiwanger also noted the positive impact of having all grades together, "You're talking about everybody from first grade to twelfth grade went to the same school. So it was a small, intimate group of people, and so were the teachers. I mean, you could tell the bond that they had." Mrs. Mackey's and Mr. Haltiwanger's comments illustrate that the family within the school was created by deep relationships fostered throughout the students' entire education at Richlex School. Dr. Martin shared similar thoughts on the school:

I think it also stood out that it was very clear that they all had a vested interest in me. My brother is 12 years older than me, so when I was in first grade, he was a freshman in college. He had been the valedictorian at Richlex and all. It was very easy for me in a lot of ways, because they'd say, 'Oh, that's James's sister.' There was just a lot of respect and support.

In some cases, previous generations had been taught by the teachers who later joined the Richlex faculty, as Mr. Reeves observed in his recollection of Mrs. Emma Bowman:

> She was my mom's teacher and my dad's teacher. So, when I was in first grade, my mom wanted Ms. Emma to be my teacher, too. But the class was so crowded that Ms. Martha Corley said, 'Well, I'll teach him,' and she said, 'Okay.' So, that's why I wasn't a legacy under Emma at the time. But my mom always remained a loyalist to Emma all the way throughout her life.

These decades-long bonds between students, siblings, parents, and faculty helped to create the Richlex community and also helped the school transmit this feeling of family.

The entire community came together to support the school and its students, and this included community members who did not have children in the school. Reeves told stories about members of the Lorick family:

> They were just active in the community a lot. And they spent a lot of time around the school too, boosting. Even before the cafeteria was there functioning at Richlex, and brought food to the school back in the trunks of the cars, pulled around the backside of the school there, brought out things in the trunks of the cars so that people could eat. And these were people that didn't have a kid anywhere near Richlex.

The Harbison faculty also fostered a family climate, contributing to students' lives in ways typically associated with close friends and family members. Like Mrs. Boulware having Richlex students over on Saturday mornings, Pauline Richardson recalled visiting the home of Harbison's Mrs. Jennie Young as a student, "We would walk up from the school up to her house and we would sit on the steps. And she would have little crackers over there with a little drink or something for us, and we always enjoyed that." Mrs. Morris told the story of the Harbison faculty's involvement in her wedding:

> Mrs. T.B. Jones was living here at the time. She used to like to entertain. So when she heard that I was getting married, she wanted to have a shower for me. Somebody else wanted to furnish the cake. Ms. Newbie (sp), she said 'Well, if I play for your wedding, could I come?' Mrs. Jones, in addition to doing the bridal shower, took pictures. I don't know what it would have been if they hadn't done all this for me.

The students' stories highlight the familial bonds created at both Harbison and Richlex. The teachers, students, and community developed in-depth relationships that were strengthened by their commitment to one another in both the school and the community. These bonds transcended the student-teacher dynamic, with teachers and staff more closely resembling extended family nurturing students through all phases of their development.

RESISTANT CAPITAL AT HARBISON AND RICHLEX

The two schools were key sites in developing resistant capital, a form of cultural capital generated as groups work against inequality and challenge existing hierarchies (Yosso, 2005). Resistant capital can be manifested as communities affirm and lift up their members as they navigate and work against systems that were designed to exclude or oppress them. Community cultural wealth is the "array of cultural knowledge, skills, abilities, and contacts possessed by socially marginalized groups that often go unrecognized," and the continued development of community cultural wealth is an act of resistance (Yosso & Solorzano, 2005, p. 129; Yosso, 2005). The Harbison and Richlex students described their schools' importance in helping students find joy and creating cultural wealth. Richlex participants also described the ways in which their teachers encouraged them to challenge inequality.

Harbison's teachers helped students discover life-long passions and provided the community with opportunities to come together. Leon Smith, John Corley, and Gladys Henderson recalled the Harbison choir, noting that it provided students with opportunities to travel and compete in other cities. Mr. Smith stated that his love of music began at Harbison "and I still enjoy singing today." As an adult living in Washington, D.C., Mrs. Henderson attended operas, an interest she developed while at Harbison. The faculty created opportunities for the community to share these experiences. Mrs. Riley recalled:

> They would come to Harbison, they just kind of looked to Harbison for leadership. That's where they got the plays and the education. Mama said they would come from up there to the different cantatas and things that they had at Harbison, and they just loved Harbison. They had beautiful music, and you know that was kind of rare for us to have pianos and this kind of thing. But she said they had some beautiful plays there.

Mrs. Schumpert stated that Harbison provided the opportunity for the community to "come in and see some things that they wouldn't have seen ordinarily, right there at Harbison."

When Harbison closed in 1958 following a period of declining enrollment, Richlex inherited Harbison's role as a center of community life, building resistant capital through activities that fostered pride and unity (Helsley, 1988; Vidal & Mooneyhan, 2006). Richlex hosted events and plays for the surrounding Black communities. Mr. Reeves recalled some of these events:

> We used to plant the maypole at the schools. We get together and the school, the communities would get together at Richlex on the ball field on May 1st, or if it was over the holiday, over the weekend, we would get together on Friday or whenever May 1st was. And we would plant the maypole, all the communities got together to plant that maypole and have May Day festivities, and it was a way for all the communities to get together. We'd have food they would bring, it was a lot like a community-style based picnic. It was great, great kind of stuff. I remember that from early on, I knew that Richlex became the social hub for everything that went on and all the communities...

...All the communities, we didn't know it at the time, but when I look back on it, all the communities were represented in the play. We had Ellen Bowers from Chapin, Brenda Eichelberger from Pleasant Spring, you had Rosetta Brannon from right there in Irmo, right off Irmo Drive, down that way. You had James Washington, Pine Grove, you had Mike Reeves from right there on Oak Grove. And then Hopewell, you had Bertha Eargle or somebody like that, in the play. We didn't know it at the time, but then when you look back and say, oh wow, we had all of these people from all the.... So when it came time for that play or the operetta, the whole community was there as one group in the gymnasium or on the ball field, with all that kind of stuff. So whether they did it by accident or whether it was just by plan, it gave a sense of community that it was one big community and not segregated communities or segmented communities so much.

Richlex teachers also exposed students to direct ways of challenging inequality. Mrs. Boulware aligned her roles as an educator, parent, and wife of Harold Boulware to connect her students to major state and national events. Mr. Reeves said that during the Saturday visits to her house, Mrs. Boulware:

...talked about who was being active and it was in an inactive way of activating us, if you kind of catch it a little bit. Matthew Perry was one of the associates that we used to hang around a lot. He used to be there with the Boulwares a lot. And she would introduce, she said, 'You know who Matthew is now, don't you? You know he's involved with...' such and such and such.

This case that TM... They called Thurgood TM. They used to call him TM. TM and Pops. Judge Boulware was called Pops. And she said, 'Pops, TM, and Matthew are working on those cases,' and all that kind of stuff. 'It's down in the country. It's down in the country, but it's going to be coming this way.' That's what she used to always say, she said, 'Pay attention, pay attention. It's going to be coming this way.'

Black educator displacement during desegregation has been well-documented in other sources, and this trend too was present in District 5. Black educators' continued presence in schools in the face of mass discrimination and displacement was an act of resistance. The former Richlex faculty who were reassigned to Irmo High after desegregation included Mrs. Riley, Mr. Cecil Haltiwanger, and Mr. Fred Godbold. These educators encouraged the development of resistant capital in their students as they navigated the desegregated environment. Dr. Martin described their efforts in encouraging Black students to integrate extracurricular activities:

Well, I think because I was the first Black cheerleader, and I was a Civinette. Every time there was something that we were going to be a part of for the first time, Ms. Riley and Mr. Haltiwanger would call me to their room and say, 'Okay, you've got to represent us.' It was almost like they wanted me to be the face for the Black community, and as a result, that's what happened. When they said, 'It's time for a Black cheerleader, who can we get to run?' They came to me. I was a very introverted person, but I think because my skin was lighter, that they felt it may be easier for acceptance to occur if that makes sense....

...Like I said, I was really introverted. But Ms. Riley even came to my house to let my family, parents know that, 'She really needs to run. We need to do this. It's time for the school to have a Black cheerleader.' We were starting the Civinettes, which was a group, and I think it was Mr. Haltiwanger came or Godbold saying, 'Again, we need to integrate this group. We need someone who will do this for us. Shirley needs to be that person.' That's how all of that would happen. Of course, my mom felt, 'Well, you need to do this.' And so I did.

Resistant capital is developed when communities directly challenge racism and when they sustain and develop cultural wealth in the face of such forces. The students of Harbison and Richlex shared numerous stories of how their school cultivated cultural wealth, and the Richlex students identified ways in which their teachers taught them to resist the status quo. Both types of resistant capital added to the cultural capital present in the Black communities in the Chapin, Dutch Fork, and Irmo areas.

"LIFT HIGH HER BANNER...FORWARD, UPWARD, ON"—THE LEGACIES OF HARBISON AND RICHLEX

Harbison and Richlex served the Black students of the Chapin, Dutch Fork, and Irmo communities for more than a half century. During that time, they partnered with the communities to create and communicate social, familial, and resistant capital. The students' stories of Harbison and Richlex demonstrate the schools' value as educational institutions, as developers of cultural wealth in the community, and points of pride in the history of Black education. Despite their successes and rich histories, neither Harbison Junior College nor Richlex School are a part of the educational opportunities available in the communities of Chapin, Dutch Fork, and Irmo today.

The rise of Richlex coincided with the rapid decline and eventual closing of Harbison. A 1941 fire resulted in the temporary closure of the school, and the high school enrollment never recovered (McMillan, 1952). The opening of Richlex further diminished demand for Harbison as the area's Black community finally had a public high school for their children. The Presbyterian Church closed Harbison in 1958 after it endured two more fires in the early 1950s and saw continued declines in enrollment. The campus was donated to Midlands Technical College in 1978 (Vidal & Mooneyhan, 2006).

Richlex School, the former Rosenwald School that opened in 1918, was converted into Irmo Junior High when District 5 fully desegregated in 1968. The campus became Dutch Fork Elementary School in 1971 (R. L. Floyd Foundation, Inc., 1996). The decision to rename and repurpose Richlex School was unpopular with its alumni and the Black community. In March 1975, after several days of unrest at Irmo High, Black parents and students met with school and district leaders. The parents shared concerns about the school's staffing and curriculum, but they also raised questions about the renaming of Richlex (District 5, March 10, 1975). This issue would be raised again in subsequent decades (District 5, May 7, 1990; District 5, November 25, 2002).

No students have attended Harbison since 1958, and Richlex's last graduates received their diplomas just a decade later. The tight-knit families created by the two schools can still be felt and seen. Former Harbison students came together to share their rich memories of their beloved school in the documentary referenced throughout this chapter, and they have worked with Midlands Technical College to preserve the school's history with an annual Harbison History Day (Midlands Technical College, 2020). Richlex alumni continue to host reunions and celebrations (R. L. Floyd Foundation, Inc., 1996; Richlex Alumni, 2017). In 2018, Dutch Fork Elementary School celebrated the centennial of the Rosenwald School and the campus's history, and James Washington served as a keynote speaker.

The two schools also live on in their former students' work to continue the development of cultural capital. Though Harold Boulware's leadership on the *Briggs* case is perhaps the most well-known achievement of a Harbison or Richlex alumnus, each of the participants in this study has generated cultural wealth in their communities throughout their lives. In 2014, Larry Haltiwanger became only the third Black member of the District 5 school board in its entire history. Norma Jean Corley Mackey served her community as a social worker, working with children in the Department of Juvenile Justice. Dr. Shirley Portee Martin served as a teacher, principal, and district superintendent, striving to create environments where all students felt welcomed and could flourish. Michael Reeves protested segregated businesses in Orangeburg, South Carolina while attending South Carolina State. He was one of the protesters present when police opened fire and killed two South Carolina State students and one high school student on the evening of February 8, 1968, an event that came to be known as the Orangeburg Massacre. Returning to Irmo following his retirement, James Washington chaired the 2016 Richlex reunion, led discussions and panels related to student experiences at Richlex, assisted Dutch Fork Elementary with its celebration of the Rosenwald/Richlex centennial, and is currently leading an oral history project with local churches. The Richlex alma mater called on the students to "Lift high her banner," and the alumni have done just that, lifting the Richlex banner high and proud as they carried the community "Forward, Upward, On" (Floyd, n.d.).

The stories of the former students demonstrate the critical role that Harbison and Richlex played in the development of cultural capital, and the works of the schools' alumni over the last fifty years demonstrate the multi-generational impacts of the community cultural wealth generated at both schools. The successes of Harbison and Richlex hold valuable lessons for those seeking to address educational inequities in the present-day. Modern practitioners and scholars must understand the contributions of the segregated Black schools as well as the values and practices that made the schools so important to their students and communities. Instead of repeating the mistakes of desegregation and discarding the traditions, beliefs, and philosophies of Black educators and schools, it is critical that marginalized voices and experiences be centered as we plan for the future of our educational systems.

REFERENCES

Allen, D. B. (2019). The forgotten Brown case: Briggs v. Elliott and its legacy in South Carolina. *Peabody Journal of Education*, *94*(4), 442–467. https://doi.org/10.1080/0161956X.2019.1648954

Alridge, D. P. (2015). The ideas and craft of the critical historian of education. In A. M. Martinez-Aleman, B. Pusser, & E. M. Bensimon (Eds.), *Critical Approaches to the study of higher education: A practical introduction* (pp. 103–129). Johns Hopkins University Press.

Alridge, D. P. (2020). Teachers in the movement: Pedagogy, activism, and freedom. *History of Education Quarterly*, *60*(1), 1–23. https://doi.org/10.1017/heq.2020.6

Anderson, J. D. (1988). *The education of Blacks in the South, 1860–1935*. The University of North Carolina Press.

Appleby, J. (1998). The power of history. *American Historical Review*, *103*(1), 1–14.

Baker, R. S. (2006). *Paradoxes of desegregation: African Americans struggles for educational equity in Charleston, South Carolina, 1926–1972*. University of South Carolina Press.

Berry, T. R., & Cook, E. J. B. (2019). Critical race perspectives on narrative research: Centering intersectionality. In J. T. DeCuir-Gunby, T. K. Chapman, & P. Schultz (Eds.), *Understanding critical race research methods and methodologies: Lessons from the field* (pp. 86–96). Routledge.

Biddle University. (1904–1919, 1921). *Annual session* or *Annual catalog*. https://lib.digitalnc.org/

Board of Missions for Freedmen of the Presbyterian Church in the United States of America. (1907). *Forty-second annual report of the Board of Missions for Freedmen of the Presbyterian Church in the United States of America*. https://archive.org/details/reportsofmission1907pres/page/n1411/mode/2up

Board of Missions for Freedmen of the Presbyterian Church in the United States of America. (1910). *Forty fifth annual report of the Board of Missions for Freedmen of the Presbyterian Church in the United States of America*. https://ia600205.us.archive.org/31/items/reportsofmission1907pres/reportsofmission1907pres.pdf

Board of Missions for Freedmen of the Presbyterian Church in the United States of America. (1912). *Forty-seventh annual report of the Board of Missions for Freedmen of the Presbyterian Church in the United States of America*. https://archive.org/details/reportsofmission1912pres/page/n7/mode/2up

Boulware, H. B., Sr. (1980, September 23). *Interview by G. J. McFadden* [Video recording]. Quest for Civil Rights, University of South Carolina. Moving Image Research Collections.

Bullock, H. A. (1967). *A history of Negro education in the South: From 1619 to the Present*. Praeger Publishers.

Callison, T. C. (n.d.). *Questions on interpretation of different phases of the 1951 School Reorganization Act*. School District Five of Lexington and Richland Counties Archived Materials.

Carr, E. H. (1961). *What is history?* Vintage Books.

Connelly, F. M., & Clandinin, D. J. (1990). Stories of experience and narrative inquiry. *Educational Researcher*, *19*(5), 2–14.

Crenshaw, K. W. (2011). Twenty years of critical race theory: Looking back to move forward. *Connecticut Law Review*, *43*(5), 1253–1352.

Dobrasko, R. (2005). *Upholding 'Separate but Equal:' South Carolina's School Equalization Program: 1951–1955* [Master's thesis]. University of South Carolina.

Donnor, J. K. (2019). Understanding the why of Whiteness: Negrophobia, segregation, and the legacy of White resistance to Black education in Mississippi. In J. T. DeCuir-Gunby, T. K. Chapman, & P. Schultz (Eds.), *Understanding critical race research methods and methodologies: Lessons from the field.* (pp. 13–23). Routledge.

Du Bois, W. E. B. (1935). *Black Reconstruction in America: 1860–1880*. The Free Press.

Floyd, J. (1973). *A study of displaced Black high school principals in the state of South Carolina: 1963–1973* [Doctoral dissertation]. Northwestern University.

Floyd, J. M. (n.d.). *Richlex Alma Mater*.

Fisk University. (2001). *Rosenwald fund card file database*. http://rosenwald.fisk.edu/

George, A. A. (1955). *The History of Johnson C. Smith University: 1867 to the Present*. [Doctoral dissertation]. New York University.

Glesne, C. (2016). *Becoming qualitative researchers: An introduction* (5th ed.). Pearson.

Harmon, C. V., & Harmon, A. L. (1951, November 26). *Order of school district reorganization*. School District Five of Lexington and Richland Counties Archived Materials.

Hartshorn, W. N. (1910). *An era of progress and promise: 1863–1910: The religious, moral and educational development of the American Negro since his emancipation*. Priscilla Publishing.

Hawkins, W. C. (1973, April 6). *Letter to John E. Tolbert*. School District Five of Lexington and Richland Counties Archived Materials.

Helsley, A. J. (1988). Harbison College: Metamorphoses of a dream. *The Proceedings of the South Carolina Historical Association: 1988–1989*. The South Carolina Historical Association. https://dc.statelibrary.sc.gov/handle/10827/23839

Hine, D. C. (2004). The Briggs v. Elliott legacy: Black culture, consciousness, and community before Brown, 1930–1954. *University of Illinois Law Review, 2004*(5), 1059–1072.

James, J. C. (1970). Another vanishing American: The Black principal. *The New Republic, 163*(13), 17–20.

Janesick, V. J. (2010). *Oral history for the qualitative researcher*. Guilford Publications.

Johnson C. Smith University. (1922–1926, 1928–1930, 1934). *Annual Catalogue*. Johnson C. Smith University. https://lib.digitalnc.org/

Johnson, D. D. (2009). *Shhh...Big Momma and dem' left last night: Shifting violent memories and the African American chain migration, Abbeville, South Carolina to Evanston, Illinois, 1910–1940* [Master's thesis]. University of Wisconsin-Madison.

Ladson-Billings, G., & Tate, W. F. (1995). Toward a critical race theory of education. *Teachers College Record, 97*(1), 47–68. https://doi.org/10.4324/9781315709796-2

Lynn, M. (2019). Foreword: Moving critical race theory in education from a problem-posing mindset to a problem-solving orientation. In J. T. DeCuir-Gunby, T. K. Chapman, & P. Schultz (Eds.), *Understanding critical race research methods and methodologies: Lessons from the field.* (pp. viii–xii). Routledge.

Malagon, M. C., Huber, L. P., & Velez, V. N. (2009). Our experiences, our methods: Using grounded theory to inform a critical race theory methodology. *Seattle Journal for Social Justice, 8*(1), 253–272.

McMillan, L. K. (1952). *Negro higher education in the state of South Carolina*. South Carolina State Library. https://dc.statelibrary.sc.gov/handle/10827/32146

Midlands Technical College. (2020). *5th annual Harbison History Day at MTC*. https://www.midlandstech.edu/news/5th-annual-harbison-history-day-mtc

Montgomery, W. M. (2002). *Columbia schools: A history of Richland County School District One, Columbia, South Carolina, 1792–2000.* The R. L. Bryan Company.

Moore, A. D., III, & Anderson, C. K. (2018). A thorn in the side of segregation: The short life, long odds, and legacy of the law school at South Carolina State College. *American Educational History Journal, 45*(1), 71–89.

Morris, J. E., & Parker, B. D. (2019). Historical/archival analyses. In J. T. DeCuir-Gunby, T. K. Chapman, & P. Schultz (Eds.), *Understanding critical race research methods and methodologies: Lessons from the field.* (pp. 24–33). Routledge.

Polkinghorne, D. E. (1995). Narrative configuration in qualitative analysis. *International Journal of Qualitative Studies in Education, 8*(1), 5–23.

R. L. Floyd Foundation, Inc. (1996). *Richlex High School Anniversary Yearbook: 1956, 1960, 1962, 1964, 1967.*

Richings, G. F. (1903). *Evidences of progress among Colored people, tenth edition.* Geo. S. Ferguson, Co.

Richland County Recreation Commission (n.d.). *Rosenwald School.* https://richlandcountyrecreation.com/rosenwald-school/

Richlex Alumni. (2017). *Richlex School.* Irmo SC. https://sites.google.com/site/richlexschool/home

South Carolina State Department of Education. (1953–54, 1954–55, 1955–56, 1956–57, 1957–58, 1958–59, 1959–60, 1960–61, 1961–62, 1962–63, 1963–64, 1964–65, 1965–66, 1966–67). *School Directory of South Carolina.* https://dc.statelibrary.sc.gov/

School District Five of Lexington and Richland Counties (District 5). (1953–2007). *Board Meeting Minutes.* School District Five of Lexington and Richland Counties Archived Materials.

Solorzano, D. G., & Yosso, Y. J. (2002). Critical race methodology: Counter-storytelling as an analytical framework for education research. *Qualitative Inquiry, 8*(1), 23–44.

Tolliver Cleveland Callison Papers. (n.d.). *Biographical or historical note.* South Carolinian Library, University of South Carolina.

Vidal, E. M., & Mooneyhan, B. (Producers). (2006). *In their own words: A history of Harbison Institute: 1911–1958* [Video file]. https://www.youtube.com/watch?v=KzU80HbAuqc

Walker, V. S. (1996). *Their highest potential: An African American school community in the segregated South.* The University of North Carolina Press.

Walker, V. S. (2000). Valued segregated schools for African American children in the South, 1935–1969: A review of common themes and characteristics. *Review of Educational Research, 70*(3), 253–285. https://doi.org/10.3102/00346543070003253

Yosso, T. J. (2005). Whose culture has capital? A critical race theory discussion of community cultural wealth. *Race Ethnicity and Education, 8*(1), 69–91. https://doi.org/10.1080/1361332052000341006

Yosso, T. J., & Solórzano, D. G. (2005). Conceptualizing a critical race theory in sociology. In M. Romero & E. Margolis (Eds.), *Blackwell companion to social inequalities* (ProQuest Ebook Central, pp. 117–146). John Wiley & Sons, Incorporated. https://doi.org/10.1002/9780470996973.ch7

CHAPTER 7

DOUGLASS HIGH SCHOOL (1891–)

A Place of Justice and Hope in Oklahoma City

Autumn B. Brown and Lucy E. Bailey[1]

Oklahoma State University

Jim Crow era laws, though meant to cement Black people as inferior in society, raised the standard of education in segregated schools. This chapter highlights one such school, Douglass High School, located in Oklahoma City, Oklahoma. Douglass, named after the abolitionist Frederick Douglass, has been serving Black students on the "east side" since 1891, 16 years before Oklahoma statehood, and is still active today. Using oral histories from Douglass alumni and select archival documents spanning decades, this chapter explores the relationship between Douglass High School and the communities it served. Through key aspects of Tara J. Yosso's (2005) conceptual framework of community cultural wealth, we foreground how Douglass both served—and continues to serve—as a site of racial equality, economic growth, resistance, aspiration, and political empowerment for Black youth, teachers, and administrators.

---

[1] Autumn Brown collected the majority of data for this study while Lucy Bailey took the lead on writing and historical data.

Black Cultural Capital: Activism That Spurred African American High Schools, pages 135–156.
Copyright © 2023 by Information Age Publishing
www.infoagepub.com
All rights of reproduction in any form reserved.

Keywords: Historically Black high Schools; Community Cultural Wealth; Oral History, Resistance, Aspiration, Capital

INTRODUCTION

Literacy and learning have been integral to the freedom of Black people in virtually every period of history (Brown, 2021). Despite centuries of tactics intended to cement Black people as inferior in society, Jim Crow-era attitudes, laws, and practices also propelled the establishment of Black schools, which raised the standard of education and contributed to uplifting the Black race (Fairclough, 2000). In Oklahoma City, Oklahoma (hereafter, OKC or The City), Douglass High School, named after the abolitionist Frederick Douglass, is one such institution. It endures today as a point in the direction of racial equality. What later became Douglass School was founded in 1891, 21 years after the establishment of the historic Dunbar High in Washington D.C. (Stewart, 2013), 16 years before Oklahoma statehood, and nearly 30 years before the "revolutionary" opening of Booker T. Washington High in Atlanta, Georgia (Driskell, 2014). The OKC Board of Educa-

The School that Became Douglass. Courtesy of Metropolitan Library System of Oklahoma County

tion met on January 5, 1891, passed a motion, and the "colored school" was born. The school served Black children as economic growth beckoned families to the area. In 1895, Principal Jefferson Davis Randolph was allowed to establish an "all grade school" and in 1898, the new principal, J. W. Sharpe, led its christening as Frederick Douglass School (*Register*, 1989). In May, 1903, the school graduated its first class of eight young men and women (*Register*, 1989).

Douglass High is still active today—a century after its founding and through varied relocations—in representing a legacy of justice and hope to the surrounding community. This chapter traces these contributions in showcasing how this "Black school" was integral to a web of institutions which fostered relationships and community flourishing throughout its existence. In doing so, we highlight how the school represented and facilitated community cultural wealth (Yosso, 2005) through its prominent leaders, teachers and central role in community life. It also nourished accomplished artists, scholars, leaders, athletes, and activists involved in the Civil Rights Movement. From its history as a segregated school to the present, the school has remained a powerful site of resistance, aspiration, and political empowerment for Black youth, teachers, and administrators.

As of 2021, the school enrolled over 400 students in grades 9–12, 97% of whom are African American. It is a site of historical memory that centers Black educational growth and community. Yet, like many historically Black high schools in the Southern United States which have been abandoned or face funding pressures (Natanson, 2020), Douglass remains vulnerable to closure or consolidation. Current pressures include competition for the school building from community charter schools, year-end data yielding low academic achievement, and teacher turnover (U.S. News, 2020). The surrounding neighborhoods, too, face threats from gentrification as White businesses and families move into a historical locus of Black community life with little awareness of its robust history.

OVERVIEW

This chapter explores Douglass High within OKC community life using examples from across the century. We first articulate key components of Yosso's (2005) conceptual framework of community cultural wealth that we connect to Douglass' history. We then overview the school's development situated in secondary literature on Oklahoma Black educational history (e.g., Cayton, 1977; Franklin, 1994, 2007; Moon, 1978; Teall, 1971). We highlight influential leaders and attendees and link the curriculum with the broader community it served. Then, drawing from archival sources and six oral histories from Douglass students across a 45-year span (1955 to 2002), we use Yosso's (2005) framing to foreground how Douglass, among other robust sites of community life (e.g. bustling businesses, churches, and neighborhoods), centered Black lives and aspirations.

The oral histories demonstrate, in Yosso's (2005) terms, the forms of wealth manifested in alumni experiences. In Lomawaima's (1994) history of Native American resistance to boarding school life, she refers to oral narrators as living "memory bearers" who remain vital resources about the past. Similarly, we honor the OKC narrators' perspectives of the capital the school helped generate. We aim to show how this staple in the OKC community remains a point of pride in fostering achievements and networks that stretch throughout the state and nation at large.

Although scholars have studied aspects of the state's Black educational activism and history (e.g., Franklin, 1982; Teall, 1971), particularly in a series of robust dissertations (e.g., Cayton, 1977; Hadley, 1981; LeSure, 1982; Moon, 1978; Saxe, 1969; Strong, 1961), much of Oklahoma's rich Black educational history remains to be told. Several OKC histories refer to Douglass High (Arnold, 2010; Hadley, 1981; Moon, 1978), as does an Oklahoma Black history sourcebook (Teall, 1971). One biographical study centered on Frederick Douglass Moon (hereafter, F. D. Moon), a beloved activist instrumental to the schools' development between 1940–1961. Moon's (1978) study is unique in foregrounding Douglass High. Our study augments this history through analyzing community capital and highlighting Douglass alumni who point to the school's continuing legacy.

CONCEPTUAL FRAMEWORK

Yosso's (2005) framework of community cultural wealth (CCW) offered an important critique and extension of Bourdieu's concepts of social and cultural capital that he formed from his analysis of French culture. In her now well-known article, Yosso (2005) drew from critical race theory to critique Bourdieu's concepts as centering a White middle-class set of norms that can result in evaluating communities of color as somehow 'lacking' (p. 70) influential forms of capital that might propel conventional forms of success. Resisting this dismissive framing, Yosso (2005) created transformative conceptions of capital that collectively convey the robust cultural wealth within communities of color. She categorizes these forms of wealth as aspirational, linguistic, familial, social, navigational, and resistant (Yosso, 2005). Several components of Yosso's model are salient to Douglass' history in *reflecting* and *fostering* CCW in its surrounding communities. We primarily deploy four forms of capital surfacing in our research—aspirational, familial, social, and resistant—that in turn align with Morris' (2004) conception of Black social capital for group advancement. Morris (2004) underscores the power of Black social capital "for survival and success in a segregated world bounded by the omnipresent forces of racism and discrimination— forces that limited their opportunities beyond the Black community" (p. 102).

Yosso (2005) describes aspirational capital as community methods to "maintain hopes and dreams for the future" in the face of challenges (p. 77). This form of capital focuses on nourishing visions of the future that can transcend the barriers (perceived and actual) that limit opportunities (Yosso, 2005). We argue that Douglass fostered aspirational capital through school programs, role models, and a vibrant community life. Collectively, these structural components helped to foster "dream[s] of possibilities" beyond the children's "present circumstances"

(Yosso, 2005, p. 78). Another resource in Douglass history, familial capital, focuses on "those cultural knowledges nurtured among familia (kin) that carry a sense of community history, memory and cultural intuition" (Yosso, 2005, p. 79). Yosso (2005) embraces a supple conception of family as "extended networks" which "model lessons of caring, coping, and providing" education as well as providing funds of knowledge (p. 79).

The third category we use is social capital, referring to

> networks of people and community resources. These peer and other social contacts can provide both instrumental and emotional support to navigate through society's institutions.... [such] social contacts and community resources may help a student identify and attain a college scholarship. (Yosso, 2005, pp. 79–80)

This dynamic is evident in Douglass's community members' circulation of information through local newspapers and community gatherings. Social capital involves emotional or concrete support to seek educational or work opportunities or extend resources within networks (Yosso, 2005). Lastly, resistant capital is also evident in Douglass community life, as people learned skills and practices grounded in the "legacy of resistance to subordination" (Yosso, 2005, p. 80). Communities of color have long histories of teaching skills to resist inequities (Yosso, 2005), whether through elders demonstrating resistant behaviors, questioning taken-for-granted assumptions and beliefs, or working actively to transform conditions. The school's existence, itself, we argue, represented such resistance.

OVERVIEW OF DOUGLASS HIGH'S HISTORY

> I believe in the Douglass High School and in the things for which it stands: HEALTH in MIND and BODY, SERVICE to others and to myself, SOCIAL ADJUSTMENT, ECONOMIC SECURITY and REVERENCE FOR THE SPIRITUAL. I believe in LOYALTY to our school and to its traditions. I pledge upon my honor to help in all its undertakings; in all that will make it a stronger and nobler school. And I promise to do all in my power to become a student to match its ideals. Douglass High School Creed. (Moon, 1978, p. 391)

Douglass was the first Black high school in OKC and likely the oldest in the state (Teall, 1971). In 1891, it was a key development for Black children in The City. From its humble beginnings, to its numerous locations downtown in early 1900, to its place today on the Eastside, Douglass has remained a site of community achievement and pride, fostering a wide range of capital across a century. Its legacy is thus tied as much to its symbolic and historical role for the Black community as its shifting brick-and-mortar site. From the last decade of the 19th century to the first of the 20th, the numbers of Black people migrating to Oklahoma and Indian territories grew quickly, tripling by 1910 (Cayton, 1977). Teall (1971) describes the first high school as occupying a two-room house on one city block,

FIGURE 7.2. Photo of F. D. Moon, Principal of Douglass High (1940–1961). F.D. Moon [Oklahoma Publishing Company Photography Collection/OHS]

which later moved to a two-story building on the next block. The school adopted Douglass's name in 1894. In fall of 1903, after honoring the first graduating class, someone burned down the school (Teall, 1971). By 1908, the year after Oklahoma became a state, the school had almost 600 pupils (Teall, 1971). By 1910, the Black population in the City was 6,700 people (*Register*, 2007, p. 8) which intensified the need for schools. Douglass remained downtown until 1934. That year, changes in the Deep Deuce and (what is now called) Bricktown neighborhoods required relocating to the Eastside of OKC.

The school building Douglass occupied from 1933–1955 was originally built in 1910 to serve White elementary students. Classified as a red brick "Classic Revival" architectural style of the late 19th and early 20th century, the school grounds occupied approximately three acres of land at 600 N. High in an active residential neighborhood (*Register*, 2007, p. 1). The school site offered 88,000 square feet of growing room. As enrollment grew and needs changed, construction teams expanded the building, plastered walls, added concrete floors, and put in a swimming pool. When Douglass's needs as a Junior Senior school again outgrew its available space, this building became Old Douglass. In 1989, it was included on the register of historic places. It represents, notes the register application, "the most important school in the Separate School system of the city... [and] the community's efforts to overcome the inherent inequality of the system" (*Register*, 2007, p. 6). Douglass moved several additional times.

The principals in the first 50 years included J. D. Randolph, a teacher, then early principal; J. W. Sharpe (1898–1903); James Henry A. Brazelton (1903–1915); Inman Edward Page (1921–22), and F. D. Moon (1940–1961). Moon was an utter force in advancing Black education in The City. He held various leadership positions in three separate schools, including as principal of Douglass (Teale, 1971). His influence was of such note that when the new 1955 high school adopted the Douglass name, leaving the junior high without one, "over 24 organizations and 40 churches" (Moon, 1978, p. 275) voted unanimously to adopt F. D. Moon Junior High as the new name. One former student's oral history speaks to Moon's legacy. As Donta Stepeny (2020), 2002 alumnus and former Douglass educator, noted, "F. D. Moon was like President Barack Obama in Oklahoma."

More broadly, the Eastside was a site of community flourishing during segregation, akin to Yosso's (2005) description of resistant capital. Douglass was a hub of activity, "a place that the community could call their own home," and "a central gathering place" (*Register*, 2007, p. 13). It hosted musical, theater, social, health, and political events. During the 1940s and 1950s, Moon (1978) described Douglass as an active "community school" packed with events, such as public meetings, library and gym activities, swimming, and adult education courses. Adults learned "tailoring, millinery, clothing, typewriting, shorthand, and art" (Moon, 1978, p. 195) or pursued college courses in the Langston University Extension Center. The school promoted vocational courses which expanded to carpentry, brick masonry and electrical training in 1950–1951. Douglass reflected an extended familial structure for students, teachers, and leaders. Yosso (2005) might describe such relationships as familial capital given Douglass's "commitment to community well being" (Moon, 1978, p. 79).

Moon worked steadily to secure financing and space for the growing school during its two decades on High Street. Because Douglass was The City's only Black high school, Moon stressed its importance to the school board: "[students] come here from the four corners of the city" (Moon, 1978, p. 246). Yet the reach of Douglass stretched beyond that. Moon (1978) noted that enrollment since 1945 had grown steadily and, of the new 163 enrollees, many joined from outside the county and state; Moon tallied, for instance, 52 from the county, 65 from elsewhere in Oklahoma, and 46 from elsewhere in the nation. When the new school opened at the fairgrounds in 1954–1955, it opened to record enrollment.

Anita G. Arnold (2020), an artist, writer, and activist, remembered this transition. She entered Old Douglass, which she called the "Douglass Next Door," in 8th grade and graduated in 1957 from the new school. She remembers the energy of that time:

> If you went to Douglass High School you had experiences that nobody else, I'm sure, in the country had like we had... students... participated in statewide competitions, we were winners all the time. We had more trophies than the law should have allowed, in everything, not just sports but we're talking about public speaking, we're talking about mathematics, we're talking about auto mechanics. It was a fully integrated curriculum, there was something for everybody; those who were going on to college, and those who were going to pursue a vocation.

As scholars have noted, despite the 1954 *Brown* ruling, the pace of desegregation across the nation was uneven. Segregation in the OKC schools primarily stretched throughout the 1960s and early 1970s until they instituted forced bussing. As Cayton (1977) noted,

> Oklahoma public schools took no action toward desegregation in the year following the decision on May 17, 1954. To be sure, there were many meetings held and some planning done; but, everywhere there was the attitude of waiting until the Supreme Court tells us what to do. (p. 112)

Rural schools moved steadily to integrate while "urban areas were procrastinating to maintain the status quo" (Cayton, 1977, p. 121). Even 7 years later, Cayton (1977) noted the City schools were "as segregated as [they had been] since statehood" (p. 121). Douglass was one of eight all-Black schools in the state and one of three situated in all-Black communities. Although "in 1961, there were no blacks attending Northeast [High] and no whites attending Douglass" (Cayton, 1977, p. 121), a family with a child attending Douglass posed a legal challenge to the continuing segregation in the schools (*Dowell v. School Board of Oklahoma City Public Schools*) that limited their child's education. A district court decided in Dowell's favor in 1963. The reverberations of the case stretched for decades, stimulating a series of changes in segregation practices (Cayton, 1977). Yet, as late as 1974, only two Eastside communities were integrated (Cayton, 1977). Many narrators in this study note the benefits of it staying that way.

DOUGLASS HIGH'S COMMUNITY CULTURAL WEALTH

Familial, aspirational, social, and resistance capital in Douglass communities are evidenced in both archival and oral history resources. Although a comprehensive history of Douglass High is beyond the scope of this essay, we focus on four aspects of Douglass's evolution to highlight these forms of capital: (a) the integration of school and community life, (b) the varied, holistic, and aspirational curriculum, (c) the role models and social networks, (d) and the effects of desegregation. We conclude with community members' enduring investment in narrating Douglass history as a symbol of Black pride and resistance.

In the early 1900s, Black schools, including Douglass, were woven into the fabric of surrounding communities. One of OKC's Black newspapers, *The Black Dispatch*, reported activities at Douglass regularly. The paper was run by the formidable Roscoe Dunjee, an OKC activist and journalist instrumental in state politics and civil rights. He was an early leader of the NAACP and a "clarion voice for freedom and justice in the mid-Southwest" (Hadley, 1981, p. 50) for decades. Dunjee's newspaper often devoted a column to Douglass, announcing cultural and musical events, demonstrations of student learning, graduation reports, and teachers' activities. For instance, columns reported on domestic science demonstrations and invited community members, parents, and friends to support the girls' making of candy, bread, and other work (Douglass High, 1918). It dedicated front page space to celebrate thousands of people attending a Douglass' graduation (Barbour Talks to Graduates, 1918, p. 1).

Community participation in school life seemed vital. For one 1918 event, teachers noted they would open an exhibition from 7:30 am to 10:30 pm "to accommodate the working people" (Exhibit, 1918, p. 8). Emphasizing the value of affirming students, the column urged visitors to "show your appreciation by coming out" and "come everybody and enjoy the day" (p. 8) to see student exhibits of sewing, furniture, and mechanical drawings. Events included athletics, music, and literary societies (e.g., Music Festival, 1918; Randolph, 1921). Circulating information about such events could both reflect and foster social capital (Yosso, 2005). The diversity of programming might provide skills to "maintain hopes and dreams for the future" (Yosso, 2005, p. 77). Some described the downtown community in these animated terms. Ralph Ellison, famed author of *Invisible Man*, graduated with honors from downtown Douglass in 1931. He was a first chair trumpet player and conductor of the school band. Oklahoma historian Franklin (1994) said of Ellison's (1914–1994) early years in OKC, "he absorbed the rhythm of black life, especially its music, and he appreciated his community's zest for living even with a society that sought to restrain black individuality" (p. 274).

The local presses commonly reported the accomplishments of Douglass teachers. The domestic art teacher in 1921, Mrs. Foster, won a "diploma" for sharing "the largest collection" and "neatest work" in an exhibit in Memphis (Randolph, 1921, p. 5). Reports about community members' activities sometimes referred to them as Douglass alumni as an apparent point of pride, such as alumni visiting the City for business. In 1918, for instance, the paper announced the military promotion of John C. Whittaker, Jr., Douglass alumnus and son of a prominent professor. Whittaker's image appeared on the front page alongside a photograph with his fellow soldiers. Other reports of service members in World War I also appeared.

The constitutive relationship between the school and community life were also evident in the oral histories of those who attended Douglass later in the century, after it moved. Nannette Allen, who grew up in a segregated OKC area in the 1960s, conveys the vitality of the community, as well as its racial boundaries.

> It was all Black. We had all Black businesses—I mean it was prominent. You had restaurants, you had cleaners, movie theatres, grocery stores, dentist's offices. And, the area which we moved in, my mom was a teacher, it was all Black. You didn't really need to go out of the community for anything... Most of the time you could even walk to church because the churches were in the community. But, you had everything right there in your own community... you probably had about 10 elementary schools. We had 2 junior highs, which are middle schools now. And then we had 2 senior high schools.
>
> In my neighborhood we had cleaners, we had...two grocery stores, we had movie theaters. Then as you went down toward 2nd street, which is now Bricktown, you had

> all types of barber shops, restaurants, hotels, Jewell Theatre….You could just name everything. It was so many Black businesses in the community. It was amazing.

The self-sustaining resources are evident in Allen's reflections as is a sense of vibrancy and belonging, as expressed in her language, "your own community." Donna Morgan-Gabriel (2020), who, like Allen, grew up during the 1960s, lived in OKC throughout her life. As a child she also lived in an all-Black community. She recalled that everyone in the community knew each other, just as she knew the young man who became her husband. These communal bonds fostered the social capital of being seen, known, and part of a broad network of resources. She shared,

> We had families that I had grown up with my entire life… My husband and I have been knowing each other since we were nine years old because we grew up in the same community…So yes, growing up there—no desegregation at all. I don't remember seeing or living with a Caucasian or an Indian or Asian child at all. School wise yes, they were there. Not very many in Douglass, but in my community none at all.

Stepeny, who graduated decades later (2002), similarly noted the networks of support circulating through and around Douglass that echoed Yosso's (2005) framing of the instrumental and emotional support characteristic of social and familial capital. He (2020) said,

> It was a real big culture as far as the sense of pride. Everybody knew everybody. It was like a big family, you should say. . . . Community-wise, we had a lot of support…from businesses to churches, parents. We had a huge parent involvement here at Douglass.

Nanette Allen (2020) noted similar patterns of connection. In particular, she described the community's respect for the school's mission and role models. The sense of kinship across community roles points to familial capital. To illustrate, Donna Morgan-Gabriel (2020) shared,

> We had respect for each other. And if the parents saw something wrong they would talk to each other about what your kid might have been doing…everybody stuck together. The teachers knew your parents, because even in school the teachers were like, "Well I know your mom, I'll just call her up."… Ya know, you had a sense of church, home, community, family, and everything. And even my neighbors now, we're just like family that I grew up with. And I've been knowing them 62 years of my life, ya know.

Most importantly, Morgan-Gabriel remembered her schoolmates were all Black. She described a "wonderful" experience in attending segregated schools in which "everybody looked like you." Although some teachers were White, "all the students were like me. The students were Black students . . . we forged everlasting friendships."

School Experiences and Curriculum

Aspirational and resistant capital were also visible in Douglass' curriculum oriented toward instilling cultural pride and knowledge, exposing students to a range of job skills, and cultivating a spirit of joy, belonging, and resistance. Cayton's (1977) study of Oklahoma Black education noted that early public-school curriculum provided only cursory information likely to further cement the inequities between Black and White citizens. Yet he notes Douglass as an "exception" (Cayton, 1977, p. 98). In 1934–35, when the school moved to High Street on the Eastside to begin a series of expansions, "it opened with a curriculum specifically designed to meet the [Black] children of its community" (Cayton, 1977, p. 98). Music and social events strengthened that curriculum. *The Black Dispatch* detailed community services at Douglass that convey these values and reflected the school as a center of community life. These services included health testing, voting, athletics, adult literacy, and veterans' services.

One example of Douglass's holistic, visionary pedagogy was the robust music program led for 40 years by Mrs. Zelia N. Page Breaux (1886–1956). Beginning in 1921, Mrs. Breaux served as a music teacher. She was instrumental in developing opportunities for the City's Black children to learn and perform music. Breaux, the daughter of Inman Page (1853–1935), principal at Douglass (1921–1922), envisioned classical music training as a vital avenue to cultivate students' life skills. In 1923, she organized a school band, which remains a point of pride today (Dickerson, 2019). She implemented glee clubs, orchestras, choruses, and supported students who grew to become remarkable musicians and artists like Ellison. Breaux's holistic pedagogical approach integrated the school and arts community. She managed the local Aldridge Theater which hosted plays and musical visionaries (e.g. Ma Rainey and Bessie Smith), further linking the school within rich artistic networks. She established the music program at Langston, an HBCU land grant institution, located about 40 miles north of OKC. These role models were sources of pride. As Stepeny (2020) remembered,

> Douglass was the place that people wanted to go. When celebrities, African American celebrities, politicians, they came to Douglass. This was the place where they actually came to break bread with people. Douglass was where everybody wanted to be in the band. They wanted to do something.

Arnold, an author and community activist, remembered the cultural knowledge and aspirational spirit that suffused Douglass. The earliest of the graduates represented in Brown's (2020) oral history collection, Arnold attended during the 1950s when F. D. Moon was principal.

> We knew that knowledge was power 'cause we heard that all the time. And we knew that we were supposed to put our best foot forward at all times to try to reach our full potential, that was just kinda ingrained in us through our education at Douglass High School. It was great.

One narrator framed this vitality as emerging from the community's full commitment to Douglass because of its unique role as a locus of belonging and aspiration for the future of the OKC Black community. The lessons at Douglass transcended course topics; her narrative reveals the teachers' modeling of aspirational and resistant capital.

> I can tell you one thing that those teachers, if they were not the most current books, they taught the hell out of us. I mean, they made sure we learned. They cared about us. Anybody that came out were pretty much scholars.

Allen (2020) also remembered the advantages of the diverse curriculum:

> You had skills in school because you had home economics where you could learn how to cook. You could learn how to sew. You had cosmetology. You had arts and crafts. You had welding. You had woodwork, woodshop, auto body. I have two classmates right now that have been very successful with their body shop from what they learned in high school.

During the 1940s and 50s, F.D. Moon embraced an expansive vision of education for Black youth oriented to aspirational capital. What others called "extra curricular" activities, were in fact, to Moon, *integral* to his philosophy of education (Moon, 1978). The trades had a long history at Douglass essential to a holistic curriculum preparing students beyond high school. Later attendees, such as Cecil McCurdy, described this curricular strength. McCurdy (2020), who attended in the 1970s, linked these skills to self-sufficiency and career development.

> The Vo-tech center right here...was incredible. I had taken workshop, I had taken printing, we literally had to set the type and send it through. We'd do stuff for the school or newspaper or the community... and we would actually do the advertising...it was awesome because you could finish here at Douglass with an apprenticeship—journeyman, electrician, seamstress, auto mechanics, brick masonry. It was so prestigious you could come out with a high school diploma and ready to start your career... find something that you can do with your hands and you can work for yourself.

More recent alumni, such as Stepeny (2020), also described the long tradition of career and technical education integral to the message of autonomy cultivated in the school.

> Vo-tech was the heart of the curriculum of the school. I don't believe that there was a lot of absenteeism, well a high absenteeism. We had a lot of kids that were involved,

and it was hands-on. I just believe that that's the reason why a lot of kids kept coming to school, even in their life situations. Kids came to school.

Vocational instructors and practitioners taught skills in technical trades in the school and on site in Black community businesses (e.g. Perry publishing, tire shops/auto mechanics, cosmetology*)*. This practice represents links between aspirational and social capital. Courses and hands-on practice taught students a trade to enable financial vitality and independence.

Stepeny (2020) remembered a variety of technical options:

> After school, they had activities. You can still work on cars, you can build on your project, you can still do cosmetology. We had a print shop. There was never a day that kids then [went] without a haircut or kids didn't [have] their hair done. That's why I think it was much pride here, because people had the tools here at school, and so they utilized it.

These examples underscore how trade skills served both students and businesses in the Black community. Stepeny (2020) emphasized, "We didn't really have to go outside the school…because we had everything we needed here at the school." The home economics program helped prepare food for athletic events. The idea the school had "everything they needed" resulted from the vo-tech programs. Although some criticized the quality of Douglass education, Nanette Allen (2020) argued the opposite, linking the high school curriculum to a successful career track:

> [T]hey claim that…one of the reasons that the *Brown v. Board of Education* wanted us to have [desegregation]— because they said that the schools …were not getting proper education and they weren't getting the most current books and things like that. Russell Perry, who's the owner of the *Chronicle,* started his business based on what he learned from printing press in high schools. So, you know, those kinds of skills were taught to us. And, they also encouraged us, a lot of us to go to college.

The Trojan tradition extended to athletics, which were another point of pride. Robert Hubbard (2020), who graduated in 1969, discussed the athletic figures and traditions that became ingrained in community memory and lore. He said,

> Growing up, especially on the Eastside, if you thought you wanted to be an athlete everybody wanted to be a Trojan. We knew about the Ben Harts, we knew about the Connie Slaters, the Prentice Gautts, all those players that we witnessed as children. Finally when we got to this place, this school, we were just enthralled to be part of it, part of the program, the tradition, the history, the winning.

The accomplishments of alumni such as Gautt became legendary in the community underscoring the aspirational capital integral to Douglass and narratives about its history. Gautt was the first Black football player at the University of Oklahoma, attending before *Brown* (1956–59), a professional football player, and later, earned his Ph.D. and coached at the University of Missouri. His story is but one example of alumni's narrative of the value of a Douglass education—a hopeful resistant curriculum that fostered belonging, transcended course content, and stretched across the years.

Educational Leaders

Meaningful teachers were integral to narrators' memories of Douglass. Arnold described a teacher who recognized and helped cultivate her love of writing and history with an assignment focused on Black history. Given that 1950s textbooks would have likely erased Black history altogether (LeSure, 1982), this research would have fostered a meaningful sense of leaders' multidimensional achievements. Anita Arnold remembered,

> I was asked by my negro history teacher to write a little book for negro history week, it was a week then, not a month. And that was my first experience at writing a little book, and I said, "I don't know how to write a book" and he said, "I'll tell you some of the things you need to know and you can write it from there." So he kinda, you know, had me divide it up into categories—science, sports, music, like that—and then go and research ... important African Americans, negroes at that time, in America. And so, I did, it was a Black history project and that was my first little published book and I still have it.

This represents a collective example of aspirational, resistant, and familial capital for children exposed to this type of assignment. It reflects the teacher's choice to sidestep dominant historical narratives to create an assignment on Black history that designated Arnold as agent and curator. Such research and writing assignments further exposed Arnold, and likely other children, to Black history and achievements (Yosso, 2005) that may have nurtured her lifelong interest in the topic.

Cumulatively, such choices might have fostered familial capital as well, "those cultural knowledges nurtured among familia (kin) that carry a sense of community history" and memory, also nourishing in the young artist a vision of aspirations for the future (Yosso, 2005, p. 78). Arnold (2020) took these lessons to heart:

> We were all taught that we should listen to our teachers, we should strive to be the very best that we could be. It didn't matter about our circumstances, we knew that. And so that's why it was important for me to write that story about our education because we felt very privileged not under-privileged. We didn't know what that was.

School attendees described how the leaders embodied such aspirations through their presence, encouragement, and commitment. Like Arnold's reflections on her history teacher, Allen (2020) described:

> A lot of people talk about the sports, but they forget that we had four Merit Scholars that [came] out of here at the same time. The time that I was here, our teachers

pushed us to the limit. They didn't just teach out the book. They added more things that we can get our hands on, you know. It was hands-on activities, also. I never remember any of our teachers even being absent from school. They were always here, and they did extra. That education here was wonderful for me.

Segregation necessitated that teachers improvise and supplement books which were incomplete or contained old information.

Allen's (2020) narrative underscored community aspirations. She described the mentors guiding, teaching, and modeling that create "dispositions to maintain hopes and dreams for the future" (Yosso, 2005, p. 77) against the backdrop of structural racial barriers. She further stated,

> They wanted us to be strong. Not only did they teach us classroom information, but they instilled in us a sense of pride and dignity in ourselves. I guess because they had so much pride in themselves, the way they carried themselves, that they instilled in us a sense of pride. Because, the whole world was, uh, you know, we were still segregated so you still had that racism going on. But they were teaching us to be a proud race.

Stepeny (2020) similarly remembered stories about the quality of educators.

> You had spectacular, I mean amazing educators. When bussing came about [...] they wanted our teachers. That's the first thing they came and got, is our teachers. Based on what I heard from people that was in that era, is that they came and got the teachers first. When you look at it, all the teachers that were here back in those days, they were professors...They became great people of Oklahoma, of this world.

Morgan-Gabriel (2020) remembered that office staff also served as role models (p. 149).

Some narrators said that Douglass helped prepare them for an integrated world. The familial networks between the school and the community created a multi-generational support system. Allen (2020) shared,

> Majority of the teachers that taught us, they taught our parents. Or they either went to school with our parents or our grandparents. So, the education here, they held us to high standards. There was no excuses. They made sure that we could compete with anybody outside of Douglass.

Desegregation Losses and Learning

Scholars have noted (e.g. Fairclough, 2004; Walker, 1996) the diverse costs of school desegregation for Black communities. Analyses of such costs focus on Black students (e.g. Irvine & Irvine, 2007) as well as teachers (e.g. Fultz, 2004). In fact, Shircliffe (2001) recognized that oral histories of pre-*Brown* schooling experiences are sometimes suffused with "romanticized memories of their school experiences" (p. 60) that emphasize the "family like" (p. 59) atmosphere of schools in segregated communities. Fairclough (2004) describes the tone of some histories as "elegiac" (p. 43). Despite the schools' structural inequities, Fairclough (2004) notes of these portrayals, "once stigmatized as symbols of Jim Crow and engines of educational failure, the black schools of the era before *Brown v. Board of Education* (1954) are now portrayed as proud institutions that provided black communities with cohesion and leadership" (p. 43).

Cayton (1977) makes this point in discussing Oklahoma desegregation; Costs of desegregation included its effects on community pride, the closure of Black schools, and teachers losing their jobs. Cayton (1977) writes, "In many communities, the only thing upon which Blacks could look with pride was their schools. When the school ceased to exist, in many instances, pride in the local community suffered" (p. 113). Some Black teachers decried the costs to their careers and insisted they were best positioned to care for the interests of Black children in a hostile world. In 1963, Willa Strong, a Black principal in Southern Oklahoma concerned about the closure of her school, argued "Black teachers knew their own children and would be more interested in them" (LeSure, 1982, p. 89) than Whites would be.

The oral histories presented here echoed this vision of nostalgia and loss. Allen and Morgan-Gabriel, who attended Douglass during the years of desegregating, noted the personal effects of a process that began in the 1960s and continued into the 1970s. Allen (2020) details the warm community in which she thrived as a child and the painful process of moving schools. Yet, Shircliffe (2001) argues that oral histories' nostalgic framing of segregated communities reflects more than a rosy story. He interprets this pattern as conveying the "value of Black school traditions" and "artful critiques of the discriminatory aspects" of school desegregation processes (p. 60). Such framing suggests that disrupting Black community schools also disrupted the familial, aspirational, and social capital that narrators experienced at Douglass. In this sense, narrating empowering stories of pre-segregation life helps forge resistant capital.

OKC narrators' stories are a form of resistant capital in reflecting how Douglass' safety and community nourished their souls, spirits, and bodies. This storying was a vital framing of a profoundly racist period. Despite desegregation's promise for accessing resources long available to White schools, Black students and teachers entering White schools experienced serious psychic, material, and learning costs as the process fragmented communities, ended teaching careers, bussed students, and eroded care. The archival resources we present about Douglass offer examples of symbolic and material community wealth fragmented through desegregation.

Nanette Allen (2020) reflects on "what might have been" without desegregation:

> I think it would have been perfect. I really do. Because, what I saw happen—they removed so many of our good teachers. And took them away....that was part of it in the 70s. Even being able to move out of the community. I think if we could've kept our businesses intact, our families intact, our schools intact and put more ener-

gies into those schools, whether we had old books or not, I think that it would've just been so much more awesome and dynamic for us as a race of a people. To have stayed together.

Moving schools exposed children to communities underprepared for integration, a process that necessitated structural support and time. Morgan-Gabriel (2020) who had to leave Douglass, noted that

> [t]he desegregation was so hard on all the students. Knives, fighting, oh yeah, I think my first week or so, maybe two weeks at Northwest Classen, we didn't even get to have class because it was so disruptive. Fighting, hollering, people throwing stuff at you and everything, it was a very hard time in the 1973 year of moving over from a Black school.

Nearly 20 years post-*Brown*, the challenges of desegregation continued. She endured violence, a long commute, and changes in her school activities, reflecting:

> [I bussed] forty-five minutes from where I lived on Northeast 27th Street all the way to 23rd and May, our school was on 25th and May, that's a long ride. The bus is full of Black students, and when we get to the school we're getting off and we're not met with, "Good morning. Let's have a great day," we're met with tension. I can remember the entire junior year, I would hate to have to go to school. Never feeling comfortable in that place called high school ... I didn't join a lot of things because I was very active at Douglass, band and speech, class president... but when I got to Northwest Classen and I couldn't keep up with the band so I got out....my interest in being involved in things went to null, it went to zero. I didn't want to be there. I don't know—I can say today that was mainly because I wanted to be a Douglass High School graduate because that's where my whole family had come from.

This narrative captures her contrasting experiences between schools, including her psychological stress, and the disruption of her family's intergenerational experience at Douglass. Yet, she also noted the new school better prepared her for the integrated world than Douglass. She was the only narrator that described this difference. For example, she remembered feeling underprepared for the new band:

> Being in a segregated school and then ... going to a desegregated school, I found out that we were not taught the same in Douglass. I was first chair flute, I played the flute, started in eighth grade I believe and then I advanced. Mr. Davis was my band teacher at Douglass and I was the first chair flute when I was a freshman—my end of freshman, beginning of sophomore year. I was a four-point student at Douglass, completely fourpoint. When I transferred...my band skills were so bad that I had to quit the band. I couldn't keep up. (Morgan-Gabriel, 2020)

The new school also provided opportunities to interact with varied racial groups, which she believed helped her working life.

Yet, for some narrators, a sense of loss remained. No other school could compare with Douglass' historical legacy and constitutive spirit born of struggle and resistance. In McCurdy's (2020) view, Douglass was the prototype for all predominantly Black schools: Douglass marched so Northeast, Millwood, and other Black schools in The City could run. Morgan-Gabriel (2020) noted that powerful spirit:

> The games were totally different, it's not the spirit of Douglass High School that they still carry. I was a part of that, and going over here, I'm like, I don't want to be here. We didn't have the class spirit that we had. …the class spirit of the camaraderie and the Glee Club, the cheerleaders, it all changed at Northwest Classen because we became a mixture.

Similarly, McCurdy (2020) pointed to the long tradition of pride that he felt simply could not be replicated.

> Douglass pride and tradition was built through struggle, through people opening up opportunities for others like us to prosper. It's just something that you can't copy. That's where a lot of kids have to understand that Douglass is the originator. If it weren't for Douglass, you wouldn't have Millwood. You won't have Northeast. It's a lot of other schools that won't be around that's predominately Black. I believe that that's where Douglass gets its pride and tradition from.

> Everybody wanted to be here. Even people cried because they couldn't go here, because they were bussing. That's why you had Millwood. When bussing, people that graduated from Douglass, they did not want their kids being bussed.

Conclusion: Pride and the 'Pathway to Greatness'

The enduring pride about Douglass' history, we argue, is one expression of resistant capital that is reflected in the narrators' rich experiences and shared historical narrative of community resilience and thriving. The school is associated with notable figures and achievements across a century of racial tyranny (Arnold, 2018). Its name, like other toponymic symbols, reflects a pattern of aspirational naming tied to significant figures in Black history. The attachment to Douglass High today reflects the attachment to its proud history. Stepeny (2020) noted the relief when in 1998, Douglass "went back to a neighborhood school" after the disruptive three decade practice of forced bussing ended in the OKC schools. Stepeny (2020) remarked,

> I did love when we became a neighborhood school, because our friends were, you know, they'd stay across the street, but they'd be going to another high school. I loved every bit of it, because now we went from going to different schools to now being at the same school. We played community football with each other, and now it's like bringing the family back together and everything.

Some narrators noted external threats to Douglass's future. Allen (2020) mentioned, "I still think eventually… they may try to change Douglass." Increased property values in the area and expanding gentrification has brought in more

Whites acting "like they own the place" (Allen, 2020). As some remarked, newcomers seem to have little sense of the rich history of the Black community they were entering. In 2020, a "Pathway to Greatness" plan began, stimulating the consolidation of schools due to low enrollment. Stepeny (2020) noted that "a lot of people have moved away from the Eastside and will likely have a hard time coming back." The community changes, in turn, affect the schools.

Yet, as our chapter reveals, Douglass is more than a building. It is a powerful example of Black resistance, pride, aspiration, and history enduring for more than a century. Stepeny's (2020) comments reflect broad investment in the origin story of Douglass High and concern for its future—a site of community cohesiveness deeply imbricated in OKC civil rights history. He reflected,

> I want Douglass to be remembered as a place of being original, a place of legacy, a place of pride, a place where nobody can copy. We were the standard. We were the bar that everybody wanted to be.
>
> [...] don't take the history away. Don't take away people that fought sweat, tears, and blood that was here. I'm going on and on because I can think of the Civil Rights leaders that we had here, that graduated from here, that taught here, that marched to have equality. And at the same time, we can't erase that, because those people actually made it and put a stamp here on Douglass. That's the scary part, and I hope that it doesn't change and get into the wrong hands.

Although the current Douglass school remains under threat, in 2007, the National Park Service approved for protection as a historic site the Old Douglass building that served as the heart of the community from 1933–1955 (*Register*, 2007, pp. 8–9). The narrative application detailing the school's influence underscores our analysis here. Douglass, the form notes,

> is more than just the name of a school or a facility where Black students attended school from 1933 to 1974. It is a facility that hosted *an experience for students,* [emphasis added] teachers, parents, and a community culminating in the American dream of earning the priceless gift of an education. It was an experience that transcended the physical limitations of a school building. (*Register*, 2007, pp. 8–9)

It remains, in short, a community school, a site of resistance and belonging, a marker of historical triumph, and a symbol of hope for the future.

NOTE

Autumn Brown collected the majority of data for this study while Lucy Bailey took the lead on writing and historical data.

REFERENCES

Allen, N. (2020). *Interview by A. Brown* [Tape recording]. *Activism in education in the Civil Rights Movement.* [Oral History interview collection]. *Education in Northeast Oklahoma City* (Call number, box number, TBA.). Oklahoma State University.

Arnold, A. (2020). *Interview by A. Brown* [Tape recording]. *Activism in education in the Civil Rights Movement.* [Oral History interview collection]. *Education in Northeast Oklahoma City* (Call number, box number, TBA.). Oklahoma State University.

Arnold, A. G. (2010). *Oklahoma City music: Deep deuce and beyond.* Arcadia Publishing.

Arnold, A. G., & Johnson, J. A. (2018). *Oklahoma City's African American education.* Arcadia Publishing.

Barbour talks to graduates. (1918, May 31). *The Black Dispatch 5(*18), 1. https://gateway.okhistory.org/ark:/67531/metadc152082/?q=The%20Black%20Dispatch%201918

Brown, A. B. (2020). *Activism in education in the Civil Rights Movement* [Oral History interview collection]. *Education in Northeast Oklahoma City* (Call number, box number, TBA.). Oklahoma State University.

Brown, A. B. (2021, February). Two Black Oklahoma women who defined American activism. *The Black Wall Street Times.* https://theblackwallsttimes.com/2021/02/09/two-black-oklahoma-women-who-defined-american-activism/

Cayton, L. (1977). *A history of Black public education in Oklahoma.* [Unpublished doctoral dissertation]. University of Oklahoma.

Dickerson, B. (2019, Aug 16). *Douglass "Pride of the East Side" marches into its 96th year.* . feepressokc. https://freepressokc.com/douglass-pride-of-the-east-side-band-marches-into-its-97th-year/

Douglass High. (1918, Feb 1). *The Black Dispatch* 5(2), 4.

Driskell, J. W. (2014). *Schooling Jim Crow: The fight for Atlanta's Booker T. Washington High School and the roots of Black protest politics.* University of Virginia Press.

Exhibit. (1918, May 10). *The Black Dispatch* 5(15), 8.

Fairclough, A. (2000). Being in the field of education and also being a negro...seems... tragic: Black teachers in the Jim Crow south. *The Journal of American History, 87*(1), 65–91.

Fairclough, A. (2004). The costs of *Brown*: Black teachers and school integration. *The Journal of American History, 91*(1), 43–55.

Franklin, J. L. (1982). *Journey toward hope.* University of Oklahoma Press.

Franklin, J. L. (1994). Black Oklahomans and sense of place. In D. Joyce (Ed.), *'An Oklahoma I had never seen before': Alternative views of Oklahoma history* (pp. 265–279). University of Oklahoma Press.

Franklin, J. L. (2007). Black Oklahomans: An essay on the quest for freedom. In D. Joyce (Ed.) *Alternative Oklahoma: Contrarian views of the sooner state* (pp. 36–51). University of Oklahoma Press.

Fultz, M. (2004). The displacement of Black educators post-*Brown*: An overview and analysis. *History of Education Quarterly, 44*(1), 11–45.

Hadley, W. J. (1981). *Roscoe Dunjee on education: The improvement of Black education in Oklahoma, 1930–1955.* [Unpublished doctoral dissertation]. University of Oklahoma.

Hubbard, R. (2020). *Interview by A. Brown* [Tape recording]. Activism in education in the Civil Rights Movement [Oral History interview collection]. *Education in Northeast Oklahoma City* (Call number, box number, TBA.). Oklahoma State University.

Irvine, J. J., & Irvine, R. W. (2007). The impact of the desegregation process on the education of Black students: A retrospective analysis. *Journal of Negro Education, 76*(3), 297–305.

LeSure, L. L. F. (1982). *Willa A. Strong: An historical study of black Education in southeastern Oklahoma*. [Unpublished doctoral dissertation]. University of Oklahoma.

Lomawaima, T. (1994). *They called it prairie light: The story of Chilocco Indian School*. University of Nebraska Press.

McCurdy, C. (2020). *Interview by A. Brown* [Tape recording]. Activism in education in the Civil Rights Movement [Oral History interview collection]. *Education in Northeast Oklahoma City* (Call number, box number, TBA). Oklahoma State University.

Moon, M. C. (1978). *Frederick Douglass Moon: A study of Black education in Oklahoma*. [Unpublished doctoral dissertation]. The University of Oklahoma.

Morgan-Gabriel, D. (2020). *Interview by A. Brown* [Tape recording]. Activism in education in the Civil Rights Movement [Oral History interview collection]. *Education in Northeast Oklahoma City* (Call number, box number, TBA.). Oklahoma State University.

Morris, J. (2004). Can anything good come from Nazareth? Race, class and African-American schooling and community in the urban south and Midwest. *American Educational Research Journal, 41*(1), 69–112.

Music festival at Douglas school. (1918, May 17). *The Black Dispatch 5*(16), 1.

Natanson, H. (2020, Jan 4). 'We refuse to let people forget': In Virginia, a push to remember historically Black high schools before they disappear. *Washington Post.* https://www.washingtonpost.com/local/education/we-refuse-to-let-people-forget-in-virginia-a-push-to-remember-historically-black-high-schools-before-they-disappear/2020/01/03/3ddd3dea-2e2f-11ea-bcd4-24597950008f_story.html

Randolph, C. (1921, Oct 27). Douglass high school. *The Black Dispatch 6*(47), 5.

Register. (2007). *United States Department of the Interior National Park Service National Register of Historic Places Registration Form*. https://npgallery.nps.gov/GetAsset/9a991625-0503-43bd-a9d1-30df0f21c084

Register. (1989). *United States Department of the Interior National Park Service national register of historic places registration form*. https://npgallery.nps.gov/GetAsset/9a991625-0503-43bd-a9d1-30df0f21c084

Saxe, A. (1969). *Protest and reform: The desegregation of Oklahoma City*. [Unpublished doctoral dissertation]. University of Oklahoma.

Shircliffe, B. J. (2001). 'We got the best of that world': A case for the study of nostalgia in the oral history of school segregation. *The Oral History Review, 28*(2), 59–84. https://doi.org/10.1525/ohr.2001.28.2.59

Stepeny, D. (2020). *Interview by A. Brown* [Tape recording]. Activism in education in the Civil Rights Movement [Oral History interview collection]. *Education in Northeast Oklahoma City* (Call number, box number, TBA.). Oklahoma State University.

Stewart, A. (2013). *First class: The legacy of Dunbar, America's first Black public high school*. Chicago Review Press.

Strong, E. R. (1961). *The historical development of the Oklahoma association of Negro teachers: A study in social change, 1893–1958*. [Unpublished doctoral dissertation]. University of Oklahoma.

Teall, K. (1971). *Black history in Oklahoma: A resource book*. Oklahoma City Public Schools.

U.S. News & World Report. (2020, April 13). *Overview of Douglass High School.* https://www.usnews.com/education/best-high-schools/oklahoma/districts/oklahoma-city/douglass-high-school-156034

Walker, V. S. (1996). *Their highest potential.* The University of North Carolina Press.

Whittaker, J. C. (1918, Oct 4). *The Black Dispatch*, 5(36), 1. https://gateway.okhistory.org/ark:/67531/metadc152099/?q=The%20Black%20Dispatch%201918

Yosso, T. (2005). Whose culture has capital? A critical race theory discussion of community cultural wealth. *Race, Ethnicity and Education, 8*(1), 69–91.

CHAPTER 8

A LABOR OF LOVE

The Origin, Development, and Legacy of A.H. Parker High School in Birmingham, Alabama

Penny S. Seals
The University of Alabama at Birmingham

In the fall of 1900, through the coordinated efforts of a group of African American citizens, Negro High School, later known as Industrial High School became the first 4-year public high school for African American students in Birmingham, Alabama. In 1939, Industrial High was renamed A.H. Parker High School after the inaugural principal, Dr. Arthur Harold Parker, and at one point in history was known as the "largest and best high school" for African American students in the country (World's Biggest, 1950). Drawing on archival documents, including Parker's 1932 autobiography entitled, *A Dream That Came True: Autobiography of Arthur Harold Parker*, this chapter describes the origin, development, and abiding legacy of an ethos of care that historically existed within Parker High School. Through a critical examination of social and cultural capital, this chapter explores (a) the establishment and early history of A.H. Parker High School; (b) the caring attitudes, beliefs, and practices of administrators, faculty, and staff, and their contributions to the development of this learning environment; (c) the institutional policies and structures resulting in its student body's academic and social success; and, (d) the impact of Birmingham's unique sociopolitical history and the unintended consequences of desegregation, namely, the reassigning of well-trained African American teachers and the declining enrollment of African American students, in the contemporary schooling environment of A.H. Parker High School.

Keywords: A.H. Parker High School, Social and Cultural Capital, African American High School, African American Education, Birmingham, Alabama

African Americans have long subscribed to the ideology that education meant freedom and liberation from an oppressive state. To obtain an education was an act of resistance; it served as an indicator of freedom and full citizenship. When southern Whites attempted to impede their educational pursuits, African Americans used creative solutions to circumvent the obstacles. Similarly, discussions of public secondary education for the African American youth of Birmingham, Alabama, was met with massive resistance. Nevertheless, in the fall of 1900, through the coordinated efforts of a group of African American citizens, Negro High School became the first 4-year public high school for African American students in Birmingham, Alabama. In 1910, with the addition of industrial focused coursework, the school became known as Industrial High School. Later, in 1939, the school was renamed A.H. Parker High School after the inaugural principal, Arthur Harold Parker. A.H. Parker High School became known as the "largest and best high school" for African American students in the country (Feldman, 1999; *World's biggest Negro High*, 1950).

Parker's philosophy of teaching emphasized that "real teaching is from the soul, not the mouth and what the teacher is, develops and grows in his pupils... [it] is a labor of love" (Parker, 1932, pp. 18–19). Guided by Christian principles, Parker sought to assemble faculty committed to preparing students for academic and social success within the broader Birmingham community. Similar to the universal themes found in the literature on African American students' positive schooling experiences in segregated schools (Morris & Morris, 2000; Siddle Walker 1996; Sowell, 1976), the administrators, faculty, and staff of A.H. Parker High School created a nurturing educational environment that motivated students

A.H. Parker High School. (Birmingham, Ala. Public Library Archives)

to excel both academically and socially. However, this feat was not accomplished without significant challenges.

During the late nineteenth and early twentieth centuries, varying degrees of racist educational ideologies ranged from moderate to extreme viewpoints concerning implementing universal public schooling for both African Americans and Whites (Anderson, 1988). A coalition of White southerners, opposing the idea of a "classical or college preparatory" schooling environment, were amenable to the idea of a limited moral or vocational education for African American students as it served the self-interests of many White southerners seeking to maintain social order and increase their economic wealth (Anderson, 1988; Loder-Jackson, 2015). Conversely, many White southerners who benefited from an uneducated class of Black laborers opposed the idea of universal education as they deemed it "unnecessary" and a potentially dangerous threat to their economic and political security, as it would position African Americans to be more competitive in the job market, and raise their social consciousness causing them to reject White supremacist ideals (Anderson, 1988; Armbrester, 1993).

Despite conflicting arguments about the need and methods for educating African Americans, in general, White southerners collectively upheld racist notions of White supremacy. For example, in 1900, an editorial in the *Montgomery Advertiser* stated, "The undeniable truth is that the Negro is not fitted to [successfully perform] any work which requires skill, patience, or mental capacity. There is something lacking in their brain and in their body" (Armbrester, 1993; Bond, 1994). Additionally, Dr. John Herbert Phillips, Birmingham City Schools' first superintendent, stated that, "The Black race is to all intents and purposes a young race; therefore, it is imitative…in anything that requires reasoning—in mathematics, for instance—the negro soon falls behind" (Archer, 1910, p.129). While Phillips's perceptions of Black intelligence reflected the hegemonic ideals of the Confederate South, he advocated for the establishment of African American educational institutions (Anderson, 1988; Loder-Jackson, 2015). Harris noted, "The school alone, [Phillips] believed, could make Blacks an asset instead of a burden to the South" (Harris, 1985, p. 396). Phillips' advocacy aligned with his beliefs that African Americans needed to take responsibility for the development of the race. Furthermore, the establishment of educational institutions converged with the interests of the coalition of White southerners who espoused an industrial education for African Americans.

Through a critical examination of social and cultural capital, this chapter explores (a) the establishment and early history of A.H. Parker High School; (b) the caring attitudes, beliefs, and practices of administrators, faculty, and staff, and their contributions to the development of this learning environment; (c) the institutional policies and structures resulting in its student body's academic and social success; and, (d) the impact of Birmingham's unique sociopolitical history and the unintended consequences of desegregation, namely, the reassigning of well-trained African American teachers and the declining enrollment of African

American students in the contemporary schooling environment of A.H. Parker High School.

THEORETICAL FRAMEWORK

Traditional theories of social and cultural capital assert that these forms of capital are the accumulated knowledge, skills, practices, traditions, relationships, and social networks that are class specific and have the potential to reproduce inequitable class structures within society (Bourdieu, 1984, 1986). Bourdieu's theory of social and cultural capital prioritizes White, upper, and middle-class values and contends that these communities have an abundance of generationally transmitted capital, which ultimately leads to increased social mobility. Subsequently, these traditional theories infer that non-White communities are deficient in social and cultural capital, often leading to the reproduction of social and economic inequities. Whereas traditional theories of social and cultural capital have neglected to highlight the unique voices, experiences, and cultures of non-White groups, an examination through a critical lens reveals that historically, African American community leaders and educators utilized social and cultural capital to develop and sustain educational institutions for African American students (Franklin, 2002; Yosso, 2005). Historian V. P. Franklin (2002) defined cultural capital as the "sense of group consciousness and collective identity that serves as an economic resource for the financial and material support of business enterprises aimed at the advancement of an entire group" (p. 177). Franklin's definition is paramount to an understanding of the essential work of the African American community with establishing secondary schools for African American students. Despite limited resources and oppressive social structures, they created innovative learning environments that sought to meet the needs of the whole child and the larger community (Foster, 1993; Franklin, 2002; Siddle Walker, 1996). Historically, it was the combination of the social and cultural capital of the African American community that provided students with opportunities to excel academically, socially, politically, and economically within the broader society.

Like Franklin, Yosso's (2005) scholarship challenges traditional definitions and perspectives of social and cultural capital. Examining social and cultural capital through a Critical Race Theory lens challenges the notion that non-White communities are socially and culturally deficient. Additionally, this approach centers the voices, experiences, and cultural values of marginalized groups and positions their histories as significant. A framework of community cultural wealth identifies six forms of capital that exist within communities of color. These include aspirational, navigational, social, linguistic, familial, and resistant capital. Yosso (2005) defined aspirational capital as the ability to "maintain hopes and dreams for the future, even in the face of real and perceived barriers" (Yosso, 2015, p. 77). Navigational capital includes the skills that individuals possess that allows them to maneuver successfully through social institutions. Social capital refers to the complex social networks and community resources. Linguistic capital refers to the communication skills and experiences that individuals possess. Familial capital can be understood to be "cultural knowledges nurtured among familia (kin) that carry a sense of community history, memory and cultural intuition" (p. 79). Resistant capital includes the skills and knowledge that individuals cultivate through resistant behaviors that challenge inequality (Yosso, 2015). These forms of capital have been instrumental to the establishment and success of African American educational institutions. Aspirational capital was displayed in their resistance to notions of intellectual and social inferiority that propelled them to cultivate their own educational environments so that African American students would have the opportunity to full citizenship and freedom through education.

Furthermore, Siddle Walker's (1996) scholarship on the value of African American segregated schools asserted that African American community leaders and educators made financial sacrifices through their respective social networks and served in advocacy roles to ensure African American students' success. Anderson (1988) aligned this tradition of "self-help" with the double taxation that African Americans experienced throughout the South. According to Anderson, African American southerners were obligated to pay direct and indirect taxes for their public schools. School taxes were primarily utilized for the establishment of schools for White students. Subsequently, African American communities had no choice other than to make private donations to fund their schools (Anderson, 1988). Often, the financial contributions and donations provided by the local African American community surpassed those provided by southern Whites and northern philanthropic agencies (Loder-Jackson, 2015).

Historically, the faculty and staff within A.H. Parker High School served as institutional agents for African American students. They provided students with the knowledge, experiences, and material resources needed to excel within a society that deemed them inherently inferior. This chapter provides a counternarrative to the unique ways African American community leaders and educators developed and maintained complex social networks in pursuit of educational avenues for African American students.

METHODOLOGY

For this historical inquiry, a qualitative research design was utilized to investigate the historic significance of establishing the first public secondary school for the African American youth of Birmingham, Alabama. Qualitative methods provide depth to the research topic. Rossman and Rallis (2012) suggested two features that are unique to qualitative methods. First, the researcher is the means through which the study is conducted. Second, the purpose is to learn about an aspect of the social world. Ultimately, the primary aim of qualitative research is to improve the human condition. Typically, the objective of qualitative research is to identify those factors that have the potential to assist with generating undiscovered data that is appropriate for researching populations that have previously been silenced or ignored (Creswell, 2007).

Furthermore, a qualitative historical inquiry has the potential to increase the understanding of how A.H. Parker High School, as a historic educational institution in Birmingham, Alabama, developed particular events, people, and circumstances that influenced and shaped the school community (Rury, 2002). Moreover, McDowell (2013) contended that the goal of historical research is to provide insight into the "significance of past events and not merely regard these events as an unconnected series of facts" (p. 10). Additionally, archival research was employed to collect relevant data and to identify emerging themes.

Data Analysis

Drawing on historical archival documents from the Birmingham Public Library Archives Department, including Parker's 1932 autobiography entitled, *A dream that came true: Autobiography of Arthur Harold Parker*, this chapter describes the origin, development, and abiding legacy of an ethos of care that historically existed within A.H. Parker High School. This chapter relies heavily on secondary resources from historical African American newspaper articles, such as, the *Birmingham Mirror*, and *Birmingham World*. Additional historical newspapers include *Birmingham News*, *Birmingham Post*, *Birmingham Age-Herald*, *Christian Science Monitor*, and *School Life*. Furthermore, excerpts from scholarly works include James Anderson's *The Education of Blacks in the South, 1860–1935;* Adam Fairclough's *Black Teachers in the Segregated South: A Class of Their Own;* Margaret Armbrester's *Samuel Ullman and "Youth": The Life, the Legacy;* and Tondra Loder-Jackson's *Schoolhouse Activist African American Educators and the Long Birmingham Civil Rights Movement.*

Additionally, both published and non-published historical documents and reports were reviewed and analyzed to provide a detailed understanding of the institutional narrative of Parker High School. These historical documents include school records, school board minutes, and excerpts from selected texts. The secondary sources utilized in this study were used to build upon and interpret primary sources. Primary and secondary sources were organized and coded to identify emerging patterns and themes relevant to historical accounts and events. A thorough analysis provided a comprehensive understanding of the historical significance of A.H. Parker High School. Preset concepts and those that emerged as analysis progressed are discussed in the findings section of this chapter.

FINDINGS

The following section documents the findings and the relevant themes that were extrapolated from select primary and secondary resources. This discussion examines the establishment and early history of A.H. Parker High School, the caring attitudes, beliefs, and practices of administrators, faculty, and staff, and their contributions to the development of this learning environment, the institutional policies and structures resulting in its student body's academic and social success, and the impact of Birmingham's unique sociopolitical history and the unintended consequences of desegregation.

A.H. Parker High School's Establishment and Early History

In Birmingham, Alabama, the task of educating Black children was assumed by the local Black community as funding for schools was disproportionately distributed to support White communities and schools. In the late 1800s, a group of African American citizens led by Dr. William Reuben Pettiford, Mr. B. H. Hudson, and his wife, Hattie Hudson, organized and led a campaign to develop the first public high school for the African American youth of Birmingham, Alabama (Anderson, 1988; Feldman, 1999). A prominent African American leader within the Birmingham community, Pettiford was a former school principal and educator, pastor of the Sixteenth Street Baptist Church, and president of Alabama Penny Saver's Bank (Fallin, 2007). With the endorsement of Birmingham's Board of Education President, Samuel Ullman, African American leaders were able to gain approval to establish a public high school for African American students (Armbrester, 1993; Fallin, 2007; Feldman, 1999; Loder-Jackson, 2015). As the President of the Birmingham Board of Education, Ullman's support and advocacy was instrumental to the board's approval for the establishment of A.H. Parker High School. However, while they advocated for African American educational initiatives, White educational leaders, such as Ullman and Superintendent Phillips, embraced motives and ideals embedded in White supremacy. Ullman held that a curriculum that included a combination of a classical and industrial education would benefit African Americans while maintaining the status quo (Armbrester, 1993). In fact, Ullman stated, "Nearly all our domestic help are colored, and as such are in daily contact with our children; hence the duty of raising their moral standard [is] indicated as much as their educational standard" (p. 39). Rather than arguing the moral position for educating African Americans, Ullman's argument was rooted in the interests of southern Whites who desired for their children not to be influenced by uneducated domestic workers. Although Superintendent Phillips had reservations concerning this pursuit, he was ultimately persuaded by the coalition of African American leaders as they guaranteed that the cost of the public high school would be supplemented by the tuition of enrolled students (Harris, 1985; Parker, 1932).

Superintendent Phillips selected Arthur Harold Parker, a close friend and protégé of Pettiford, to serve as the new high school principal. Parker stated, "To this day I do not know why he selected me from the many from whom he could select. I gave him my word that I would roll up my sleeves and go to work with all my might" (Parker, 1932, p. 34). With an initial enrollment of 18 students, Negro High School was birthed in a single classroom on the second floor of the Cameron Elementary School (Brown, 1959; Fairclough, 2007; Parker, 1932). The Cameron School was a likely choice for the initial space for the high school as it was an established African American elementary school where A.H. Parker had previously served as an educator and later as a principal (Feldman, 1999; Parker, 1932). Parker recalled the first morning, "I remember Mrs. B.H. Hudson, Reverend Wilhite, Reverend Williams, Dr. Pettiford, and a few others. We were so happy over beginning that first morning that we made speeches, sang and prayed almost the entire morning" (Parker, 1932, p. 35). This coalition of African American leaders pledged their full support to ensure the school's success (Brown, 1959; Parker, 1932). By the end of the first year, enrollment had reached 45 students. As was customary for all schools in Alabama, enrolled students at Negro High School paid a monthly tuition rate of $1.50.

In 1904, Negro High held its first commencement ceremony at the Sixteenth Street Baptist Church, where 15 students, 5 boys and 10 girls, became the first graduates. Parker quickly realized that the school was outgrowing its current location. His ultimate dream was to build a school for the African American youth of Birmingham that would benefit students and the greater African American community.

Due to increasing enrollment, in September of 1910, the school was relocated to a wooden frame building that was previously known as Lane's Auditorium. While the physical shape of the building was not equivalent to educational institutions that were built for White students, Parker noted, "The character of the building in which we worked never dampened the unbounded enthusiasm for the work" (Parker, 1932, p. 45). In addition, this larger space allowed Parker to hire additional African American teachers and offer more courses that specifically focused on industrial work. With the addition of formal industrial training courses, the school became known as Industrial High School. Similar to Booker T. Washington, A.H. Parker embraced an industrial curriculum for the uplifting of the African American community. Parker believed that schools should teach students how to efficiently and effectively perform the "everyday" (Parker, p. 35) tasks and duties available to them. Consequently, initial courses at Industrial High included woodworking, carpentry, gardening, and sewing. However, with the addition of new faculty, J. R. Coffey, there was more interest in teaching classical than industrial courses, such as "…science, philosophy, and the languages" (p. 36). While Parker's autobiography does not further expound on Coffey's interest in classical coursework, it does highlight Parker's willingness to accommodate the interests of his faculty.

The following years brought many firsts to Industrial High School. In 1911, Parker established the first night school for adults in Birmingham, enrolling 60 students the first year (Parker, 1932). Additionally, in 1912, Parker established the first summer school for African American educators in Birmingham at Industrial High School. The summer institute lasted for six weeks and served three primary purposes for African American teachers—providing preparation to meet the standard requirements for the teacher's examination for Alabama, improving teacher scholarship in special topics, and preparation for more effective and efficient instruction in industrial coursework (Parker, 1932).

However, during the summer of 1914, the city inspector condemned Industrial High School due to the dilapidated wooden structure. Parker negotiated with the city commissioner to secure an appropriate building that would house students. The entire student body assisted with moving into the new space and transforming the rooms into classrooms (Fairclough, 2007; Parker, 1932). The boys reconstructed the rooms and painted the building interiors, while the girls cleaned and decorated the classrooms (Fairclough, 2007; Parker, 1932). Next door to the new location was a lot that contained 14 cottages. Again, Parker negotiated with the City Commissioner and Superintendent Phillips to secure this lot and the accompanying cottages for the school's use. While the Board of Education only made provisions for the paint, the community and the students of Industrial High School renovated and furnished the 14 cottages (Parker, 1932). Parker (1932) recalled, "While we were thus building and making our own schoolhouses—there was being built into the [fiber] of the spirit of the school a strength and purpose that made it irresistible" (p. 65). As Franklin (2002) noted in his scholarship, "members were willing to donate money, energy, time, and other resources to support these 'business enterprises' because these institutions were perceived as beneficial to an entire group" (p. 177). Educational pursuits within the African American community have not been viewed as social or cultural capital that benefited students or the larger community. However, the Industrial High School community displayed social capital through their collective efforts to support the schooling environment. The Industrial High School community realized the importance of having an educational institution that would afford African American students the opportunity to gain an education.

As the only public secondary school for African American students in Birmingham, Industrial High School enrolled students across socioeconomic statuses. However, some middle-class African Americans criticized Industrial for focusing on an industrial curriculum and opted to enroll their children in local private schools (Feldman, 1999; Loder-Jackson 2015). Moreover, the school was criticized by some within the African American community as giving preferential treatment in hiring practices to lighter-skinned educators (Feldman, 1999). However, Parker attempted to create an atmosphere where all students were treated equally. For example, an article in the *Birmingham News* provides an account of a local, White news reporter's visit to the school. Mistaking the girl sweeping the floor as a "janitress," Parker corrected the news reporter and responded that the girl is a student and the daughter of one of the "most wealthy Negroes of the city" (Childers, 1933, para 6). Furthermore, Parker stated, "there is no difference who they are...when they enter high school, they know that they're going to have to work with brooms as well as with books (Childers, 1933). Industrial High School did not just benefit the students who attended, but it benefited the entire community. It was a source of pride for the students and the larger African American community in Birmingham, Alabama. The African American communities surrounding Industrial High School supported the school's educational pursuits by attending events and contributing to efforts to sustain the community institution. For instance, the community attended school concerts, programs, and commencement exercises. The African American community desired to support the efforts of the school, but also benefited from these programs as they served as cultural experiences that were often limited to African Americans in the early history of the school (Feldman, 1999). Moreover, an article in the *Birmingham Age-Herald* noted that in the spring of 1913, the mothers, and teachers, seeing the need for a more inexpensive method of dressing young girls, together decided to implement student uniforms. In another instance, the Mother's Improvement Association furnished the medicines for nursing students, and in 1920 when the school organized a band, students borrowed instruments from the local Black community members (Feldman, 1999). These instances provide examples of the ways in which the community collaborated with the educational institution by making personal sacrifices and lending their own resources that the African American youth of Birmingham could be educated.

In 1932, Industrial High School reached an "enrollment of nearly 3,000 students" making it the largest high school for African American students in the Country (Caliver, 1932, p. 11). Angela Davis, renowned political activist, author, and alumna of Parker High School stated,

> If Parker was the 'largest high school for colored pupils,' it was for the same reason that there was not a single public high school in Harlem and the same reason that the education of Black youth in South Africa doesn't merit a grain of consideration. (Davis, 1974, p. 99)

Davis's statements acknowledge the storied histories of African American educational pursuits and how White supremacist notions of the inferiority of African Americans permeated through all aspects of society, primarily the establishing of educational institutions. To this end, the cultural capital that was harnessed to establish and sustain Parker High School was essential, particularly because of the large number of African American students that were served by this singular high school.

Brown (1959) stated, "Few high schools in the South…had graduated more students than Parker. From 1904, when the first class of 15 students graduated… through May 1959, a total of 18,599 students had been awarded the high school diploma" (p. 38). Industrial High School would later be renamed A.H. Parker High School after the inaugural principal, Arthur Harold Parker. Parker's school colors would become purple and white, and the Bison served as the school mascot. Through the years, the school's nickname became "The Thundering Herd."

Determined to provide Birmingham's African American youth with a complete education, Parker created an environment where students excelled academically and socially. In addition, the students, faculty, and staff espoused a spirit that reflected strength and purpose. Despite discriminatory policies and less than adequate resources, Parker attributed the success of this schooling environment to the unrelenting spirit of the students, faculty, and staff.

THE LEGACY OF BLACK EDUCATORS AT A.H. PARKER HIGH SCHOOL

Students within historical African American schools were not only prepared to be academically successful but were prepared for life. Many African American educators possessed a political clarity that allowed them to have insight into the interior lives of their students. They were familiar with the everyday experiences of their students and thereby sought to prepare them academically and socially for a racist society that deemed them intellectually and socially inferior. Within A.H. Parker High School, administrators and teachers were remembered for their zeal and dedication towards the students within this community school.

Arthur Harold Parker's Visionary Leadership

Arthur Harold Parker was born May 7, 1870, to two former slaves. His father was born a slave in Decatur, Alabama, but at the age of 12, he escaped by way of the Underground Railroad, ultimately making it to Canada. Parker's father remained in Canada until the end of the Civil War and then relocated to Springfield, Ohio, where he met and married Parker's mother. Parker's mother was also born into slavery but was granted freedom with the passage of the Emancipation Proclamation in 1863 (Parker, 1932). According to Parker's autobiography, upon his mother's freedom, she and her three sisters were provided funds for an education, and each was provided a home by their former owner, who was also their biological father (Parker, 1932). After high school, Parker's plans to study law at Oberlin College in Ohio were interrupted when his father fell ill. So instead, Parker worked as a barber in his father's barbershop until he decided to seek opportunities in the South.

Parker arrived in Birmingham, Alabama, in August of 1887. At the persuasion of his uncle on his father's side, who was teaching in the Birmingham School System, Parker took the teacher's examination and received a third-grade teaching certificate. Superintendent Phillips appointed Parker to serve as a teacher at the Slater School. Thus, Parker became the 13th African American teacher to serve in the Birmingham Public School system (Fairclough, 2007; Loder-Jackson, 2015; Parker, 1932). Immediately, Parker became captivated with the profession. "Right at the very first I became fascinated with the work of teaching, and as much so, with the prestige that such a position carried among my own people" (Parker, p. 12). To supplement his income as a teacher, Parker continued to barber. In 1892, Parker was appointed principal of Cameron Elementary School.

Early on, Parker adopted a philosophy of care that was evident through his perspectives on the role and responsibility of the teacher. Broadly, Parker believed that all individuals were teachers and were obligated to function within that purpose. Specifically, Parker held teachers in high esteem and cautioned that teachers have a great responsibility to students. In fact, Parker (1932) argued that "By taking the position of the teacher, all responsibility is assumed, a responsibility not only for what is done but for what is not done, and there is no escaping the responsibility" (p.17). Additionally, Parker expressed that:

> Real teaching is from the soul, not the mouth, and what the teacher is, develops and grows in his pupils. The boys and girls of today must draw in deep and holy inspirations and form noble and lofty ideals. The profession of teaching needs the best product that the race produces. It needs men and women who are morally, mentally, and physically strong and sound. Real teaching must truly be a labor of love. (Parker, 1932, pp.18–19)

Initially, Parker's fascination with the profession was superficial as he enjoyed the prestigiousness of the position. However, as Parker's philosophy evolved, he understood the importance and significant responsibility educators had to the students and the larger African American community.

Through his service to the community and the educational landscape of Birmingham, Parker became respected by many in the African American community and by those within the White community. Parker considered Superintendent Phillips a friend and even grieved over the loss of his dear friend after his passing (Parker, 1932). Likewise, Superintendent Phillips held Parker in high esteem and often boasted about the great work that Parker was doing at Industrial High School. Moreover, in early 1900, Parker was elected President of the Alabama State Teachers' Association (Loder-Jackson, 2015; Parker, 1932). And, in 1933, Parker was awarded an honorary doctorate by the Miles Memorial College, later known as Miles College, a historically Black college in Fairfield, Alabama.

While Dr. Parker was touted as a great leader by faculty, staff, and students, some criticized his desire to implement an industrial curriculum and accused him of adopting accommodationist perspectives (Loder-Jackson, 2015). For instance, in 1924, W.E.B. Du Bois hurled verbal attacks at Parker in the *Fisk Herald,* calling him "A Negro tool lickspittle," ultimately accusing Parker of acquiescing to the White citizens of Birmingham, most notably, Superintendent Phillips (Du Bois, 1924). Subsequently, Juliet Bradford (1925), one of Parker's faculty at Industrial and an alumnus of Fisk University, wrote back to Du Bois in defense of Parker:

> I regret the unwarranted attack very much that was made upon my principal here. I am a teacher in the Industrial High School and know that the charges made against prof. A.H. Parker are untrue. He has labored faithfully here since the very beginning of the school and has stood for every progressive movement. He has not hindered but has been a wonderful help in the progress of our community educationally. (Bradford, 1925).

The faculty and staff at Industrial valued the work that Parker did for the students and the larger African American community. They believed in his vision to establish and enhance Black education in Birmingham and supported his efforts.

Parker's dream was to build a high school for Black students. In 1924, that dream would be realized with the erection of a high school building. After 50 years of service within Birmingham's educational system and 38 years as principal of Industrial High School, Parker retired in the Spring of 1939 (Jackson, 1939). In recognition of Parker's service to the educational community of Industrial High School, the Board of Education approved a resolution that changed the name of the school from Industrial High School to A.H. Parker High School (Birmingham school named for principal, 1939). However, in August of that same year, Parker died after a long illness, but with his dream of creating a school for African American students in Birmingham realized.

Remembering the Principals

As the inaugural principal of Industrial High School, A.H. Parker set a high standard for administrators, faculty, and staff. While there is a significant amount of documentation on Parker's principalship, largely due to his autobiography and work to establish A.H. Parker High School, there is limited information on the work of many of the administrators who served as principals at Parker. In the history of the school's 121 years, approximately 11 principals have served the educational institution. This section provides brief sketches of notable principals who have contributed to the work and maintenance of the Parker school community after Dr. Parker's tenure.

William Bennett Johnson was born in Selma, Alabama, April 3, 1894 (United Alumni Association, 2000). W.B. Johnson, a graduate of Industrial High School, attended Wilberforce University and in 1917 earned a degree in mathematics. W.B. Johnson began teaching mathematics at Industrial High School in February 1919. However, in 1926, he was called to serve as principal of Lane Elementary School. During this time, Mr. Johnson enrolled at Columbia University in the summers and received a Master of Arts degree in education. Shortly after this accomplishment, Mr. Johnson was appointed assistant principal of Industrial High School and in 1939, upon Arthur Harold Parker's retirement, Mr. Johnson assumed the position of the second principal of A.H. Parker High School. W.B. Johnson served as principal from 1939 through 1947 (United Alumni Association, 2000).

Robert Charles Johnson was born in Oberlin, Ohio, August 11, 1903 (United Alumni Association, 2000). R. C. Johnson earned a bachelor's degree in chemistry from Talladega College and completed a master's degree from Fisk University. R. C. Johnson, a former science teacher at Parker, was appointed principal of Parker High School in 1947 after the death of W.B. Johnson. Remembered as an administrator that was respected and well-regarded by students, he was best known for remembering the names of all his students. R. C. Johnson was principal at A.H. Parker High School during the implementation of Birmingham's desegregation court orders and policies. Under the leadership of R. C. Johnson, Parker implemented a Guidance Program which included two full-time positions for a Girls and Boys club advisor. Furthermore, the Student Council along with other student organizations expanded their involvement to include district, state, and national activities. Parker High School received accreditation by the Southern Association of Colleges and Secondary schools in 1953. Moreover, following in the footsteps of Dr. A.H. Parker, Mr. R. C. Johnson served as the president of the Alabama State Teachers Association (ASTA) from 1948–1950. R. C. Johnson's two daughters, Alma Vivian and Barbara Rose both attended Parker High School. Alma Vivian is the widow of the late Colin Powell, who served as the first African American secretary of state. Mr. Robert Charles Johnson served as principal for 22 years before retiring in 1969.

In 1969, Edward Bennett Thompson, affectionately known as "Bubba," was appointed to serve as the fourth principal of Parker High School (United Alumni Association, 2000). Mr. Thompson was a 1943 graduate of Parker High School and the nephew of W.B. Johnson, the second principal of Parker. It was the hope of Thompson to reignite the spirit of Parker's past while achieving new academic milestones. Thompson served as principal of Parker High School for almost 20 years and retired in 1989 (United Alumni Association, 2000).

Lovie Hayden was appointed interim principal from 1989 to 1990. Previously, Hayden served as a mathematics instructor and department head at Jackson-Olin High School in Birmingham, Alabama before serving as the Assistant Principal at Parker High School. Moreover, while Hayden's tenure as principal was brief, Lovie Hayden was the first and only woman that has served in this role.

Darrell Hudson was appointed principal in 2013. In 2018, Hudson was named District 5 high school principal of the year (Council for Leaders in Alabama Schools [CLAS], 2018). According to Hudson, it is his mission as principal to ensure that all students "reach their maximum potential through engaging lessons taught by skillful educators" (CLAS, 2018, para 2). Mr. Hudson is the current principal of Parker High School.

Remembering the Teachers

Historically, African American educators in segregated schools are remembered for their commitment and dedication to educating African American students. Many teachers viewed their profession as a "calling" or "mission" to make a difference in the life of students (Beauboeuf-Lafontant, 2005; Foster, 1993; Kelly 2010; Morris & Morris, 2000; Siddle Walker, 1996, 2000). Despite inequities and lack of resources, African American teachers were able to create an educational environment for students to excel. They aimed to exhibit an ethos of care that acknowledged students' social, economic, and political positions within the larger society (Rolón-Dow, 2005). Like the narratives of exemplar African American educators within the literature that deemed it their "mission" and "responsibility" to teach and care for students, A.H. Parker High School served as an incubator for student success and racial uplift. Parker's philosophy of care for students was evident throughout the institution. For example, the 1962 student handbook stated:

> Parker High School teachers believe education in a democratic society is an evolutionary process changing, as needs arise, to suit the time and place. Since this is our belief, we hope to enrich the pupil's experiences in life and to develop their potentialities and interests so that they may continue to grow into useful citizens. We hope, further, to increase their abilities to think independently and to develop a sensitivity to individual and social values. We believe that we should help them find and to prepare for work suitable to their mental ability and personality so that they may lead full and happy lives. We believe that our pupils should feel that a good life is one in which a contribution is made to society in which a man's work is well done. (Parker High School Student Handbook, 1962, p. 8)

Parker's teachers deemed it their responsibility to prepare students academically and prepare students for life.

Orlean Kennedy was one of those educators who reflected Parker's philosophy of care. Kennedy, an English teacher, and girls' advisor joined the Industrial faculty in year three. In 1937, Kennedy was honored for 50 years of commitment and dedication to teaching within the Birmingham Public School system and heralded as having the "longest record of service in the entire school system" (School honors teacher, 1937). Kennedy opened her home and served as a foster parent to young orphan girls through the years. According to Kennedy, at least 30 of the girls she cared for followed in her footsteps and became an educator. Like Parker, Kennedy wanted to see the African American youth of Birmingham excel. Through her service as an educator, she embraced an ethic of care necessary for the times.

In 1917, Mr. John T. "Fess" Whatley joined the faculty and organized the printing department and the high school band. School instruments were donated by members of the community (Feldman, 1999). Whatley, affectionately known as "Fess," an abbreviated form of "professor," was remembered as an instructor who demanded discipline and excellence from students. Whatley believed that a music career was one of the few professions open to African Americans (Griffin, 1975). In 1939, Whatley organized a chapter of the American Federation of Musicians union as African Americans were not permitted to join the chapter already in existence due to segregation. Many former students of Whatley experienced great success in the profession. These included Erskine Hawkins, Cleveland Eaton, and Sun Ra (Griffin, 1975).

Within Parker High School, many African American teachers were remembered for their sternness and insistence on excellence and discipline. Mrs. Ossie Ware Mitchell, a 1935 graduate of Parker stated,

I remember crying an entire class period when my sewing teacher made me rip out a seam that wasn't straight. But if I need to make a dress today, I can do it. And if I had to cook for a living, I'd be a very good cook because of what I learned at Parker High School. (Stewart, 1998, p. 25)

Sandra Humes Weems is a retired educator within the Birmingham City Schools. Mrs. Weems was a 1972 graduate of A.H. Parker High School and served as the student body president under the leadership of principal Edward Thompson. Additionally, Mrs. Weems later became a highly regarded faculty member within A.H. Parker High. Students recall that Mrs. Weems instilled the importance of knowing the history of Parker High School into students, requiring them to learn the mission statement and school song (University of Alabama at Birmingham, 2017). In 2018, Parker's Alumni Association inducted Mrs. Weems into its first class of inductees for the Teacher Hall of Fame. These educators were recognized for their commitment to educating the youth at Parker, length of service, going above and beyond their duties, and attempting to keep Dr. Parker's dream alive by nurturing and showing compassion for pupils.

Likewise, Mr. Barry McNealy, a 1985 graduate of Parker, is a current history teacher at Parker. McNealy stated in a recent news interview that his primary aim as an educator is to give to current students what was given to him (WVTM 13 News, 2021). African American educators have and continue to assume the responsibility to care for the students enrolled at Parker to ensure that they are prepared to be the torchbearers for the race.

AN ETHOS OF INSTITUTIONAL CARING

According to Siddle Walker (1993), institutional care "seeks to meet psychological, sociological, and academic needs but provides for those needs to be met directly or indirectly through explicit school policies" (p. 65). Thus, institutional caring reinforces interpersonal interactions and relationships by establishing supportive school policies and structures that seek to meet the needs of the whole child. Historically, Black educators have recognized the importance of both interpersonal caring and institutional caring, as they developed relationships with students and their families, but also created structures and policies within the schooling environment that prepared students for life inside and outside of the classroom (Morris & Morris, 2000; Rolón-Dow, 2005; Siddle Walker 1996, 2000).

The Homeroom Plan

The faculty and staff at Parker High School provided students with opportunities to gain knowledge about civic engagement and responsibility despite the lack of opportunities within the larger society. For example, the homeroom plans provided students with opportunities to learn about the components and processes of a democratic society. Each homeroom functioned as an individual county with its own president. Parker served as the chief executive. Therefore, "if the chief executive, Mr. Parker, wants to tell the counties (the classes) something he tells it to the presidents and they will in turn give the message to the citizens of the counties (students of the classes)" (Class and School Problems, 1932, p. 19). Through this method, Parker provided students with the agency to make decisions while also teaching leadership skills. As a result, the students took their responsibilities seriously and realized how their actions and behaviors were reflected in high school. The following excerpt concerning the homeroom program reflects their commitment to their responsibility: "Let us as individuals do our bit to help exalt the character of this school. It is very true that we are the ones who make the school, and since we are builders, let us build this school" (Class and School Problems, 1932, p. 19). A.H. Parker's homeroom plan is an example of the aspirational and navigational forms of capital that existed within the schooling environment. While African American students were not allowed to exercise their civic duties within the larger society because of obstacles created by federal and local legislation, educators attempted to create opportunities to teach students how to navigate through political processes while also instilling in them the desire and necessary responsibility of participation in civic activities.

Commencement Exercises

Likewise, student commencement exercises provided A.H. Parker High School students with educational opportunities and experience in planning and constructing programs for the Greater Birmingham community. Additionally, because of the massive size of Parker's student body, two commencement ceremonies were had. Students were primarily responsible for selecting the theme and planning the commencement program. For the Parker High School community, commencement provided students with the opportunity to display the brilliance within the school's walls to the Greater Birmingham community. Moreover, commencement became an occasion to educate the students and community on important issues to the students who attended Parker High School and addressed issues that were relevant to the larger African American community in Birmingham, Alabama. For instance, in 1926, the theme of the commencement exercises was "Character Education Through Work." The graduates presented the audience with demonstrations and recreated scenarios to persuade and inform the audience of the importance of industrial work. Other themes for commencement ceremonies included "The Spirit of the Negro" and "Some Achievements of the American Negro" (Parker, 1932).

Extracurricular Activities, Clubs, and Organizations

While primarily noted for the varied opportunities for industrial education, A.H. Parker High School excelled and was widely known for their excellency in other areas including, local and state oratorical contests, band and athletic teams, and choir that performed locally and nationally. Additionally, a 1962 student handbook revealed that Parker High School had over 50 extracurricular activities, clubs, and organizations for students to participate. For example, options included the Hi-Y club, whose purpose was to create, maintain, and extend throughout the school and community high standards of Christian character. The Flower Club was an organization that was established to improve the school's appearance. Students raised money and purchased shrubbery and flowers across campus. Other organizations included a host of special interest clubs, such as art and architecture, ceramics, creative writing, diversified occupations, and photography. Finally, other options included clubs that prepared students for careers in certain vocational areas, such as the Future Nurses club, Future Teachers of America, Future Scientist of America, and New Homemakers of America.

From its beginning, Parker High School had an outstanding and well-known music department. Each year, Orlean Kennedy would orchestrate an annual musical. According to Parker (1932), "the entire city anticipated these performances" (p. 41). Superintendent Phillips was deeply moved by the Industrial High School choir, particularly the old Negro spirituals. At the suggestion of an orchestra instructor for Industrial, Phillips responded, "you will get an instructor of orchestra on one condition, and that is that you will always sing these old songs" (p. 58). Fairclough (2007) asserted that Parker utilized this "Old South nostalgia" (p. 269) to gain support with fundraising efforts for meeting the school's needs. According to a 1985 article in the *Birmingham News*, in the Spring of 1937, First Lady Eleanor Roosevelt attended an assembly program at Parker (Dizier, 1985). She praised them for their performance upon hearing the students sing.

In 1945, during a World War II war bond campaign drive, Parker High School students were the recipients of an $80,000 Navy Wildcat fighter plane after contributing more bond sales than any other high school, both Black and White, in Jefferson County, Alabama (Birmingham School Wins, 1945). Parker students surpassed their anticipated quota by 319 percent. The Wildcat fighter plane was placed on the school grounds to serve as a memorial trophy for their work and contributions to the war efforts.

Historically, these forms of social and cultural capital have largely been ignored and unacknowledged. However, it was through the contributions, personal sacrifices, and innovative instruction that the faculty and staff were able to develop and maintain an ethos of care that was reflective of the "spirit" that Dr. Parker proclaimed was the guiding force of this African American educational institution.

THE CONTINUING LEGACY OF A.H. PARKER HIGH SCHOOL

Since the establishment of A.H. Parker High School in the fall of 1900, there have been many changes within the school and the greater Birmingham community. This section addresses the impact of Birmingham's unique sociopolitical history and the unintended consequences of desegregation, namely, the reassigning of well-trained African American teachers and the declining enrollment of African

American students in the contemporary schooling environment of A.H. Parker High School.

In 1954, the Supreme Court ruled that segregated schools were "inherently unequal" (*Brown v. Board of Education*, 1954). However, the objective to preserve racial segregation in Birmingham, Alabama, continued through overt and subtle means. It would be 9 years after the *Brown v. Board of Education* decision that schools in Birmingham finally started the process of desegregating schools (Loder-Jackson, 2015). Like most African American segregated schools nationwide, A.H. Parker High School remained a predominantly African American school. Local and national legislative efforts contributed to the reassigning of highly qualified African American educators to White schools and declining enrollment in the community school.

In the late 40 and 50s, Parker's enrollment reached a height of almost 4,000 students. However, during the 2019–2020, A.H. Parker High School had an enrollment of 669 students (U.S. Department of Education). In 1987, a local newspaper article highlighted the fact that the school has continued to lose teachers due to the school board's formula of assigning teachers by the number of enrolled students (Mangels & Butgereit, 1987). Furthermore, like the many predominantly African American schools located with urban centers, Parker High School faces challenges with declining student achievement. In 2016, Parker was added to the State's Failing Schools list; however, in 2019, the school was able to get off the state's list. Principal Darrell Hudson attributed this advancement to the collective efforts of the students, educators, and greater Parker School community. Hudson stated, "…The teachers, the clerical staff, the maintenance staff, the child-nutrition staff, everybody plays a key role in student achievement here at A.H. Parker High School" (Wright, 2019, para. 17).

While the school has experienced significant challenges within the past few years, there still exists an unyielding love and pride for the institution. A.H. Parker High School's Alumni Association has an active presence within the institution, providing supplies and scholarships for current students. In 2011, A.H. Parker High School opened a new $32 million structure with state-of-the-art features and technology. Several of the new buildings are named for notable educators throughout the history of the school. For example, the school's auditorium bears the name of Robert C. Johnson, Parker's third principal, and Robert Bobby Jones. Additionally, Parker's library is named for Dr. Dannetta K. Thornton Owens, the 1955 valedictorian of Parker High School and a longtime educator and District 5 leader of Birmingham City School Board. Furthermore, Parker has and continues to produce alumni that contribute to the uplifting of the race, community, and the broader society.

The alumni of A.H. Parker High School have varied accomplishments, locally, nationally, and internationally. To note, Judge Orzell Billingsley, Jr., civil rights activist, and attorney, was one of the first African Americans admitted to the Alabama State Bar (Dickson, 1998; United Alumni Association, 2000). Additionally, Billingsley organized and founded 12 towns in Alabama. Oscar W. Adams, a 1940 graduate of Parker High School, was the first African American Alabama Supreme Court. Nell Carter, famed singer and actress, was a 1968 graduate of Parker. Sun Ra, Jazz musician and poet, graduated from Parker High School in 1914. Odessa Woolfolk, educator and civic activist, was the leading force in obtaining funding and developing the Birmingham Civil Rights Institute (United Alumni Association, 2000). Erwin Prentiss Hill, a 2001 graduate of Parker, founded and currently serves as Executive Director of the Chicago-based Black College Sports Group 360 (BCSG). This nonprofit organization uses sporting events at Historically Black Colleges and Universities to promote educational opportunities to urban youth (Crenshaw, 2017). Kamil Goodman, a 2020 graduate of Parker High School, was a finalist in the 2018 NextGen Pitch Competition through the Economic Development Partnership in Birmingham. Goodman's pitch encouraged the creation of a leadership forum for youth leaders to share their ideas with Birmingham's elected officials (Wright, 2018).

Arthur Harold Parker's dream continues to be realized through the continuation of A.H. Parker High School and the quest of the faculty and staff to educate the students of Birmingham, Alabama. The social and cultural capital that was and continues to be nurtured within this predominantly African American schooling environment serve as protective factors that motivate students to excel and to adopt the "spirit" that Dr. Parker identified in that first inaugural class. A.H. Parker High School's song is a testament to this continuing legacy.

> There's no other high school
> We love as Parker High
> Now we'll sing her praises
> Until the day we die.
> We'll cheer for white and purple,
> The colors that we love.
> They will lead us in the conflict
> And our triumph prove.
> We'll cheer for thee, Dear Parker
> In each victory
> Thy love of truth shall guide us
> Through each adversity.
> Bless her name and shout her praises,
> Make the rafters ring.
> Hail to thee our dear old Parker,
> Hail to thee we sing

REFERENCES

Anderson, J. (1988). *The education of Blacks in the South, 1860–1935*. University of North Carolina Press.

Archer, W. (1910). *Through Afro-America, an English reading of the race problem*. Chapman & Hall, Limited.

Armbrester, M. E. (1993). *Samuel Ullman and youth: The life, the legacy*. University of Alabama Press.

Beauboeuf-Lafontant, T. (2005). Womanist lessons for reinventing teaching. *Journal of Teacher Education, 56*(5), 436–445. https://doi.org/10.1177/0022487105282576

Birmingham school named for principal. (1939, May 20). *The Chicago Defender*, p. 9.

Birmingham school wins $80,000 plane in war bond drive. (1945, December 15). *New Journal and Guide*, p. A11.

Bond, H. M. (1994). *Negro education in Alabama: A study in cotton and steel*. University of Alabama Press.

Bourdieu, P. (1984). *Distinction: A social critique of the judgment of taste*. Harvard University Press.

Bourdieu, P. (1986). The forms of capital. In J. G. Richardson (Ed.), *Handbook of theory and research for the sociology of education* (pp. 241–258). Greenwood Press.

Bradford, J. R. (1925, March 13). *Letter from Juliet R. Bradford to WEB. Du Bois*. W. E. B. Du Bois Papers (MS 312). Special Collections and University Archives, University of Massachusetts Amherst Libraries. http://credo.library.umass.edu/view/full/mums312-b027-i467

Brown, C. A. (1959). *The origin and development of secondary education for Negroes in the metropolitan area of Birmingham, Alabama*. Commercial Printing Co. https://hdl.handle.net/2027/uiug.30112118439535

Brown v. Board of Education, 347 U.S. 483 (1954).

Caliver, A. (1932, April 21). Students share activities of Birmingham high school: Largest Negro high school in country. *Philadelphia Tribune*, p. 11.

Childers, J. (1933, May 28). Where pupils study books and brooms. *The Birmingham News Age-Herald*. Birmingham Public Library Digital Collections https://cdm16044.contentdm.oclc.org/digital/collection/p4017coll2/id/1466/rec/1

Class and school problems discussed. (1932, April 21). *Philadelphia Tribune*, p. 19.

Council for leaders in Alabama schools. (2018). *Parker High School principal named district 5 high school principal of the year* [Press release]. https://clasleaders.org/docs/default-source/public-relations/poy-19-20/district-5-hspoy---darrell-hudson.pdf?sfvrsn=2

Crenshaw, S. (2017, April 27). Meet the Parker High School grad whose sports firm is becoming an HBCU powerhouse. *Birmingham Times*.

Creswell, J. W. (2007). *Qualitative inquiry and research design: Choosing among five traditions*. Sage Publications.

Davis, A. Y. (1974). *Angela Davis: An Autobiography*. Random House.

Dickson, J. (1998, March 4). Orzell Billingsley, Jr. judge attorney unsung hero of A.H. Parker High school. *Birmingham World*.

Dizier, B. (1985, May 24). Parker High long way from single room. *Birmingham News*. Birmingham Public Library Digital Collections. https://cdm16044.contentdm.oclc.org/digital/collection/p4017coll2/id/1453/rec/1

Du Bois, W.E.B. (1924). *Fisk Herald, 33*(1), 6. (Series 2, Box 2, Folder 18). The Richetta Randolph Wallace Papers, Brooklyn Historical Society.

Fairclough, A. (2007). *A class of their own: Black teachers in the segregated South*. Harvard.

Fallin, W. (2007). *Uplifting the people: Three centuries of Black Baptist in Alabama*. University of Alabama Press.

Feldman, L. B. (1999). *A sense of place: Birmingham's Black middle-class community, 1890–1930*. The University of Alabama Press.

Foster, M. (1993). Educating for competence in community and culture: Exploring the views of exemplary African American teachers. *Urban Education, 27*(4), 370–394. https://doi.org/10.1177/0042085993027004004

Franklin, V. P. (2002). Introduction: Cultural capital and African American education. *The Journal of African American History, 87*, 175–181.

Griffin, J. (1975). *Fess Whatley*. Omeka at Auburn. https://omeka.lib.auburn.edu/items/show/1975

Harris, C. V. (1985). Stability and change in discrimination against Black public school: Birmingham, Alabama, 1871–1931. *The Journal of Southern History, 51*(3), 375–416.

Jackson. E. O. (1939, August 22). Dr. Arthur Harold Parker's funeral rites impressive; Lofty tributes to educator. *Atlanta Daily World*, p. 3.

Kelly, H. (2010). What Jim Crow's teachers could do: Educational capital and teachers' work in under-resourced schools. *The Urban Review, 42*(4), 329–350. https://doi.org/10.1007/s11256-009-0132-3

Loder-Jackson, T. L. (2015). *Schoolhouse activist: African American educators and the long Birmingham civil rights movement*. State University of New York Press.

Mangels, J., & Butgereit, B. (1987). Proud Parker High is paying a price for school integration. *Birmingham News*. https://bit.ly/37qBPEe

McDowell, B. (2013). *Historical Research: A Guide*. Routledge.

Morris, V. G., & Morris, C. L. (2000). *Creating caring and nurturing educational environments or African American children*. Greenwood Publishing Group.

Parker, A. H. (1932). *A dream that came true: Autobiography of Arthur Harold Parker*. Printing Department of Industrial High School. https://cdm16044.contentdm.oclc.org/digital/collection/p4017coll8/id/1481/rec/4

Parker High School handbook: leadership, scholarship, dependability, and service. (1962). A.H. Parker High School Student Council.

Rolón-Dow, R. (2005). Critical care: A color(full) analysis of care narratives in the schooling experiences of Puerto Rican girls. *American Educational Research Journal, 42*(1), 77–111. https://doi.org/10.3102/00028312042001077

Rossman, G. B. & Rallis, S. F. (2012). *Learning in the field: An introduction to qualitative research* (3rd ed.). Sage Publications.

Rury, J. L. (2002). *Education and social change: Themes in the history of American schooling*. Lawrence Erlbaum Associates, Inc.

School honors teacher's half century of service. (1937, November 16). *Birmingham Post*.

Siddle Walker, V. (1996). *Their highest potential: An African American school community in the segregated South*. University of North Carolina Press.

Siddle Walker, E. V. (2000). Valued segregated schools for African American children in the South, 1935–1969: A review of common themes and characteristics. *Review Educational Research, 70*(3), 253–285. https://doi.org/10.3102/00346543070003253

Sowell, T. (1976). Patterns of Black excellence. *The Public Interest, 43*(26), 26–58.

Stewart, S. W. (1998, February 26). A tribute to A.H. Parker High School. *Birmingham World*. https://cdm16044.contentdm.oclc.org/digital/collection/p4017coll2/id/1499/rec/2

U.S. Department of Education. (2021). *Institute of Education Sciences, National Center for Education Statistics*. https://bit.ly/3rVBz9J

Ullman, S. M. (1915, June 13). *Birmingham Industrial High School factor in the city's development*. The Birmingham Age-Herald.

United Alumni Association. (2000, May, n.d.). *The record, special edition: Parker High School, a dream that came true*. https://cdm16044.contentdm.oclc.org/digital/collection/p4017coll8/id/6414/rec/9

University of Alabama at Birmingham. (2017, February 25). *UAB's Birmingham 101: Parker High School* [Video]. YouTube. https://www.youtube.com/watch?v=agQXXwrPxzQ

World's biggest Negro High School: Birmingham's Parker has largest June graduating class, highest enrollment. (1950, June, n.d.). *Ebony*, 5(8), 15–20.

Wright, B. (2018, May 11). Parker High School teacher, Huffman High student win Next-Gen competition. *The Birmingham Times*. https://bit.ly/38qkxeq

Wright, E. (2019, November 21). Here's how A.H. Parker High School got off the state's failing list. *Birmingham Times*. https://bit.ly/3Mdt0QS

WVTM 13 News. (2021, February 9). *Black History Month special: Parker High School paves the way*. https://www.youtube.com/watch?v=iXqGdkH34f8

Yosso, T. J. (2005). Whose culture has capital? A critical race theory discussion of community cultural wealth. *Race Ethnicity and Education*, 8(1), 69–91.

CHAPTER 9

A PORTRAIT OF COMO HIGH SCHOOL, FORT WORTH, TEXAS

Altheria Caldera
Howard University School of Education

This chapter presents a narrative of the brief history of Como Junior-Senior High School in Fort Worth, Texas. The Como community—comprised of Black working-class citizens—opened a school for its children in 1914. By the mid-1950s, the original one-room school had developed into an elementary school serving K–5 and a junior-senior high school serving students in grades 6–12. Como High School was beloved and supported by the tight-knit Como community. It was the unifying force in a Black community surrounded by White neighborhoods yet segregated from them. Using ethnographic research methods, the researcher reveals how the school's closing after just 14 years disrupted the lives of students and teachers and shuttered the Como community. It contributes to knowledge about segregated Black schools and the way they were impacted by desegregation mandates.

Keywords: Como High School, Black Critical Theory, Social and Cultural Capital, Community

INTRODUCTION

I was visiting Como Elementary School to discuss my research project with the assistant principal and a few of her staff when a woman stumbled upon our conversation about the closing of Como Junior-Senior High School.

Black Cultural Capital: Activism That Spurred African American High Schools, pages 181–199.
Copyright © 2023 by Information Age Publishing
www.infoagepub.com
All rights of reproduction in any form reserved.

"I never understood why they did that to us, why they closed our school," she lamented.

"Were you at Como High when the school closed?" I asked.

"No, I was in elementary school. I was so disappointed. As little children, we looked forward to the day that we'd attend Como High. I used to wonder why the community didn't fight for our school."

"I'm sorry that happened to you. Thank you for sharing this with me."

The tears scuttling down her face suggested her despondency. Like me, she had questions about the closing of Como High. But her questions stemmed from her personal connections to this place. The Como community had been hers. The school, her inheritance. She represented one of three groups of students who participated in this study: (a) elementary students who dreamt of one day attending Como High School, (b) students who were attending Como High School at the time of the closing, and (c) students who had graduated from Como High. Students yet to graduate spoke with envy of those who had graduated from Como

Como High School. Note. This is the exterior of Como Junior-Senior High School, Fort Worth, Texas, when it was newly built in 1956. University of Texas at Arlington Libraries, Special Collections. Located in the Fort Worth Star-Telegram Collection, AR406-6 09/07/1956 3664. NonCommercial 4.0 International (CC BY-NC 4.0) http://creativecommons.org/licenses/by-nc/4.0/

High between 1957, the year the first class graduated, and 1971, the year of the last graduating class. I cannot help but notice the irony. Though segregated Black schools are often viewed through a deficit lens, graduates of Como High saw themselves as privileged. They believed that they were lucky to have attended Como High. I am reminded of Nikki-Giovanni's poem "Nikki-Rosa," in which the speaker reflects on what might be apprised as a difficult childhood. The speaker concludes her poem with a keen observation—outsiders only see Black suffering where there is also Black joy:

> And I really hope no white person ever has cause
> To write about me
> Because they never understand
> Black love is Black wealth and they'll
> Probably talk about my hard childhood
> And never understand that
> All the while I was quite happy (Giovanni, 1968).

Like the speaker in the poem, the students who attended Como High experienced conditions that could be deemed "hard"—being both segregated and under-resourced—but they were still "quite happy."

THEORETICAL FRAMEWORKS

Two theories can shed light on the study's findings—Black critical theory (Dumas & ross, 2016) and social and cultural capital theory (Bourdieu & Passeron, 1977). Black critical theory, or *BlackCrit,* an extension of critical race theory, helps to illuminate the specificity of anti-blackness by revealing the counterstories of Black people experiencing racism. *BlackCrit* "helps to explain precisely how Black bodies become marginalized, disregarded, and disdained, even in their highly visible place within celebratory discourses on race and diversity" (Dumas & ross, 2016, p. 417). In other words, *BlackCrit* is useful in revealing ways Black people are distinctly dehumanized in institutions, resulting in Black suffering. Three main ideas define *BlackCrit* and help us understand the racial oppression experienced by Black people in general and the Como community specifically: (a) Anti-blackness is central to the functioning of society, (b) Blackness clashes with neoliberalism's celebration of diversity and multiculturalism, and (c) *BlackCrit* makes space for a "Black liberatory fantasy" that is decolonized and envisions social change.

Social and cultural capital, as a theoretical framework, can be traced to the work of Bourdieu and Passeron (1977) but has been re-envisioned by other scholars (Franklin, 2002; Yosso, 2005). According to Bourdieu and Passeron (1977), individuals receive social and cultural capital in the form of knowledge, skills, and abilities mainly from their homes and families and rely upon this capital to effectively navigate in institutions outside the home, in schools for example. They contend that children from White, middle class homes have access to social and cultural capital that is aligned with societal norms and, therefore, hold knowledge that can be easily transferred to and developed in schools. Consequently, society reproduces inequities generationally because students of color are denied access to these forms of social and cultural capital. Yosso (2005), in her critique of Bourdieu's and Passeron's theory, suggests that their theory positions White, middle class culture as the "standard" or "norm" by which all other cultures are judged. She argued, instead, that ethnic cultures have knowledge that is valuable to students and their families but is often devalued in schools. The challenge, according to Yosso (2005), is for schools to align with students' home cultures. In his examination of the role of cultural capital in African American schooling, Franklin (2002) defines cultural capital as "the sense of group consciousness and collective identity that serves as an economic resource . . . aimed at the advancement of the entire group" (p. 177). In Black segregated communities before 1960, families, community members, organizations, and churches shouldered the responsibility for educating their own children. Said differently, they relied upon their cultural capital as a resource to create educational opportunities. These theories will be further developed in the findings section.

RESEARCH QUESTIONS AND METHODOLOGY

I began this research project during my first year of doctoral studies in the fall of 2012 as a member of a research team led by my advisor, Dr. Reynolds, and comprised of a small group of graduate students in Curriculum Studies. Though the study we designed was historical in nature, we were not education historians. My advisor had convened this group of novice researchers because she wanted us to develop skills in conducting culturally sensitive research while immersing ourselves in a marginalized community in our city (Mullings, 2000; Tillman, 2002). This type of experiential learning would be quite a departure for most students at our private, predominantly White university— an institution nestled in one of the most exclusive communities in Fort Worth. Dr. Reynolds had no specific questions, and the nebulous nature of the project caused me, a goal-oriented, instruction-following doctoral student, much angst. I wanted to know exactly what we hoped to learn about the community (research questions) and why (rationale), but Dr. Reynolds offered us no such direction. "Get to know a local community, go on community walks, meet the residents, help-out at the community center" was the sum of her instructions. "I'll guide you through the journey."

The team started by brainstorming to select a community that would be the focus of our study. Remembering a conversation I had with a student during my previous work at a community college, I added "Como" to the Fort Worth communities under consideration. With our research team, I shared a summary of a conversation I had had with a community college student about why he, in his mid-fifties, was "late," in his words, to finish his college degree. Don (pseudonym) had been among the students who were pushed out of school when their all-Black high school closed during desegregation, and he was forced to attend a nearby White high school. I remember his piercing pain as he described his experiences. His furrowed brows, glassy eyes, and bowed head spoke emotions that his words could not.

The research group was instantly attracted to this idea, and Como was chosen as the community we'd "get to know." We decided that we wanted to learn more about desegregation in Fort Worth by studying the all-Black high school, Como, and the integrated White high school, Arlington Heights. Several of my colleagues focused on Arlington Heights, but I knew that I wanted to focus on the closing of Como High. I defined my own questions for this study, based on my conversation with Don several years ago:

1. What was it like to grow up in the Lake Como (or simply *Como*) community?
2. What was Como High School like?
3. What circumstances led to the closing of Como High School?
4. What effects did the school closing have on students and the community?

Through ethnographic research consisting of semi-structured interviews with Como High students and teachers, Lake Como community members, and residents of Fort Worth; analyses of artifacts, such as archival newspapers and Como High School yearbooks; and observations of the present-day Lake Como community, I was able to answer my four guiding questions. Before the examination of the school, I begin with an overview of the Lake Como community.

LAKE COMO, A *SELECT* COMMUNITY

I was drawn to this project, in part, because of the immense pride held by those connected to the Lake Como community, hereafter Como. Not being a Fort Worth native, I was intrigued by the love expressed by Como residents I had met through the years. During my first year in Texas, the school counselor at the middle school where I taught enthusiastically and proudly described the community where she had grown up and still lived. She invited me to the community's signature event—the Como 4th of July Parade. I didn't attend the parade and had never visited Como prior to this project.

The byline of an episode of the documentary *One Square Mile-Texas* described Como as "an island" that has been home to many generations of African-Americans, many of whom had moved to Como to work as domestic laborers in the affluent neighboring communities, Ridglea Country Club and Arlington Heights (Crum & Crum, 2010). When Como was being settled, the Black residents earned the city's lowest incomes while residents in the neighboring country club were noted as being among those with the highest incomes (Gandy, 2020). In an article entitled, "FW's Como Area Lives in Isolation from Surrounding Affluence," in *The Dallas Morning News,* Como's distinction is noted:

> Como poses what may be Fort Worth's most jarring study in social contrasts. Only a few blocks from the Ridglea and Arlington Heights neighborhoods—where man-

sions are protected by private security guards—shotgun shacks surround empty lots used as impromptu dump sites.

The "Como-Ridglea dynamic" reflects the residential segregation of the time but also sheds light on race-related income disparities (Gandy, 2020). Though they were neighboring communities, Como residents were worlds away from its closest neighbors (Gandy, 2020). Study participants pointed out Como's strange positioning. A lifelong Como resident described his community:

> Como was isolated because we had the lake and the park was the boundary on the east side. On the west side was the Ridglea corridor and a wall there in the town . . . that separated the black community in Como from the rest. In the north section, Camp Bowie the commercial corridor and there was the rail yard, Vickery on the far south end. We were pretty much walled off, so to speak.

Similarly, a White teacher who taught at Arlington Heights and lived in the Arlington Heights neighborhood noted Como's isolation, "They had a wall that kept them in . . . there was no way they could get into Ridglea, from Camp Bowie to Vickery." Though separated by a physical barrier, Como's proximity to White communities was unlike other Black communities in Fort Worth, which were not located close to wealthy White communities. A former Como teacher who lived outside Como expressed what she saw as benefits of this unique location:

> Well first of all, I loved the community. It was something about the compactness of that community. I tell you what. They tried to compare it with Kirkpatrick, but it was not like that. Como was lucky in that they were on the very end of the Fort Worth elite. We had parents who worked in the richest and the most prominent people's homes in Arlington Heights.

She went on to describe the material advantages to Como's contiguity to its wealthier neighbors:

> We had parents who worked in the richest and the most prominent people's homes in Arlington Heights. To me, when you would go through Como at Christmas time, you'd see the little Christmas lights and all that, probably were giveaways from the elite.

I imagine that these second-hand items were both valued and despised by recipients. This transferral of discarded, or leftover, items from White families to Black families reinforced existing racial and class hierarchies.

Como's unique geographic location—a Black community physically separated from other Black communities in Fort Worth and surrounded by Whiteness—undoubtedly contributed to the residents' unity and closeness, words often used to describe the community by those who grew up in Como. A lifelong resident of Como described her childhood community as "a whole big family." While Como's designation as the poor amidst the wealthy is well-documented, it is important to note that the residents of the community were not *just* servants in the homes of their wealthy neighbors. Como was a self-contained, autonomous community with entrepreneurs who provided important services to the community. Como had Black-owned grocery stores, barber shops, beauty salons, daycares, a pharmacy, a movie theater, a shoe repair shop, a dry-cleaners, weekly newspaper, restaurants, and more. But, unquestionably, the heart of Como was Como Junior-Senior High School. A former student surmised, "The school was the community, and the community was the school."

THE BIRTH OF A COMMUNITY SCHOOL

The first school in Como was "a small frame one-teacher, eleven pupil school" opened in 1914 and was organized by local families who saw a need for formal education (Como High School, 1971). This time corresponds with the period during which Texas passed, repealed, and re-passed compulsory attendance laws, with the law finally taking effect in 1916 (Clay et al., 2012) and with the period in which public elementary schools became available to the majority of southern Black children (Anderson, 1988). During this time, members of the community supplied everything needed for instruction because "they recognized the value of literacy and schooling" (Franklin, 2002, p. 176). After the first year of operation, the elementary school in Como closed for two years due to a decrease in enrollment, but after reopening in 1917, there was a steady increase in student enrollment accompanied by physical expansion and additional teachers. By 1935, the growth necessitated a new site and larger building. In the next decade, Como Junior High was created and would later be expanded to Como Junior-Senior High. This expansion is worthy of deeper examination.

ESCAPING INTEGRATION: THE FORMATION OF COMO JUNIOR-SENIOR HIGH SCHOOL

Como schools were a part of the Fort Worth Independent School District (FWISD), the school district where I taught middle school English from 2003–2004. School district leadership had grappled with implementing the *Brown v. Board of Education* mandate from the time of the ruling in 1954 until the early 1970s. Like many school districts throughout the U.S., "rather than seeking positive solutions to systemic racism, the Board used the power of local bureaucracy to resist desegregation for 17 years after Brown" (Gandy, 2020, p. 50). It is clear that the formation of senior high schools in Fort Worth was an attempt to escape integration. At the time of *Brown*, Fort Worth had only one high school for Black students—I.M. Terrell. In the years following *Brown*, three additional junior high schools (grades 6–9) were gradually expanded into senior high schools: Dunbar, Kirkpatrick, and Como. Tenth grade was added in 1954, 11th grade in 1955, and 12th grade in 1956. Together, these four schools—I.M. Terrell, Dunbar, Kirkpatrick, and Como—became the first Black high schools in Fort Worth. (Only Dunbar still exists as a high school in 2021. Though neighborhood composition changes have resulted in an increase in the Latino student population, Dunbar's historical significance causes it to still be seen as a Black high school.) Although Fort Worth now had Black high schools to serve its Black communities, the district's schools were still segregated. Attorney L. Clifford Davis, the attorney who sued to desegregate FWISD and a participant in this study, confirmed the reason behind the district's expansion of grade levels to create high schools in Black communities:

> So what they did, because the original thought [about integration] was to go to the school nearest your home. Fort Worth said we can fix that. We will put a high school in the Black areas. So in Como, they added a grade a year, to move it up to a high school and the same was true in Kirkpatrick and the same was true in Dunbar. They thought that insulated them from any attack, because those kids were going to the school nearest their home. So we brought that suit and ultimately brought integration to Fort Worth ISD.

The lawsuit, *Flax, et al. v. Potts (1959),* prosecuted by Attorney Davis, led to the eventual desegregation of FWISD. In the *Flax* ruling handed down in 1962, the Court decided that the school district had "taken no step to abandon their policy of racial segregation." Even after this ruling, FWISD refused desegregation and litigation continued for almost another decade. To comply with *Flax's* desegregation mandates, FWISD board of trustees decided to close Como High School and send its students to neighboring white schools.

COMO SENIOR HIGH SCHOOL: A FALSE START, AN UNFULFILLED PROMISED

Como Junior-Senior High School has had a short, memorable and glorious history.
—*Principal's message in 1971 yearbook*

The establishment of Como Senior High School can be regarded as a false start and an unfulfilled promise. The first class graduated from Como in 1957, the last class in 1971. Como students yet to graduate either transferred to Western Hills High School or Arlington Heights High School, nearby predominately White schools. The decision to close Como High disrupted the educational experiences of hundreds of children and fragmented a community once bonded through a shared school with its traditions and celebrations. This decision was made, not because the students were failing, not because the school was overrun by violence, or any other reason that might be given for closing Black schools today. FWISD's response to the desegregation mandate established by *Brown* was to put the burden unduly on the Black community, exacting its power and privilege on a community victimized by racism and classism. Rodgers (as cited in Siddle Walker, 2000) described the typical Black segregated school as a "world of its own, dynamic quality and its own ecological structure" (p. 265). This was true of Como. The motto for the 1967 Como High School yearbook reflected the school's charm, "Our Own Little World." In a 2007 *Fort Worth Star-Telegram* article, columnist Bud Kennedy, writing on the 50th anniversary of the first graduating class from Como Junior-Senior High School, surmised, "They were victims of blatant discrimination. But they also had a true neighborhood school" (Kennedy, 2007).

School desegregation in Fort Worth created a psychological tension that forced Como residents into an impossible quandary. Desegregation symbolized progress, but with this progress came tremendous loss. A former Como schools' student who still lives in the community expressed these paradoxical feelings, "I was excited about desegregation. Then when I saw what it did to our community, it broke my heart," she lamented. Another former student expressed, "I think our community leaders let that [school closing] pass . . . because they were looking at the advancement of our community." I sensed that Como residents were caught in a morass, wanting the seemingly impossible—*freedom from* the bars of segregation and *freedom to* continue being a haven, or perhaps heaven, for its children. Como residents had invested significantly in Como High by drawing upon their collective social and cultural capital to create a school that was theirs. The school closing stripped them of this ownership. Remnants of the purple and gold Lions are still evident in the Como community. Places like the community center, re-purposed high school, elementary school, and a daycare center show the efforts of devoted residents to preserve the old Como by displaying the high school's memorabilia.

Black Critical Theory, which presupposes that "antiblackness is endemic to, and is central to how all of us make sense of the social, economic, historical, and cultural dimensions of human life" (Dumas & ross, 2016, p. 429) can explain why Como Junior-Senior High School was devalued by those outside the Como community. FWISD's decision to close this, and the other Black high schools, supports Black Critical Theory's belief that systemic practices are rooted in the dehumanization of Black bodies. As such, FWISD and school systems across the country disregarded the ways desegregation—facilitated through Black school closures—might destabilize Black families and communities, interrupt the development of healthy Black racial identities, and damage the socio-emotional well-being of Black children (Dumas & ross, 2016) —all of which are evident in this study. Though we know how Como High School's story ends, it is important to shed light on the school's "short, memorable and glorious history."

COMO HIGH: TANGIBLY POOR, INTANGIBLY RICH

Como High possessed an intangible richness though situated in a tangibly poor community. Lasseter Doggett (1927) wrote,

> The Negro high school is called upon to render a much larger service than its facilities and capacity justify. The increasing number of children attending high school gives rise to a crowded condition and in many situations immoderately large classes. (p. 24)

This was true of Como High. In Kennedy's (2007) article, a former Como football player described using worn-out football equipment that was handed down from

White high schools. Noting their lack of resources, a former student described the schools as "Fun, educational, very educational with what they had." Still, lack is not the whole story of Como High School. Morris and Morris (2002) argued that "much too often, separate African American schools were characterized as having poor teachers and administrators, poorly operated academic programs and activities, uncaring and neglectful parents, dilapidated school buildings, and scarce instructional resources" (p. 2). Siddle Walker (2000) cautioned against this singular assessment of Black schools: ". . . confining explanations of the education in the schools to descriptions of resources has not adequately explained the kind of education African American teachers, principals, and parents attempted to provide under externally restrictive circumstances" (p. 254). Como students rarely mentioned the school's deficits, focusing instead on the richness of the education they received even in the face of insufficiency.

Viewing these schools only in terms of deficits creates an imbalanced depiction and neglects of the affirmative aspects of Black schooling, the enviable attributes to which future students looked forward, the never-experienced treasures that make grown women teary with longing. My research broadens this assessment of Black segregated schools and provides a more comprehensive picture of Como schools, producing counternarratives that broaden the stories often told in master narratives. Stanley (2007) described counternarratives:

> Perspectives that run opposite or counter to the presumed order and control are *counternarratives*. These narratives, which do not agree with and are critical of the master narrative, often arise out of individual or group experiences that do not fit the master narratives. (p. 14)

Counter narratives serve to deconstruct the master narratives, and they offer alternatives to the dominant discourse in educational research. A Como High School graduate saw a need for a counter perspective and called upon researchers to paint "the whole picture . . . if you're going to tell the story of Como."

From interviews with more than a dozen Como students, teachers, and residents emerged a salient truth expressed as an understatement: Como High School was deeply loved. In this next section, I center the voices of research participants in explaining the richness of Como schools and why they were loved by those who knew them. While conceding the schools' lack of material resources, research participants described schools that (a) were extensions of home, (b) had impressive parental/community involvement, (c) offered culturally relevant extracurricular activities, and (d) boasted impactful teachers. Du Bois (1935) believed that "there is no magic . . . in segregated schools," (p. 335) but these findings suggest that there was something *magical* about Como. These are the counter-narratives.

Extensions of Home

Two Como students described Como Elementary as "an extension of home." This anecdote explains why:

> I remember my very first day at school, leaving the house with a bag and some books. Scared because it was a new experience. I didn't go to kindergarten. My mother taught me how to read and a lot of the basics. I felt I was ahead of the class when I got there, but I hadn't learned in a group setting. It felt a little different, so I was nervous. It's funny how I can remember, it's been a long time ago now. Walking along Horne Street, those two blocks, walking slow. I guess I started making up my mind that I was going to go. When I got to that corner, just by Zion, over the big hedge, it's not there anymore, but I was walking and I just ... and sat behind that hedge. I don't think I was thinking of not going, but I was just slowing the pace, I was real nervous. My mother must have been watching me because after a few seconds, she turned that same corner that hedge and looked down. She didn't fuss. I just remember her getting my hand, so she walked me to the school. That front door right there, that first door is the hall where all the primary grades were. She walked me into the room and put my hand in the hand of Mrs. Briscoll, my first grade teacher. It was something powerfully symbolic about that. It was from my mother to my mother on campus. That's how Mrs. Briscoll embraced the class, embraced me, the most powerful education experience that I can imagine. It certainly set me on a trajectory of success and acceptance and belief in myself.

This story demonstrates how teachers were a form of social capital. The relationships between parents and teachers were important resources for students to draw upon (Franklin, 2002). Stories of this kind make it easy to see why Como schools were deeply loved by its students, parents, and community members. I found myself wondering, here and many times throughout this project, how we might recreate these aspects in today's climate but also lamenting that this is likely a time that has come and gone. My dream of educative spaces that humanize Black children is supported by *BlackCrit's* idea of a Black liberatory fantasy. Schools not only extended the care students experienced at home, but, according to participants, they also perpetuated values of Como families, values like hard work, respect, and dignity. Similarly, disciplinary practices at home, oftentimes whippings, were mirrored with spankings at school. One student admitted, "We had all black teachers who believed in paddling and discipline and everything . . ." Former Como students interviewed for this study seem to have appreciated the physical punishment given to them by their teachers and no one suggested that the punishment crossed the line to abuse. Viewing Como schools as "extensions of home" is consistent with Yosso's (2005) theory of social capital. She saw social capital as networks who students can draw upon for knowledge and support. These networks played a prominent role in student success at Como.

Other prevailing features that added value to the educational experience at Como schools were parental/community involvement, extracurricular and social activities, and, of course, the exceptional teachers. Each of these elements is explicated in the sections that follows.

Parental/Community Involvement

Like other Black communities in the segregated South (Chafe et al., 2014), Como was a strong, supportive community. In the 1957 Como Junior-Senior High School yearbook commemorating the first graduation class, the principal, Mr. O.M. Williams, Jr., offered special appreciation to the parents: "Your cooperation has been of such magnitude that it has strengthened the bond between school and home" (Como High School, 1957). The testimonies of several participants, both students and teachers, also evidence Como's parents' involvement in the local schools. This story from a former teacher is particularly poignant:

> The parents were involved. The PTA was very involved with the kids. If I had problems with a child, I didn't hesitate to call the parents. I remember one time, one of my students came to me and said, "Mrs. Roberts, Herbert has your car." I said, "My car?" I had left my keys on the table. He had gone to pick up some girls and told them that Mrs. Roberts said that it was alright for him to pick them up. When he came in, I didn't report him to the principal. When he got home, I was sitting in his living room with my legs crossed.

Pictures in the 1959 Como Junior-Senior High School annual show many P.T.A. (Parent Teacher Association) members and officers filling several rows in an auditorium. This level of involvement on the high school level is particularly remarkable considering that parental involvement wanes in the upper grades. Gonzalez (2002) argued, as have others, that parental involvement is linked to high academic achievement, time spent on homework, positive attitudes toward school, persistence, and college aspirations. A former student added his perspective on parental involvement, "When the parents came to school, they were always updated on what went on. Your parents were present. They were involved." Sadly, this level of parental involvement seemed to diminish after Black high schools were closed. Mrs. Roberts, a teacher who taught at Como Junior-Senior High School and at Arlington Heights High School, noted the lack of involvement by Black parents once their children were transferred to Arlington Heights. Their lack of involvement was likely due to discomfort in the new environment and the school's distance from their neighborhood. Social and cultural theory can help to explain this perceived disengagement. Black parents likely didn't possess the knowledge of social and cultural norms at the White schools and may have feared encountering values that were inconsistent with their own.

Similarly, churches were an instrumental part of the Como community and, consequently, Como schools. A former student commented, "Most of the people in Como went to church out here. The churches, they were part of the school and everybody at the school had a pastor of their church that spoke for the churches and for them." Several former and current Como residents attested to this community, school, and church triangle. A Fort Worth resident observed this link, "In those days, parents' and community support was detrimental [sic] because you knew those people. They lived in that neighborhood. They went to church with you." The depth of community involvement can be seen in a reflection by a former student:

> We didn't have after school programs per se, but we did have some members of the community who offered different things after school. I remember Mrs. Campbell. She offered dance classes and etiquette classes, and I remember taking ballet and tap and all of those kinds of things at Como Elementary.

Yosso (2005) argued that minoritized cultures hold valuable knowledge, skills, and abilities—or cultural capital—that are valued within their communities but are often devalued in school contexts. Cultural capital theory is also predicated on the belief that capital, a byproduct of culture, is transmitted implicitly and explicitly by the family (Louque & Latunde, 2014). The findings of this study affirm cultural capital theory. Como school students possessed cultural capital that was also valued at their Black schools. Because they attended schools that were congruent with their culture, they were able to navigate within these institutions with ease.

Mrs. Campbell's teaching classes shows the dedication of community members who supplemented Como Elementary School's instruction and curriculum and contributed to the holistic development of its students. It also attested to the shaping of curriculum—formal and informal—around the needs and interests of students, a characteristic of the Progressive Education Movement that influenced Black high schools (Kridel, 2018). Undoubtedly, the collaboration between teachers, parents, and the community at large contributed to the sentiment of connectedness expressed in the narratives of all the participants. Como was a community united by a common goal—the success of its children. This strong sense of unity made the closing of their school and the dispersing of the children difficult for its residents.

Extracurricular and Social Activities

Extracurricular activities were an important part of life in Como schools. The junior-senior high school's purpose as stated in several yearbooks include the following: "acquisition and maintenance of good physical, mental, and emotional health" and "development of an appreciation of aesthetic values," among others (Como High School, 1971). Several participants told stories of Como's exceptional sports teams, particularly basketball and football teams. A community member expressed,

> We took ... once the high school was closed, the trophies from the high school was just thrown in storage down under the field house, the main field house ... our alumni went and restored as many as they can, and we have them here at our center.

That's another point of pride for us to know that we're still preserving some of those things here within this community center.

The Como Community Center has become a museum displaying many of the trophies earned by these teams. In addition to athletics, the 1971 yearbook depicts active student organizations: Speech Club, Art Club, Band, Debate Team, Usherette, Science Club, Cultural Club, and French Club. Participants recalled experiences such as their annual Como Homecoming and May Day events, full of excitement and pageantry. Another opportunity for Como students to showcase their talents and creativity was through the community's Independence Day Parade, a Como tradition that still takes place. After being canceled because of the COVID pandemic in 2020, the 2021 Como Parade was a celebration of the Como community, the 4th of July, and Juneteenth. In the 24th Anniversary Supplement to the Como Weekly (community newspaper), students are pictured as cheerleaders, chorus members, and carnival-goers. Undoubtedly, the availability of such extracurricular activities helped to make Como Junior-Senior High School a treasured learning environment that was longed for years after the school closed. A former student expressed this sentiment, "We knew in our hearts that we'd never get it back. There was always thoughts one day we'll have our high school back, but that never appeared."

Exceptional Teachers

The most celebrated and appreciated aspect of Como schools was the faculty. This should not come as a surprise as "teachers held the highest status jobs in the Black community" (Chafe et al., 2014, p. xxx). These teachers were thought to be exceptional for a variety of reasons, namely their care, knowledge, high expectations, and disciplinary approaches. In her insightful study into teachers at Black schools, Tillman (2004) described these teachers in ways that echo the students' stories. "These teachers saw potential in their Black students, considered them to be intelligent, and were committed to their success. Teachers and principals collaborated to help students build on their strengths and improve their weaknesses" (p. 282). A teacher who taught at Como High School from its first year to its last year voiced sadness and worry about the closing,

> I was unhappy because I didn't know what the future held for those kids. And that's the reason I chose, I asked to go to Arlington Heights because I wanted to be there with them. I figured they would need me.

Each student interviewed for this project fondly remembered experiences with caring teachers. In fact, this level of care and dedication was often cited as missing in teachers at the integrated high school. A former student described his experience with Como teachers, "I have to admit that the teachers at our middle school, to me in my experience, pushed us and cared more about us than when we went to Arlington Heights." Similarly, a former student and present community leader who is active in area schools commented on today's teachers as compared to teachers in Como:

> We lost that ability for them to have Black teachers who really cared. I look at our elementary school now and yes, we know there are white people in this day that care, but there a lot of them that still don't. They just funnel our children through and they're not teaching them from the skills and things they need to make it in society.

As mentioned earlier, the teachers' care was combined with strong discipline, which sometimes included corporal punishment. According to a former student,

> The teachers were strict but loving and they really cared about teaching us. They wanted to make sure that we were taught well. I can remember one, Ms. Gardner, who was my second grade teacher, who every morning lined us up to make sure our hair was combed, our teeth was brushed and all of that kind of stuff and would get on us if it hadn't been done.

Part of Como's teachers' exceptionality was their expertise in their subjects. They possessed knowledge that was inspiring to their students:

> They were very knowledgeable about their subject. If it wasn't their major in school, they became knowledgeable about it. They intended to inspire you. I had an English teacher that was from London. She was very well read in the classics and everything. I had never given any thought to doing a lot of classic literature and Greek theatre, Greek literature, even much grammar at all. But she inspired the ability to write. She wanted you to know how to write.

A former student expressed, "We excelled because we were taught through our coaches and through those around us that we couldn't just be as good as, we had to be better." This mentality yielded much success as evidenced by the achievements of alumni. In addition to these student narratives, Como Junior-Senior High School 1971 yearbook show teachers whose dedication was reflected in their sponsorship of many clubs and organizations. According to the 1971 Como Junior-Senior High School yearbook, all teachers held bachelor's degrees, with almost a third with a master's degree. One of the teachers, Mr. Rudy Eastman, founded and directed The Jubilee Theater, a Black treasured theater company that still offers rich theatrical performances in downtown Fort Worth. The 1971 teacher-of-the-year and mentor to Gospel superstar Kirk Franklin, Ms. Jewell Kelly, became an award-winning choir director whose contributions to education were recognized by having a street named in her honor.

IMPLICATIONS

As a graduate of a Historically Black College/University (HBCU), I could relate to these findings on a personal level. I, too, saw my college as an extension of home. This project also resonated with me professionally. As a teacher educator and scholar whose research centers the education of Black students, I found this study meaningful to my work. In fact, my article (Caldera, 2020a) outlining a disposition I name *Black cultural reverence* was inspired by this examination of Como High School. In this article, I propose standards for educating Black students. For example, to cultivate the success of Black students, school leaders must "recognize the strengths of Black culture and see Black culture as an asset" and "hold Black culture in high regard" (Caldera, 2020a). Other keys to success are below.

1. Since school closures impact neighborhoods, school boards need to include community members in discussions. The community members had little to no influence on the decision to close their high school, a decision that was detrimental to their neighborhood. Research reveals that forced school closures, like those that happen when states close schools for low academic performance, continue to disrupt communities of color and, therefore, should be eliminated as a reform strategy (Sunderman, Coghlan & Mintrop, 2017).
2. The children of Como held social and cultural capital that were assets at school. This is the premise of culturally sustaining pedagogy. Black children need culturally sustaining schools that are "extensions of home." These schools employ strategies that "sustain the lifeways of communities who have been and continue to be damaged ad erased through schooling" (Paris & Alim, 2017, p. 1) and do not require the identity shifts and negotiations experienced when Black children attend schools characterized by whiteness (Caldera, 2020b).
3. Black children need exceptional teachers whose care is demonstrated through high expectations, culturally relevant discipline, and knowledge to prepare for an unjust society (Beauboeuf-Lafontant, 2002, 2005; Ladson-Billings, 2009). Franklin (2002) identified committed Black teachers who saw themselves as community leaders and role models and who viewed teaching as a calling as an important form of cultural capital.
4. Black children need schools that respect the roles that families and parents play in educating their children. Latunde and Clark-Louque (2016) found that Black families contribute to their children's learning in many ways, namely through helping with learning at home and exposing children to educational activities outside the school. Drawing upon Yosso's (2005) theorizing, it is important for educators to demonstrate value for the knowledge and skills families of color impart to their children.

CONCLUSION

Through this study, I came to understand the tears of the stranger I encountered in the library of Como Elementary School. I realized why, decades later, she was still heartbroken by the school's closing, a closing brought about in the name of

FIGURE 8.1. Image of a Broken Bell From 1971 Yearbook

desegregation. Although desegregation was hailed as a gateway to advancement for African Americans, the story of Como High School reveals that FWISD's desegregation efforts had adverse effects on this Black community, leaving it forever fractured, as symbolized by the broken bell in the last Como High School yearbook (See Figure 8.1). I am reminded of the research participant who surmised,

> The schools were the identities or the pillar of those communities. Think about it like this. Remember that in the segregated day, you spent most of your time in your community—church and school. So a lot of things gravitated towards to the schools. To close a school [was seen as] a failure on the community.

However, it is important to emphasize that the Como residents did not fail; the Fort Worth school system failed Como.

The dedication in the Como Lions United Class Reunion commemorative book encapsulates former students' hope: "May the purple and gold spirit forever linger in our hearts and minds." Fifty years after the school's 1971 closing, spirit is all that remains.

DEDICATION

This chapter was intended to be a part of a monograph reflecting what our research team learned about the Como community, but our project came to an abrupt end when my professor and mentor, Dr. Sherrie Reynolds, in year two of our study, suddenly became ill and passed away a few months later. I dedicate this chapter to her and to the participants in this study who deeply loved Como High School.

REFERENCES

Anderson, J.D. (1988). *The education of Blacks in the South, 1860–1935.* The University of North Carolina Press.

Beauboeuf-Lafontant, T. (2002). A womanist experience of caring: Understanding the pedagogy of exemplary Black women teachers. *The Urban Review, 34*(1), 71–86. https://doi.org/10.1023/A:1014497228517

Beauboeuf-Lafontant, T. (2005). Womanist lessons for reinventing teaching. *Journal of Teacher Education, 56*(5), 436–445. https://doi.org/10.1177/0022487105282576

Bourdieu, P., & Passeron, J. (1977) *Reproduction in education, society and culture*. Sage.

Caldera, A. (2020a). Eradicating anti-Black racism in U.S. schools: A call-to-action for school leaders. *Diversity, Social Justice, and the Educational Leader, 4*(1), 12–25. https://scholarworks.uttyler.edu/dsjel/vol4/iss1/3

Caldera, A. (2020b). Toward wholeness: Anzaldúan theorizing used to imagine culturally accepting educative spaces for Black girls. In M. Cantu-Sanchez, C. de Leon-Zepeda, & N. E. Cantu (Eds.), *Teaching Gloria E. Anzaldua: Pedagogy and practice for our classrooms and communities* (pp. 33–46). University of Arizona Press.

Chafe, W. H., Gavins, R., & Korstad, R. (2014). *Remembering Jim Crow: African Americans tell about life in the segregated South*. The New Press.

Clay, K., Lingwall, J., & Stephens Jr., M. (2012). *Do schooling laws matter? Evidence from the introduction of compulsory attendance laws in the United States*. NBER Working Paper Series. https://www.nber.org/system/files/working_papers/w18477/w18477.pdf.

Como High School. (1957). *Como Lion Yearbook*.

Como High School. (1971). *Como Lion Yearbook*.

Crum, C., & Crum, E. (2010). *One Square Mile-Como*. https://www.imdb.com/title/tt1617261/

Du Bois, W. E. B. (1935). Does the Negro need separate schools? *The Journal of Negro Education 4*(3), 328–335.

Dumas, M. J., & ross, k. m. (2016). "Be real Black for me": Imagining BlackCrit in education. *Urban Education, 51*(4), 415–442. ttps://doi.org/10.1177/0042085916628611

Franklin, V. (2002). Introduction: Cultural capital and African American education. *The Journal of African American History, 87*, 175–181.

Gandy, B. (2020). *"Trouble up the road:" Desegregation, busing, and the national politics of resistance in Fort Worth, Texas, 1954–1971*. [Master's thesis]. Texas State University. https://digital.library.txstate.edu/bitstream/handle/10877/9881/GANDY-THESIS- 2020.pdf?sequence=1

Giovanni, N. (1968). *"Nikki-Rosa." Black feeling, Black talk, Black judgment*. Broadside Press.

Gonzalez, A. R. (2002). Parental involvement: Its contribution to high school students' motivation. *The Clearing House, 75*(3), 132–134. https://doi.org/10.1080/00098650209599252

Kennedy, B. (2007, July 4). Graduates of Como High, it will always be 'our school'. *Fort Worth Star-Telegram*.

Kridel, C. (2018). *Becoming an African American progressive educator: Narratives from 1940s Black progressive high schools*. Museum of Education, Wardlaw Hall.

Ladson-Billings, G. (2009). *The dreamkeepers: Successful teachers of African American children* (2nd ed.). Jossey-Bass.

Lasseter Doggett, D. (1927). *Survey of Fort Worth's Negro schools*. [Master's thesis]. Texas Christian University Archives. (43566)

Latunde, Y., & Clark-Louque, A. (2016). Untapped resources: Black parent engagement contributes to learning. *Journal of Negro Education*, *85*(1), 72–81. https://doi.org/10.7709/jnegroeducation.85.1.0072

Louque, A., & Latunde, Y. (2014). Cultural capital in the village: The role African-American families play in the education of children. *Multicultural Education*, *21*(3/4), 5-10.

Morris, V. G., & Morris, C. L. (2002). *The price they paid: Desegregation in an African-American community.* Teachers College Press.

Mullings, L. (2000). African American women making themselves: Notes on the role of Black feminist research. *Souls: A Journal of Black Politics, Culture, and Society*, *2*(9), 18–29. https://doi.org/10.1080/10999940009362233

Paris, D., & Alim, H. S. (2017). *Culturally sustaining pedagogies: Teaching and learning for justice in a changing world.* Teachers College Press.

Siddle Walker, V. (2000). Valued segregated schools for African American children in the South, 1935–1969: A review of common themes and characteristics. *Review of Educational Research*, *70*(3), 253–285. doi:10.3102/00346543070003253

Stanley, C. A. (2007). When counter narratives meet master narratives in the journal editorial review process. *Educational Researcher*, *36*(1), 14–24. https://doi.org/10.3102/0013189X06298008

Sunderman, G. L., Coghlan, E., & Mintrop, R. (2017). School closure as a strategy to remedy low performance. *National Education Policy Center*, https://files.eric.ed.gov/fulltext/ED574706.pdf

Tillman, L. C. (2002). Culturally sensitive research approaches: An African American perspective. *Educational Researcher*, *31*(9), 3–12. https://doi.org/10.3102/0013189X031009003

Tillman, L. C. (2004). (Un)Intended consequences? The impact of *Brown v. Board of Education* decision on the employment status of Black educators. *Education and Urban Society*, *36*(3), 280–303. ttps://doi.org/10.1177/0013124504264360

Yosso, T. J. (2005) Whose culture has capital? A critical race theory discussion of community cultural wealth, *Race Ethnicity and Education*, *8*(1), 69–91. doi:10.1080/1361332052000341006

CHAPTER 10

BEYOND THE YEARS

Dunbar High School 1916–1968

M. Francyne Huckaby, Stephanie Cuellar, Michelle Nguyen, Leslie Ekpe, Rachel Brooks, Kellton Hollins, and Jonathan W. Crocker

Texas Christian University

Dunbar High School flourished in Texarkana, Texas, for 7th to 12th grades, offering a community-based education to generations of Black families from 1916–1968. In 1968, the high school closed to integrate the Texas High School (THS). The Dunbar Buffalos, who were not yet alumni, joined the Texas Tigers to complete their high school careers. This chapter, Beyond the Years, amplifies the voices of Dunbar alumni interviewed 50 years after the closing of the school during the occasion of their all-classes reunion. Their oral histories of educational experiences reveal countless victories for African American education prior to the Reconstruction Era. Turning to arts-based inquiry, the authors combine film and ethnography. As critical researchers, they filmed semi-structured interviews to illuminate Dunbar alumni experiences prior to, during, and after integration. The project archives individual interviews electronically and themed short films that are integrated into the chapter with QR Codes. This chapter, "Beyond the Years," explores Dunbar and attends to Black character and confidence, integration, athletics, comparisons with early 21st century education, and visions alumni have for contemporary education.

Keywords: Intergenerational storytelling, Cultural Capital, Dunbar High School, Texarkana, Texas

BEYOND THE YEARS: DUNBAR HIGH SCHOOL 1916–1968

Dunbar High School (Dunbar) (see Figure 10.1) flourished in Texarkana, Texas, offering a community-based education to generations of Negro, Black, and African American families from 1916–1968. Each morning four teachers would stand on the corners of the property to invite students into the school, and the principal, standing in the entrance hall, greeted everyone as they walked into the building. Dunbar was a fortress against the hardships 7th to 12th graders and their communities faced in the racialized South of the United States of America. In 1968, the high school was closed to integrate Texas High School (THS). Students, who had not yet graduated, joined the Texas Tigers to complete their high school careers. Nonetheless, Dunbar Buffalo pride and its community extended beyond the years of the school's existence. In 2018, Dunbar alumni from across the nation gathered in Houston, Texas to remember the Blue and Gold and share in their Buffalo Pride.

This chapter, "Beyond the Years," explores Dunbar and attends to Black character and confidence, integration, athletics, comparisons with early 21st century education, and visions alumni have for contemporary education. This work draws heavily from the oral histories and stories told by Dunbar alumni. Throughout the chapter are embedded hyperlinks and QR codes that allow direct access to

FIGURE 10.1.   Dunbar High School

QR Code 1. Dunbar 1916–1968 Project. https://franhuckaby.com/dunbar/

Dunbar: 1916–1968, a film project and digital archive of the Dunbar oral historians and storytellers. Their remembrances tell of an educational institution that prepared generations of Negro, Black, and African American youth to succeed in a world bent on holding them down. The terms *Negro, Black*, and *African American* are used in this text for historical reasons. In keeping with the practice before the 1960s, we most often use Negro. After the 1960s, we use Black or African American (Martin, 1991). At times, our language parallels the usage of the Dunbar alumni who offered oral histories. We turn to African American to connect the past to the present and Black to signify intergenerational and diasporic relations. Throughout, we capitalize both White and Black. Another approach would take note from Crenshaw (1991) and capitalize Black but not White. Citing Mackinnon, Crenshaw explains that "like Asian, Latinos, and other 'minorities', constitute a specific cultural group and, as such, require denotation as a proper noun" (Crenshaw, 1991, p. 1244). Brown would be capitalized for the same reason. Because *White* "is not a proper noun, since Whites do not constitute a specific cultural group," Crenshaw (1991, p. 1244) writes it in lower case. This logic also leads to writing "women of color" in lower case letters.

This is a project about witnessing, hearing deeply, and sharing the storytelling, accounts, and records in hopes that we may be heirs to the legacy left by a community that wrapped caring adults around its youth. This is an arts-based inquiry that understands the power form has to inform (Eisner, 1981; Finely, 2005) and turns to film to illuminate and amplify (Huckaby, 2018, 2019) the experiences of Dunbar. In many ways, the Dunbar experience addressed the critiques and expectations of education theorized by William Edward Burghardt Du Bois (1973), Carter Godwin Woodson, and Anna Julia Cooper (Grant et al., 2016). Dunbar is an exemplar of Negro education, not just for the historical record, but also for the 21st century and beyond as it provides tangible recommendations for rectifying issues within contemporary education systems. Dunbar educators understood Dubois when he made clear that the teacher of Negro students,

> Has got to be able to impart his [*sic*] knowledge to human beings whose place in the world is today precarious and critical; and the possibilities and advancement of that human being... and acquainted too with human beings and their possibilities. (DuBois, 1973, p. 78)

Dunbar was committed not to the mis-education that Woodson theorized, an education that directed students and graduates away from the needs African Americans, but toward a proper education for Negro students that was academic, redemptive, and consistent with Cooper's ideals (Grant et al., 2016).

INTERGENERATIONAL STORYTELLING

One fall weekend, my mother and I (M. Francyne Huckaby) were in her kitchen. She was cooking breakfast and sharing information and updates on things important—family, events, plans—as she usually does. Sitting at the breakfast bar, I watched and listened, making mental notes, asking questions, and adding my occasional commentary. The upcoming Dunbar High School all-class reunion drifted into the conversation. My research at the time focused on the public education struggles communities face (Huckaby, 2017a, 2017b, 2018, 2019). I was curious and asked if I could go to the reunion. A few weeks later, I was on a telephone call with the Houston alumni planning committee. My mother told them about my research and filmmaking, and the committee was curious about documenting the reunion. I addressed their questions about options, and then they engaged in discussions without me. Occasionally, my mother would call to ask questions on behalf of the group. I was eventually invited to film their storytelling at the pre-reunion luncheons and to film oral history interviews at the luncheons and reunion. This invitation was indeed an honor, and it was a privilege to offer a means to record and preserve the storytelling of my elders.

Storytelling, an African American intergenerational tradition (Fabius, 2016), was an essential part of my childhood and has remained important in my family. Sometimes the stories were/are directed toward children; other times they are told for all present and in earshot of youth. This film project of Dunbar historians and storytellers on the occasion of their all-class reunion 50 years after the school's closing is situated in this Black tradition in four ways. First, the project focuses on the oral histories and stories of alumni who lived in segregated and desegregated America. Second, the films and digital archives now hold the orations of the Dunbar experience online for the alumni and their families. The individual accounts and short films offer multiple vantage points that are also available to broader communities of youth, students, educators, scholars, and citizens of the world interested in this history. Third, Dunbar stories are part of my family history. My mother attended Dunbar for a year when she lived in Texarkana with her eldest sister, Aunt Connie. Known by Dunbar historians as Ms. Alton, the math and home economics teacher and spouse of Mr. Arthur Alton, the third of four principals (see Figure 10.2). Uncle Arthur led Dunbar from 1935 to 1966 just two years before the school was closed due to integration with THS. My cousins, the children of two of my aunts, were around my mother's age and also attended Dunbar. Despite these connections to Dunbar Alumnus, Vernon Johnson describes as "one of the finest Black educational institutions that was ever created for Black people during the era of segregation," I knew little about Dunbar. Fourth, the hearing of the stories of the alumni have made clear to me the ways I am an heir of this educational institution that has continued to live through its students and their descendants as Mr. Alton wrote in "A Message FROM MY PRINCIPAL,"

It should be your purpose to arouse yourselves to the vast vision that lies before you, prepare yourselves through college work to achieve the success placed

FIGURE 10.2. Dunbar Principles from 1916–1968v

before your vision by those who have gone before you and sacrificed their lives that you might enjoy the blessings of life, liberty, and the pursuits of happiness.... And to this end you as high school graduates should launch to accomplish a more respectful, a more resourceful, a more perfect and more enjoyable world for posterity to enjoy. (African American Life in Texarkana, 2019a, para. 5)

For Cynthia Dillard (2012) and Dillard with Chinwe Okpalaoka (2011), people of the African diaspora are African Ascendant people. Ascendant, unlike the more common descendant, describes African diasporic peoples "upward and forward moving nature" (Dillard, 2012, p. 16) instead of a "falling or tumbling down" (Marina, 2016, p. 29). This connection of ancestors, elders, and youth informs the methodology of this project. Drawing upon endarkened feminist praxis (Dillard & Okpalaoka, 2011), we have sought to establish and maintain intergenerational

QR Code 2: Dunbar Oral Historians. vimeo.com/showcase/dunbarhistorian

 QR Code 3: Dunbar Storytellers https://vimeo.com/showcase/storytellers]

and reciprocal relationships of responsibility. For similar reasons, we include first names and last names of academic scholars as well as Dunbar oral historians and storytellers. This feminist approach creates space to acknowledge people more fully, including the gender cues first names may offer. To ensure the Dunbar oral historians and storytellers are held on equal status with academic writers, we introduce their words and quotations from the collection of films with present tense verbs as the films exist. We also use the titles for school personnel that were either spoken by the Dunbar oral historians and storytellers or written in archival sources. This is collective and transformative work of hearing histories from within a community of youth who have become our elders and amplifying the stories told within an intergenerational, interracial research team.

Dunbar alumni are of the Silent Generation and Baby Boomers, while the research-filmmaking team consists of Generation X, Millennials, Generation Y and Generation Z. In logistical terms, the project has entailed filming activities and oral history storytelling at two pre-reunion luncheons held in Houston in 2017 and Texarkana in 2018. The luncheons raised funds for the reunion, encouraged participation in the reunion, and offered a mini reunion for people who might not attend the formal one. During the luncheons, alumni talked with old classmates, played trivia games, told stories, and laughed. These were joyous events. I had an opportunity to address alumni at the luncheons, pass out informed consent forms, and point out the locations of the cameras. The luncheons provided an opportunity to inform alumni about the interviews that would be filmed at the reunion and to conduct a few oral history interviews in Texarkana. I also toured and filmed the school grounds and Bell Park in Texarkana with two of the primary organizers of the reunion, Vernon Johnson and Larry Mathis. Twenty-four alumni participated in the filmed interviews conducted by Michelle Nguyen and me in 2018. Michelle Prokof (2018–2019), Stephanie Cuellar (2019–2020), and I (2017–2020) reviewed the footage and edited thematic short films (2019–2020). Leslie Ekpe, Rachel Brooks, and Kellton Hollins joined us in 2020 and Jonathan Crocker in 2021 to write from our study of the films and raw footage. Three research team members are African American, one is second-generation Vietnamese-American, one is Mexican American, and two are White. We are a diverse research team, and

QR Code 4: https://dunbar19161968.com/dunbar-high-school-2018-reunion/]

our perspectives and positionalities show through our writing. This chapter and the African Ascendent Elder stories in text, image, film, and digital archive are the result of our efforts to chronicle and study narratives of oral historians and elder storytellers of Texarkana's Dunbar High School. Throughout the remainder of the chapter, we honor the intellectual work of the Dunbar oral historians and storytellers who participated in this project by name.

BEFORE DUNBAR

An increasing Negro population in Texarkana brought to bear the question of a public school around 1880 (Doan, 2019; Williams & Woolridge, 2007). At the time, public schools were accessible to the public and supported and controlled by the public (Huckaby, 2019; Reese, 2007). Because of Jim Crow and segregation, Negro youth could not go to these schools, as they only taught White students. In response, Texarkana's Negro community built their own school. Because Oak and Elm streets on the Texas side of Texarkana were central for the community, the school was first held in Mount Zion Baptist Church at Fourth and Elm Streets with Professor Dillard serving as the principal and Mrs. Dillard as the assistant (Williams & Woolridge, 2007). Later the school moved to its own property on Seventh and Elm streets, where Professor Williams (principal) built the school facing Sixth Street. Because of its proximity to the Negro community, it was named Central.

The Williams and Woodridge (2007) historical account entitled, 1916 Paul Laurence Dunbar High School, notes that Central passed through several leaders over the years before it became Dunbar. (This particular archival account of Dunbar High School, with the exception of 1880 and 1916, provides a series of school personnel that excludes dates of service.) Professor Spencer built a four-room, two-story building facing Sixth Street during his first term. Teachers during this time included Mrs. Spencer, Mrs. Hattie Dawson, Mrs. Campbell, Miss Fannie, Rev. Plant, Mrs. Plant, Miss R. Webb, and Miss Eva Webb. Professor W. T. Daniels served for a year during Principal Spencer's years. Professor M. C. McCowan followed Spencer. Teachers during the McCowan term were Mrs. Lula Long, Mrs. Jessie Johnson, Professor Jetie Weaver, Mrs. Cora Jones, Miss Susie Fridia, among others. During this time, a brick building facing Seventh Street was added. Professor B.A. Jackson, a graduate of Fisk University and Harvard Law School and former Paul Quinn College professor of mathematics, became principal in 1916 and proposed the name change to Paul Laurence Dunbar after the American writer of poetry, plays, short stories, and novels.

Other Negro schools in the area that were established after Dunbar included Orr, NewTown, and Macedonia schools. The Orr School building was erected in Arkansas in 1880, and the school commenced in 1886, six years after the start of the Texarkana, Texas, school. Negro children including Scott Joplin, a composer and the Father of Ragtime Music attended the school (Arkansas Historic Preservation Society, 1976). A donation to the Black community funded the two-story school which was rebuilt as a one-story school after a fire (Watts & G.W., 2006). NewTown elementary was established at the request of Harrison G. Goree, who was hired as principal of Sunset Elementary in 1912. Instead of taking the Sunset post, he started NewTown and served as principal until 1916. NewTown was held in a two-room house on Taylor Street (Day & Woolridge, 2007; Texarkana Independent School District, 2016). Macedonia School, a one-room, one-teacher school was built for grades 1 to 11 in 1917 (African American Life in Texarkana, 2019) with the help of the Rosenwald Fund, which materially aided Booker T. Washington's efforts to build rural public schools (McCormick, 1934).

This history chronicles Dunbar and its antecedents as the first school for Negro youth in Texarkana, giving it nearly a 90-year history of serving the Black community in Texas from 1880 to the late 1960s. While data about the size of the school's student body over its years of existence is unavailable, *Figure 3* charts the number of seniors by year for the years available from the Texarkana Genealogy Society between 1928 and 1965 (http://dunbartexarkana.org/Gene/). Dunbar was part of the increase in Negro education that DuBois (1973) claimed "by all measurements has been a little less than marvelous" (p. 65). Over the decades,

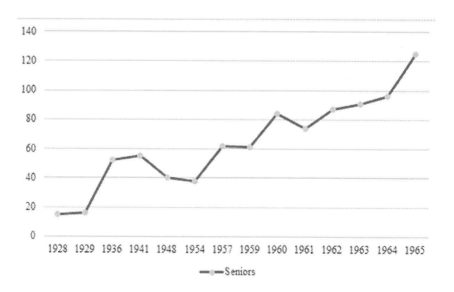

FIGURE 10.3. Dunbar Seniors 1928–1965

the school served an increasing population of students from 7th to 12th grade. An important aspect of education was the character and confidence Dunbar students developed.

DUNBAR CAPITAL

Pierre Bourdieu and Jean-Claude Passeron (1977) theorized about "the disadvantage attached to social origin" as they pertained to "educational channeling" (p. 83) and found that the two are, in fact, strongly correlated. This dynamic makes for the general predictability based on social, cultural, and economic backgrounds of which students are likely to complete or excel. Thus, existing educational systems determine who will fail and who will succeed based on the backgrounds students bring with them instead of what they will gain. The measure of whose capital is valuable—human, social, linguistic, or cultural—is also a measure of which social classes will meet with success (Bourdieu & Passeron, 1977). The fact that wealth and race determine educational success and progress is precisely why the relationship between education and social origin must be questioned.

U.S. education was built on an oppressive system that exclusively valued one kind of capital, that of White wealth. Considerations of the capital Black students contributed were dismissed. Desegregation, however, forced the issue,

> A situation of nascent crisis is an opportunity to discern the hidden presuppositions of a traditional system and the mechanisms capable of perpetuating it. ... It is when the perfect attunement between the education system and its chosen public begins to break down that the 'preestablished harmony' which upheld the system so perfectly as to exclude all inquiry into its basis is revealed. (Bourdieu & Passeron, 1977, p. 99)

The education Bourdieu and Passeron (1977) describe is a self-fulfilling one. Rich White people who speak, write, and learn in similar ways teach White children to do things that way and so the culture is passed down from generation to generation. The system reproduces itself by giving an education, which grants social capital, to the classes the system defines as already worthy of that capital. The "nascent crisis" of desegregation is a moment of change, a chance to learn, to look behind the curtain of the system and see the lie of the wizard. Education does not lift people up to social capital, it redistributes social capital among those who already have it and ensures those without it never receive it.

Dunbar capital offered an anecdote to the social capital that denied them, and that was destined to misshape them. For Dunbar alumni, as their stories and remembrances demonstrate, Dunbar capital was about realizing the "lovely precious dream" Nina Simone sings—To Be Young, Gifted and Black (1970). That the play and song title lack the Oxford comma after gifted makes clear that young-gifted-black are to be thought together as a unity, not separate entities that only come together on occasion in a few. An adaptation of the play by the same name written by her friend and playwright, Lorraine Hansberry, Simone sings:

> We must begin to tell our young
> There's a world waiting for you
> Yours is the quest that's just begun

Dunbar faculty and staff believed this of their students and the community and held steadfast to this vision even when students made mistakes or failed. Teachers, classmates, and the local community were there to support and uplift students in a network of reciprocal relationships that wrapped care, support, expectations, and aspirations around individuals, classes, and the school. In the sections that follow we share through the wisdom of Dunbar historians and storytellers tangible examples of Dunbar capital in action manifest in developing of character and confidence, overcoming failure, and refusing exclusion.

Developing Character and Confidence

Dunbar oral historians do not tell stories about capital, nor do they talk about linguistic or social capital or how the system was fought. Instead, they offer narrations about how their teachers were good people who taught to make them good people. These are the things—the relationships and the character—that often get ignored in talk about "the system" of education. Faye Price Banton, Dunbar Class of 1968, explains "I carry with me the lessons I have learned from all the people along the way. I took a little bit of every teacher that ever taught me and made it into me." She goes on to list individual teachers and specific situations she would apply toward her own development. She remembers her Dunbar teachers for how they contributed to her growth and how they helped her develop her own strategy of facing the world. When it came to student learning, the teachers at Dunbar were persistent. Whether it be sewing a zipper into a blouse, learning social graces, science, or business, Dunbar teachers required students to master the curriculum. Pat Dizer Odom, Dunbar Class of 1961, recounts how involved teachers were in the classroom: They wrote on the board, called on students routinely, and required each individual play an active role in their learning. The system that succeeded at Dunbar was not a cookie cutter one that produced uniformity, but one that allowed each student the chance to become, with support and guidance from faculty. For Carol Jean Afford, Dunbar Class of 1968, the high standards upheld at Dunbar, from dress code to addressing teachers, are noteworthy "when you went to Dunbar High School you learned how to act anywhere you go. You could go to the White House and you would be appropriate." Dunbar teachers knew that the system was made by and for White people. They had been barred from it, as were their parents and Negro progenitors, for the same reason—social origin. The tradi-

 QR Code 5: Character Development vimeo.com/460673831]

tional system was a White system, and even with integration, the new system was just as White even with the addition of Black students. The teachers at Dunbar set high standards for their students because the system was not going to. They created educational experiences for African Ascendent youth who contribute to the world. Carol Jean Afford, class of 1968, describes the mentality Dunbar instilled in her as "you ought to make a difference in life... If you want to be different in the world then you ought to be the difference in the world today."

Dunbar alumni, like Diane Gaines, THS Class of 1970, understand that "school is just not about education, it's about how you learn how to treat people and it gives you character, and I thank God for the character that I have from Dunbar." This is why Black schools matter, because Black teachers and Black communities support Black students. Black students may not have had the social capital or the linguistic capital that the school system expected and perpetuated, but they had strong and healthy communities which shared a common. They had their own social and linguistic capital, which was valued within Dunbar and the surrounding community, because it was shared. That is precisely what Dunbar protected. Dunbar proved that the old system was not the only one that could work, and the White wealth version of capital was not the only one worthy of value.

For numerous alumni, this attention to building character fostered more. Reverend Willie Stephens, Dunbar Class of 1956, remembers Mr. Bell who taught him, "you decide on who you want to be, what you want to do, and where you want to go." These are not things young Black men could have heard from a White teacher in a segregated school, or even in an early integrated school. They had to have heard it from a Black community member, be it parents, coaches, church leaders or teachers, and they heard it at Dunbar. Character, now that is some true capital. Dunbar offered a form of character development that led to confidence of a particular kind that made for success of Negro youth in a hostile environment—Black confidence. Wardell Richardson, Dunbar Class of 1965, for example, notes that "the training and the coaching and the teaching that was instilled in us at Dunbar High School has made me a better person today." The character and confidence built through the Dunbar experience occurred in the community, classroom, relationships, and athletics.

Athletics—Overcoming Failure

Sports are staples to the state of Texas. Friday night high school football is a significant piece of Lone Star culture. But in segregated schools, only White athletes in White schools were allowed to play on this day nationally known for football. As Brenda Dizer North, Dunbar class of 1964 and public school teacher, ex-

QR Code 6: Confidence vimeo.com/460678059]

plains, "Unless you were at a school that had its own football stadium, you didn't play on Friday night. The White people played on Friday nights. You played on Wednesday and Thursday nights." Luckily Dunbar students had their own stadium, giving them the chance to showcase their abilities under what has become known as the Friday night lights. Not only reserved for the football team, the stadium had a half-track providing the school's track athletes a place to work out and practice. Dunbar also had a gymnasium situated in the middle of the campus that served the entire student population and was the center of school social life.

The Dunbar storytellers express pride in their sports facilities, but despite having a stadium and gymnasium to themselves, having things of their own was limited. The athletes received hand-me-down gear and equipment from surrounding schools, such as THS, and the band played used instruments. Due to the unequal and inadequate funding Negro and segregated schools received, resources and materials were limited. Often, "the resources needed for basic instruction, including blackboards, pencils, books, chairs, desks, even land and buildings, had to be supplied by members of the local Black communities" (Franklin, 2002, p. 176). Additionally, the lack of funding left little to no room for resources for extracurricular activities, especially sports. With the primary focus being education because of its association with freedom in the Black community, it would have been easy to push athletics aside at Dunbar. Fortunately, that was not the choice made. Dan Haskins, a Dunbar alumnus, joined Dunbar as the head football coach in 1965 after a year of all losses in 1964, along with Richard Tolbert, football co-captain, Samuel Aikins and John Walton. Frances Brewster, class of 1956 and daughter of Mr. and Mrs. Alton remembers her mother "saw 'good' in him" even as he tried "to go in the other direction." She continued in a text message "Mom was his math teacher and knew he was smart. She begged Dad to let him pass to the next grade. She told him, if we hold him back, we're going to lose him." Coach Haskins brought a commitment to athletes at Dunbar. Saul Washington recalls,

> When Coach Haskins came, the new thing changed. What he did I'll never forget… First, they got rid of all the jerseys because we were wearing jerseys from [other schools]. We never got anything different from that. He came in and burned a lot of that stuff up.

As a result of Coach Haskins actions, Dunbar's football team had a new look. "We came in one day, and we had all brand-new stuff, and we felt like kids at Christmas," Phillip Pegues jokes. In addition to new gear, the football team won the title of district champions before forced integration.

Winning adds to the experience of being a student-athlete and creates camaraderie along the journey to the primary goal. The Dunbar team spirit among athletes was demonstrated through the way they looked out for one another. As a testament to the community at Dunbar, football players would take turns making a menu and bringing in dishes to feed themselves and their teammates on the bus rides to away games. Players would also do a war cry they called the "Dunbar Spirit" on these bus rides. The chant, "would go around until every player on the bus had a chance to exemplify the Dunbar Spirit." After losing the first game of the district season one year, Samuel Aikin, Dunbar Class of 1967 and football co-captain, recalls Coach Haskins getting on the bus after the game and telling the team they were acting more like cheerleaders than a football team. Their coach was insinuating the players spent more time chanting their Dunbar Spirit, than focusing on playing the game. Consistent with many teachers at Dunbar, the coaches never gave up on the team. Aikin remembered, "From that moment on, he began to work with us... We gathered around that failure, and we became a successful football team." Commitments to resources, character building, and confidence, in return, provided student-athletes the opportunity to play at the college level. One such athlete was Wardell Richardson, Dunbar Class of 1965, one of three Black football players for Texarkana College in 1965. Coach Haskins, along with Dunbar students, integrated THS as coach. He became the first Black THS principal. Frances Brewster remembers hearing stories and laughter about Coach Haskins around the dining room table. He was a great coach and principal "because whatever the kids tried to do, he had already done." Dunbar coaches and teachers' delicate balance of discipline and compassion provided space for students to explore their interests, learn from their failures, succeed, and develop a sense of self.

INTEGRATION—REFUSING EXCLUSION

The demand to integrate U.S. public schools, upheld by the Supreme Court, focused on race and socio-economic class to foster economic and social equality as well as stability of the democracy. After the 1954 Brown v. Board of Education ruling on integration was delayed in Texas and Arkansas schools (Doan, 2019), the Texarkana community responded unfavorably to the court ruling, and even the 1955 call (Ogletree, 2004) for slower integration "with all deliberate speed" caused anxiety (Doan, 2019). Dunbar remained a segregated school for Negro youth until 1968. Starting with the 1st grade in 1964, Texarkana Independent School District (TISD) desegregated grade level by grade level, year by year until 1968 via the "Freedom of Choice" policy, which allowed students to stay in Dunbar or move to THS. Ed Johnson remembers this "story of forced integration."

> First, they told us they were going to give us what they called 'freedom of choice'....
> But they only wanted certain people. I definitely wasn't one of them. But anyway,
> that didn't work. Then they came up with mandatory busing. But nobody got bussed

QR Code 7: Integration Awareness vimeo.com/460674684]

to Dunbar. Everybody had to leave, and they really stripped the whole school. They tried to pick the best teachers and the best students.... They actually welcomed some of the football players, the athletes, over there and they started playing the first year.

In 1968, all remaining Dunbar students were transferred to THS. Dunbar remained a junior high school, graduating its last class of 9th graders in 1969 before it was shut down and closed.

Integration is often touted as one of the most effective methods for enriching student lives. For Dunbar students, however, this was not always the case. Integration in Texarkana did not rectify inequities. Much like integration across the nation, it was another iteration of the dominant social group exerting and maintaining its dominance. Dunbar offered deep connections between teachers and students as well as athletes and coaches. When students were forced to integrate with THS, they lost these connections within the school setting. The students recognized this disconnect as they tried to understand their own value. Ed Johnson recalls, "When we got there, we said, wait a minute, they got the football team on the field right away," but the school lacked any African American representation in the student council, cheerleaders, band, and majorettes. Student, Mary Jacki Washington, THS Class of 1972, recalls that they were told about prerequisites, like the two years of pep squad needed to try out for the cheer and two years junior high experience for the band and majorette team, but "there were no prerequisites for the athletes because they needed those bodies for the football team and the basketball team." The discrepancy between Black student involvement in sports and their involvement in student council and other clubs and organizations demonstrated and communicated where, how, and to what degree Black students were valued at THS. Betty Pickett Stuckey, THS Class of 1970, explains,

> Everybody worked and lived together; culturally aware that everything you needed was right there in the community. The transition was difficult from Dunbar to Texas High. I feel like I lost out on so much more if I had continued to be at Dunbar. When you go from being leaders in your school, being in charge of various things, and then going where you [pause], for lack of better word [pause], low on the totem pole, then you miss out on a lot.

Dunbar's student-leaders were excluded from engagement with school activities, and student-athletes were only valued for their athleticism. This dynamic is an uncomfortable parallel to the institution of slavery. Black student-athletes performed physical labor while being led and directed by White coaches not unlike the ways Black bodies executed manual labor for the benefit of those who enslaved them. As Du Bois (1973) noted, enslaved people "were not supposed to be subjects for education at all" (p. 10). To exacerbate the linkages between athletics and slavery, a confederate flag hung in THS entry for students to see as soon as they walked into the school. The flag was eventually removed thanks to a brave group that decided to protest.

Taught to standup for themselves and to value their contributions, students from Dunbar resisted the discrimination and exclusion. Ed Johnson reminisces, "But at that time we had been taught some things... about a guy named Nat Turner, a person named Denmark Vesey, someone named Gabriel Prosser—these were revolutionaries." This focus on Black history and sociology in the Dunbar curriculum was consistent with the education Woodson—the founder of *Negro History Week*, the *Negro Bulletin*, and the *Home Study Program*—theorized (Grant et al., 2016). Mary Jacki Washington continues narrating the history about a protest around the flagpole.

> We tried to do it in a civil manner. We went before administration; we had our own little committee and the whole bit... and we told them, "This is not fair.".... My mother lectured me for two weeks to stay out of it. But as soon as it broke out, I was right in the middle of it, because I was the only African American in my [enriched] academic classes.... We were up on the hill... huge, everything. That evening we were on the news. As a result of that, we were expelled from school—forever.

Yvette Goree-Harris, Dunbar student and THS alumna, notes of her involvement in the protest, "If I didn't do it, who was going to do it?" In actuality the students only missed five weeks of school, because they filed and won an injunction against THS. The court ruled that the constitutional rights of the expelled students were violated when they were not offered adequate due process for their expulsion. They were not given enough time and preparation to properly defend themselves and were unrightfully expelled during the spring semester of their school year. Thankfully, the court did not uphold the expulsions and allowed students to come back to school and finish out their school year. When they returned, they noted marked changes in THS within a year. Within 2 years, African American students were cheerleaders and members of the homecoming court. This legacy of the students who stood up for their right for representation within their own educational experience has not been forgotten (*Texarkana ISD v. Lewis*, 1971).

Despite the lack of adequate resources and funding, Dunbar served as a success that met the educational needs of the community it served. Like many other Negro schools, Dunbar was integral to the community and offered a strong educational base for thousands of children. Desegregation threatened these communal ties. As a small community, Dunbar parents and teachers had strong partnerships that supported students in educational attainments. At THS bigotry circumvented the education of students from Dunbar. While integration was, for many, the loss of Black community and solidarity, somehow Dunbar maintained its community, and 50 years after desegregation alumni gathered to celebrate their education. The significance of community is an essential theme throughout the Dunbar alumni stories. The integration stories of Dunbar historians are noteworthy—not because they demonstrate the common phenomenon of the local authorities, school districts, and communities systematically working to preserve White schools, while diminishing and closing schools for people of color and restricting access to equitable opportunities—but because they demonstrate Dunbar's persistence, brilliance, character, and confidence. These narrations of Dunbar history reveal the solidarity built in the community that transcended the school building into family, culture, and religious partnerships (Coleman, 1988).

EDUCATION THEN AND NOW

Dunbar historians describe their educational experiences in comparison to the academic experiences they have observed of their own children, grandchildren, and other young relatives in the decades following integration. Some alumni juxtapose the immediate changes in educational environments and practices as they transitioned from Dunbar to THS, holding their Dunbar experiences in high regard as the standard for which education should strive. In fact, Judge Evelyn Palfrey McKee, a romance novelist, claims that Dunbar was "an experience that [she] would wish for all of the students today—not just the Black ones." Dunbar historians express their preference for Dunbar curriculum, instruction, and structure, alongside their disapproval of how teaching practices have evolved over the years. They discuss the nurturing environment created by teachers and school leaders as well as the intentional instructive strategies as components of education that should be emulated in 21st century schools. They value the broad, foundational Dunbar education that allowed them to explore various interests and become aware of their capabilities and talents. They remember the overwhelming support and care they received at Dunbar. Dr. Alda Faye Moore, a Gestalt psychologist, shares that Dunbar was "the campus where everybody was somebody." Dunbar created a sense of community and belonging not unlike that experienced by Cooper in her own education; the kind of belonging that informed her theorizing and pedagogy (Grant et al., 2016). Despite appearance, background, or level of intelligence, students knew they were loved by their instructors, principals, parents, and peers. Standards were set high as were structures of support to assist students in achieving. Dunbar teachers worked in close partnership with parents to ensure accountability and success. According to Judith Sims Cox-Reaves, Dunbar Class of 1964, if a student missed school, it was not uncommon for their teacher to make a visit to their home. As keepers of a lived historical record, Dunbar alumni note the lack of parental involvement in contemporary schools as a stark contrast to the close teacher-parent alliance they experienced at Dunbar. Students, as Loretta Rhoads-Sanders, Dunbar Class of 1965, describes, also received support from peers, who ensured no one showed up to class with incomplete assignments.

 QR Code 8: Education Then and Now vimeo.com/460676348]

These community strengthening structures drastically contrast the individual responsibility expected in subsequent generations.

Unsurprisingly, Dunbar historians notice the drawbacks of standardized tests and the consequences to students and schools when they fail to meet the established expectations. Contrarily, Dunbar was described as a safe space for students to fail. Failure was considered part of the learning experience rather than a result that negatively impacts student, school, and community options. Dunbar alumni affirm these notions by sharing their experiences with the "tough love" from the teachers. Diane Gaines, THS Class of 1970, recalls that when she found herself pregnant in high school, her teacher assured her that she was college-bound regardless of the circumstance. Conversely, rather than teaching to a test, Dunbar teachers took the time to ensure students fully understood and could apply their knowledge to various concepts and situations. Instead of attending to passing grades and presenting content regardless of whether students were digesting the information or not, Dunbar teachers were focused on genuine learning experiences that met students where they were with respect to their circumstances. Consistent with intellectuals such as W. E. B. Du Bois (1973) and Anna Julia Cooper (Grant et al., 2016), Dunbar teachers were preparing students for college, to be intellectual leaders not just laborers or wage earners. Pat Dizer Odom, Dunbar Class of 1961, shares that she does not see the Dunbar level of involvement or accountability in contemporary education. Dunbar leaders were far less concerned with administering a test and checking the boxes required for their job. Instead, Dunbar was an intimate educational environment dedicated to the holistic development and success of students.

Judge Evelyn Palfrey McKee notes how easily children are labeled discipline problems and the role disciplinary records have in sustaining a school to prison pipeline. At Dunbar, every student mattered. Every student was encouraged, supported, and loved. In the words of Virgil Bursey, a veteran of the Marines and Air Force, "It was a personal thing at Dunbar." It was also a collective effort. Samuel Aikin, Dunbar Class of 1967, describes the community-based approach practiced at Dunbar by referencing the ancient West African proverb—It takes a village to raise a child. Church leaders, neighbors, teachers, and parents alike all contributed to student upbringing, growth, and success. David Earl Evans, Dunbar Class of 1967, shares that when his family did not have enough to eat, his neighbors ensured they did not miss a meal. When Diane Gaines, THS Class of 1970, did not have enough money to purchase fabric for her sewing project, her teachers provided. Dunbar students never went without because, according to Samuel Aikin, Dunbar Class of 1967, the "larger community of people…looked out for each other." These elements of social capital distributed throughout the community provided the assurance of achievement that may otherwise have not been possible (Coleman, 1988). Teachers also took personal interests in ensuring each student succeeded. This supportive and nurturing approach by the community and the school to student development fostered the success of Dunbar alumni even though, as Faye Banton Price, Dunbar Class of 1968, observes, society "did not want to see Black students succeed."

Robert Melvin Lee Jr., Dunbar Class of 1963, speaks of the stark contrasts between the community-based education at Dunbar and the lack thereof in schools that came later.

> What I see happening today.... You don't have that community involvement for multiple reasons. Sometimes it's economics, depending on where the schools are, and you don't have schools necessarily in the community where the parents can be involved... that's what I think we need to get back to is having more involvement of parents and others with the kids in the schools... I do feel that if education could move...back closer to the community it would help the children and help us as a community.

The contrasts made between Dunbar and education that came over the subsequent 50 years is glaring. Whether it be the importance placed on standardized tests over the attention to student learning or the decline in parental and community involvement, the differences are unfortunate. Because the Dunbar oral historians and storytellers had the opportunity to attend a school full of loving and supportive teachers, principals, and peers, they noticed the differences to early 21st century education quite easily. Their hopes for students is that education resurrects elements of the Dunbar educational experiences for current and future schools. Black schools and their communities, such as Dunbar, lost much in the transition into integrated schools. The experiences of Dunbar historians shed light on the need for educational systems to appropriately involve Black communities, to consider their contributions and needs of students and teachers. To be in the struggle for racial equity, education must commit to the Black community (Yosso, 2005). The need for reform to undo damage of earlier reforms of U.S. education systems persists and requires attention to the oppressive structures that created and maintain barriers to educational equity. Considerations of how race has been misused in such detrimental dynamics is crucial for future educational policy and practice.

VISION FOR EDUCATION

One might think that the outdated, early 20th century segregated education model would be inappropriate for envisioning the future. However, when asked about their visions for education, many Dunbar historians reflected on the characteristics of their own experiences. The sense of community and high levels of support from teachers and peers are key features of their hopes for students in schools. They envision a more holistic and inclusive learning environment for future generations.

QR Code 9: Vision for Education vimeo.com/468165714]

Institutions exist and succeed because of the trust engendered by them. Without a high level of trustworthiness, institutions, including successful schools, simply could not exist (Coleman, 1988). Students, families, and communities of such schools come to trust the systems the institutions put into place. To create productive learning environments that catalyze student learning experiences, school systems, including teachers, administration, and policy, need to establish and maintain trust based on the realities of the context. They avoid spin doctoring and manipulating discourse. Such an approach would entail transparency and a mutuality between students and authority figures, as well as between the community, the school, and municipality leadership. Dunbar alumni consistently praise their teachers and school administration and attribute their success to the support they received from educators and leadership they could trust. An aspect of this trust is collectivism, a phenomenon noted within communities from similar ethnic and cultural backgrounds (Coleman, 1988), which is more easily achieved in spaces such as Dunbar. For Dunbar alumni like Richard Tolbert, Dunbar Class of 1967, attending to the communal notion of education includes criticism of standardized testing, "you've got to customize education and make it more community-based, instead of teaching to a test." Standardized testing and the lack of individualization in public schools inhibits the learning experiences of many students and focuses too much on reaching school and district goals. Such an approach does not benefit students but diverts functions of teaching in pedagogically unproductive ways that end up negating the educational endeavor (Bourdieu, 1987).

Communities, school administration, teachers, and students all benefit when there is a sense of community that is based on a shared goal of learning and shared experiences, as was true for Dunbar. For Coleman (1988) this is a form of shared capital that benefits the generations that come after. Dunbar alumnus Richard Tolbert specifically mentions such sharing of ideas and experiences across generations is the best way to improve education. For Carol Jean Afford, Dunbar Class of 1968, such engagement may lead to a future where "every child knows the value of education." Investing in the education of students will impact their children and subsequent generations. Dunbar alumni want to pass along learning environments that are community-based and carry the potential to create life-changing opportunities for all students. They want youth to have the same educational privileges their education provided them.

CONCLUSION

This work is an amplification of the storytelling of Dunbar's historians in text and film. While the Dunbar teachers no longer stand at the corners of the school property to welcome students into a school that transformed youth of a Black rural community into productive citizens, their wisdom continues through the historians and storytellers and the digital archive they so generously created with their remembrances and stories. May their stories be heard and cherished by countless

FIGURE 10.4. Dunbar Graduates 1956

generations; may their wisdom last beyond the years because as Nina Simone orates,

> There's a million boys and girls
> Who are young, gifted and Black
> And that's a fact

Dunbar alumni experienced a positive, supportive and demanding learning community committed to their growth, well-being, and success. Their history and community were central to the curriculum as was an anticipated, expected engagement with the nation and the broader world. Dunbar offered a holistic learning environment that was nested in reciprocal community relationships that offered a fortress against White supremacy and the oppression of Black communities. Their education not only steeled for the hardships integration brought, but made possible refusals in the face of exclusion. This work offers essential insights for contemporary education, schools, and curricula that too often fail to highlight a truthful and comprehensive history. Equally important, are the Dunbar dispositions and relationships educators and school leaders should strive to foster. May these lessons from Dunbar extend beyond the years.

AUTHOR NOTE

M. Francyne Huckaby https://orcid.org/0000-0002-4000-6285
Stephanie Cuellar https://orcid.org/0000-0003-3601-1134
Michelle Nguyen https://orcid.org/0000-0003-2851-8891
Leslie Ekpe https://orcid.org/0000-0002-1353-5560
Rachel Brooks https://orcid.org/0000-0002-3774-712X
Kellton Hollins https://orcid.org/0000-0002-7742-3699
Jonathan W. Crocker https://orcid.org/0000-0001-9012-7731
We have no known conflict of interest to disclose.

Correspondence concerning this article should be addressed to M. Francyne Huckaby, Texas Christian University, TCU Box 297040, Fort Worth, TX 76129. Email: f.huckaby@tcu.edu.

REFERENCES

African American Life in Texarkana. (2019). *Schools*. https://blacktexarkana.wordpress.com/2019/04/29/the-journey-begins/

Arkansas Historic Preservation Program. (1976, July 30). *Orr School*. https://www.arkansasheritage.com/docs/default-source/national-registry/mi0045-pdf.pdf?sfvrsn=48de85f3_0

Bourdieu, P. (1987). *A social critique of the judgment of taste*. Harvard University Press.

Bourdieu, P., & Passeron, J. (1977) *Reproduction in education, society and culture*. Sage.

Crenshaw, K. W. (1991). Mapping the margins: Intersectionality, identity politics, and violence against women of color. *Stanford Law Review, 43*(6), 1241–1299. https://doi.org/10.2307/1229039

Coleman, J. S. (1988) Social capital in the creation of human capital. *The American Journal of Sociology, 94*, S95–S120. https://doi.org/10.1086/228943

Day, D. M., & Woolridge, G. A. (2007). *NewTown Elementary School history*. Texarkana Genealogy Society. https://sites.rootsweb.com/~txkusa/schools/newtown.htm

Dillard, C. B. (2012). *Learning to (re)member the things we've learned to forget: Endarkened feminisms, spirituality, & the sacred nature of research & teaching*. Peter Lang.

Dillard, C. B., & Okpalaoka, C. (2011). The sacred and spiritual nature of endarkened transnational feminist praxis in qualitative research. In N. K. Denzin & Y. S. Lincoln (Eds.), *The Sage handbook of qualitative research* (4th ed., pp. 147–162). Sage.

Doan, K. A. (2019). *Equal but separated: Desegregation of Texarkana public schools*. Plan II Honors Theses-Openly Available. https://repositories.lib.utexas.edu/handle/2152/75439

Du Bois, W. E. B. (1973). *The education of Black people: Ten critiques 1906–1960*. Monthly Review Press.

Eisner, E. W. (1981). On the difference between scientific and artistic approaches to qualitative research. *Educational Researcher, 10*(4), 5–9. https://doi.org/10.3102/0013189X010004005

Fabius, C. D. (2016). Toward an integration of narrative identity, generativity, and storytelling in African American elders. *Journal of Black Studies, 47*(5), 423–434. https://doi.org/10.1177/0021934716638801

Finely, S. (2005). Arts-based inquiry: Performing revolutionary pedagogy. In N. K. Denzin & Y. S. Lincoln (Eds.), *The Sage handbook of qualitative research* (3rd ed., pp. 681–694). Sage.

Franklin, V. P. (2002) Introduction: Cultural capital and African American education. *The Journal of African American History, 87*(2), 175–181. https://doi.org/10.1086/jaahv87n2p175

Grant, C. A., Brown, K. D., & Brown, A. L. (2016). *Black intellectual thought in education: The missing traditions of Anna Julia Cooper, Carter G. Woodson, and Alain LeRoy Locke*. Routledge.

Huckaby, M. F. (2017a). Becoming cyborg: Activist filmmaker, the living camera, participatory democracy, and their weaving. *International Review of Qualitative Research, 10*(4), 340–359. https://doi.org/10.1525/irqr.2017.10.4.340

Huckaby, M. F. (2017b). *Public education | Participatory democracy after neoliberalism.* scalar.usc.edu/works/publiceducation/

Huckaby, M. F. (2018). Cyborg scholarship: Films for the people. In M. F. Huckaby (Ed.), *Making research public in troubled times: Pedagogy, activism, and critical obligations*: Vol. *Qualitative Inquiry: Critical ethics, justice, and activism* (pp. 99–119). Myers Education Press.

Huckaby, M. F. (2019). *Researching resistance: Public education after neoliberalism.* Myers Education Press.

Marina, B. (2016). Mentor myself? The juxtaposition of identity development for women of color in higher education. *The Sophist's Bane, 8*(1), 29–33.

Martin, B. (1991). From Negro to Black to African American: The power of names and naming. *Political Science Quarterly, 106*(1), 83–107. https://doi.org/10.2307/2152175

McCormick, J. S. (1934). The Julius Rosenwald Fund. *The Journal of Negro Education, 3*(4), 605–626. https://doi.org/10.2307/2292184

Ogletree, C. J. (2004). *All deliberate speed: Reflections on the first half century of Brown v. Board of Education.* WW Norton & Company.

Reese, W. J. (2007). *History, education, and the schools.* Palgrave Macmillan. https://doi.org/10.1057/9780230104822

Simone, N. (1970). *To be young, gifted and black* [Song]. On Black Gold. RCA Victor.

Texarkana Independent School District. (2016, December 14). *Press release: TISD to Host Dedication ceremony for renaming of facility to Goree Academic Learning Center.* http://www.txkisd.net/headlines/news.asp?id=570

Texarkana ISD v. Lewis, 470 S.W.2d 727 (1971). casemine.com/judgement/us/5914c753add7b049347e1ba4#91

Watts, J., & G. W. (2006). *Orr School: Texarkana, TX.* Texarkana Genealogy Society. http://dunbartexarkana.org/Gene/orr.htm

Williams, B., & Woolridge, G. A. (2007). *Paul Laurence Dunbar High School: Texarkana, TX 1916–1968.* http://dunbartexarkana.org/Gene/dunbarhs.htm

Yosso, T. J. (2005). Whose culture has capital? A critical race theory discussion of community cultural wealth. *Race Ethnicity and Education, 8*(1), 69–91. https://doi.org/10.1080/1361332052000341006

CHAPTER 11

FOR THE GOOD OF THE WHOLE

Restor(y)ing the History of Georgia's First Black Public High School

Amber M. Neal-Stanley
Purdue University

Originally constructed in 1914 as Reese Street School, it was later renamed Athens High and Industrial School (AHIS) to become Georgia's first accredited four-year Black public high school in 1922[1]. Yet, when AHIS opened its doors, the local Black community in Athens, Georgia had already successfully opened and operated numerous private, county and city public schools for decades, serving as central hubs of the community. This chapter suggests that what rooted the collaborative efforts of the local Black Athens community was a distinctive communal ethos and practice. Black Athenians viewed education as valuable capital, which served to benefit the community as a whole. As such, this is not a success story of one school, but the relentless struggle to resist White supremacy, anti-Black racism, and exclusion from predominantly White institutions by radically developing educational institutions in accordance with communal needs and future aspirations. This is a story of refusal

---

[1] Booker T. Washington was the first Black secondary public school in Atlanta. Ware was the first public high school for Black students. Athens High and Industrial was the first Black public high school that was accredited in the state of Georgia.

Black Cultural Capital: Activism That Spurred African American High Schools, pages 223–246.
Copyright © 2023 by Information Age Publishing
www.infoagepub.com
All rights of reproduction in any form reserved.

and restoration, and a local Black community's success in effectively altering the educational, sociopolitical, and economic landscape in Athens, Georgia, for years to come.

Keywords: Athens High and Industrial School, AHIS, Social Capital, History of Black Education; Segregated Schools, University of Georgia, Athens, Georgia

As was the case across the United States, immediately following their emancipation in 1865, formerly enslaved Black people in Athens, Georgia, began to vigorously search for ways to secure their freedoms. Though they began the period of "Jubilee" in unrestrained optimism, Black Athenians would soon learn that their endeavor would be plagued by disease, poverty, disenfranchisement, violence, and White supremacy (Thurmond, 2019). They were faced with the monumental task of building a free culture and society, all their own. Churches needed to be built, separated families needed to be reunited, organizations needed to be founded, and businesses needed to be established.

Knox Institute, founded by the Freedmen's Bureau in 1868, was the first Black school in Athens, Georgia. (Taken by the Author in 2020). In 1933, Athens High and Industrial School (AHIS) relocated to the previous site of Knox Institute, located here.

These enterprises were wholly dependent on various forms of capital including financial capital: money to pay for raw materials and labor; human capital: the skills, talents, abilities, and expertise of the workers and managers; and physical capital in the form of land, machines, and other types of equipment and tools (Franklin, 2002; Wimberly, 2013). However, social capital served as the foundation of the entirety of their endeavors. A complex social network—comprised of Black parents, farmers, ministers, doctors, politicians, and educators, as well as community and neighborhood groups, churches, social organizations, and voluntary associations—leveraged its collective resources to help secure Black people's collective socioeconomic, political, and educational futures. Together, they facilitated the development of the local Black Athens community, and established social, cultural, and educational institutions as a result.

This chapter demonstrates the ways in which the local Black Athens community promoted a distinct form of social capital to advance pioneering educational institutions. One salient example is the development of Athens High and Industrial School (AHIS). Originally constructed in 1914 as Reese Street School, it was later renamed Athens High and Industrial School (AHIS) to become Georgia's first accredited four-year Black public high school in 1922. Yet, when AHIS opened its doors, Black Athenians had already successfully opened and operated numerous private, county and city public schools, which served as central hubs of the community.

This chapter suggests that what rooted the collaborative efforts of the local Black Athens community was the distinctive communal ethos and practice. Black Athenians viewed education as valuable capital, which served to benefit the community as a whole. As such, this is not a success story of one school, but the relentless struggle to resist White supremacy, anti-Black racism, and exclusion from predominantly White institutions by radically developing educational institutions in accordance with communal needs and future aspirations. This is a story of refusal and restoration, and a local Black community's success in effectively altering the educational, sociopolitical, and economic landscape in Athens, Georgia for years to come.

A BRIEF HISTORY OF ATHENS, GEORGIA

In 1785, Abraham Baldwin drafted legislation to the Georgia General Assembly for Franklin College. The charter effectively initiated the University of Georgia (UGA), then Franklin College, as the nation's first state-supported university (Boney, 1984; Coulter, 1950). Due to financial difficulty, however, the college did not open to students until 16 years later when a committee from the school's board of trustees was commissioned to secure a site for the university (Dyer, 2004). Over the next two centuries, the small liberal arts college grew into a major research university whose influence extends far beyond the boundaries of the state (Dyer, 2004).

In 1801, Clarke County was established, named after Elijah Clarke, a Revolutionary War officer and Georgia legislator. Subsequently, Athens, Georgia, was established as a town in 1806, patterned after the center of classical learning and culture in Greece (Coleman, 1968). When the town was incorporated, it had "seventeen families, ten framed dwellings, and four stores" (Thomas, 2004). Yet, it grew in tandem with the college as people began to move to this sparsely inhabited area to attend and support the school.

Athens became home to business owners, merchants, college professors, and aristocrats looking to educate their sons and enjoy the culture the college encouraged (Thomas, 2004). In 1833, a group of businessmen financed the construction of one of Georgia's first railroads, connecting Athens to Augusta, GA, in 1841, and to Atlanta (then Marthasville) in 1845 (Storey, 2006). Because of the transportation and industrial developments and the growing influence of the University of Georgia, Athens became known as one of the state's most important towns during the antebellum period (Hynds, 1974). On the University of Georgia campus and within the local Athens community, however, the institution of slavery governed the lives of many Black people.

The University's Legacy of Slavery

Each year, the Board of Trustees approved budgets to hire enslaved workers who labored on behalf of the students and faculty of the University of Georgia. In line with the practice of "hiring out," the labor of enslaved people would often be rented from local enslavers. For example, the Prudential Committee, an administrative board responsible for overseeing much of the maintenance of the university, contracted with local enslaver, Sarah H. Harris in 1842 for the labor of several enslaved people, who worked as "college servants" for $100 each (University of Georgia Prudential Committee, 1842). They completed routine repairs to college buildings and tended to university property (University of Georgia Board of Trustees, 1855). Some—like Patrick and Henry—were skilled craftsmen, appointed to take care of the university's botanical garden (University of Georgia Prudential Committee, 1842). Enslaved college servants cleaned dormitories, made fires in professors' rooms, and were "at the beck and call of every student in Old and New College" (Hull, 1906, p. 176).

Despite the widespread contributions of enslaved people to the development, construction and maintenance of the University of Georgia, Black people were barred from attending and strictly prohibited from the campus, a rule fiercely enforced by students and faculty alike. In minutes from an 1827 meeting of the Board of Trustees, in regard to servants, it states, "it shall be the duty of the Faculty [sic] to prohibit all other Colored persons from entering the College Buildings [sic] for any purpose whatsoever except by special permission from one of the Body [sic]" (University of Georgia Board of Trustees, 1827, p. 186). For many White students and faculty, the utility of Black people on this campus of higher learning was exclusively of servitude; and these beliefs manifested in violent assaults, on and off campus. An excerpt of the minutes from an 1823 faculty meeting, for example, described an incident where student, John Clark confessed to "violently assaulting and maiming a negro without provocation." Three other assailants were also found guilty of "cruel and barbarous treatment to a poor deranged negro man" (University of Georgia Faculty, 1823, p. 15). The violent assault, maltreatment, and exploitation of enslaved and free Black people in the city of Athens is indicative of the White supremacist ideologies that permeated Franklin College.

Moreover, several of the college's first administrators enslaved Black people. Sources suggest that Josiah Meigs, who served as the second president of the university from 1801–1810, owned enslaved Black people while living in Athens. In an 1803 letter to a relative, he writes "we have had no death except of my favorite Negro female slave and her child, an infant" (Meigs, 1887, p. 101). Moses Waddel, university president from 1819–1829, also owned enslaved people. His son, John Waddel, claimed that his father had been a "most humane master...no cruel treatment was ever known or permitted, and every reasonable liberty was allowed them [enslaved people]" (Waddel, 1891, p. 119–120). Alonzo Church, the 6th president of the college from 1829 until 1859, held the longest-serving presidential term in UGA history. In his will, he leaves six enslaved people—Louisa, Hanson, Caroline, Alfred, Sophia, and Elvir (a little girl)—to his descendants (Enslaved People, n.d.). Other administrators and university personnel, while not enslavers, were explicit in their beliefs about the sanctity of the slave system. In 1844, for example, Patrick Hues Mell, a Baptist minister and president of the university from 1878–1888, published a pamphlet, entitled "Slavery: a treatise, showing that slavery is neither a moral, political, nor social evil." In it, he advanced several arguments to demonstrate his stanch support of the institution of slavery including using Biblical grounds for enslavement and White supremacy (Williams, 2010).

In summary, although the University of Georgia, as an institution, did not own enslaved people, it benefited greatly from the peculiar institution of slavery, and remains an integral—and often neglected—part of the university's history. In fact, in 2015, an expansion project on Baldwin Hall came to a halt when construction workers discovered human remains on the site. Subsequent DNA tests revealed what the local Black Athens community and many historians already knew: these were the remains of formerly enslaved people. This discovery, as well as the local response that followed, forced the University of Georgia to reckon with the often forgotten legacy of slavery, and (re)member (Dillard, 2012) the significance of the local Black Athens community to the development of the university and the city of Athens.

The Antebellum and Postbellum Black Athens Community

In 1810, the enslaved population constituted 31% of the Athens population, however, the rise of "King Cotton" increased the population significantly. During the 1820s, Athens became the center for textile manufacturing, powered by the Oconee River and supplied by local cotton plantations and slave labor. With steady economic growth as a result of the booming cotton industry, Athens became an important trade center, "the second largest inland cotton market in the state and the sixth largest in the world" (Doster, 2002, p. 1). Yet, the majority of enslaved people worked as domestics and service workers in the homes of prominent, wealthy, White families that moved to Athens for education, business, and agricultural purposes; others, on textile and paper mills (Coleman, 1968).

Despite the growing numbers of enslaved Blacks in the city of Athens and within county limits, a relatively small number of Whites were enslavers and an even smaller number owned 20 or more enslaved persons. With this sharp delineation between those relatively few Whites who owned enslaved people and those who did not, historians have noted that by 1840 "a fairly well-defined class system at the top and half the population living in slavery at the bottom" (Thomas, 1992, p. 31) had developed . Still, the enslaved population continued to rise so that by 1850, Clarke County had joined the Black Belt of the South, with its enslaved population outnumbering its free population (Woofter, 1913; Young, 2020).

By 1860, enslaved people comprised nearly half of the total population in Clarke County (Stegeman, 1964). These numbers steadily increased during the Civil War as plantation owners permitted enslaved people to "hire out" to earn wages while they went to battle. Though no major battles took place in Athens during the Civil War, it was a major gathering point for Confederate soldiers and a haven for refugees from more active areas of the war (Stegeman, 1964). As the war continued, faculty and students at the University of Georgia served in the Confederate army, prompting the school to close in October of 1863 when enrollment dropped to 78 students.

The Confederacy summoned all campus buildings, using them to house soldiers and evacuees. The chapel on campus became an army hospital, and in 1864, a prison for captured Northern soldiers (Stegeman, 1964; Thomas, 2004). Clarke County lost more than 300 men (out of a total White male population of 2,660), and more than 100 university students and alumni died in the Civil War (Thomas, 2004). Yet, when the university reopened in January 1866, nearly 5,000 enslaved Black people in Clarke County were freed. With their newfound freedom, the dynamics in the city of Athens began to change, drastically (Thurmond, 2019).

Education as a Communal Core Value

During and after the Civil War, educational opportunities for Black people throughout the South arose primarily from the vigorous efforts of the Black community themselves (Anderson, 1988; Franklin, 2002; Span, 2002; Webber, 1978). Indeed, the concerted efforts of missionary organizations and freedman's associations helped to formally establish schools throughout the South; however, Black people had long initiated the educational process whenever, and however possible. The desire for literary and formal education became a "core value" in the Black cultural value system as a result of the experience of enslavement, educational exclusion, and continued legalized oppression and discrimination (Franklin, 2002).

Defying the stringent laws that prohibited the education of enslaved people, the antebellum Black community established clandestine schools, home school networks, rural schools, as well as Sunday and Sabbath schools (Anderson, 1988; Webber, 1978; Williams, 2005). They established these educational enterprises for a number of reasons, including an intrinsic value of literacy, being able to read the Bible, understanding their rights after the Civil War, and being able to buy and lease land (Span, 2002). They likewise associated literacy with freedom. As a result, they relied wholly on social and community networks to facilitate their collective liberation. According to Franklin (2002), "African Americans were willing to contribute their time, energies, and financial and material resources to support [these] educational institutions because they knew they were important for the advancement of African Americans as a group" (p. 178). As a result, education for Black people was a collective effort that yielded communal benefits, for the present and future.

THEORETICAL FRAMEWORKS

Social capital, as a framework, helps us to examine how the local Black Athens established pioneering educational institutions. Social capital is defined as "the network of social organizations, cultural institutions, voluntary civic associations, family and kinship groups in a community that assist in the development of an economic enterprise" (Franklin, 2004, p. 36). While early Black schools were not regarded as economic enterprises (Span, 2002), the social relationships and networks therein lead to the accumulation of human capital and yielded communal economic benefits. In the case of the local Black Athens community, the collective resources from collaborative social networks supported the educational attainment of Black youth and adults, and the development of highly valued skills, literacies, and knowledge. The efforts to improve the lives of the Black community also emanated from the rise of individual community leaders, who first improved their own lives through education, and in return, used their knowledge in service of their community, demonstrating a distinctive form of capital (Bourdieu, 1984, 1986; Yosso, 2005). Academic capital is a mode of investment wherein the knowledge, expertise and skills gained by individuals are then reinvested and transmitted back into the communities from whence they came, to then continue the cycle. Academic capital then provided a means to empower the Black community educationally, economically, socially, and politically, with implications for communal return.

THE MAKING OF THE FREE BLACK ATHENS COMMUNITY

Black Athenians worked diligently to bind their community together after emancipation and created social, cultural, religious, political, and educational institutions that would benefit the entire community. As such, in 1866, the first Black fire company was established as well as the first Black church, Hill First Baptist

Church (Thurmond & Sparer, 1978), named in honor of its first minister, Reverend Floyd Hill, who led the church without the ability to formally read or write (Burkhart, 2012). Though rare in most southern cities, Black people in Athens also had a strong presence in the press, launching three newspapers, the *Athens Blade*, *Athens Clipper*, and the *Progressive Era* (Thurmond, 2019). During the Reconstruction era, newly freed Black Athenians endeavored to forge a new social, political, and economic life (Thurmond, 2019). This meant challenging the pervasive caste system in their own backyard at the University of Georgia.

Around 1866, a group of local Black Athenians confronted Chancellor Patrick Hues Mell with demands that their sons be granted admission and "have the same privileges extended their people that were enjoyed by the White people in the University" (Mell, 1895, p. 225). According to his son's account, Chancellor Mell responded by saying,

> Your demand will not be respected, because this is the White man's college, and you are perfectly powerless to help yourselves. You are now surrounded by armed and determined men who are only waiting for my orders to fire into [sic] you on every side. If you will quietly disperse and go to your homes you will not be hurt; if you refuse, I will command these men to fire and not one of you will leave this campus alive. (Mell, 1895, p. 225)

Eventually, the group of Black men scattered after hearing these threats and realizing they were outnumbered and surrounded by heavily armed White students and residents of the town. However, this interaction reveals how Black Athenians utilized their collective power, and in multiple ways. First, they came together to rebel against the social orders that relegated Black people to the margins of society. They also resisted the discriminatory admissions policies that excluded Black people from White educational institutions. Finally, for the sake of the whole Black community, they would later utilize their social capital to form their *own* institutions. Though their efforts to desegregate the university were ineffective at the time, it demonstrated the lengths that the local Black Athens community would go to actualize their newfound civil and human rights.

In 1868, following Congress' passing of the Reconstruction Acts to rebuild the South, Black voters came out in record numbers to elect two formerly enslaved men as Georgia's first Black delegates to the Georgia State Legislature from Clarke County (Thurmond, 2019). Black Athenians were also involved in civic engagement and political activism in hopes of establishing economic independence. According to the Freedman's Bureau, just two years after gaining their freedom, more than 70 Black families purchased homes in the Athens area (Thurmond & Sparer, 1978). However, due to discriminatory housing policies, White landowners purchased the most promising land. Consequently, property ownership among Black Athenians was concentrated in the most undesirable and underdeveloped parts of town. Yet, the population of newly emancipated Black people created their own settlements. So much so that toward the end of the 19th century many Black Athens natives resided in the Reese Street and West Hancock Avenue neighborhoods, effectively establishing two of Georgia's oldest remaining Black neighborhoods (National Register of Historic Places, 1987, 1988).

Black residents of the Reese Street and West Hancock Historic Districts worked as carpenters, masons, seamstresses, shopkeepers, blacksmiths, and in other skilled trades. These areas were also home to prominent Black professionals, including Dr. William H. Harris, one of Athens' most prominent early Black physicians and co-founder of the Georgia State Medical Association of Colored Physicians, Dentists and Druggists, and Ira Mae Hiram, the first Black woman to be licensed to practice dentistry in the state (McCarthy, 2017). Drs. Harris and Hiram both operated their practices just a few blocks from their homes at the Morton building, founded in 1910 by Monroe "Pink" Morton, a formerly enslaved Black man who owned approximately 30 buildings and became the second Black postmaster in the city of Athens (Thurmond, 2019). Despite marginalization, continued disenfranchisement, and bitter hostility from White Athenians, emancipated Black people banded together to resist these oppressive structures and establish supportive, affirming, self-sustaining communities in accordance with their cultural traditions and communal ethos.

Black codes and other racist state laws, however, were enacted throughout the South to curtail the rights of Black citizens by restricting their ability to purchase land, vote, and use public facilities, and by denying them access to employment (Ogbu, 1978; Thurmond & Sparer, 1978). In 1879, Athens' first Black weekly newspaper, the *Athens Blade*, suggested the continued prejudice of Whites immediately following emancipation and throughout Reconstruction was the main cause of persistent poverty and low educational attainment by local Black people (Knight, 2007). Yet, William A. Pledger, one of the owners of the newspaper, believed that the resolution to this hostility and violence was to raise the standard of education (Heard, 1928; Heard & Pledger, 1879).

From the era of enslavement, Black Athenians firmly believed that literacy and formal education would be their means of reaching true liberation (Anderson, 1988; Thurmond & Sparer, 1978). This is evidenced in the story of Lucius Henry Holsey. UGA professor, Richard Malcolm Johnston, enslaved Holsey, who worked as a carriage driver, house servant, and gardener. But Holsey always felt a deep desire for education, only deepened once he arrived in Athens. He stated,

> I was then fifteen years of age. As soon as I arrived in Athens, I felt an insatiable craving for some knowledge of books, and especially I was anxious to learn to read the Bible. What must I do? I was a slave and could not attend school, and it was considered unwise, if not dangerous for slaves to read and write… So I determined to learn to read at all hazards, and take whatever risks there might be connected with it. (Holsey, 1898, p. 16)

Holsey eventually learned to read and after emancipation became a licensed preacher in the African Methodist Episcopal (AME) Church. He later founded

Paine College, a historically Black college in Augusta, Georgia. This deeply rooted desire for education remained central to the development of the Black educational landscape, resulting in the establishment of several Black schools in Athens and throughout Clarke County, including the first accredited Black public high school in the state of Georgia.

THE FORMATION OF BLACK SCHOOLS IN ATHENS, GEORGIA

In 1859, a free public school system for Whites was established in Athens, Georgia, sponsored in part by the state's Poor School Fund, which provided financial support for children unable to pay for tuition at private schools (Coleman, 1968). This endeavor was abandoned soon thereafter due to the enormous financial burden on the city. However, renowned private, semi-private and public institutions for Whites continued to thrive in the city of Athens, including the Lucy Cobb Institute, the Center Hill Classical Academy, R.P. Adams School, the Cobbham Academy, University High School and Collegiate Institute, Georgia College of Agriculture, the State Normal School, and of course, the University of Georgia. Because of the volume of educational institutions, Athens became recognized as the Classic City, or an "educational center" in Georgia (Coleman, 1968, p. 7).

In spite of the widespread availability of White primary, secondary, and postsecondary institutions in the city of Athens, the possibility of public education for Black people evoked fear and anger for local Whites. Black people were central to the rebuilding and industrial development of Athens during the Reconstruction era, so Whites believed that formal education was unnecessary for their tasks (Walker, 2000). Whites also feared the implications of the educational progress of Black people, concerned that it would jeopardize their inherent superiority, as well as the southern political and social economy that maintained their supremacy (Thurmond & Sparer, 1978). As a result, the Black community endeavored to build educational institutions, all their own.

Private Schools

As soon as 2 years following emancipation, Black Athenians were diligently pursuing possibilities to expand their access to education by opening several private schools. With the help of the Freedmen's Bureau and local Black churches, Knox Institute was established in 1867 in the Reese Street Historic District as the first Black school in Athens (O' Brien, 1999; Thurmond & Sparer, 1978). Although the Black community appreciated and benefited from the efforts of Northern philanthropists and organizations, they resisted "infringements that threatened to undermine their own initiative and self-reliance" (Anderson, 1988, p. 12). The land for the school was purchased in 1867 by three local Black men: Mr. Courtney Beal, a property owner; Reverend Floyd Hill, a formerly enslaved man who established the first Black Baptist church in Athens; and Madison Davis, who together with Alfred Richardson, became the first of their race to be elected to the Georgia State Legislature from Clarke County in 1868 (Thurmond, 2019).

Freedmen's Bureau schools were usually taught by White northern women who felt religiously or morally compelled to instruct the formerly enslaved population. The local White Athens community, however, vented their resentment by disrupting classes at Knox, forcing White teachers to leave soon after its opening (Thurmond & Sparer, 1978). As a result, Knox teachers were exclusively Black men and women, typically trained at Black colleges like Atlanta and Fisk Universities. Along with their roles and responsibilities as teachers, they also lived and worked within the Black community, typifying a staunch communal ethos.

One of the most influential figures in the development of the first Black school in Athens was Reverend L. S. Clark, who became principal of Knox in 1887 and remained in that position for nearly 40 years. In the December 28, 1917 edition of the *Athens Daily Herald* newspaper, Rev. Clark discussed the school's development from a four room building, with no planned course of study, and few students in attendance to one with modern architecture, a maximum enrollment of 460, students from across the nation and a well-developed curriculum that included college preparatory courses, domestic science, art, teacher training, printing, and music, serving grades K–8 (Clark, 1917a). He spoke proudly of Knox's contributions to the economic development of the city of Athens, but more so about the development of Knox graduates. Alumni of Knox worked in every area of the country, engaged in professions such as teaching, dentistry, law, religion, agriculture, and other important positions. Rev. Clark attributed the success of the school to unwavering faith in God, hard work, and sacrifice, exhibiting a distinct educational philosophy. "The work is practical," he said,

> It seeks to develop students along all lines—'his intellect, his heart, his hands'… The school is endeavoring to help the young people who attend here to become producers as well as consumers and to make not only a living, but a life. (Clark, 1917b, p. 2)

Under the tutelage of Rev. L. S. Clark, Knox grew from a small ungraded school with few students to be one of the top ranking schools for Black people (Thurmond & Sparer, 1978), ushering in a pioneering model of holistic education for other Black schools in Athens.

The Black Athens community continued to open private Black schools to meet their educational needs including a Methodist school in 1876 and Jeruel Academy in 1881 (O'Brien, 1999; Thurmond, 2019). Jeruel was a private school supported by a cadre of rural Black churches: the Jeruel Baptist Association, the American Baptist Home Mission, and the Women's Missionary Baptist Society (Thurmond, 2019). In accordance with their desire for independence, Jeruel was the only Black school in the city, and the foremost in Northwest Georgia, operated and controlled exclusively by and for Black people (Thurmond, 2019). The purpose of the school was to develop Black men and women for occupations as teachers, preachers, and leaders in the community.

In 1886, a new facility was constructed at Jeruel Academy and headed by Professor J. H. Brown, who served as its principal for approximately 36 years (Thurmond, 2019). In addition to agriculture, industrial training, and domestic service courses, Black youth were offered college preparatory courses in English, Greek, Latin, French, history, theology, mathematics, and public speaking. In 1924, the school consolidated with three other institutions to become the Union Baptist Institute and continued providing high quality education for the Black Athens community until 1956, when it merged with Athens High and Industrial School (AHIS).

This local private school remained open longer than any other local Black private school in Athens. Today a historical marker near Brumby Hall at the University of Georgia commemorates its former site. The development of private schools in Athens, Georgia, demonstrates the ways in which members of the Black Athens community provided material resources and financial capital to support educational institutions for Black students, and for generations to come.

Public City Schools

With the local Black Athens community providing the majority of the labor for Athens's business and industrial development throughout the Reconstruction era, the teaching of newly freed Black people became a central concern of White Athenians. As such, many local Whites refused to support Black public education (Knight, 2007). Some Whites, one historian suggests, were envious of the local Black private schools because they were nearly free and there were no free White schools in all of Clarke County (Knight, 2007; Schinkel, 1971). However, Thurmond and Sparer (1978) note that both Black and White community members supported the opening of public city schools, as they believed that the development of "free schools for everyone" (p. 84) would advance future prosperity of the city of Athens.

In 1885, local Athenians joined efforts to establish a free Black and White public school system, nearly two decades after the establishment of Athens' first Black school (Branson, 1886). In 1886, the Board of Education in Athens, Georgia, erected two, two-story, 10-roomed brick buildings, one for each race (Branson, 1886; Rowe & Barrow, 1923; Thurmond & Sparer, 1978). Yet, from its inception, the White Athens City School Board made certain that the Black schools were substandard by providing them with inadequate funding, fewer and less qualified teachers, and minimal supplies (Fultz, 1995a, 1995b; Knight, 2007; Thurmond & Hester, 2001). Records suggest that while White schools were stocked with science apparatuses, globes, maps, and reading, number, and music charts, Black teachers saved "every scrap of paper and every pencil" (Hill as cited in Hester, 2001, p. 104) they could find to have enough supplies for their students (Branson, 1886; Knight, 2007).

The Black public school was located on Baxter and Pope Streets and the White school was located miles away on Washington Street. In 1893, however, the Baxter Street School was remodeled for use by White students, and the Black students were subsequently relocated to two smaller, six-room frame buildings on the east and west side of Athens, possibly to accommodate the burgeoning Black student population. The East Athens School had three teachers, served elementary grades, and was first supervised by John R. Mack. The other school, West Athens School, had five teachers who served students in middle grades. In 1894, Archibald J. Carey, Sr., former principal of Baxter Street School, was given principalship of the West Athens School, and through his leadership, the school expanded to also include early high school grades (Thurmond & Sparer, 1978).

Despite these provisions and massive community support, severe overcrowding at the East and West Athens schools remained one of the major problems of early public education for the Black community (Knight, 2007). As public school enrollment increased, Black students continued to attend classes taught by a total of 14 instructors in the two original wood-frame buildings (Woofter, 1913). Some Black Athens educators and community leaders, however, sought other financial support for schools outside of local taxes and thus, were unrestrained by the school board.

In 1903, Judia Jackson Harris left her teaching post in the public school system to open a rural school 5 miles outside of Athens, the Model and Training School, later renamed the Judia C. Jackson Harris School. She endeavored to create a school that would accommodate rural Black children and families who, because of distance or work obligations, were unable to attend the city public schools (Knight, 2007). Along with basic grammar, math, and history, students were trained in art, drama, and music, often performing musical pageants at the Morton Theatre in Athens. After a fire of unknown origin completely destroyed one the school buildings, Harris temporarily held classes in her home. She also solicited donations from Black and White businessmen in Athens to raise funds to rebuild the structure, including White philanthropist, Julius Rosenwald. The Rosenwald Fund contributed to the construction and improvement of over 5,000 rural Black schools in the South and was the primary financier for the rebuilding of the Harris School.

In recognition of the overcrowded conditions of the Black schools, Athens public school system added a four-room grade school building in 1911–1912, named Newtown School. Nonetheless, this addition did little to alleviate the overcrowded conditions in the city public schools for Black students. Moreover, the demand for education among Black Athenians was so great that many were turned away because of the lack of sufficient space in schools (Thurmond & Sparer, 1978). Nonetheless, a Phelps-Stokes study of the Black Athens schools reported, "Under conditions such as this it is hard to do any work of merit, and yet several unexpected visits to the school showed that the children were learning very well what was put before them" (Woofter, 1913, p. 26). Despite the enormous obstacles, the Black community in Athens succeeded in providing nurturing educational environments for Black students to learn in, culminating with the first accredited Black public high school in the state of Georgia.

THE FIRST ACCREDITED BLACK HIGH SCHOOL IN GEORGIA

In 1913, the Athens Board of Education adopted plans to construct a new Black public high school. Originally known as Reese Street School, it would later be renamed Athens High and Industrial School (AHIS). The new building was modern for its time: high windows, steam-heated, electric lighted and contained all new equipment. AHIS offered a full curriculum of vocational training, as well as rigorous academic coursework in Latin, Greek, literature, history, chemistry, physics, and music—a pioneering educational model for many local schools. In the December 28th, 1917 issue of the *Athens Daily Herald* newspaper, AHIS is described as "a regular high school of the four year course, the only real high school in Georgia for colored youths" ("Athens Colored Schools," 1917, p. 2). Yet, ideological debates about the purposes of this school were widespread among Blacks and Whites alike from its inception.

Industrial vs. Classical Education Debate

Some Black Athenians viewed AHIS with apprehension because the curriculum initially focused on service work instead of intellectual endeavors. Constructing schools with a focus on manual labor skills, they believed, would essentially deny Black students access to the skills needed to challenge the oppressive southern political economy (Knight, 2007). Black and White supporters of classical education expressed concern that the industrial educational model was designed to merely reinforce the existing social order of the South instead of facilitating racial uplift (Anderson, 1988; Du Bois, 1903, 1969; Spivey, 1978; Washington, 1900). This concern added to an ongoing controversy about what was educationally best for Black children—the historic classical versus industrial education debate.

Some within the local Black community believed that industrial education would assist them in gaining economic independence. White southerners generally supported the industrial education model due to the belief that it would save inferior Black people from laziness and sustain the economic superiority of Whites. Tension soon developed between the supporters and opponents of industrial education among the Black community in Athens. They confronted the Athens City School Board about their concerns, as well as the lack of curricular options, insufficient resources, and decaying conditions of the remaining Black public schools (Knight, 2007). Samuel F. Harris, a well-known educator in the city, was instrumental to the pioneering industrial *and* classical educational model adopted by the newly constructed Black public high school.

The Influence of Samuel F. Harris

Harris, a local Black Athenian, returned to his hometown in 1896 to begin his teaching career. He started teaching second grade at East Athens School, but noticed that the Black public elementary schools in Athens were solely providing literacy courses, which he believed were insufficient, as these did little to help students gain vital industrial and vocational training (Harris, 1910). In the early 1900s, newly opened White businesses and factories in Athens required a larger, cheaper labor force. While Whites refused these jobs, Black people began moving to Athens to fill these vacancies. A report by Woofter (1913) posits that almost 94% of Black Athenians over the age of 16 were working in the skilled trades, domestic and hotel services, and unskilled labor at the turn of the century. As more of these positions became available, centralized training for these jobs became necessary and as a result, industrial education became a key curricular component in both the public and private schools of Athens (Woofter, 1913). Similar to Booker T. Washington, Harris believed that classical, academic training and literacy alone were inadequate for the growing economy in the city of Athens, which at the time were wholly dependent on manual labor and domestic service of Black men and women (Gardner, 1975). As such, industrial education of the Black working class through practical, manual skill development, became central to his educational reform endeavors.

Only 2 years after he began his career, Harris was selected as the new principal of the East Athens School. However, he quickly realized that he wanted to shape the direction of older students and transferred to the West Athens School in 1903. Within a year, Harris developed an agricultural self-help program, primarily focused on the development of a community garden. He believed that this endeavor would help feed local impoverished Black families, while teaching Black students important life skills. Soon, the work at West Athens School community garden began to get noticed. First, by local White Athenians who complained that White children were not being provided with equal opportunities as Black children—ironically, during the time of state sanctioned segregation—and second, by the school board.

After receiving a letter from Millie Rutherford, the President of the prestigious Lucy Cobb Institute, regarding the work of Samuel Harris, the Athens school board decided in 1905 to add manual and industrial training to their annual budget. The decision to implement industrial education may also be attributed to the ascendancy of America's industrial bourgeoisie after emancipation. Nonetheless, in July of the same year, Harris designed cooking and gardening classes at both East and West Athens schools. The next month, he was presented with a check from George Peabody to continue the development of the manual training programs at the Black public schools. With these newly acquired funds, Harris expanded his project and designed a series of technical and vocational courses in Athens public schools to develop the Black community's workforce training skills. These included night classes that offered housework, needlework, gardening, and cooking. The flexible class schedule allowed Black youth and adults to work during the day and develop their industrial skills in the evening. The donations also helped to acquire more resources for the schools, hire an additional teacher, and facilitate the construction of a new building (Gardner, 1975).

Despite these resources, overcrowding, insufficient staffing, and miniscule salaries worked to quell Harris's industrial endeavors. He believed that the conditions of the Black public schools and the relative inattentiveness of the school board to address these issues hampered his ability to truly develop industrial training programs. Subsequently, in 1906 Harris took matters into his own hands. Determined to bring quality industrial education to Black students in Athens, Harris diligently collected funds from wealthy, northern Whites (Knight, 2007; Thurmond & Sparer, 1978). His persistence and knowledge about vocational training allowed him to quickly gain notoriety throughout Athens and beyond, and donations and funding for his efforts soon followed (Moss, 1910).

Whites generally agreed with Harris's model, in line with Northern philanthropic projects to invest economic support for industrial education for Black people (Anderson, 1988). Yet, Harris had a plan to use the strength and political power of the White elite to support the enfranchisement of the local Black Athens community. Harris understood that many Whites felt a paternalistic obligation to help the "inferior race," and as such, utilized their support to fund industrial efforts for Athens Black public schools. One of the reasons that Harris became so popular with both the Black and White Athens community was that he was a strong proponent for education that taught the practical duties of life (Knight, 2007).

Harris remained highly regarded, in the Black and White Athens community, as an educator, leader of the race, and bridge builder. Because of his reputation, and the successful development of agricultural and industrial programs at both East and West Athens schools, Harris was appointed as principal of AHIS and promoted to supervisor of all Black schools in Athens in 1913. Harris was instrumental in ensuring that AHIS was fully equipped with a manual training shop and a vocational night school. Under Harris's supervision, AHIS became a pioneering high school, successfully blending both classical and industrial education. In 1922, AHIS earned the distinction of being Georgia's first accredited four-year public high school for Black students.

A Legacy of Leadership

In 1933, AHIS relocated to the previous site of Knox Institute—founded by the Freedmen's Bureau in 1868—to accommodate its steady growth. Over the years, the school continued to grow, and eventually became one of the most prestigious Black public schools in the city of Athens, and in the state. Hundreds of students enrolled, and represented counties spanning the state of Georgia. Principal Samuel F. Harris led AHIS for nearly 20 years until his death in 1935, leaving a legacy of strong school leadership, community involvement, and a pioneering educational model.

Assistant principal, Annie H. Burney assumed the role as interim school leader after Harris's passing. In addition to her leadership duties at school, Burney continued her work as an 8th and 9th grade math teacher, often providing housing for Black people who came to Athens to teach (AHIS/BHHS Alumni Association, n.d.). Burney devoted 50 years to education, with 42·of those years exclusively at Athens High and Industrial School. Burney spent her entire career instilling the values and principles that would help her students become successful men and women who would go out into the world and make contributions toward the progress of their community (Harris, 2012).

Aaron Brown served as the principal of AHIS and supervisor of Black public schools in Athens from 1936–1945. During the first year of his principalship, Brown spoke publicly regarding the vital importance of Black schools in the development of the Black Athens community. He argued that the "nobler purpose" of these schools, and education more broadly, was to enable the Black community to "think wisely, love sincerely, act justly [and]…exhibit a reverent attitude" toward one another. He believed that the Black community would be better equipped to work together in the struggle against economic, social, and political oppression if grounded in a communal purpose (Brown, 1935). This educational philosophy was imperative to the continued success of Athens Black public schools (Knight, 2007).

Brown also encouraged the implementation of extra-curricular activities in Athens's Black schools, which he believed would inevitably advance the physical, socioemotional, and spiritual development of Black students (Thurmond, 2019). During his tenure, he added numerous departments to Black schools in Athens, including athletic associations, debating clubs, drama, a Glee club, and the Try-Hi-Y club (to enhance Christian values) (AHIS/BHHS Alumni Association, n.d.; Knight, 2007). Brown also developed a "Negro History" course in Athens Black public schools, recognizing the importance of racial identity development and Black history knowledge. From 1938–1945, Charles Duval served as the principal of AHIS, a particularly difficult time as the school became in jeopardy of losing its accreditation due to financial difficulty. Nonetheless, AHIS continued to thrive under the strong leadership of highly regarded community members, each grounded in a fierce resolve on providing quality education for the Black Athens community and improving the lives and futures of Black Athenians.

In 1945, Homer T. Edwards assumed the principal position of Athens High and Industrial School (AHIS) and remained for more than two decades. He led during some of the most pivotal times in the school's history, including the school's renaming, the inauguration of school desegregation, and its relocation to a new building. In 1954, Edwards successfully negotiated plans to close the original AHIS building, merge the school with Union Baptist Institute, and construct a new AHIS building (Knight, 2007). Construction for the new school building began in 1956, just a few blocks away from the original school.

One of the biggest benefits of the merged schools was the unification and increase of extracurricular programs offered to Athens's Black high school students. In line with the legacy of its founding, the new AHIS continued to offer Black students a wide array of courses blending industrial and classical education elements. Courses included mathematics, science, and English, in addition to numerous extracurricular activities like the historical society, speech, library, and choir. Students were also expected to take a foreign language course, physical education, and several vocational courses, such as home economics, industrial arts, and printing (Harris, 2012). AHIS endeavored to cultivate Black students to become well-rounded individuals and contribute to their community, and society, writ large.

(Re)membering the Legacy of AHIS

In 1964, a coalition of parents, students, teachers and community leaders spearheaded a movement to have the high school renamed. The proposal was in recognition of how generations of Black Athenians' lives had been touched by the work of its founding leaders. The same year, with approval from the Clarke County Board of Education, AHIS was renamed Burney-Harris High School (BHHS) to honor its first leading administrators, Annie H. Burney and Samuel F. Harris, who each worked dutifully for decades advocating for educational equity for generations of Black Athens youth. In the 1965 yearbook, Principal Edwards remarked that there was a "swell" of community support for the name change of the school. He hoped that the new name would "inspire the youth" who pass through the school's doors "for generations to come" (Edwards in Yellow Jacket Staff, 1965, as cited in Knight, 2007, p. 167). And it did.

Ileane Nesbit Nunnally, a native Athenian, graduated from AHIS in 1947 at the age of 16. She then attended and graduated from Clark College in Atlanta where she majored in French and minored in English. In 1951, at the age of 20, Nunnally returned to Athens to teach at the East Athens Elementary School. After 3 years, she was transferred to her alma mater, AHIS, later Burney Harris High School, where she remained for 32 years. Nunnally recalled that as many as four generations of Black Athenians had built strong relationships with both Samuel Harris and Annie Burney as educators, school administrators, and community leaders (AHIS/BHHS Alumni Association, n.d.; Knight, 2007). Yet, Burney and Harris were only two of the many memorable staff members at AHIS-BHHS who helped the students to edify the Black Athens community. When alumni speak on the impact of the school, they recall with reverence for the teachers and community leaders that helped to guide them through a dehumanizing time in American history, the era of Jim Crow segregation (Knight, 2007). Yet, it was in this space that Black students in Athens were equipped with the tools to navigate these oppressive structures and later returned to help others do the same.

The Unintended Consequences of School Desegregation

After the tenure of Homer T. Edwards, Ernest T. Roberson served as AHIS's final principal during the school's last year in existence as a new era of desegregated schools ushered in the closing of groundbreaking Black schools. As was the case in many Black schools across the nation, the strong educational community that Black Athenians worked tirelessly to develop began to dissolve, largely as an unintended consequence of school desegregation. In 1970, following the federal mandate of the desegregation of schools, the high-achieving school for Black children, Burney-Harris High School (formerly Athens High and Industrial School), and the high school for White children, Athens High School, merged to establish Clarke Central High School. Consequently, Black students were bused across town to White schools while influential Black teachers and administrators lost their previous political and social status, were demoted, or pushed out of the profession altogether (Thurmond & Hester, 2001); many of whom had been born, raised, and educated in Athens.

Siddle Walker (2009) argues that the displacement of Black teachers and administrators not only impacted their professional and personal lives, but worked to eliminate an educational system that "both sought to eradicate injustice and foster psychological resilience in the face of overt oppression within black boys and girls" (p. 273). What replaced it was an educational system that proved inhospitable and antagonistic toward Black cultural ways of knowing and being in schools, as well as to those who sought to preserve it, aiding as a factor in the displacement of Black teachers in Athens schools. Bob Paris, for example, a 1947 graduate of Burney-Harris High School, and one of the first Black teachers placed at the previously all-White schools suggested,

> There are certain things that you did black on black, you couldn't do black or white or white on black. What I could say to a black kid in a black situation [segregated school setting]... I couldn't say in integrated. It would be out of place, it wouldn't fit the situation and then you could get in a lot of trouble. (as cited in Harris, 2012, p. 309)

Paris argued that when he instructed Black students at segregated Black schools, he could teach them things that would edify them as a whole, but that changed drastically once schools were desegregated. At the same time, notable Black school buildings were vacated, left to deteriorate, or demolished completely due to gentrification and citywide revitalization projects. Too often the places where noteworthy Black history happened have been unrecognized for the essential role they played in the fabric of American society. Yet, on the corner of Pope and Reese Street in Athens, Georgia, Athens High and Industrial School still stands.

A LEGACY CONTINUED

Denied but not defeated, the local Black Athens community used their collective energies to develop quality schools for Black children that ultimately resulted in Athens High and Industrial School. Black Athenians endeavored to prepare Black children with industrial, religious, political, *and* classical education to combat the wiles of an oppressive, White supremacist sociopolitical system. As such, for more than a century, they leveraged financial, social, cultural, academic, and physical capital to sustain Black schools. The men and women who served as leaders at AHIS, and at other pioneering educational institutions across Athens, endeavored to cultivate Black children who would become integral figures in the social, political and economic development of their community (Thurmond & Sparer, 1978). Supporters included educational pioneers like L.S. Clark, Samuel F. Harris and his wife, Judia Jackson Harris; farmers like Floyd Kenny; politicians like Madison Davis; ministers like Reverend Floyd Hill; business owners like William A. Pledger and Pink Morton, as well as many other Black men and women whose names we may never know. The contemporary value of these schools is demonstrated through a legacy of refusal, strong leadership, integrated curricula, caring teachers, community and parental involvement, and educational advocacy that remains embedded in the local Black Athens community through networks like Black churches, lodges, and social organizations.

The value of social capital is well-established and evident in the local Black Athens community's triumph in establishing groundbreaking educational institutions. Yet, what lies under the surface of these collective actions is a form of cultural capital, a sense of group consciousness that serves a resource aimed at the advancement of the entire group. The local Black Athens embodied a communal ethos that suggested that Black people were beholden to each other, and what one does to benefit another, simultaneously benefits the self. This way of thinking manifested as a duty and commitment to being collectively responsible for the setbacks and victories of the community. As a result of this ethos of communal responsibility, accountability for the education of a child was not solely the onus of the teacher but relied on the action of the entire community. Collective responsibility supported individuals, while advancing the well-being of the family, neighborhood, and the overall common good of the whole. The adoption of this communal ethos in contemporary times has the potential to radically transform the trajectory of students, families, communities, and educational systems. And the story of Black Athenians provides a necessary blueprint for the cultivation of family, school, and community connections.

REFERENCES

AHIS/BHHS Alumni Association. (n.d.). *A brief history of Athens High and Industrial School and Burney-Harris High School*. The Yellow Jacket. http://www.theyellowjacket.com/history.html

Anderson, J. (1988). *The education of Blacks in the south, 1860–1935*. The University of North Carolina Press.

Athens Colored Schools Are Keeping Pace With Progress of Community. (1917, December 28). *Athens Daily Herald*. p. 2, section 2. https://gahistoricnewspapers.galileo.usg.edu/lccn/sn88054118/1917-12-28/ed-1/

Boney, F. N. (1984). *A pictorial history of the University of Georgia*. University of Georgia Press.

Bourdieu, P. (1984) *Distinction: A social critique of the judgment of taste*. Harvard University Press.

Bourdieu, P. (1986). The forms of capital. In J. Richardson (Ed.), *Handbook of theory and research for the sociology of education* (pp. 241–258). Greenwood Press.

Branson, E. C. (1886). *Report of the Athens city schools*. Banner Print.

Brown, A., Jr. (1935, December 5). *Letter from Aaron Brown, Jr. to W. E. B. Du Bois*. W. E. B. Du Bois Papers (MS 312). Special Collections and University Archives, University of Massachusetts Amherst Libraries. https://credo.library.umass.edu/view/full/mums312-b073-i234

Burkhart, A. (2012). *Hill First Baptist Church celebrates 145th anniversary*. Athens Banner Herald Online. https://www.onlineathens.com/faith/2012-03-22/hill-first-baptist-church celebrates-145th-anniversary

Clark, L. S. (1917a, December 28). Athens colored schools are keeping pace with progress of community: Knox Institute and Industrial School. *The Athens Daily Herald*. https://gahistoricnewspapers.galileo.usg.edu/lccn/sn88054118/1917-12-28/ed-1/seq-2/

Clark, L. S. (1917b, December 28). Knox Institute and Industrial School. *Athens Daily Herald*. https://gahistoricnewspapers.galileo.usg.edu/lccn/sn88054118/1917-12-28/ed-1/seq-2/

Coleman, K. (1968). *Confederate Athens*. University of Georgia Press.

Coulter, E. M. (1950). Franklin College as a name for The University of Georgia. *The Georgia Historical Quarterly*, *34*(3), 189–194. http://www.jstor.org/stable/40577234

Dillard, C. B. (2012). *Learning to (re)member the things we've learned to forget: Endarkened feminisms, spirituality, & the sacred nature of (re)search & teaching*. Peter Lang.

Doster, G. L. (2002). *A postcard history of Athens, Georgia*. Athens Historical Society.

Du Bois, W. E. B. (1903). *The souls of Black folk*. A. C. McClurg & Company.

Du Bois, W. E. B. (1969). *An ABC of color: Selections chosen by the author from over a half century of his writings*. International Publishers.

Dyer, T. G. (2004). *The University of Georgia: A bicentennial history, 1785–1985*. University of Georgia Press.

Enslaved People of Alonzo Church. (n.d.). Mentioned in Probate Record, *African American Experience in Athens*. Retrieved August 10, 2021, from https://digihum.libs.uga.edu/items/show/37

Franklin, V. P. (2002). Introduction: Cultural capital and African American education. *Journal of African American History*, *87*(2), 175–181. https://doi.org/10.1086/JAAHv87n2p175

Franklin, V. P. (2004). Cultural capital and Black higher education: The A.M.E. colleges and universities as collective economic enterprises, 1865–1910. In V. P. Franklin & C. J. Savage (Eds.), *Cultural capital and Black education: African American communities and the funding of Black schooling, 1865 to the present* (pp. 35–47). Information Age.

Fultz, M. (1995a). African American teachers in the south, 1890–1940: Powerless and the ironies of expectation and protest. *History of Education Quarterly, 35*(4), 401–422. https://doi.org/10.2307/369578

Fultz, M. (1995b). Teacher training and African American education in the South, 1900–1940. *Journal of Negro Education, 64*(2), 196–210. https://doi.org/10.2307/2967242

Gardner, B. T. (1975). The educational contributions of Booker T. Washington. *Journal of Negro Education, 44*(4), 502–518. https://doi.org/10.2307/2966635

Harris, S. F. (1910). It's beginning. In C. J. Hood, H. H. Dean, W. T. Bryan, J. E. Talmage, R. R. Maddox & J. D. Moss (Eds.), *The Black Mammy Memorial or Peace Monument, Athens, Georgia*. Banner Printery. Hargrett Rare Book Library, University of Georgia.

Harris, T. A. (2012). Value, networks, desegregation, and displacement at one of Georgia's Black high schools, Athens High and Industrial School/Burney-Harris High School, 1913–1970 [Doctoral dissertation]. Georgia State University. ScholarWorks @ Georgia State University. https://doi.org/10.57709/2773754

Heard, W. H. (1928). *From Slavery to the Bishopric in the A. M. E. Church: An Autobiography* (Electronic Resource). A. M. E. Book Concern. https://docsouth.unc.edu/neh/heard/heard.html

Heard, W. H., & Pledger, C. W. A. (1879). Prejudice. *The Athens Blade, 1*(21), 2. https://research.libs.uga.edu/undb/newspapers/1832

Hester, A. L. (Ed.). (2001). *Athens memories: The WPA federal writers' project interviews*. Green Berry Press.

Holsey, L. H. (1898). *Autobiography, sermons, addresses, and essays of Bishop L. H. Holsey, D. D.* (Electronic version). Franklin Print and Pub. Co. https://docsouth.unc.edu/neh/holsey/holsey.html

Hull, A.L. (1906). *Annals of Athens, Georgia, 1801–1901*. Banner Job Office.

Hynds, E. C. (1974). *Antebellum Athens and Clarke County, Georgia*. University of Georgia Press.

Knight, M. D. (2007*). Seeking education for liberation: the development of black schools in Athens, Georgia from emancipation through desegregation* [Doctoral dissertation]. University of Georgia Libraries.

McCarthy, R. (2017). *The Hiram House was home to Georgia's first Black female dentist*. The Flagpole. https://flagpole.com/news/city-dope/2017/12/06/the-hiram-house-was-home-to-georgias-first-black-female-dentist/

Meigs, W. M. (1887). *Life of Josiah Meigs*. J. P. Murphy.

Mell, Jr., P. H. (1895). *Life of Patrick Hues Mell*. Baptist Book Concern.

Moss, M. J. D. (1910). The Black Mammy Memorial. In C. J. Hood, H. H. Dean, W. T. Bryan, J. E. Talmage, R. R. Maddox, & J. D. Moss (Eds.), *The Black Mammy Memorial or Peace Monument, Athens, Georgia*. Banner Printery. Hargrett Rare Book Library, University of Georgia.

National Register of Historic Places. (1987). *Reese Street Historic District, Athens, Clarke County, Georgia.* National Register #87001990.

National Register of Historic Places. (1988). *West Hancock Avenue Historic District, Athens, Clarke County, Georgia*. National Register #88000227.

O'Brien, T. V. (1999). *The politics of race and schooling: Public education in Georgia, 1900–1961*. Lexington Books.

Ogbu, J. U. (1978). *Minority education and caste: The American system in cross-cultural perspective*. Academic Press.

Rowe, H. J., & Barrow, D. C. (1923). *History of Athens and Clarke County*. H. J. Rowe.

Schinkel, P. E. (1971). *The Negro in Athens and Clarke County, 1872–1900* [Unpublished master's thesis]. University of Georgia.

Siddle Walker, V. (2009). Second-class integration: A historical perspective for a contemporary agenda. *Harvard Educational Review 79*(2), 269–284.

Span, C. (2002). "I must learn now or not at all": Social and cultural capital in the educational initiatives of formerly enslaved African Americans in Mississippi, 1862–1869. *The Journal of African American History, 87*, 196–205. https://doi.org/10.2307/1562463

Spivey, D. (1978). *Schooling for the new slavery: Black industrial education, 1868–1915*. Greenwood Press.

Stegeman, J. F. (1964). *These men she gave: Civil War diary of Athens, Georgia*. University of Georgia Press.

Storey, S. (2006, November 3). *Railroads*. New Georgia Encyclopedia. https://www.georgiaencyclopedia.org/articles/business-economy/railroads

Thomas, F. T. (1992). *A portrait of historic Athens and Clarke County*. The University of Georgia Press.

Thomas, F. T. (2004, July 27). *Athens*. New Georgia Encyclopedia. https://www.georgiaencyclopedia.org/articles/counties-cities-neighborhoods/athens

Thurmond, M. L. (2019). *A story untold: Black men and women in Athens History*. Athens Historical Society.

Thurmond, M. L., & Hester, C. (2001). *A story untold: Black men and women in Athens history* (2nd ed.). Green Berry Press.

Thurmond, M. L., & Sparer, D. (1978). *A story untold: Black men and women in Athens history*. Clarke County School District.

University of Georgia Board of Trustees. (1827). Prohibition of "Colored Persons" in College Buildings in Board of Trustees Minutes (Vol 2: p. 186). *African American experience in Athens*. Retrieved August 10, 2021, from https://digihum.libs.uga.edu/items/show/73

University of Georgia Board of Trustees. (1855). Slave labor in Board of Trustees minutes (Vol. 3, p. 349). *African American experience in Athens*. Retrieved August 10, 2021, from https://digihum.libs.uga.edu/items/show/86

University of Georgia Faculty. (1823). An attack and cruel treatment of enslaved people by students, faculty meeting minutes. (Vol. 1, p. 15). *African American Experience in Athens*. Retrieved March 9, 2021, from https://digihum.libs.uga.edu/items/show/96

University of Georgia Prudential Committee. (1842). Mention of enslaved workers on campus, Prudential Committee Meeting Minutes, 1834–1857. (pp. 15–16). *African American Experience in Athens*, Retrieved March 9, 2021, from https://digihum.libs.uga.edu/items/show/152.

Waddel, J. N. (1891). *Memorials of academic life: Being an historical sketch of the Waddel Family, identified through three generations with the history of the higher education in the south and southwest*. Presbyterian Committee of Publication.

Walker, V. S. (2000). Valued segregated schools for African American children in the south, 1935–1969: A review of common themes and characteristics. *Review of Educational Research, 70*(3), 253–285. https://doi.org/10.2307/1170784

Washington, B. T. (1900). *The future of the American Negro* (2nd ed.). Small Maynard & Company.

Webber, T. L. (1978). *Deep like the rivers: Education in the slave quarter community, 1831–1835*. Norton.

Williams, D. S. (2010). *From mounds to megachurches: Georgia's religious heritage*. University of Georgia Press.

Williams, H. A. (2005). *Self-Taught: African American education in slavery and freedom*. University of North Carolina Press.

Wimberly, G. (2013). Chapter three: Understanding social capital and the African American school experience. *Counterpoints, 383*, 37–52. https://www.jstor.org/stable/42981247

Woofter, T. J. (1913). Phelps-Stokes Fellowship Studies #1: The Negroes of Athens, Georgia. *University of Georgia Bulletin, 14*(4). (1913). Schomburg Center for Research in Black Culture, Jean Blackwell Hutson Research and Reference Division, The New York Public Library. https://digitalcollections.nypl.org/items/510d47df-9d97-a3d9-e040-e00a18064a99

Yosso T. J. (2005) Whose culture has capital? A critical race theory discussion of community cultural wealth. *Race Ethnicity and Education, 8*(1), 69–91. 10.1080/1361332052000341006

Young, J. R. (2020, September 30). *Slavery in Antebellum Georgia*. New Georgia Encyclopedia. https://www.georgiaencyclopedia.org/articles/history-archaeology/slavery-in-antebellum-georgia/#:~:text=In%201820%20the%20enslaved%20population,of%20the%20state's%20total%20population

CHAPTER 12

TURN AROUND, REACH BACK, LEAD

Legacy and Lives of the Howard W. Blake High School

Vonzell Agosto, Jacqueline K. Haynes, and Ann Marie Mobley
University of South Florida

Drawing on the strand of social capital theory that has been contextualized in communities of color, this chapter provides a historical account of Howard W. Blake High School in Tampa Florida. Centered are first-person accounts of a former principal and her mentee whom she met while working at Blake H.S. during her 10 years there. Their intertwined narratives provide insight into the forms of social capital (i.e., navigational, familial) that were exchanged and used by the authors and members of the community who struggled to maintain access to public education and offer a unique account of one of the first and still remaining schools serving Black, and primarily African American, students. More specifically, this historical account portrays the dispersals of capital that have supported equity focused leadership across generations at Blake and in the surrounding communities. It is a history situated amid the politics of racial segregation that illustrates how court orders, land disputes, bussing, and curricular tracking have affected the status, place, and relationships of the school and those invested in its past and future and therefore its legacy.

Keywords: Blake High School, Racial Segregation, Educational Leadership, Social Capital Theory, Curriculum

This chapter adds to the historiography of one of the first Black high schools in Tampa, Florida. The Howard W. Blake High School (Blake or Blake H.S.) was established in 1956. By Black school, we mean schools in which most, if not all, of the students enrolled are of African descent and tend to identify ethno-racially as African American. As told through academic literature thus far, Blake High School's history is situated in race-related turmoil caused by different perspectives and practices regarding racial segregation, integration, desegregation, and resegregation policies (Kimmel, 1992; Shircliffe, 2001, 2002, 2006). Additionally, the role of leadership has been often framed within neoliberal discourse and related outcomes such as school closures, re-openings, and other market-driven approaches such as closing schools (Johnson, 2012). Black schools' histories can help to rescue Black history from distortions and orient it towards present-day struggles to exist (Levine, 2000). Yet school histories are often neglected as a sub-discipline of heritage studies (Haupt, 2010), and stories of any type that emerge from the benefits of White privilege risk silencing the experiences of People of Color (Solórzano & Yosso, 2002). Needed are counter-narratives of those who challenge miseducation of (and about) *the Negro* (Woodson, 1933) and mis-leadership within schools serving Black students (Brooks, 2012).

Howard W. Blake High School (2022)

We sought to understand Blake H.S. as a source of Black life by focusing on two authors, one was once an administrator (Haynes) and one, a student at Blake H.S. (Mobley). As doctoral candidates in the same program, they are connected to the author/professor (Agosto) and to Blake's social network. Thus, our professional journeys are bound by fictive, familial, and professional kinships. We interpreted their first-hand accounts using social capital theory and critical race theory (i.e., community cultural wealth). Our guiding question was this: How was community cultural wealth activated in the context of leading a historically Black school? In this counter-narrative to the history of Blake High School, is also a reconsideration of *turnaround* leadership and the companion dominant narrative that the only schools needing to be turned around are those primarily serving Black students (Khalifa & Briscoe, 2015). This history of a school, and school building (Yanow, 1995), illustrates how some educators have bonded within and around an organization to combat the forces of anti-Black racism (i.e., spirit murdering, majoritarian narratives, erasure, interest divergence, colonization).

SOCIAL CAPITAL THEORETICAL FRAMEWORK: CRITICAL RACE NARRATIVES OF CULTURAL WEALTH

There are several strands of social capital theory that differ in terms of what they emphasize (Allard, 2005). James Coleman's (1988) theorization of social capital emphasized families, rationality, and social control. Bourdieu (1977) and Bourdieu and Wacquant (1992) emphasized the reproduction of the social order and the individual use of capital and habitus (i.e., dispositions) to alter the norms of the social field. Putnam (2000) emphasized the collective or communal relations that can be amassed and shared as a network of social capital. Each strand offers strengths and limitations. While we were interested in kinship and professional bonds that develop in school as sources of capital (Stanton-Salazar, 2001), we were also interested in legacy and heritage or how social capital can be passed on only to be mediated by individuals (as members of groups) who can collectively or singularly use their influence to increase or decrease others' successful use of capital.

According to Allard (2005), Bourdieu (1993) provided three dimensions of social capital: relationships (e.g., membership, contacts) with others, the quality, and types of interactions constituting those relationships add up to potential or actual opportunity to access and make good use of resources. In other words, social capital is not inherent within an individual but is a dynamic outcome that hinges on who people are and how they are affiliated or connected and enabled by the social field of actors and institutional norms and practices to do as they please or need in order to translate potential capital to desired outcomes. By way of Bourdieu and his attention to the relativity of relations of power within social fields, we find Yosso's (2005) differentiation of types of capital useful.

Yosso (2005) developed the community cultural wealth framework as a critical race theory-based challenge to versions of social capital theory that ignored the culturally influenced ways people of color have negotiated their lives in relation to other people and organizations. Her framework offers an asset/wealth-based approach highlighting the strengths found in the communities and homes of ethno-racially minoritized people: *aspirational, navigational, social, linguistic, familial, and resistant capital*. Forms of capital make up the basis of cultural wealth and as a framework, it brings attention to how those who are vulnerable to harm associated with racism are able to mediate relationships and determine which resource, or recourse, is suitable. Fashioned through the lens of critical race theory, cultural wealth treats forms of capital as resources that can be negotiated. *Navigational, aspirational, familial,* and *resistant capital* are prevalent forms working in tandem within this account of Howard Blake's legacy and the continued existence of his namesake school as a symbol and source of cultural wealth.

This historiography of Blake H.S. confronts anti-Black racism by positioning the school as a site of survival for Black people and their resistance to exterminating practices identified via critical race theory in law and education such as spirit murdering (Williams, 1987). Spirit murdering expresses racism as a crime that is not only deeply painful and assaultive, leading to a slow death. Such assaults are not necessarily hostile or physically violent, as they can occur politely and be psychically violent (Williams, 1987). Following in the tradition of Carter G. Woodson (1933), knowledge of the history and cultural contributions made by people of African descent intervenes in miseducation and the erasure of heritage and therefore the social capital network ties that come from knowing and feeling connected to others and the good they have done.

METHODOLOGY

The following definition of life history is suited to our purpose and is consonant with our process and theoretical framework. Life history "is an elaborate, connected piece of talk presented in a social situation consisting of an informant and an ethnographer" (Agar, 1980, p. 223). An attribute implicated in this definition of life history is the relationship between researchers and informants. Life history is not simply a way for researchers to focus on factual accuracy or coherence of the story, but also a way to focus on the meaning the story has for the respondent/informant (Dhunpath, 2000).

The ethnographer as interviewer and the informant as a source of experience are both storytellers. However, these roles are blurred when both are informant and researcher (authors two and three), and when the research process is duo or trioethnographic (Agosto et al., 2015; Sawyer & Norris, 2015). Each of us authors interpreted talk transcribed from interviews between authors two and three and storied incidents as part of the analytical and documentary process. We share responsibility for breaking the stories into segments and creating order and disorder in the im/balanced life history honoring the storytellers and seeking to provide a deeper understanding of Blake High School.

Methodologically, we expand life history as a narrative genre focused on people to include places. By taking a life history approach to study a place, we risk inciting concerns among readers who may have competing views about what constitutes life. In order to diminish some initial concerns rather than settle paradigmatic differences we assert the following: We do not aim to flatten life to include only that which is composed of matter (i.e., school buildings). We do not intend to limit the meaning of life to only that which mirrors the common capacities of human beings (i.e., moving, breathing). We do not aim to assign regard for all living things according to a single non-hierarchical, moral code. Instead, we begin from the view that schools and related spaces (e.g., campuses, playgrounds, cafeterias) become animated in response to the natural environment where they were built and the social environment that gets built around them as people interact on different planes—locally, nationally, internationally. The life of the school is a life the school gains over time as a gathering place where people map out the course of their lives.

To bring focus to this historical account of Blake H.S., we organize the narratives around critical incidents that link the school history to the work of leading schools and school districts. More specifically, this humanistic perspective begins with the father of author three and his influence on her leadership as a principal at Blake High School and continues with her para-social mentoring of another (author two) who was a student at Blake H.S. Others have detailed accounts of the school's history we point to along the way. This version of Blake's history is vital to these authors and their development as educators, scholars, or practitioners adding to the research base on the advancement of Black women in educational leadership to *turnaround* (improve) schools.

THE FOUNDING AND FOLDING OF BLAKE HIGH SCHOOL: A DAUGHTER'S NARRATIVE

The Don Thompson Vocational School (Thompson V. S.) was established in a warehouse during 1945. It was named after Don Thompson, who was a Caucasian man once in charge of all vocational educational high schools in Hillsborough County (Cridlin, 2003). The school offered African American students an opportunity to receive a diploma, vocational training, and receive admittance into an all-Black college. However, Thompson V. S. had limited facilities and workspaces. It did not have an auditorium, library, nurse's office, or main office. What it did have was a notable coach, James J. Williams, who was Chair of the Physical Education Department.

When *Brown v Board of Education* (1954) was decided by the United States Supreme Court, making *de jure* racial segregation of public facilities unlawful, many schools were closed or redesigned. This included the Don Thompson V.S., which was closed to make room for a comprehensive high school that was built and opened in 1956 to educate Black (mainly African American students) from the West Tampa and Ybor City communities (grades 10th–12th). This new school, named after an African American man, was Howard W. Blake Senior High School. Howard W. Blake died in 1954 after serving 21 years as a principal of another school in the district that primarily served Black students, Booker T. Washington Junior High School. He was a former athlete and athletic coach who was instrumental in organizing the Florida Athletic Association (Canning, 2003). Blake H.S. was already known to have a strong athletic program (Kimmel, 1992). Athletics, vocational trades and (an emerging) arts programs were in place when the school closed.

Jacqueline Haynes: My father, Frank Kennedy, attended Blake, which, at that time, was the only Black high school in West Tampa/Ybor City/Central Park. He was part of the first graduating class of 1957, which was an honor and source of pride for my father who understood himself to be part of the legacy of Black education. High school graduation from a Black school was a milestone in history at that time. My father later received a baseball scholarship to Allen University, Columbia, South Carolina, where he earned his bachelor's degree in Elementary Education. After graduating, he returned to Tampa in the 1960s to become an Elementary Education teacher at Meacham Elementary, located in the historical Black area of Tampa named Central Park.

Meacham Elementary, was named after the first African American principal in the Tampa area, Christine Meacham (1865–1927), who worked at the rebuilt Harlem Academy School in 1914, which was the first public school in the Hillsborough area (Harlem Academy School Committee, 2007). Originally, Meacham Elementary was built in 1926 to serve "descendants of freed slaves who settled the area called the Scrub in the late 1800s" (para. 6), which was Tampa's version of Harlem in New York, and by 1945 it was the school serving the largest number of Black students (Sokol, 2016). In 1954, it was the site for a meeting of African American principals working in Florida at the time. There, my father was known for having high expectations and standards for his students, which was not un-

FIGURE 12.1. Frank Kennedy (first person left, back row) in Front of Meacham Elementary School.

common for Black educators prior to integration. Meacham Elementary closed in 1964 while talks about its reopening have continued for at least a decade (Sokol, 2016).

Throughout his teaching career, I heard and watched my father place an emphasis on building relationships with students. Many knew and respected him (aka Mr. K.). His connections with students lasted for years as he continued his work in the community. Many of his students attended his funeral and recalled stories of his support for them. Their stories reiterated his passion for providing a quality education to students. His fight for equity, justice, and fair treatment of students above all was displayed on a continuous basis. I sensed his satisfaction with the quality of life at Blake H.S. and witnessed its effects on his life more generally. He continued to embrace formal education and retired after 31 years of serving Hillsborough District. In him, I had a role model who was a family member and I witnessed what others have described as the good qualities of segregated (all Black students) schools with their "family-like atmosphere" (Shircliffe, 2001, p. 59). My father instilled in me the belief that education was a priority and attending college was an expectation, not an option. Little existing research directly examines the impact of race and class on school quality or provides a consistent explanation of how middle-class Blacks, in particular, fare in life with regard to the specific characteristics of the schools they attended (Davis & Welcher, 2013). Even less examined is the sense of purpose instilled in students that manifests through *familial* and *resistance capital* to end racial injustice.

DESEGREGATION AND THE DEMISE OF THE ORIGINAL BLACK H.S.

Despite the Supreme Court decisions in *Brown I* (*Brown v. Board of Education of Topeka*, 1954) and *II* (*Brown v. Board of Education*, 1955), to desegregate with *all deliberate speed,* it was not until the 1970s when districts' efforts intensified as a result of the United States Supreme Court's decision to uphold a court-ordered "busing for integration" plan in Charlotte, North Carolina (*Swann v. Charlotte-Mecklenburg Board of Education*, 1971). Hillsborough County followed suit and implemented a county-wide school desegregation plan involving mass busing of students (Kimmel, 1992; Shircliffe, 2002). This plan modified the previous plan that was inspired by a lawsuit (*Mannings v. the Board of Public Instruction of Hillsborough County, FL*, 1970) that was filed in 1958 with rehearings continuing to 1970 when Blake was still a high school and had "an all Negro student population of 887" (*Mannings*, 1970, p. 3).

The constant use of *navigation capital* was demonstrated by families and organizations, such as the National Association for the Advancement of Colored People (NAACP) and their Youth Councils, to dismantle racial segregation across the state of Florida (Saunders, 1992). Saunders (1992), a parent of a Black student, described how in the 1960s parents were criticized for seeking an end to racial segregation in schools, newspapers printed editorials attacking desegregation efforts, and school districts used stalling tactics rather than work with haste to achieve unitary status.

As critical race theorist and Civil Rights attorney Derrick A. Bell (2004) argued, the phrase "all deliberate speed" confirmed that the 1954 *Brown* decision was "more symbolic than real" (p 19). Furthermore, the institutional power (authority) of the courts was inadequate to overcome the *resistance capital* (oppositional behavior to equity or inequity) of White people who resorted to hostility, violence, and other forms of legal protest to undermine the intent of the battles that culminated in the 1954 decision and the 1955 directive to integrate public schools. The broader political context is part of the network of power relations and expressions of capital into which the history of Blake is reticulated.

Desegregation resulted in Blake High School closing after the 1970–71 school year with its students being bussed to Plant High School, where White students predominantly attended. Despite the public protests to save Black and Middleton high schools, the District approved the plan, and described in the petition from the Biracial Advisory Group as "a punitive blow" (Kimmel, 1992, p. 41) to the Black community. Blake was reopened in 1972 having been converted into a seventh-grade center. "School officials converted most schools in [B]lack communities into sixth- or seventh-grade centers" (Shircliffe, 2002, p. 140), while White schools and communities stayed intact. The nuances of desegregation plans and orders affecting Blake H.S. and the court-mandated bussing plans that occurred between the 1970s to the 1990s are described in detail by Shircliffe (2002, 2006). Members of the local Black community fought to keep the high school open. However, low student enrollment, and the low enrollment of White students specifically, led to the closing of Blake High School in 1996.

The disparate outcomes were damaging to the spirit of the Black community members who had affiliations with Blake H.S. via organizational, cultural-historical, or emotional ties. The dissolution of the championship football team is one example of how school spirit and community pride was undermined through the transition of Blake to a 7th grade center (Shircliffe, 2002). Referring to Blake and Middleton, Groulx (2016) asserted "the community did not want to see the high schools become junior highs because the bands and athletic teams would lose the prestige that they had built up over the past decades" (p. 144). Captured by Groulx, was a comment made by a former principal of Middleton H.S. about the effect the closing of the schools had on members of the community. He stated, 'it did something to our psyche. We were hurt because our identity was being removed to some extent' (Groulx, 2016, p. 144).

Adding insult to injury, the lives of White people were made convenient with desegregation efforts as desegregation plans tended to require Whites to do less bussing (fewer years/grades). To the extent the cache of the location and programming in the arts would bring value to the White community their support followed. It wavered when the potential site was in closer proximity to historically Black and less affluent communities (Shircliffe, 2002). The conditional support reflects

Bell's (1980) principle of interest convergence and in this case, divergence. As Kimmel (1992) describes, White, moderate parents were willing to accept Black children into their neighborhood schools but would not allow their children to be bused into schools in Black neighborhoods. The zoning changes and bussing arrangements tended to increase White students' access to arts in place of vocational education and sports. In other words, their *navigational capital* was less taxed with desegregation plans that increased their proximity to such arts programs when decisions about navigating land and space were decided in their favor (i.e., via rezoning and subsequent relocation of the re-established Blake to the downtown area rather a community highly populated by Black residents).

Amid continuing debates, deliberations, and machinations, Black people continued to remain skeptical that efforts to desegregate would eventually bring equity, parity, or justice for Black students and schools. For example, the only Black member of the school board, Dorris Ross Reddick, was the only one to vote against a plan to cluster schools and increase Magnet programs. Also, then president of the Hillsborough County branch of the NAACP, Sam Horton, expressed doubts about the plan. He stated,

> There's still a reluctance by some to go to an inner-city school, no matter what you call it ... There's not much difference between what you can put in a magnet school and a conventional school, so when they don't deliver, people go back to their original schools. (Johnston, 2001, para. 17)

Despite being authority figures, their refusal to vote in favor of plans and their public expression of doubt did not stop the desegregation plan. In other words, their *resistance capital* did not overcome the *resistance capital* of those who held opposing views and other types of cultural capital, such as Whiteness, within a hierarchical network of power relations. The social capital that one has or does not have depends upon interpersonal relationships of power and domination (Dika & Singh, 2002), both of which can be exponentially multiplied, compounded, sedimented, or defunded in relationships between people and institutions. As such, the cultural wealth can be im/mobilized. The history of relations leading up to the re-establishment of Blake is also a history of race relations and a racial gap in the education of Black students and Blake's students. Hillsborough County Public Schools continued to have dual status, a Black and a White system of education, until 2001 (Johnston, 2001; Shircliffe, 2002; United States Commission on Civil Rights, 2007).

THE RE-ESTABLISHMENT OF BLAKE IN CONTEXT—1997

After 25 years, the community rallied to re-establish Blake as a high school. Alumni of the Don Thompson-Blake High School convened for a reunion. Howard Blake's widow (Margaret Blake Roach), who was the assistant principal when Blake opened, worked with other organizers of the reunion to start a petition and engage Black community leaders (Shircliffe, 2002). This was the time when schools were converted to middle schools and magnet schools were promoted to assist with desegregation. These reform efforts provided a window of opportunity to transition Blake from a 7th grade center to a high school and meet the increasing number of students in the district.

Extending from alumni efforts, a group was formed called *Blake Alumni and Friends* to lead the efforts to re-establish Blake and determine its fate through being vocal during community meetings, court hearings, and school board meetings. They argued that Blake should become a comprehensive high school that could house a magnet school program and as such would restore a sense of pride to the neighborhood and stimulate business interest in the area (Shircliff, 2002). According to Shircliffe (2002), "alumni focused on 'returning' a high school to the black community," while "school officials wanted a school that would attract students throughout the county" (p. 133)—a performing arts magnet school.

Despite the desire of some Black community residents and members of *Blake Alumni and Friends* to locate the school in a neighborhood of Black families, others pushed to locate the school "downtown," which was approximately three miles away. For instance, then superintendent Walter Sickles advocated for a site near the Hillsborough River to build a new Blake rather than renovate the old Blake. Backlash came as politicians, banks, and newspapers pushed for a riverfront site and opponents argued that the location was influenced by political brokering and catering to White parents. The battle over the site ended with the riverfront site being designated the future home of the new Blake High School of Performing Arts rather than the larger site where the Clara Frye Memorial Hospital, the only hospital for African Americans during segregation, was located (Shircliffe, 2002).

Once the site was proclaimed, the newly established Blake H.S. needed to be built. With a total construction cost of $57 million, Blake H.S. was the most expensive school ever built in Hillsborough County up to that time. It was also the only high school built in the heart of the city on prime waterfront property with a scenic downtown view and overlooking the Hillsborough River. It was designed by an African American architect to serve grades 9–12 and accommodate a fine arts magnet component featuring fine, visual, and communication arts. It housed

FIGURE 12.2.   Distant view of Howard W. Blake High School

a state-of-the-art theater that was designed with the assistance of architect-professors from the University of Florida (UF). Students from UF, majoring in architecture, often tour the facility as part of their university studies.

The original Blake H.S. was a comprehensive high school that had vocational education and a college preparatory curriculum. It was also known for its outstanding music program, including its band, which started in 1954 when the institution was still called the Don Thompson Vocational Institute (Groulx, 2016). The band was started by Mr. Thomas Jefferson (T. J.) Simpson, who then became the band director at Howard W. Blake H.S. when it opened in 1956 and led it to participate in the Florida Association of Band Directors (FABD) events where they earned superior ratings at district and state competitions (Groulx, 2016). Simpson was followed by John C. Turner (1969) and Dean Page, who was a White band director and the last one to serve at the original Blake High School. When Blake was converted to a 7th grade center it lost its band. However, it was re-established as a fine arts magnet and has since maintained a strong, successful music program (Groulx, 2016).

Students also reaped the rewards of Blake's band program. One, a cousin of the former principal of Blake H.S. (co-author) Jacqueline Haynes, was Doug Hammond. After graduating from Blake, Hammond became a renowned Detroit Jazz Musician, drummer, and professor of music at Anton Bruckner Private University, in Linz, Austria. He has numerous major recordings.

Through a community wealth lens, we relate this legacy of those who worked at Blake H.S. who were sometimes described as kinfolk—some students considered Band Director Simpson "to be like a second father" (Groulx, 2016, p. 138). As such, *familial capital* is a source of *aspirational capital* that students like Hammond use to pursue their dreams. Simultaneously, their ability to translate their *navigational capital* into action is mediated by their ability to maneuver within unsupportive or even hostile environments that can characterize schools. However, their *resistant capital* is continually needed for Black men whose success is a process and outcome of countering dominant narratives that deemphasize their positive attributes, artistry, and outcomes. In 2005, a successful campaign to name the school's auditorium after its original namesake resulted in the Don Thompson Performing Arts Theatre. Then principal Brinson expressed the view that connections between the past and present should be part of the education of students. He stated, "It's important that we take the history that was shared here and pass it along to the students that are here" (Cridlin, 2003). Just as the heritage of a community is told through its efforts to name schools or areas within them, some have argued that school histories should include the heritage of communities (Haupt, 2010). Don Thompson, Howard W. Blake, and Dr. Lewis Brinson (former area superintendent) are a few of the iconic figures in the history of Blake H.S. who have supported the education of Black students through their leadership at the school or district level. They used their *navigational capital* as Black men to advance within the district, set the tone for future administrators, and model the relationship between history making, heritage pride, and counter-narratives reflecting the importance of education for Black people. In the following accounts of life at Blake H.S. is a para-social mentoring relationship between two women (authors two and three).

PRINCIPAL HAYNES AND THE DEVELOPMENT OF LEADERSHIP AT BLAKE HIGH SCHOOL IN THE 2000s

I began my service as the Assistant Principal for Curriculum at Blake High School in 2001. I recall walking the halls on my first day and noticing that classes were identifiable. For instance, Black students were tracked into remedial and on-level courses, and White students were tracked into honors and advanced placement courses. I could count the number of Black students in honors and advanced placement classes on one hand. Several teachers had low expectations of students of color and often vocalized their displeasure at having to *water down* curriculum if students were placed in higher-level courses. Some acted as gatekeepers for higher-level courses and were unwilling to teach differently as indicated by the *Miseducation* site showing a racial gap between Black and White students in advanced placement courses (ProPublica, n.d.).

I worked to build the belief that students could achieve in honors and advanced placement courses and should have access to higher-level coursework. I worked to shift the mindsets of teachers and change their practices such as identifying students who could be successful in the higher-level courses, removing barriers preventing their access to such courses, and building support systems for students. However, changing the culture and view to one in which open access to higher-level courses was understood as a right and not a privilege was a challenge. To overcome this challenge, courageous conversations about race had to occur. I thought we needed to examine the racial opportunity gap and racial discipline disparities. However, I was inexperienced in navigating the topic of race, let alone courageous conversations about race. In my experience up to that point, the topic of race was not openly discussed in the school district. My task was to bring educators to an awareness of their implicit biases, address their attitudes about race, and increase their willingness to admit they were part of the problem.

At one point early in my tenure as assistant principal, I was unsettled by the realization that teachers at Blake H.S. did not have true/authentic or trust-filled relationships with students. This was particularly noticeable among teachers in their relationships with students who were positioned differently from them, primarily as students of color—mainly Black. This was also the case for students transitioning or questioning their gender identification, practicing different religions, or not fitting the typical American family mold that was reflected in television sitcoms of the 1950s and, albeit to a lesser extent, today. These differences in identities, experiences and values were the subject of many unnecessary parent conferences and disturbing conversations that echoed racial stereotypes. These disturbing conversations, rife with deficit language about students, were instigated by White teachers and teachers of color regardless of their gender. In other words, the cultural wealth of the students was seldom recognized.

This portrayal of teachers at Blake avoids the racial essentialization of teachers of color as inherently empathic, knowledgeable, or competent in educating Black students. Teachers were different in terms of their indifference toward students and their circumstances and there was more than one way to do right or wrong by Black students. Characteristic of critical race theory is the attempt to avoid essentializing people and people of color specifically (Capper, 2015). The social capital teachers can amass within broader forces of institutional inequity (e.g., underfunding) can serve to inhibit educational achievement. Furthermore, social and cultural capital within an organization can intertwine with power at various levels (Stanton-Salazar, 2001). Despite me being someone who had kinfolk who had previously attended Blake and was savvy in terms of linguistic and cultural norms and practices, the forms of capital in which I was rehearsed (e.g., *familial, linguistic, cultural*) were not necessarily influential in my work to attain the best outcomes for students.

The Hillsborough County School District's plan to return to neighborhood schools resulted in the student population at Blake having 49% residing in the zoned area and 51% auditioning to enter the performing, visual, fine art programs. The auditioning students tended to be White (Caucasian) and were bussed in from all corners of Hillsborough County. I was intent on unifying a school that had become divided into two schools; the haves (magnet student population) and the have nots (traditional students). The traditional student course offerings were limited to Career and Technical Programs in Hotel and Restaurant Management, Cosmetology, and Culinary Arts. The community was extremely concerned, for fear that students were learning to make beds and clean rather than prepare them for advanced careers and college opportunities. These concerns were not unlike those identified in the 1970s as segregation continued in the classrooms with Black students being substantially overrepresented in special classes for the disabled rather than those associated with talent/arts (Kimmel, 1992).

Appointed as the Principal

After 2 years as assistant principal, I was appointed as Principal of the Howard W. Blake High School in 2003. A news article of my appointment was on the front page of the *Tampa Tribune* and included as a special news spot on NBC entitled What's Great in Tampa Bay that was featured on the nightly news. As the first African American woman to be appointed as the high school principal at Blake H. S., and the first in Hillsborough County, I was proud to have been selected. It was also a proud moment for my family, especially for my father. I felt a divine connection to the school that traced back to my father being a student there when it first opened. For the 12 years I was principal there, from 2003–2015, I found its alumni to be very involved and invested in ensuring that the history of Blake is preserved and passed on to every student enrolled there.

As principal, I implemented many strategies to improve instruction, school climate, and community relations. These and all of the other tasks can be extremely complex and difficult, especially when a school district does not have or does not allocate the proper resources to support your efforts. Studies have found that school funding is strongly related to school quality (Darling-Hammond, 2004; Kozol, 2005). Funding supports the recruitment of educators with high-quality credentials, the sustainability of programs requiring the replacement of high-quality equipment (e.g., pianos, paints), and the maintenance of facilities (e.g., theatre seats, stage lights), which help to provide a suitable environment for learning (Davis & Welcher, 2013). However, given the links between racial subordination, race/class residential segregation, and the reliance of school funding on taxes based on property values, "the schools black students attend, even middle-class black students, might have fewer resources to support high achievement" (Davis & Welcher, 2013, p. 472).

Principled Use of Capital by a Principal

Principals are responsible for closing the achievement gap and providing every student with quality curriculum and instruction that prepares them for postsecondary education. Second only to teachers, school leaders profoundly affect student achievement (Leithwood & Levin, 2011) and their decisions affect students' life changes. So, I began to research professional development opportunities within the district that could lead to assisting the faculty and staff in addressing diversity concerns in a meaningful and non-offensive way. To my dismay, I found limited options. The work of Ruby Payne was at the forefront and a few more courses assisted with ways to address the problem. Educators teaching and leading must be taught to grapple with race, culture, and intersecting identities and oppressions through courageous, but critical, dialogue and personal reflection (Asher, 2007; Osanloo et al., 2016), but nothing was available to me as a new principal on how to begin discussions with my faculty and how to challenge their beliefs.

Intuitively, I drew on my cultural wealth. Having been raised in the culture of Black churches, I learned to practice deference toward elders and witnessed leadership rooted in a greater purpose in connection to a greater being for the greater good. As a principal, I took this spiritual based ethic of justice into leadership and gravitated toward a positive approach to organizing school that emphasizes appreciation (Orr & Cleveland-Innes, 2015). I later learned during my doctoral studies of the appreciative inquiry (AI) approach to leadership, which is guided by five principles that can support teams in leading organizations such as schools and school districts: Positive Principle, Constructivist Principle, Principle of Simultaneity, Poetic Principle, and the Anticipatory Principle.

According to Orr and Cleveland-Innes (2015), leading according to the Constructivist Principle is "to know and understand an organization as a human construction, as ever changing" (p. 236). Leading via the Principle of Simultaneity, "the questions we ask and the changes we make are not separate moments but are considered to be simultaneous" (p. 236). The Poetic Principle guides leadership to make "the story, and its unfolding, explicit. Each participating author of the story is [sic] acknowledged and validated for contributing, wherever the story may go" (p. 236). The Anticipatory Principle is future-oriented wherein leading involves envisioning "new, even multiple, future realities. This plays out as a communal forum which involves all its participants" (p. 237). The Positive principle orients the outlook and uses positivity as a frame of reference wherein "positive affect, caring, shared meaning, and purpose fuel change efforts" (p. 237). Such principles can help guide the school as well as guide how the history of the school is considered and created—with questioning, caring, crafting, contributing, and considering how it changes as we construct it. Guiding schools around such principles with shared goals helps to avoid mis-leadership and the reproduction of inequities (Brooks, 2012). Appreciative leadership in organizations shares the positive or asset orientation towards communities of color evident in the cultural wealth model. Unfortunately, an asset orientation has seldom been extended to communities of color, and Black students more specifically, once *de jure* (by law) segregation ended.

Racialized Discipline and Disciplinary Disparities

Despite the end of *de jure racial segregation, de facto* (in effect) segregation continues. School districts continue to operate as a dual system or have schools that are being or have been resegregated. According to the ProPublica website titled *Miseducation,* segregation between Black and White students in Hillsborough County remains high with their uneven distribution across the district. Even when the district was deemed to have unitary status, Black students were still overrepresented in a few schools, with 40% attending 26 schools and less than 10% attending 24 schools (Borman & Dorn, 2007). This school level demographic profile points to uneven distribution across the district. In addition, based on school grades reported at the time (2002), the schools with majority Black student populations accounted for 75% of those grade D or F and only 10% of those grade A or B (Borman & Dorn, 2007). The racial demographic profile of Blake High Schools in 2021–2022 was approximately 40% Black, 29% Hispanic/Latin descent, and 24% White, 6% multiracial, and 1% Asian (Hillsborough County Public Schools [HCPS] Website, 2022). However, this school demographic profile does not reflect the programmatic distribution of students within the school into its traditional or arts program. Racial segregation can occur with schools with a racially balanced profile.

A deficit orientation toward Black students is indicated by the behavior, not of the students but of the adults who are responsible for discipline policies that result in disparate outcomes along racial lines resulting in patterns of racial inequities. At one point, Hillsborough County was identified by the Office of Civil Rights regarding complaints about inequities in discipline, namely suspensions among students of color (Peterson, 2014). One approach to the complaint was to develop a Student Code of Conduct and monitor how discipline was being issued. Beyond that reactive approach another that could have been taken, while not new to African American communities, is called an appreciative leadership approach (Orr & Cleveland-Innes, 2015), which includes developing relationships with the community, students, parents, and teachers to mitigate the tendency to suspend students. Training faculty on sensitivity, incorporating culture within the curriculum, celebrating diversity, and being inclusive of everyone is the beginning of decreasing discipline and showing the community that diversity is a top priority.

As I began to develop training at Blake, I thought it would not be as complicated as it turned out to be to have conversations and training about such a sensitive topic. Teachers were somewhat receptive, but not truly honest about their feelings. Perhaps my *familial capital* and confidence as a Black woman was too powerful for their comfort. Many of their emotions began to erupt and some made individual attacks on others' beliefs or disbeliefs. I was amazed to see in this day and age teachers are still unable to have conversations about racial diversity without their emotions escalating. As the staff development continued, the topic became a little easier to approach and eventually we survived the storm. If I was nervous and hesitant about having these conversations for the purpose of improving our culture, decreasing suspensions, and helping teachers and students build stronger relationships, then what were other principals within our district feeling? Whereas my *resistant capital* is "grounded in the legacy of resistance to subordination exhibited by Communities of Color" (Yosso, 2005, p. 80), their legacy of resistance to subordination went uncommunicated or I failed to perceive it. The risk is that those who cannot muster resistance to inequities will labor less intensely than those of us to navigate racism and resist falling prey to racial inequities daily.

Administrators were aware that the problems existed, but either were extremely uncomfortable with how to move forward to educate staff or gave other problems higher priority rather than acknowledge racism as a primary concern. Nevertheless, some teachers at Blake H.S. began to incorporate culture in the curriculum, conversations became civil and sincere, and progress was occurring. By no means was it perfect, but the topic, once in the air, became easier to address. Teachers were paying attention, sharing cultural competency lessons with the faculty, and having conversations about improving minoritized student performance without feeling totally uncomfortable.

As my research continued, I noticed that other districts had offices of diversity that kept the topic in the forefront of their work within the district. One particular district offered staff development to assist administrators in having difficult conversations about race within the school, examples of inclusion in the curriculum were evident, and professional development in diversity was a mandate. I became overwhelmed by the difference in the amount of resources that were made available to us compared to other large districts. Prior to 2017, there was no district-level racial equity policy. Without plans to achieve racial equity in a school or school district, addressing racism tends to occur through random acts of improvement rather than sustained and coherent proactive responsiveness (Brooks, 2012; Scheurich & Skrla, 2003). In part, the stimulus for the increased attention to equity came with the shift in policy. The *Every Student Succeeds Act* (ESSA, 2015) required states to submit equity plans. Florida submitted its plan in 2017, which was approved in 2018. These statewide equity plans for public education indicate commitment to equity and excellence and compliance with federal law. At minimum, the call for plans increased the expectation to make equity more central to the work in schools and district offices.

THE QUALITY OF SCHOOL LIFE AT BLAKE H.S.

The extent to which students' affect toward schools and schooling have been found to be influential in whether or not they achieve academically as well as how they react to other aspects of the schooling experience and ultimately how schooling shapes their quality of life (Baker et al., 2003; Jackson,1968). The *quality of school life* is an outcome affected by the informal and formal aspects of school including experiences that are social and task-related and relationships, such as with peers and authority figures (Epstein & McPartlan, 1976). In other words, three common areas of measurement of a quality school in the United States have been students' general satisfaction, commitment to schoolwork, and the nature of their relationships with teachers. This third area suggests that quality in school life is dependent on the quality of the arrangements between people, namely teachers, and therefore aligns with our framework of community wealth and forms of capital that can be shared, exchanged, or diminished within a network of relationships. However, rather than this distributive approach to understanding the quality of school life, the current discourse on student engagement and turnaround leadership have both helped to emphasize the individual agency of the student and educator (administrator in the case of turnaround leadership) rather than collective, shared, or relational agentic dynamics.

Today, *student engagement* discourse emphasizes how students are psychologically committed to a place and immersed in positive relationships with teachers (rather than principals or assistant principals) as authority figures. However, much of the research on teacher-student relationships affecting Black students points to negative relationships associated with anti-Black racism that surface with educators inflicting disciplinary punishment to spirit-murder upon them (Hines & Wilmot, 2018; Love, 2016), rather than heal them from past offenses or protect them from those that are ongoing macro and micro-assaults, -invalidations, -aggressions (Osanloo et al., 2016; Pérez Huber & Solórzano, 2015).

Ann Marie Mobley: Testimonio of a Student, Educator, Researcher

In 2006, I (Mobley) was enrolled into Blake H.S. as a freshman. It was my first time going to a majority Black school and it was also the first and last time I had a Black woman as a principal other than in middle school when the principal was shortly removed after one semester before I could get to know that individual. Haynes had a longstanding presence at Blake. I remember her and the school as she led it, from the same black and yellow checkered sneakers she would wear, despite the formality of the rest of her attire, to the performances that took place. I often felt there was something to look forward to—something I would thoroughly enjoy. I now understand there was a school environment and culture that Haynes' leadership helped to create.

Blake High School was a place where being Black, White, gay, straight, and othered in various ways was accepted and even celebrated. There were policies set in place to ensure this as well. I remember going to a meeting for the gay-straight alliance with friends and attending special assemblies to celebrate heritage months or awareness meetings. I also attended *Chat and Chews* where professionals would come and talk to students during lunch about college, life goals, and other topics that pertained to our immediate needs. For me, Blake was perfect, and it was so because of what the principal allowed and welcomed.

One of the most memorable moments for me at Blake came when I experienced a great loss: the death of a family member. Despite having over a thousand other students and obligations to attend to, Haynes took the time to attend to my needs. That moment made me realize that she was the type of administrator I wanted to be. I was already inspired by the way Haynes maintained the school and provided activities and exposure to the school and community, but her taking the time to truly care and listen to the needs of a single student reached me far above all else. This account challenges the idea that the development and use of *familial capital* is limited to the boundaries of official kinship ties rather than fictive ones. *Familial capital* is characterized by a "*c*ommitment to community wellbeing" (Yosso & García, 2007, p. 164). This account also points to the development of *aspirational capital* (Yosso & García, 2007), how I, Ann Marie, then an African American girl studying at Blake H. S., was helped to envision what I hoped and dreamt of for my future. In part, my pursuit of education despite barriers faced by Black women continues as I am now in the final stage of my doctoral studies and planning to research the persistence and resistance of Black women in educational leadership.

FINDINGS POINTING TO RETICULATIONS OF STRUCTURAL RACISM

Blake's history intervenes in the strands of social capital theory that attribute the demise of organizations led by communities of color to their (i.e., Black women) inabilities (i.e., Coleman, 1966), rather than to their vulnerabilities within networks of power that promote racism. It helps to illustrate how *resistance capital* of members of the Black community has been instrumental in giving life to Blake H.S. In response to the question of *how community cultural wealth was activated in the context of leading a historically* Black high school, we found it was expressed through leadership and its development as processes in communion with the life histories of the school. We also found that leadership made public or echoed by witnesses provided archival testimonials and supported para-social mentoring between past and future generations and fictive and familial kinships with namesakes (schools, people). These networks of power-laden relationships make up the history of Blake H.S. to influence its longevity and progeny.

The relationship between characters and the forms of capital used in isolation or simultaneously is symbiotic in the way namesakes (named, named after) are symbiotic. The energy from these complex re-arrangements drive the potential translations of capitals into useable resources responsive to micro-, meso-, and macro-in/validations that threaten to murder the spirit of a school. As such, for Black schools, social networks are less a safety net and more a reticulation of social capital as moveable (i.e., writhing). A visual metaphor that pairs with the history of Blake H.S. since its inception is that of living pythons coiling and folding themselves.

Reticulating pythons is an image that conjures a sense of slipperiness whereby one or several can shift and change arrangements at various levels. Metaphorically, in a reticulated pattern forms of capital like sources of racism (e.g., racial animus, antipathy) can be integrated and mixed to work with or against one another so as to squeeze the spirit/ethos out of a place, plan, or person(s), or lie dormant until provoked.

In contrast to this image, in terms of pace of activity, *turnaround leadership* today is often described as a quick-paced response wherein the principal is the lead person or individual most responsible for whether or not the school improves or not. Those improvements are typically focused on test scores and other metrics that can be used as indicators of gains and losses and assigned an evaluative mark—a letter grade. The literature on preparation in turnaround leadership does not address turning around a school primarily serving students with racial privilege. The burden to maintain schools with a high quality of school life, especially in the continuation of colonization and anti-Black racism, rests with leadership and their responsibility to amass and use capital to undo structural racism and other forms of reticulated oppression.

Missing in the narratives of school leadership are principals who are Black women (Murtadha & Watts, 2005), the histories of schools they serve, and the testimonies of those bearing witness to the daily work they perform. We seldom learn from academic literature the intricacies of their leadership practice (Agosto & Roland, 2019). The absence of such narratives and historical accounts of their use of capital and leadership savvy undermines struggles for racial equity in schools such as Blake H.S. that primarily serve ethno-racially minoritized students. Drawing on Black Feminist Thought (Collins, 1989, 1990), we point back to the women who led the struggle to and bridged interested parties into *Blake Alumni and Friends*: Flora Dawson who organized the reunion and who, with Margaret Blake Roach, had the idea to start a petition, Carolyn Collins who drafted the resolution to re-establish Blake as a high school, and Jacqueline Haynes who was its first Black woman principal. Their lived personal experience with Blake H.S. is evidenced through Alumni relations (even marriage), reunion, and rise in rank and reflective of Black Feminist Thought as the knowledge, wisdom, and lived experiences validated by other Black women (Collins, 1989).

Given the under-representation of Black women in the educational leadership role of principal, they have fewer direct mentors from which to learn how to develop and use *navigational capital* to advance through state, district, and community processes (formal and informal) despite gendered racism. Helping to fill the absence of actual mentors are parasocial mentors; those from whom we learn through observation or archives even if they do not know us. Parasocial mentors can be historical figures (e.g., Anna Julia Cooper) or fictional characters (e.g., *City Guy,* 1997–2001; *The Steve Harvey Show,* 1996–2002; *The Affair,* 2014–2019). For example, Hamlet (2015) described how she learned from Black women characters in the movies and television how to persist in institutions of higher education with predominantly White faculty. Parasocial interaction had been documented among youth who identified with people and then shaped their behavior to reflect what they admired in them (Papa et al., 2000). Girls related to celebrities and boys related to athletic figures as authority figures or mentors (Gleason et al., 2017).

CONCLUSION

The leadership narrative of Jacqueline Haynes is not an uncommon one. Research on Black women in the role of principal has indicated reduced financial and mentoring support provided to them (Bloom & Erlandson, 2003; Lomotey, 2019; Moorosi et al., 2018). For instance, being the only Black woman principal in a district or even a district area means there are reduced opportunities for her to benefit from the bridge leadership of other Black women (Horsford, 2012). More generally, the labor of Black women is susceptible to punishment especially when there is no bridge linking their work to racial justice movements (Larson, 2016). However, what Haynes's and Mobley's narratives offer are testimonies of how forms of capital, *familial resistance and aspirational capital,* can work together to help Black women thrive as professionals building *navigational capital* education.

Turnaround leadership praxis and research, through a critical race theory lens, is also needed in schools that benefit from affluence and have access to several forms of capital (e.g., social, economic). Future studies could examine how schools benefit from the displacement of Black educators, how Magnet programs intended to promote racial integration provide culturally responsive or unresponsive curriculum, and how concerns over land (i.e., is the area expansive and located ideally) mitigate decisions over who will be assigned to lead the school, who will be its namesake, where it will be located, and what curriculum it will offer.

REFERENCES

Agar, M. (1980). Stories, background knowledge and themes: Problems in the analysis of life history narrative. *American Ethnologist, 7*(2), 223–239. https://doi.org/10.1525/ae.1980.7.2.02a00010

Agosto, V., Marn, T., & Ramirez, R. (2015). Biracial place walkers on campus: A trio-ethnography of culture, climate, and currere. *International Review of Qualitative Research, 8*(1), 109–126. https://doi.org/10.1525/irqr.2015.8.1.109

Agosto, V., & Roland, E. (2019). Intersectionality and educational leadership: A critical review. *Review of Research in Education, 42*(1), 255–285. doi: 10.3102/0091732X18762433

Allard, A. (2005). Capitalizing on Bourdieu. How useful are concepts of 'social capital' and 'social field' for researching 'marginalized' young women? *Theory and Research in Education, 3*(1), 63–79. doi: 10.1177/1477878505049835

Asher, N. (2007). Made in the (multicultural) U.S.A.: Unpacking tensions of race, culture, gender, and sexuality in education. *Educational Researcher, 36*(2), 65–73. https://doi.org/10.3102/0013189X07299188

Baker, J. A., Dilly, L. J., Aupperlee, J. L., & Patil, S. A. (2003). Developmental context of school satisfaction: Schools as psychologically healthy environments *School Psychology Quarterly, 18*(2), 206–221. https://doi.org/10.1521/scpq.18.2.206.21861

Bell, D. A. (2004). *Silent covenants: Brown v. Board of Education and the unfulfilled hopes for racial reform*. Oxford University Press.

Bell, D. A., Jr. (1980). Brown v. Board of Education and the interest-convergence dilemma. *Harvard Law Review, 93*(3), 518–533.

Bloom, C. M., & Erlandson, D. A. (2003). African American women principals in urban schools: Realities, (re) constructions, and resolutions. *Educational Administration Quarterly, 39*(3), 339–369. https://doi.org/10.1177/0013161X03253413

Borman, K. M., & Dorn, S. (2007). *Education reform in Florida: Diversity and equity in public policy*. State University of New York Press.

Bourdieu, P. (1977). *Outline of a theory of practice* (R. Nice, trans.). Cambridge University Press.

Bourdieu, P. (1993) *Sociology in Question*. SAGE.

Bourdieu, P., & Wacquant, L. J. D. (1992). *An invitation to reflexive sociology*. University of Chicago Press.

Brooks, J. S. (2012). *Black school, White school: Racism and educational (mis) leadership*. Teachers College Press.

Brown v. Board of Education of Topeka, Shawnee County, Kansas et al., 349 U.S. 294 (1955) (Brown II).

Brown v. Board of Education of Topeka, Shawnee County, Kansas et al., 347 U.S. 483 (1954) (Brown I).

Canning, M. (2003, April 11). *The legacy of an educator endures*. Tampa Bay Times. https://www.tampabay.com/archive/2003/04/11/the-legacy-of-an-educator-endures/

Capper, C. A. (2015). The 20th-year anniversary of critical race theory in education: Implications for leading to eliminate racism. *Educational Administration Quarterly*, *51*(5), 791–833. https://doi.org/10.1177/0013161X15607616

Coleman, J. S. (1966). *Equality of Educational Opportunity summary report*. U.S. Dept. of Health, Education, and Welfare, Office of Education.

Coleman, J. S. (1988). Social capital in the creation of human capital. *American Journal of Sociology*, *94*, 95–120. doi: https://doi.org/10.1086/228943

Cridlin, J. (2003, April 27). School's history lives on in hall name. *Tampa Bay Times*. https://www.tampabay.com/archive/2003/04/27/school-s-history-lives-on-in-hall-name/?outputType=amp

Collins, P. H. (1989). The social construction of Black feminist thought. *Signs*, *14*(4), 745–773. http://www.jstor.org/stable/3174683

Collins, P. H. (1990). *Black feminist thought: Knowledge, consciousness, and the politics of empowerment*. Routledge.

Darling-Hammond, L. (2004). Inequality and the right to learn: Access to qualified teachers in California's public schools. *Teachers College Record*, *106*(10), 1936–66. doi: 10.1111/j.1467-9620.2004.00422.x

Davis, T. M., & Welcher, A. N. (2013). School quality and the vulnerability of the Black middle class: The continuing significance of race as a predictor of disparate schooling environments. *Sociological Perspectives*, *56*(4), 467–493. https://doi.org/10.1525/sop.2013.56.4.467

Dhunpath, R. (2000). Life history methodology: "Narradigm" regained. *International Journal of Qualitative Studies in Education*, *13*(5), 543–551. doi: 10.1080/09518390050156459

Dika, S. L., & Singh, K. (2002). Applications of social capital in educational literature: A critical synthesis. *Review of Educational Research*, *72*(1), 31–60. https://doi.org/10.3102/00346543072001031

Epstein, J. L., & McPartlan, J. M. (1976). The concept and measurement of the quality of school life. *American Educational Research Journal*, *13*(1), 15–30. https://doi.org/10.3102/00028312013001015

Every Student Succeeds Act, 20 U.S.C. § 6301 (2015). https://www.congress.gov/bill/114th-congress/senate-bill/1177

Gleason, T. R., Theran, S. A., & Newberg, E. M. (2017). Para-social interactions and relationships in early adolescence. *Frontiers in Psychology*, *8*(255), 1–11. https://doi.org/10.2289/fpsyg.2017.00255

Groulx, T. J. (2016). Influences of segregation and desegregation on the bands at historically black high schools of Hillsborough County, Florida. *Journal of Historical Research in Music Education*, *37*(2), 129–149. https://doi.org/10.1177/1536600616638793

Hamlet, J. (2015). Still standing, still here: Lessons learned from mediated mentors in my academic journey. *The Popular Culture Studies Journal*, *3*(1), 232–299.

Harlem Academy School Committee. (2007). *Our history*. https://harlemacademyschool.org/Our_History.php

Haupt, P. M. (2010). The school as a microcosm of communities and their heritage and the need to encapsulate this in the writing of school histories. *Yesterday and Today*, *5*, 15–21. http://www.scielo.org.za/scielo.php?script=sci_arttext&pid=S2223-03862010000100006

Hillsborough County Public Schools (2022, Jan 21). Demographic report, *Ethnic enrollment by school: School year 2020–21*. HCPS. https://www.hillsboroughschools.org/cms/lib/FL50000635/Centricity/Domain/4/DemographicReport.pdf

Hines, D. E., & Wilmot, J. M. (2018). From spirit-murdering to spirit-healing: Addressing anti-black aggressions and the inhumane discipline of Black children. *Multicultural Perspectives*, *20*(2), 62–69. https://doi.org/10.1080/15210960.2018.1447064

Horsford, S. D. (2012). This bridge called my leadership: An essay on Black women as bridge leaders in education. *International Journal of Qualitative Studies in Education*, *25*(1), 11–22. https://doi.org/10.1080/09518398.2011.647726

Jackson, P. (1968). *Life in classrooms*. Holt, Rinehart & Winston, Inc.

Johnson, A. W. (2012). Turnaround as shock therapy: Race, neoliberalism, and school reform. *Urban Education, 48(*2), 232–256. doi: 10.1177/0042085912441941 uex.sagepub.com

Johnston, R. C. (2001, March 28). Hillsborough, Fla., district declared 'unitary.' *Education Week*. https://www.edweek.org/leadership/hillsborough-fla-district-declared-unitary/2001/03#:~:text=One%20of%20Florida's%20longest%2Drunning,to%20operate%20racially%20divided%20schools

Khalifa, M., & Briscoe, F. (2015). A counternarrative autoethnography exploring school districts' role in reproducing racism: Willful blindness to racial inequities. *Teachers College Record*, *117*(8), 1–34. https://doi.org/10.1177/016146811511700801

Kimmel, E. (1992). Hillsborough County school desegregation busing and Black high schools in Tampa, Florida April 1971–September 1971. *Sunland Tribune*, *18*(1), 37–45. https://scholarcommons.usf.edu/sunlandtribune/vol18/iss1/7

Kozol, J. (2005). *The shame of a nation: The restoration of Apartheid schooling in America*. Three Rivers Press.

Larson, E. D. (2016). Black Lives Matter and bridge building: Labor education for a "New Jim Crow" era. *Labor Studies Journal*, *41*(1), 36–66. https://doi.org/10.1177/0160449X16638800

Levine, D. (2000). Carter G. Woodson and the Afrocentrists: Common foes of mis-education. *The High School Journal*, *84*(1), 5–13. *Gale Academic OneFile*. Retrieved May 24, 2022, from link.gale.com/apps/doc/A68864181/AONE?u=anon~ef131c22&sid=googleScholar&xid=7db0f540

Leithwood, K., & Levin, B. (2011). Understanding how leadership influences student learning. In J. Sanna (Ed.), *Social and emotional aspects of learning* (pp. 251–256). Elsevier Science.

Lomotey, K. (2019). Research on the leadership of Black women principals: Implications for Black students. *Educational Researcher*, *48*(6), 336–348. https://doi.org/10.3102/0013189X19858619

Love, B. L. (2016). Anti-Black state violence, classroom edition: The spirit murdering of Black children. *Journal of Curriculum and Pedagogy, 13*(1), 22–25. https://doi.org/10.1080/15505170.2016.1138258

Mannings v. Board of Pub. Instruction of Hillsborough County, 427 F.2d 874, 878 (5th Cir. 1970).

Moorosi, P., Fuller, K., & Reilly, E. (2018). Leadership and intersectionality: Constructions of successful leadership among Black women school principals in three different contexts. *Management in Education*, *32*(4), 152–159. https://doi.org/10.1177/0892020618791006

Murtadha K., & Watts D. M. (2005). Linking the struggle for education and social justice: Historical perspectives of African American leadership in schools. *Educational Administration Quarterly, 41*(4), 591–608. https://doi.org/10.1177/0013161X04274271

Orr, T., & Cleveland-Innes, M. (2015). Appreciative leadership: Supporting education innovation. *International Review of Research in Open and Distributed Learning, 16*(4), 235–240. https://www.learntechlib.org/p/161847/

Osanloo, A. F., Boske, C., & Newcomb, W. S. (2016). Deconstructing macroaggressions, microaggressions, and structural racism in education: Developing a conceptual model for the intersection of social justice practice and intercultural education. *International Journal of Organizational Theory and Development, 4*(1), 1–18.

Papa, M. J., Singhal, A., Law, S., Pant, S., Sood, S., Rogers, E. M., & Shefner-Rogers, C. L. (2000). Entertainment-education and social change: An analysis of parasocial interaction, social learning, collective efficacy, and paradoxical communication. *Journal of Communication, 50*(4), 31–55. https://doi.org/10.1111/j.1460-2466.2000.tb02862.x

Pérez Huber, L., & Solorzano, D. G. (2015). Racial microaggressions as a tool for critical race research. *Race, Ethnicity and Education, 18*(3), 297–320. https://doi.org/10.10 80/13613324.2014.994173

Peterson, Z. (2014). Federal complaint questions how Hillsborough disciplines minority students. *Tampa Bay Times* https://www.tampabay.com/news/education/federal-complaint-questions-how-hillsborough-disciplines-minority-students/2186514/)

ProPublica. (n.d.). *Miseducated.* Hillsborough County District. https://projects.propublica.org/miseducation/district/1200870

Putnam, R. D. (2000). *Bowling alone: The collapse and revival of American community.* Simon & Schuster.

Sawyer, R., & Norris, J. (2015). Duoethnography: A retrospective 10 years after. *International Review of Qualitative Research, 8*(1), 1–4. https://doi.org/10.1525/irqr.2015.8.1.1

Saunders, R. W. (1992). A profile of school desegregation in Hillsborough County. *Sunland Tribune, 18*(1) 73–79. https://digitalcommons.usf.edu/cgi/viewcontent.cgi?article=1234&context=sunlandtribune

Scheurich, J. J., & Skrla, L. (2003). *Leadership for equity and excellence: Creating high-achievement classrooms, schools, and districts.* Corwin Press.

Shircliffe, B. (2001). "We got the best of that world": A case for the study of nostalgia in the oral history of school segregation. *The Oral History Review, 28*(2), 59–84. https://doi.org/10.1525/ohr.2001.28.2.59

Shircliffe, B. J. (2002). Desegregation and the historically Black high school: The establishment of Howard W. Blake in Tampa, Florida. *The Urban Review, 34*(2), 135–158. https://doi.org/10.1023/A:1015362316709

Shircliffe, B. J. (2006). School and community loss, yet still imagined in the oral history of school segregation in Tampa, Florida. In D. Cobb-Roberts, S. Dorn, & B. J. Shircliffe (Eds.), *Schools as imagined communities* (pp. 125–142). Palgrave Macmillan.

Sokol, M. (2016, May 18). New plan to replace the historic Meacham school: An urban garden. *Tampa Bay Times.* https://www.tampabay.com/news/education/k12/new-plan-to-replace-the-historic-meacham-school-an-urban-garden/2277257/

Solórzano, D. G., & Yosso, T. J. (2002). Critical race methodology: Counter-storytelling as an analytical framework for education research. *Qualitative Inquiry, 8*(1), 23–44. https:// doi.org/10.1177/107780040200800103

Stanton-Salazar, R. D. (2001). *Manufacturing hope and despair: The school and kin support networks of U.S.-Mexican youth*. Teachers College Press.

Swann v. Charlotte Mecklenburg Board of Education. (1971). 402 U.S. 1.

United States Commission on Civil Rights. (2007). *Becoming less separate? School desegregation, Justice Department enforcement, and the pursuit of unitary status.* U.S. Commission on Civil Rights.

Williams, P. (1987). Spirit-murdering the messenger: The discourse of fingerpointing as the law's response to racism. *University of Miami Law Review, 42,* 127–157.

Woodson, C. G. (1933). *The mis-education of the Negro*. Associated Publishers.

Yanow, D. (1995). Built space as story: The policy stories that buildings tell. *Policy Studies Journal, 23*(3), 407–422. https://doi.org/10.1111/j.1541-0072.1995.tb00520.x

Yosso, T. J. (2005) Whose culture has capital? A critical race theory discussion of community cultural wealth. *Race Ethnicity and Education, 8*(1), 69–91. doi:10.1080/1361332052000341006

Yosso, T. J., & García, D. (2007). "This is no slum!": A Critical Race Theory analysis of community cultural wealth in culture clash's Chavez Ravine. *Aztlan: A Journal of Chicano Studies, 32*(1), 145–179.

EPILOGUE

Vanessa Garry, E. Paulette Isaac-Savage,
and Sha-Lai L. Williams

On February 1, 2023, *The New York Times* article, "The College Board Strips Down Its A.P. Curriculum for African American Studies," revealed the never-ending assault on the education of Blacks in the United States (Hartocollis & Fawcett, 2023). The College Board, accused by some to have amended the curriculum to appease White conservatives, denied this allegation. However, the actions of the College Board were likely no surprise to Black Americans. After all, throughout the history of the United States, Black Americans had no choice but to lead the way to educating their young. Such was the case for the development of Black high schools some years following the American Civil War.

In our book, *Black Cultural Capital: Activism that Spurred African American High Schools*, the authors of each chapter laid bare the Black community activists who spearheaded or played key roles in the development of Black high schools. In 1865, with the high rate of illiteracy in communities of former enslaved men and women, Black leaders knew educating the Black masses was necessary (Convention of Colored Newspaper Men, 1875). It would help the race safeguard their newly acquired civil rights. Unfortunately, educating Blacks and hiring Black teachers was not an urgent matter for the White majority (Butchart, 2010; McPherson, 1970; Rabinowitz, 1974). Therefore, Blacks did what was

Black Cultural Capital: Activism That Spurred African American High Schools, pages 273–275.
Copyright © 2023 by Information Age Publishing
www.infoagepub.com
All rights of reproduction in any form reserved.

necessary to develop schools for their children. At the close of the 19th century, Black segregated high schools were slowly populating the states across America. As Black communities sprouted up around these schools, Blacks replaced White teachers, and Black neighborhoods became self-contained communities (Rabinowitz, 1974). The inhabitants of these thriving communities spawned by segregation improved their lives through education as previous Black generations imagined for their race.

Each high school narrative illustrates its importance to the Black community from the perspective of its exceptional school leaders and teachers, the parents, and community leaders who supported it. The stories show the determination of Black leaders who, at times, put themselves in harm's way to make it possible for Black children to receive a high school education. Additionally, the stories show how Black teachers taught their students academics and life skills so the next generation could avoid life pitfalls they encountered. Black children's educational experience included college prep, business, or manual training which prepared them to either attend college or secure jobs after high school.

Throughout the early 20th century these high schools and communities flourished until the 1950s. The 1954 *Brown v. Board of Education* landmark case ushered in the promise of improved educational opportunities for Black children. The promise faded as predominantly White school districts shuttered Black schools. They also demoted Black principals, who were pillars of their communities; and they terminated many Black teachers by refusing to redeploy them to fill positions at White schools (Tillman, 2004). The *Brown* decision, implemented by White school leaders reluctant to integrate schools, disrupted Black children's lives by closing their high schools and forcing them to travel to schools outside of their neighborhoods. Their decisions had a domino effect as Black communities that derived their identities from the closed schools found their neighborhoods predisposed to decline, as discussed in several chapters.

Black community activists could not prevent the mass closures of the segregated high schools they cultivated; however, their fight for improved education for their children continued through the courts. The remnants of the overall poor implementation of the *Brown* decision manifested in continued segregated schools. The continued assault on Black children's education first witnessed after the Civil War as school districts slow-walked the development of Black schools, then shuttering them after *Brown*, eventually gave way to the "busing" phenomenon.

For example, the *Liddell v. Board of Education for the City of St. Louis*, filed in 1972 and decided in 1980 resulted in the school choice program. The program allowed Black parents of children attending St. Louis Public Schools the opportunity to enroll their children in suburban schools. The Voluntary Interdistrict School District Program in St. Louis was the dichotomy of the integrated schools Black community activists in the 1860s wished for their children. Again, the burden was placed on Blacks to select schools miles from where they lived, which required Black children to leave home early to be bused from the city to the county.

As school busing programs across the country neared the end of their life cycle, city schools remained segregated. This was mostly due to White flight from urban centers to suburbs during the 1960s. The decade's urban renewal projects designed to rebuild cities, including the construction of highways to link cities to suburbs, failed to attract the number of people cities lost during the mid-20th century. Instead, city officials recreated Black neighborhoods experiencing extreme poverty by forcing Black families to abdicate their property in segregated neighborhoods earmarked for public highways and moving them to public housing high rises. Some cities never recuperated nor did the schools, especially Black high schools given there were so few of them.

Many Black children who longed to attend the neighborhood high schools their parents, aunts, and uncles lovingly spoke about can no longer do so. The schools are either closed or are a shell of what they once were during their height of success. Instead, families without the means to move continue to live in neighborhoods in such disrepair it is hard to believe they were once communities where affluent Blacks lived. Children whose domicile remains in the city attend district schools, charter schools, facilities outside of their district, or private schools. Similar to the different schools they may attend, demographics in todays' urban schools are no longer comprised of mostly White and Black students but include a spectrum of minorities and immigrant children. What continually persists in urban spaces is the amplification of Black activists' voices that reminds the White majority that Blacks remain vigilant when it comes to the education of their children.

REFERENCES

Butchart, R. E. (2010). Black hope, white power: Emancipation, reconstruction and the legacy of unequal schooling in the US south, 1861–1880. *Paedagogica Historica, 46*(1–2), 33–50. https://doi.org/10.1080/00309230903528447

Convention of Colored Newspaper Men. (1875, August 4). *Proceedings of the Convention of Colored Newspaper Men Cincinnati*. https://omeka.coloredconventions.org/items/show/455

Hartocollis, A., & Fawcett, E. (2023, February 1). The College Board strips down its A.P. curriculum for African American studies. *The New York Times*.

McPherson, J. M. (1970). White liberals and Black power in Negro education, 1865–1915. *American Historical Review, 75*(5), 1357–1386.

Rabinowitz, H. N. (1974). Half a loaf: The shift from White to Black teachers in the Negro schools of the urban south, 1865-1890. *The Journal of Southern History, 40*(4), 565–594. https://doi.org/10.2307/2206355

Tillman, L. C. (2004). (Un)Intended consequences? The impact of the *Brown v. Board of Education* decision on the employment status of Black educators. *Education and Urban Society, 36*(3), 280–303. https://doi.org/10.1080/00309230903528447

BIOGRAPHIES

EDITORS

Vanessa Garry received her Ph.D. in Educational Leadership and Policy Studies from the University of Missouri-St. Louis where she is currently serving as an associate professor in the Department of Educator Preparation & Leadership in the College of Education. She trains aspiring principals and superintendents. Using a historical lens, her research involves the examination of urban education in the St. Louis region with an emphasis on African American leaders' influence on the development of the education of children of color during the Jim Crow era. Additionally, she examines and presents research on teachers' data use training and their implementation of the practice in schools as a vehicle to improve students' learning.

E. Paulette Isaac-Savage is a Professor of Adult Education at the University of Missouri-St. Louis. Her research projects have included an examination of adult education in the Black Church, health education behaviors of non-custodial Black men, and assessment. Currently she is exploring Black faculty and staff associations at higher education institutions. She is president of the American Association for Adult and Continuing Education.

Sha-Lai L. Williams is an Associate Professor at the University of Missouri-St. Louis. Dr. Williams teaches Social Work Practice and Human Behavior courses, utilizing her expertise as an accomplished facilitator of several nationally recognized training curricula and her experience teaching Masters-level courses at The Brown School. She teaches Human Behavior in the Social Environment as well as Social Work Practice with Individuals, Families, and Groups. Her research interests center around access to quality mental health services and service utilization among African Americans.

CONTRIBUTING AUTHORS

Vonzell Agosto is Professor of curriculum studies in the Educational Leadership and Policy Studies program at the University of South Florida. Her research agenda focuses on curriculum, leadership, and anti-oppressive education with an emphasis on how they mediate racism, anti-sexism, and disablism. Culture, aesthetics, and ethics are core concepts she engages in research that makes use of arts, narrative, and cartography to produce historical, conceptual, empirical accounts of education practice and policy.

Lucy E. Bailey is faculty in the Social Foundations of Education and the Director of Gender, Women's, and Sexuality Studies at Oklahoma State University. She conducts research and teaches courses in qualitative methodologies and diversity issues in contemporary and historical perspective. She is the editor of the historic journal, VS: The Journal of Educational Biography and the Co-editor of the book series, *Life Writing in Education* (IAP).

Rachel Brooks is a graduate student in the accelerated master's program for Curriculum Studies: Curriculum and Instruction in the College of Education at Texas Christian University. While serving as a residence assistant, L4L mentor, and as a facilitator for various student organizations, she earned a Bachelor of Science in Secondary Education and a concurrent Bachelor of Arts in English. Her research interests include the legacy of school segregation, cultural memory, and generational oppressive structures.

Autumn B. Brown earned her Ph.D. in Social Foundations of Education from Oklahoma State University where she is an assistant professor in the Edmon Low Library with the Oklahoma Oral History Research Program. Her dissertation was an educational biography of teacher activist Clara Luper (1923–2011) and Luper's work with Oklahoma City's NAACP Youth Council leading one of our nation's first sit-in. Dr. Brown uses oral history methodology to collect and preserve stories about Oklahoma City's Civil Rights Movement, (re)presenting Oklahoma City as a radically activist state. Autumn has published book chapters on Black women and sexuality, racial dimensions of life writing, and the history of all-Black schools in Oklahoma City, and journal articles on the policing of the Black woman body and the 2018 Oklahoma City teacher walkout. Autumn served as IMLS Research Scholar on the Eddie Faye Gates Tulsa Race Massacre Collection at Gilcrease Museum from 2021–2022. She was also the 2022–2023 Duane H. King Postdoctoral Fellow at the Helmerich Center for American Research at Gilcrease Museum/University of Tulsa. Dr. Brown was part of the inaugural cohort of John Robert Lewis Fellows and Scholars with the Faith & Politics Institute in Washington, D.C. Autumn runs her own research consulting business named Winona Jewel Research Consulting, LLC, serves on the Board of Directors for BLAC, inc. (Black Liberated Arts Center), and manages the Clara Luper Freedom Archive in Oklahoma City, Oklahoma.

Altheria Caldera Ph.D. is a Senior Professorial Lecturer in the School of Education at American University. She's also the CEO and principal consultant for Caldera & Associates Equity Consulting, LLC. To learn more about her work, visit www.drcaldera.com.

Loyce Caruthers began her career in the Kansas City, Missouri School District as a middle-school teacher and later served in several program and administrative roles: Career Education Coordinator, Gender Equity Coordinator, Staff Development Coordinator, Effective Schools Director, and Assistant Superintendent or Curriculum and Instruction. Her journey from the public schools and regional labs to UMKC led to her current position of Professor for the division of Educational Leadership, Policy, and Foundations where she currently serves as Program Coordinator for Pk–12 Ed. D. Education Administration. Editorial Board membership includes *Educational Studies*: A Journal of the American Educational Studies Association and past member of the *Journal of Urban Learning, Teaching, and Research* and the Regional Education Laboratory Central Governing Board.

Tasha Coble Ginn is the Director of Leadership Development for the Principal Impact Collaborative at the University of North Texas-Dallas Campus. She facilitates professional learning for K–12 campus and school system leaders in adaptive leadership, educational equity, and strategic planning. Previously she served as a middle and high school principal and principal supervisor for twelve years. Research interests include the black-white achievement gap and principal resiliency.

Marceline L. Cooley is a retired elementary teacher/administrator from the Kansas City, Missouri Public School District. She has worked in various capacities as a classroom teacher, Bilingual ESL Resource teacher, Instructional Assistant, and Principal. She attended Wendell Phillips Elementary School, R.T. Coles School, and graduated from Lincoln High School, class of 1956. She is past president of the Lincoln/R. T. Coles National Alumni Association, and Board member of the Black Archives of Mid-America, Kansas City. Research interests include collection and preservation of Black historical artifacts, curriculum instruction of Black history, and community outreach.

Jonathan W. Crocker is a Ph.D. student in Curriculum Studies at Texas Christian University. He works at the intersection of education, politics, and rhetoric and explores the possibilities of anti-authoritarian pedagogy and curriculum within neoliberal society and public culture.

Stephanie Cuellar is the DEI Post-Doctoral Fellow in the Department of Educational Leadership and Higher Education in the College of Education at Texas Christian University (TCU). She received her Bachelor of Science in Psychology and Master of Arts in Clinical and Counseling Psychology from Midwestern State University. She earned her doctorate in Higher Educational Leadership from TCU. She holds a graduate certificate in Comparative Race and Ethnic Studies with a concentration in pedagogy as well as a general pedagogy certification. Her research interests include psychological resilience among minoritized populations; ethnic-racial identity development, and increasing access to postsecondary education for low-income, first-generation college students.

Leslie Ekpe, Ph.D., is an assistant professor of higher education at Texas A&M University-Commerce. Ekpe earned her Ph.D. in Higher Educational Leadership from Texas Christian University. Her research seeks to promote access for marginalized peoples, specifically focusing on anti-racist policies and social justice in higher education and society. Ekpe's research has been published in academic journals such as Innovative Higher Education, Journal of School Leadership, Equity in Education & Society, and the I.

Jacqueline K. Haynes is the Executive Director, Acceleration School Turnaround, at the Charleston County School District, Charleston, South Carolina. She was the first African American woman appointed as a High School Principal within the Hillsborough County Public School District in Tampa, Florida. She served in that position at Howard W. Blake High School for over 10 years. Her research interests include school turnaround leadership, cultural competency, and school improvement.

Vann Holden earned his doctorate in Education Administration from the College of Education at the University of South Carolina. He is a former teacher, assistant principal, and principal and currently serves as the Director of Planning and Accountability for School District Five of Lexington and Richland Counties. His doctoral research primarily focuses on Black educational experiences during segregation and desegregation. He has also taught the course *The History of Education in the United States* at the University of South Carolina.

Kellton Hollins is a student-athlete in the Curriculum and Instruction: Curriculum Studies Master's program at Texas Christian University. While balancing the workload of athletics, he received his Bachelor of Science in Youth Advocacy and Educational Studies. Throughout his tenure at Texas Christian University, he has prided himself on being more than an athlete. Hollins has served as president of S.P.A.R.K., an organization started by TCU football student-athletes to provide motivation to local youth about the importance of education and serving the community. His research interests include the academic experiences, mental health, and holistic development of black student-athletes

M. Francyne Huckaby, Ph.D., is Associate Provost of Faculty Affairs at Texas Christian University (TCU). She holds the rank of Professor and has served as Associate Dean and Interim Dean of the School of Interdisciplinary Studies, Interim Chair of the department of Comparative Race and Ethnic Studies, director of Center for Public Education and Community Engagement, and Professor of Curriculum Studies at TCU. She is former President of the Society of Professors of Education. Her work (as pedagogue, curricularist, and scholar) has focused on creating openings and spaces for anti-oppressive discourses and practices. Her scholarship on community organizing and resistance to neoliberal education reform puts filmmaking to work as a form of inquiry and making public research and sites of resistance and struggle. Her books include *Researching Resistance: Public Education after Neoliberalism* (2019) and *Making Research Public in Troubled Times: Pedagogy, Activism, and Critical Obligations* (2018).

William P. Kladky is associated with the American Institutes of Research and occasionally lectures at the College of Notre Dame of Maryland. He is the author of many articles and reviews in history and sociology. Fascinated by the intersection of faith and the social world, his writings include an examination of the role of faith on civil and human rights advocacy in the American Reconstruction era ("Joseph Hayne Rainey and the Beginnings of Black Political Authority," in *Before Obama: A Reappraisal of Black Reconstruction Era Politicians*, ed. Matthew Lynch. ABC-CLIO, 2012).

Ann Marie Mobley is a doctoral candidate in Educational Leadership at the University of South Florida. Her research interests concern leadership, gender, and African American history. More specifically, she studies the leadership practice of Black women, school culture and climate through a historic lens, and the racial achievement gap. Currently she is a 5th year middle school teacher with aspirations of becoming a school administrator.

Amber M. Neal-Stanley, Ph.D., is an Assistant Professor of Curriculum Studies in the Department of Curriculum and Instruction at Purdue University. She received her Ph.D. from the University of Georgia. Informed by her own experiences as a Detroit Public School (DPS) student as well as appointments as a social worker and public elementary school teacher, Amber is committed to preparing the next generation of teachers to address structural inequality, (re)member Black radical traditions, and utilize intersectional analyses and humanizing pedagogical and research approaches. Areas of research interest include but are not limited to theorizations of Blackness and anti-Blackness, Black feminist theories, abolition, and spirituality in education.

Michelle Nguyen currently serves as a Project Manager for Cap & Company, an LLC focused on providing comprehensive support, guidance, and empowerment for college and graduate students. Michelle was among one of the first students to graduate from Texas Christian University with a Bachelor of Science in Youth Advocacy and Educational Studies in May of 2019. After graduation, Michelle spent a year abroad as an English teacher in Salatiga, Central Java, Indonesia, through the Fulbright Scholars program. She is passionate about educational equity and believes the solution to solving social injustice is through investing in public education. Her research interests include the identity development and self-discovery process amongst students who are self-proclaimed activists.

Molly O'Connor holds a Ph.D. in Education from Rutgers University-New Brunswick, specializing in Black internationalism in education and history. She also holds a graduate certificate in Africana Studies and master's degrees in Education and International Affairs. Dr. O'Connor's research examines the connections between politics, education, and Black leadership in the early 20th century. Her writing appears in *Educational Studies* and the *Journal of African American History*.

Bradley Poos is currently the Associate Director in the Institute for Urban Education (IUE) at the UMKC. As Associate Director, Dr. Poos is responsible for teacher pathway programs, community partnerships and engagement, and student support. Dr. Poos has experience in both k–12 and higher education. Most recently, Dr. Poos was a faculty member and coordinator of the Grow Your Own program at Avila University in Kansas City, Missouri. His research focuses on issues related to the historical and social context of schooling. Dr. Poos is interested in the history of urban education, urban teacher preparation, social justice education, and diversity and educational equity. Dr. Poos has written and published broadly in these areas and has presented his work around the country. He has long been committed to work around equity and justice in education and the community at large.

Penny Seals, Ph.D., serves as the Associate Director of the Academic Success Center at Samford University, in Birmingham, Alabama. She earned her Ph.D. in Educational Studies in Diverse Populations from the University of Alabama at Birmingham (UAB), a master's degree in clinical psychology from Wheaton College in Wheaton, Illinois, and a bachelor's degree in psychology from Samford University. Her current research interests center the history of African American education in the South, with a particular focus on examining the historical relationship between race and education.